CALLING:
A MEMOIR OF MINISTRY

By Jeri Rowe

ISBN (Paperback): 979-8-9913233-6-9

Published by Cardinal Hound Publishing

"If you pour yourself out for the hungry and satisfy the desire of the afflicted, then shall your light rise in the darkness and your gloom be as the noonday."
— Isaiah 58:10

"Pain or love or danger makes you real again."
— Jack Kerouac

For Katherine, Will & Elizabeth
For making my life richer, more than I deserve

Table Of Contents

The Rev. Frank Dew held communion during every service of New Creation Community Presbyterian Church in all kinds of places, including Iona, an island off Scotland.

An Introduction

A Weathervane for America

"All too often today people are looking for the perfect church. But there are no perfect churches because there are no perfect people. There are more people like Groucho Marx. You know, he once said, "I don't want to belong to any club that will accept me as a member." But those people who are like Groucho Marx — people we disagree with or even dislike — are the very people who can help us grow. We can learn how to forgive and be forgiven, and we begin to understand what it means to experience grace and to give grace."

The Rev. Frank Dew

Everybody I know calls him Frank. So, I called him Frank. And the Rev. Frank Dew, let me just say, will surprise you.

He comes across as a laid-back Southerner, a curious amalgam of Jimmy Buffett and Ernest Hemingway because of his salt-and-pepper beard. He loves to fish, loves a shrimp sandwich when he vacations on Ocean Isle, and loves to pull for his beloved Demon Deacons. "You know," he'll tell everybody willing to listen, "*this* could be the year."

Everywhere he goes, from a church sanctuary to a trip to see his three grandkids outside Chicago, he'll wear his workaday uniform: running shoes, khakis, and a collar shirt that carries one of the most favorite hues of blue from his home state. Of course, that's Carolina blue. When you listen to his sermons — and I have — Frank exudes this aw-shucks demeanor that reminds me of "The Andy Griffith

Show." It's not because of his relaxed Southern accent. It's because of his anecdotes and stories. They all are incredibly relatable, full of details that are very North Carolina, very much imbued with what first helped shape him: his hometown of Lumberton, the small Robeson County city beside the Lumber River. Wherever he has preached, Frank will drive home a point he believes important by raising his voice ever so slightly, making a statement that seeps deep, and pausing for a second — or two — to look over the congregation in front of him and say with a slight smile, "Amen?"

I first heard Frank's spiritual exclamation mark during a sermon at Greensboro Urban Ministry. In Greensboro, we all know it as GUM. It's the go-to spot for those without a home, without a support system, in need of a safe place to land away from the storm of their life. Nearly 20 years ago, I came to GUM to see Frank because I was working on a story. As a metro columnist at the News & Record, the city's daily, I lived with a notepad in my hand. I chased stories across central North Carolina, and on a weekday in the fall of 2007, I came to GUM to see its chaplain, its first chaplain. That's Frank. I came to talk to him about the city's new loitering ordinance that Frank thought squeezed out the compassion the city needs for those in need. Frank sees them as "the least, the last, and the left out." For Frank, they have first names, full of heart-tugging stories. They are the very ones Frank encourages us to channel our inner Jesus and reach out to with a helping hand.

Back then, I didn't know Frank. I just knew of Frank. Everybody in Greensboro knew of Frank, I think. He had become one of the city's most recognizable faces of social justice. I knew he had spoken to governors about his opposition to the death penalty, stood on a downtown street corner every week for years protesting the death penalty, and worked daily to help those who felt invisible and forgotten. Frank helped them feel seen and heard.

That's all I knew of Frank when I followed him that afternoon years ago down a hall at GUM. I walked into his windowless cave of an office and on the edge of his desk sat a small stone. I asked, and Frank responded with what didn't surprise me. I grew up Southern

Baptist; Frank grew up Presbyterian; and I knew the story of the stone, a parable of forgiveness and mercy from the Book of John. I think I first heard it trotted out when I lost my two front teeth as a first grader in my hometown of Charleston, South Carolina. That was the first of many, many times.

Must be a Southern thing. I don't know. But it's definitely a Frank thing.

"Oh, the stone," Frank told me. "It reminds me — should remind all of us — that we're all sinners. You know the Bible verse? Where Jesus saves the woman from being stoned? 'Let anyone among you who is without sin be the first to throw a stone against her.' We all need to remember that. By the way, can you stick around for our noon service?'"

Of course, I said. Let's see what I can get, I told myself. At least that's what I told myself then. But as I've gotten older, I've come to realize there are no coincidences in life. All of us stumble into moments that can give us a new perspective on life. That is, if we only pay attention. Many times, when I was younger, I didn't pay attention. I saw life only through the lens of the stories I discovered with a notepad in my hand. That was it. But this meet-up with Frank stuck with me. Back then, I didn't know why. Only years later did I find the answer.

* * *

On that weekday in the fall of 2007, I walk into what passes for a sanctuary. It's merely a room, a little larger than a two-car garage. To the right is an upright piano. On the wall is a Celtic cross, about three feet tall. In loose rows are folding chairs. Soon, a dozen or so men and a few women start wandering in, and I see that Frank knows many of them. He calls them by first name. He shakes hands with the ones he can and hugs more than a few. Soon, the service begins. The men pick up a hymnal from a nearby shelf, and an older woman named Betty sitting at the piano starts to play. The room booms. It becomes full-throated with both on-key and off-key baritones and a few sopranos doing their best to find the melody. I listen. I even sing. I know these hymns. Like many of those around me, I grew up singing them. After we finish, Frank begins.

He delivers a sermon about love and hope and the need to feel worthy no matter what hand life has dealt us. His sermon is no more than 10 minutes. He finishes with his spiritual exclamation mark, "Amen?" Then, Betty begins to play. The room booms once again. After the hymn, Frank circles everyone up. They hold hands, and Frank ends the service with a prayer. Then, a few around him pray. These men and women around me wrestle with heartache and uncertainty, addiction and mental illness, depression and anxiety. They often don't know where they will find their next meal or their next place to stay beyond an underpass, a sidewalk, an alcove, a doorway, or a tent in the woods. Yet, you hear unbridled enthusiasm in their voices as they pray. They squeeze their eyes shut and talk, almost shout, about the idea of being alive, of sharing their life with others and saying, "Thank you for waking me up this morning!"

The service is about 30 minutes, and when it ends, Frank stops and talks to everyone he can around him. The compassion I see unfold in front of me convinces me to tell Frank afterward, "Frank, let me know if you ever run into something that needs to be written about. A person with a story. An injustice that needs to see the light of day. Call me. I trust your judgement. And what I saw today was something. Keep me in the loop."

That's the gist of what I said. And that's how our professional relationship evolved into a friendship. Years ago, Frank asked me, "Would you be interested in helping me with my biography?" Back then, I laughed. Really. I was living on roller skates. I was writing three columns a week for the News & Record and freelancing as often as I could as layoffs in our newsroom continued and salary increases never happened for nearly a decade. Life was a blur.

"Frank, I wish I could," I told him. "But I have no time."

Years later, I made sure I had the time.

* * *

It was the fall of 2020, a time when fear, hatred and unfounded conspiracies had trumped facts and decency, civility and truth. We all watched in mute disbelief, sometimes screaming disbelief as a second-rate TV celebrity, a racist New Yorker intoxicated with his own perceived importance, vied for a second term in the White House, our House. This convenient Christian used the Bible to hoodwink evangelicals and manipulate the military to do his bidding. It was enough for me to lose my religion and unleash my share of F-bombs as nouns, verbs, and a string of adjectives on many days. Especially that summer. I saw dozens of National Guard troops standing guard on the steps of the Lincoln Memorial. They arrived to prevent protesters from vandalizing or destroying a shrine that we Americans see as sacred.

The irony of it all.

Inside that iconic American temple of marble were the words from Abraham Lincoln's Second Inaugural Address. They're chiseled into the north interior wall. On a Thursday in March 1865, a few months before the Civil War ended, Lincoln urged all Americans to put aside their bitterness. He wanted everyone to work together, to be compassionate toward one another and take to heart these words: *"With malice toward none, with charity for all."*

I remember how I felt when I first saw those words as a 10-year-old on my first visit to DC. Pride. But in the summer of 2020, I remembered how I felt about what I read and what I saw. Our America needed to find our moral compass once again and lean into what one well-known minister from Atlanta called a "coalition of conscience."

That's when I thought of Frank.

We talked about his biography again. I didn't have to think about it. I said, "Yes."

* * *

My professional life was no longer a treadmill. In October 2014, as layoffs began to mount and the newspaper industry started downsizing itself into irrelevance, I left the News & Record in Greensboro and accepted a job as senior writer for High Point University. By the summer of 2020, I had helped write and put together more than a few books for HPU as well as one of my own. The ripple effect of that work eased my fear of tackling a project as a big as a book. But I said yes to Frank not because of courage. I said yes because of need. I felt we needed a book like Frank's book because our country, our America, had begun to unravel. Frank had a story to tell, and I wanted to tell it because it was a story I felt we all needed to hear. We as a country had lost our way. We lacked the compassion, the empathy, the need to build bridges to understand those different from us in gender, race, nationality, political ideology, and religious beliefs — or lack thereof.

We had become an angry nation, a divided nation, a nation that addressed any difference of opinion with a raised fist, middle-school name calling, outright racism, and actual violence. Think Charlottesville, 2015. That will always be an emotional gut punch. Meanwhile, too many Americans saw journalists as the "enemy of the people" rather than the gatekeepers that kept government — and government officials — honest.

Then, of course, there was COVID-19.

In the midst of the world's first global pandemic in more than a century, the numbers were staggering. In the summer of 2020, the numbers looked this: 46 million cases worldwide, with 1.2 million deaths; in the United States, 9.4 million cases, with 236,000 million deaths.

Every one of those numbers represented someone's family, someone's loss. Yet, Americans wouldn't wear masks and protect others from infection because they saw that wearing a mask was a political statement or a sign of capitulation or some lame-brained idea that you're weak or something.

Then there was the self-absorbed man, the racist New Yorker, in our White House, the People's House. He dissed science and told us COVID-19 was behind us when he ran for reelection. At his rallies, he told his unmasked supporters doctors make lots of money by over-reporting the number of infected patients.

That's where we were. Five years later, not much has changed.

We are still angry, we are still divided, and after one term away from the People's House, our second-rate TV celebrity was voted back in for a second term. He won despite instigating an insurrection in January 2020 to overturn the election he claimed he won. He didn't. He won despite having a New York jury in May 2023 finding him liable for sexually abusing an advice columnist in 1996 and defaming her with his statements. He won despite having another New York jury in May 2024 finding him guilty of 34 felony counts for trying to illegally influence the 2016 election through hush money payment to a porn actor who said the two had sex. With the verdict, he became the first former president to be convicted of felony crimes.

As all that happened, I wrote. I talked with Frank. I talked with many others impacted by Frank. I revised and wrote, revised and wrote. I used Frank's words like pieces to a jigsaw puzzle and turned them into sermons I called "Frank on Frank" so he could explain in spiritual terms what unfolded in his life in the previous chapter. I collected photos, I talked with Frank some more, and I talked with others some more. And yes, I talked with his wife Michie a lot. I rode with Frank to Raleigh, Durham, and Lumberton to see his hometown and the Carolina Theater with the three doors: one for white, one for Black, one for a member of the Lumbee Tribe. That really started it all for Frank and his pursuit to right the wrongs of society. And now, five years later, Frank's book is finished. Finally.

Frank's story is a story of courage, resilience, and love. It shows how a middle-class kid from the small-town South became a social justice advocate unafraid to stand up for what he believed in, even if it meant getting arrested three times. He chose deliberately to walk a different professional path than many of his white peers of privilege, and along the way, he discovered a soulmate named Michie Harriss, a woman from Sanford way more direct than him. Smarter, too. "She graduated in three years, Phi Beta Kappa and cum laude," Frank likes to say. "And I graduated in four years and 'Oh, lawdy!'"

In the fall of 1972, as they posted "McGovern For President" signs across Robeson County, Michie joked, "Well, we have to get married. We are the only two liberals in Robeson County." They did, and together, they blazed a trail that helped make their corner of the South a more compassionate, more empathetic place to live.

For the brother and sister from Kansas they adopted and raised.

For the South African named Ali they befriended.

For the church Frank started.

For the psychological practice Michie began.

For the homeless Frank helped.

For the spiritually adrift Frank mentored.

For the nonprofit he initiated in the fourth quarter of his life with a corral of friends. Like he's done his entire life, he wanted to make sure those in need recover from the personal demons they face every day. The nonprofit, a program created by the Church of the Saviour in Washington, DC, has a name that works: Recovery Café.

After a half-century in ministry, Frank continues to help many. "A Calling: A Memoir of Ministry" delves into all that. In its pages, I hope we all can find a little hope and the inner drive we need to be more courageous, stand up to tyranny, and push hard against this idea that might is always right. We need to be unafraid to protest, vote, make calls, write letters, hold signs, and persist to resist. We need to gather with others and fight for an America where equality and due process are not wishes. We need to step out of our perceived comfort zones and help those who embody one of Frank's favorite phrases: "the least, the last, and the left out."

That's Frank's America. That's our America. Or what it needs to be.

As Frank's good friend, the Rev. Z Holler, said so often, "Press on, brother! Press on!"

Frank did. And does.

* * *

As I neared the finish line of Frank's book, I discovered an essay from the Pulitzer Prize winner and longtime activist Studs Terkel. It's his introduction to "Hope Dies Last," his last of 11 books before his death in October 2008 at the age of 96. "Hope Does Last" came out in 2003. What he believes resonates with so much with what we face today. Terkel wrote:

'When I was first beginning this book, I had my doubts. Hope, as a theme, seemed too abstract. My earlier works dealt with specifics, visceral stuff: the Depression, war, the job, race, age, and death. It was a matter of personal

*experience, of people dealing with what happened or was happening to them —
conditions that were imposed on them.*

*"Activists have always battled the odds. But it's not a matter of Sisyphus
rolling that stone up the hill. It's not Beckett's blind Pozzo staggering on. It's more
like a legion of Davids, with all sorts of slingshots. It's not one slingshot that will
do it. Nor will it happen at once. It's a long haul. It's step by step. As Mahalia
Jackson sang out, "We're on our way" — not to Canaan Land, perhaps, but to
a world as a better place than it has been before.*

*"It's what Kathy Kelly and her Voices in the Wilderness project is all about.
She is a direct descendent of Dorothy Day, who when asked why she was making
so much trouble for the authorities answered simply, "I'm working toward a world
in which it would be easier for people to behave decently."*

In an era where our democracy feels like sand slipping through
our fingers, we need slingshots to slay the Goliath we face and subdue
its lust for power and greed that is fed by lies, disinformation,
conspiracies, performative masculinity, and 24/7 vitriol that
encourages violence. We need to work toward a world where it's easier
for people to behave decently, where it's easier to respect one another,
where it's easier for the rule of law to be the rule of the day rather
than some whack-a-mole whimsy of leaders whose ego trumps
reason.

North Carolina's motto, adopted in 1893, is *"Esse quam videri."*
To be rather than to seem. In our era of discontent, our motto makes
me feel a bit like Goldilocks. It does feel right. To be rather than to
seem. To be like Dorothy Day. To be like Studs Terkel. To be like the
Rev. Frank Dew.

Yes, be like Frank.

That's why "A Calling: A Memoir of Ministry" matters. It's like
a weathervane. It can point us in the right direction where we can find
ways to make America — our America — what it needs to be for the
first time.

Can I hear an Amen?

-    *Jeri Rowe, April 27, 2025*

Frank Dew was the oldest of three, a kid who grew up in a loving household surrounded two sisters who called him "Buzzard." Frank and his two sisters, Sara and Phyllis, came of age in a city where the call letters of one of its radio stations celebrated its economic backbone. Lumberton's WTSB was short of Where Tobacco Sells Best.

Chapter 1

"You're A Social Gospeler"

"Some men see things as they are, and say, "Why?'; I dream things that never were and say, 'Why not?'" - Robert F. Kennedy

Frank Dew pulled out his yellow legal pad and began writing about Jesus.

It was the summer of 1969, the summer before he would start at Wake Forest. Frank was working as the summer intern at First Presbyterian Church in Lumberton, the white-columned church of his childhood, and he had spent a few days in a small room in the church's education building, writing, and rewriting in blue ink. He found himself sitting near a window, and as the light filtered through the curtains, he filled 10 pages. Frank was exhilarated as the words came in waves, culled from his years in Sunday School and sitting in the middle in a wooden pew with his family on Sunday mornings. After marking through words and scribbling down more thoughts, he read over what he had.

"Oh, this is real," he said to himself. "This'll work."

He had his first sermon. Frank was only 18, but he felt he had something to say, something he felt deep in his very bones. He believed a church should be more than a white-columned building.

The church's people, its congregation, needed to stand up and fight racism, and protest against a war that didn't make any sense to him. That all took some courage, especially in his house.

Frank was the oldest of three, the only son of a World War II veteran, a bomber pilot who never really questioned the authority of the government, let alone the decisions it made. As for racism, his father was a product of his Southern upbringing, and he felt powerless to change it. What could he do? His father asked that to himself. Yet, his son thought differently. Even as a teenager, Frank believed anyone can do a lot, everyone needs to do a lot. And in the summer of 1969, for the first time, he wrote it all down. A few days later, he walked into the office of the Rev. Bob Sloop, the slender man with wispy white hair Frank had known all his life.

Sloop had watched Frank grow up and blossom into a respected leader among the young people of the church. That particular morning, Frank sat across the desk from Sloop, and he wanted Sloop to hear his sermon and give him an idea of what worked — and what didn't. Above all, he wanted Sloop to hear what he believed faith needs to be. Frank fidgeted a bit, wondering what his minister would think. No matter, he pulled out his legal pad, and in his relaxed Southern accent sculpted by his years in Lumberton, Frank began.

"Faith needs to move from our heads and our hearts to our hands and our feet," Frank said. "We have to help the left-out and the less fortunate, and we need to march against the injustices we see around us. We need to be revolutionary, be counterculture and be demonstrative enough to turn tables over in a temple to make change happen. Just like Jesus."

Frank went on for a few more minutes. When he looked up from his legal pad, Frank met only silence. No 'That's great!' or "I love what you said there!" Nothing. Sloop was silent. With his hands folded under his chin, Sloop leaned back in his chair and stared at the ceiling. For 10 seconds, Sloop didn't say a word. Then, he spoke.

"You know, Frank, you're a social gospeler," Sloop said.

Frank leaned forward.

"What does *that* mean?" Frank asked.

"Oh," Sloop responded, pointing at Frank's legal pad. "It's what you got right there. Right there on your legal pad."

It was only years later as a seminary student when Frank realized what Sloop meant. When he did, Frank didn't think it was such a bad thing at all. Matter of fact, when he read what the Social Gospel movement was all about, he exclaimed out loud, "I've heard this before!"

The first social gospeler was a minister named Walter Rauschenbusch. He was a seventh-generation minister from New York who in the 19th century led the Social Gospel movement in America. He had piercing eyes, a stern chin, and he saw Jesus as a fighter dedicated to social reform. Rauschenbusch once said: "There was nothing mush, nothing sweetly effeminate about Jesus. He was the one that turned again and again on the snarling pack of His pious enemies and made them slink away. He plucked the beard of death, and He went into the city and their temple to utter those withering woes against the dominant class."

Rauschenbusch didn't mince any words. Neither did Frank. Frank may have been a bit more genteel in his delivery. But the rhetorical fire was the same, except with a Southern accent.

But that day in Rev. Sloop's office, Frank had no idea who this Rauschenbusch fellow was, and he sure didn't expect his minister to label him or his first sermon. But he trusted Sloop from all those years listening with rapt attention in the pews. So, when he got up to leave, Frank figured the phrase "social gospeler" must be appropriate.

"Well," Frank replied. "I guess you're right."

Frank walked out, feeling a bit confused, but happy. Sloop didn't change a word he wrote. And it was only Wednesday, and Frank knew he could fine-tune his sermon in his small room by the window before delivering it Sunday before his first congregation.

And it was a congregation where he didn't know a soul.

On Sunday morning, for his first sermon trip to the pulpit, Frank wore a Southern man's uniform: a blue blazer, tie, a light blue shirt and khakis. He slipped into the family's maroon Ford station wagon and drove 10 minutes to the mission church, the sister church of First Presbyterian.

The mission church was built of white cinder blocks with clear glass windows, wooden pews and a low ceiling. It was the home church of the working-class of Lumberton, situated in a mill village just beyond the city limits.

Many who lived there toiled at what made Lumberton wealthy — tobacco. Lumberton had 24 tobacco warehouses that covered 35 acres of space, and by 1969, the Lumberton Tobacco Market was edging close to its 75th anniversary. Since 1898, the city's tobacco warehouses had provided income for thousands and crafted the personality of this small city beside the Lumber River. All anyone had to do was tune into "Leather Lungs" Pridgen on Lumberton's WTSB to figure that out. The station's call letters stood for a four-word phrase that Lumberton believed — Where Tobacco Sells Best.

Frank had never worked tobacco. He mowed lawns for extra money. Yet, at 18, Frank was undaunted. He believed he could reach the people in the pews in front of him, and when his stomach began to twist, he kept thinking of the personal heroes he had lost in the past year to an assassin's bullet. He remembered what one of them said:

"The travail of freedom and justice is not easy, but nothing serious and important in life is easy. The history of humanity has been a continuing struggle against temptation and tyranny — and very little worthwhile has ever been achieved without pain."

Frank thought about those words from Robert F. Kennedy as he drove toward that mission church of white cinder blocks. What he was about to do was not easy, speaking in front of people he didn't know. So, when he pulled in, Frank said a prayer. He met some of the parishioners as he walked through the church doors and took a seat up near the pulpit. When he felt the butterflies of nervousness flying in his stomach, he closed his eyes and prayed again. A few minutes later, it was time.

With his legal pad under his arm, Frank stood behind the pulpit, took a breath, and began. He knew his sermon so well he barely looked down at the paper. He didn't need to turn page after page. He knew it. Frank looked at the 30 or so people in front and talked about his Jesus, about taking your faith from your heart to your hands and how we all have to make the world better for the least of these.

Twenty minutes later, Frank finished. He looked out over a congregation. They were as still as statues. Did they like it? Did it move them? Frank didn't know. He simply sat back down and left those questions unanswered. But he did it. His first sermon. At 18 years old, he had preached his first sermon and gave words to what he believed to an older congregation at least three times his age. Afterward, Frank walked from his seat near the pulpit to meet some of the church goers. His hands were slick with sweat and his throat felt as narrow as a straw. Frank didn't know what to expect. But growing up in the Dew household, where manners and graciousness prevailed, Frank knew what he had to do.

Meet them with a handshake and a smile. The parishioners smiled back and gave him his first grade.

"Thank you for being here," said one.

"Nice sermon," said another.

"Appreciate you so much," said a third. "Your words made so much sense."

"Thank you," Frank responded, beaming. "Thank you for listening."

In 2011, Frank teamed up with Jane Murden to write, "Improving Our Acoustics for Hearing the Gospel." In his book, Frank describes how working with the poor made him a better preacher. In those pages, right there on page 59, he writes about what kind of preacher he wanted to always be: "The point should be to help people to grow in hearing God's call in their lives and respond to it."

Frank wasn't much different at 18. His churning stomach had subsided; the butterflies gone. He felt good about his sermon because he spoke from his heart. As he weaved the family station wagon toward Tanglewood, the middle-class neighborhood where he lived, he kept thinking about what the Rev. Sloop said just a few days before.

"Social gospeler," he said to himself. "Whatever that means, it does seem to fit. Isn't that kinda cool?" Yes. Especially around the Dew dinner table. But those sermons were a bit more tense.

Frank on Frank

"Why Not?"

When I heard, 'You're a social gospeler,' I thought it was somewhat pejorative at first. But after leaving Rev. Sloop's office, the more I thought about it, the more I felt it did seem an appropriate label for me. It was a good thing, and I was gratified that he saw that in me. I definitely saw that in myself, especially then.

Now, you have to think of the context of that particular moment. The year was 1969. Think about all that was happening in my young life at the time. The civil rights movement. The assassinations. The Vietnam War. It was just another aspect of all those things referred to in these days as the generation gap. And that was the gap between the World War II generation and the Baby Boomer generation.

Back then, you could feel the times were a-changing even in Lumberton. But in the midst of that chaos and tragedy, there was a lot of idealism and a lot of hope for a better world. And it was born from this realization that we can't keep going on the way we were going. For me, it was grounded in the context of my faith and believing what Dr. King said, 'The arc of the moral universe is long, and it bends toward justice.'

Hope is not something based on the evidence. It's based on your own makeup and your own personality. At least for me it was.

Think about what is happening today. If you think about what's around us, all the evidence does not give anyone a sense of hope. There's climate change, the continuing need for racial justice and the continuing threats against our democracy. But what the evidence does point to is that people are recognizing that we cannot continue as we have been.

That's how it was in 1969. No matter how bleak it was, I felt there was an opportunity for change, grounded in a hope that God's purpose will prevail. I still believe that today. I believe that is a part of my calling. I work to encourage hope in others, and to me, that feels like a gift.

There's this quote that Bobby Kennedy used during his presidential campaign in 1968. He got it from George Bernard Shaw. Kennedy said, "Some men see things as they are, and say, 'Why?', I dream things that never were and say, 'Why not?'"

That has always spoken to me. It's about seeing any crisis through a lens of hope. We all have gifts. People have a gift of music or art or athletics. I see my gift as being hopeful. It's up to us, you and me, to see how we use our gifts.

In this June 15, 1967 file photo, American infantrymen crowd into a mud-filled bomb crater and look up at tall jungle trees seeking out Viet Cong snipers firing at them during a battle in Phuoc Vinh, north-Northeast of Saigon in Vietnam's War Zone D. The war ended on April 30, 1975, with the fall of Saigon, now known as Ho Chi Minh City, to communist troops from the north. Photo credit: AP Photo/Henri Huet, File

Chapter 2

"God, Please Protect Our Country"

"Dad, think about what Kennedy said about war. I heard it in class. 'Mankind must put an end to war before war puts an end to mankind.' I think Cronkite is doing a good thing. It's something we need to hear." The young Frank Dew to his father, Luther Dew, the World War II veteran, at dinner.

It was February 1968, the last Tuesday of the month, when Frank's dad, Luther Dew, took up his regular spot in the den. He had hung up his coat and sat in the high back armchair in front of the TV, still wearing his tie from his day of working real estate and building homes in Lumberton.

Luther was a coat-and-tie man, a family man, and he liked this time of day. He got to watch the CBS News with Walter Cronkite. And he got to watch it with Frank. Frank sat a few feet away on the couch, and during commercials, he'd sometimes turn to his father and spark a conversation by saying, "Gosh, did you see that?"

But on this particular Tuesday, during Frank's junior year at Lumberton High, Frank grew quiet during the commercial break. Luther did, too. For years, father and son had watched Cronkite deliver the news in just-the-facts style. But this time, as the Dews and the rest of America tuned in, Cronkite delivered his own editorial on the Vietnam War. It was Cronkite's first-ever editorial. Frank had never seen anything like it. Or Luther. They grew still and quiet, as quiet as a Sunday morning in church, and listened.

*The reporting by CBS anchor Walter Cronkite in Vietnam changed the public
perception of the war. Photo credit: National Archives*

"It seems now more certain than ever that the bloody experience
of Vietnam is to end in a stalemate," Cronkite said. "It is increasingly
clear to this reporter that the only rational way out then is to negotiate
not as victims but as honorable people who lived up to their pledge
to defend democracy and did the best they could."

Frank heard the click-click-click of plates and silverware from
the dining room, five steps up from the den.

"Dinner's ready!" his mom, Louise, yelled.

Frank got up from the couch without saying a word. He walked
up the steps into the dining room and slid into his chair, across from
his two younger sisters, Phyllis and Sara, and bowed his head over his
plate of roast beef and mushroom gravy, broccoli, cooked carrots and
a roll. Leftovers from Sunday dinner. His dad came right behind him
and sat at the head of the table, head down, wringing his hands. His
mom waltzed in from the kitchen, still wearing her charcoal slacks and
cream sweater she had worn that day.

"Hello, everybody!" Louise said in her sing-song voice.

She sat down at the other end of the table near the kitchen,
oblivious to the night's news.

"How was everyone's day?" she chimed in. "And yes, I have dessert."

Frank didn't respond. Instead, he looked up at the rosy pink walls and eyed the gift from his Aunt Frances, one of his dad's sisters. She was a talented painter, and she gave Luther and Louise her painting of a bough of a pine tree with the flag

of North Carolina in the corner. In the middle, she had painted in green letters the official State Toast of North Carolina.

Frank always liked looking at Aunt Frances' painting because he loved the line, "Where the weak grow strong and the strong grow great." He always wanted to believe that, particularly now. After hearing Cronkite's editorial, Frank had become a jumble of nerves. So, he read the whole toast to himself because he needed some sort of emotional anchor. And the State Toast of North Carolina always helped.

Here's to the land of the long leaf pine,
The summer land where the sun doth shine,
Where the weak grow strong and the strong grow great,
Here's to "Down Home," The Old North State!

Frank sighed. "Let us pray," he said.

Frank bowed his head and squeezed his eyes shut.

"God, thank you for the blessing of family and food, and for the blessing of being together," he said. "Let us pray for peace in the world and help the peacemakers and help us be the peacemakers."

After the prayer, the Dews served themselves family-style. Louise smiled, and Phyllis and Sara darted looks at one another. They could tell something was gnawing at Frank and their dad. The broadcaster Frank grew up with and the one Luther always trusted had just told millions of viewers that we Americans needed to get out of Vietnam. For a few minutes, they all ate in silence. Finally, Frank set down his fork and looked at his dad, the World War II veteran who enlisted in the Army Air Corps and flew B-24 bombers over the Pacific. Frank knew he needed to say something because of what he had just heard.

"Dad, I don't know. You've told me before that quote from Sherman, Gen. William Tecumseh Sherman, about how he said, 'War is hell.' I get that. If people don't follow orders, people get killed and everything goes to hell. I don't disagree with that. But ..."

Frank exhaled. He knew what he was walking into. His dad would raise his voice, his sisters would squirm in their seats and his mom would try to be peacemaker, saying something like, "Now, we don't have to talk about that now, do we?"

But Frank had to. He needed to. So, he took in a breath and continued.

"But Dad, if people don't follow their conscience, wouldn't it be better if we were asking, 'What's right in this circumstance?' You heard Cronkite. He believes the Vietnam War is wrong. And ..."

"Yes, I heard it, Frank," Luther said, interrupting his son, "and I have never EVER heard Cronkite say something like that. But how SMART is that to tell the whole nation? All of us. We Dews. We everyone. Right here in our den. Saying that we need to get out of the war. We have servicemen over there right now. Boys barely older than you, Frank. Trying to do the right thing and following orders, fighting the enemy and then they hear about Cronkite saying THIS?"

"But how do they know if the orders they're getting are right?" Frank asked.

"If we don't stop the Communists THERE," responded Luther, his voice rising, "where will they stop?"

Back and forth they went. Phyllis and Sara didn't look up. The dinner-table debates between their dad and Frank happened several times a month, and every time, they felt the stress rise around the table like an incoming tide. They didn't like it because they didn't want Frank, at least nine years their senior, to get in trouble. They were two sisters, a year and 10 days apart in age. Really, though, they were best friends. And they'd been best friends for years.

And for good reason.

* * *

Phyllis and Sara, Frank's two sisters as teenagers.

Sara called her sister "Phyl."

She and her older sister shared a room wallpapered with ballerinas all in pink. Sara and Phyl liked nothing better than to hop on their bikes' banana seats and just go. Phyl's bike was blue; Sara's was pink. They'd pedal fast to just past the railroad tracks two blocks from their house and mess around in the tree forts they built. Phyl was scared of thunderstorms, and when she heard the rumble and shake outside their bedroom window, Phyl would jump in bed beside her sister to feel safe. Sara didn't mind as long as her sister didn't touch her back. She traced a line with her finger down the middle of the bed, and Phyl couldn't cross it. She never did.

The girls wore matching dresses at Easter and toted to church white wicker pocketbooks with little slick flowers on them. They had nicknames for each other, and they wore those nicknames like a badge of honor. Sara was "Sadie," and Phyl was "Phylly" or "Rascal." They called Frank "Buzzard," something they had heard from "The Andy Griffith Show" when Andy said to Opie, "Oh, you little buzzard!"

The name stuck.

So, when their dinner table discussions turned heated, Phyl and Sara kept quiet and longed for their life on a banana seat rather than their life after Walter Cronkite. On the Tuesday of Cronkite's broadcast editorial on Vietnam, they waited for Mom, the peacekeeper, to intervene. She didn't. So, Phyl and Sara had to listen.

They had always looked up to Frank, and they always were a bit intimidated by their dad, the stern officer of the household. He always raised his voice, but Frank never did. He always tried to rely on logic rather than emotion.

But as a teenager, Frank never gave his dad enough credit because he didn't hear about his dad's combat experience in the Pacific Theater during World War II until he was a seminary student. And the stories he heard were more like snapshots.

He wished he knew more because he later heard from one of his aunts that Luther came back from the war a changed man.

He finished his accounting degree, worked for the state Department of Revenue for three years and later moved to Lumberton to work for a real estate firm and build subdivisions. There, in a city named after the Lumber River, was where he met Louise McLeod, the former Miss Robeson County.

When he was older, Frank remembered one story that he wished he had brought up around the dinner table during their spirited discussions when he was a teenager. He would love to know more about that one. It's the story about how his dad nearly died.

* * *

Louise and Luther Dew, Frank's parents.

Luther Dew Jr, the farm boy and paper boy from Richmond, Va., was in his early 20s. He had spent two years at UNC-Chapel Hill, pursuing an accounting degree, when he was moved to enlist in the Army Air Corps after the attack on Pearl Harbor. He learned to fly B-24s, long-range bombers known as the Liberator or the "Flying Coffin" because of its stiff and heavy controls. Luther was the handsome, happy-go-lucky Southerner, stationed in the Pacific flying bombing missions and targeting the enemy, the Japanese.

On one mission, he had to turn around because the cloud cover prevented him from dropping bombs from his plane. With the bombs still onboard, Luther knew he and his crew couldn't make it back to the base. Luther dropped the bombs, and they exploded beneath the plane. The B-24 he was flying crashed into the Pacific. Luther and the others in the plane bailed out, reassembled in the water, and swam to a nearby island. The natives on the island took them in and protected them from the Japanese. The next day, his dad and his crew were rescued.

Luther never told Frank that harrowing story. Later in life, he told it to Frank's wife. What Frank heard was how his dad got beer as part of his rations and kept the beer cool by putting it into the airplane during flights. Or, he heard how his dad bought a tennis racquet during R&R in Australia, and it got so hot in his tent the strings started to pop. Sounded like gunfire, Luther told his son.

But that's it. Frank didn't hear about his dad's survival story in the Pacific around the dinner table, but on that Tuesday after Cronkite's eye-opening editorial, Frank simply wanted to convince his dad that he was right.

"Dad, think about what Kennedy said about war. I heard it in class. 'Mankind must put an end to war before war puts an end to mankind.' I think Cronkite is doing a good thing. It's something we need to hear."

Luther began wringing his hands and looked up at his son with sad eyes. Frank didn't know what his dad had seen during his time in combat, and his dad wasn't going to start telling those stories now. Luther took a deep breath and looked at Louise. She gave him a tight smile, smoothed her hands on her slacks and scooted back her chair. She knew what her husband's look meant. Change the subject.

"Well," she said, looking bright-eyed around the table. "Does anyone want dessert? I've got a sheet of brownies with vanilla ice cream."

Louise got up from the table, followed by Sara and Phyl who wanted to help. Luther kept silent. Frank, too. Frank wanted to feel like he won. But he didn't. He kept thinking of the PT boat tie clasp his dad gave him years ago.

The tie clasp became one of Frank's favorite keepsakes, right up there with the stack of 700 baseball cards he got from Wood's Dime Store for his seventh birthday. The cost: $7, a penny a card. The baseball cards reminded Frank of the time Smokey the dog ate the rawhide rug in his room right before Christmas. Or the times he let Zipper the parakeet play in the bedsprings of his upper bunk.

The tie clasp, though, reminded Frank of John F. Kennedy.

In World War II, Kennedy was a lieutenant in the U.S. Navy, and he captained PT Boat 109. In August 1943, just south of the Solomon Islands in the Pacific Ocean, a Japanese destroyer rammed Kennedy's Patrol Torpedo boat and threw Kennedy and his crew into the water. Kennedy helped save his crew and earned the Navy and Marine Corps Medal, and the injuries he suffered during the incident qualified him for a Purple Heart.

Frank liked that story because, as a kid who slept in a room wallpapered with cowboy hats and horseshoes, six shooters and lariats, Frank liked heroes. On Saturdays at the Carolina Theater in downtown Lumberton, Frank and his cousins liked nothing better than watching the matinee movies featuring Lone Ranger or Robin Hood. Those were Frank's childhood heroes. But Kennedy was one of Frank's real-life heroes. He was young, handsome, and progressive in his views. And as Frank got more interested in politics and what he thought politicians could do to make the world a better place, Kennedy became the person who represented all that, all that was good in the world.

That's what made that one Friday in November 1963 so awful.

* * *

In 1963, Frank was a seventh grader at Joseph P. Moore Junior High. One late autumn afternoon, he sat in his last period class, in the back with his buddies in Mrs. Davenport's room. It was his mom's birthday, and his dad was going to pick him up after school, and they were going to The Fashion Bar in downtown Lumberton to pick out a birthday gift for his mom. Then, over the intercom came the announcement that the president had been shot. Frank sat there stunned. Neither he nor his friends said a word. Shortly afterward came another announcement. John F. Kennedy, the 35th president of the United States, was dead.

As Frank sat at his desk in the back of Mrs. Davenport's room, he felt lightheaded. He couldn't believe what he had just heard. The president was dead. Kennedy was dead. The man whose face graced a calendar hung on his bedroom wall was dead.

One question kept running through his mind. Why? He didn't have an answer.

After school, his dad picked him up. Neither said a word. His dad knew, Frank thought. They drove to The Fashion Bar and picked out a pink coat and a pink skirt. They got the presents wrapped, drove home and the first person Frank saw was Hattie, the family's Black maid.

When he walked into the house, carrying his mom's birthday presents, Frank found Hattie in the den standing at the ironing board. She was watching the TV, ironing clothes, her back to Frank.

"Hey, Hattie," Frank said.

Hattie didn't reply.

Frank stopped. He looked at the TV and saw the face of Cronkite. Skinny black tie. Glasses off. Rolled-up sleeves. Frank listened. He hung on every word Cronkite said.

Dallas.

Dealey Plaza.

Three shots.

From an assassin.

"Oh, no!" shouts Mrs. Kennedy.

Parkland Memorial Hospital.

The president is dead.

Frank stood still, holding his mom's present. Standing beside Hattie and hearing the sh-sh-sh of an iron going across a pair of pants, he stared at the TV and then looked at Hattie. She was crying, tears rolling down her face. Frank teared up, too. But he didn't say a word. He and Hattie simply stood together listening to the no-nonsense baritone of Cronkite delivering news that they both knew they'd remember forever. Of all days, this day, on his mom's birthday. A day of joy for his mom. A day of dashed hopes for the nation.

Later that night, Frank went to a birthday party a few blocks away. He got to hear a new group called The Beatles. Their debut album had come out nine months before. As the album played on a nearby turntable, he picked up the album cover and saw four young, happy-faced guys from England, leaning over a rail. He listened, the poppy sound of the first single spilling from a speaker nearby.

Love, love me do
You know I love you
I'll always be true
So please, eeese
Love me do
Whoa, love me do

A few of his classmates from Moore Junior High clustered around him. Everyone seemed so happy, dancing, snacking on cake, seemingly oblivious to the events of the day. Frank wasn't. He couldn't shake what he had heard in Mrs. Davenport's class and what he had seen on TV standing beside Hattie. So, he talked to some of the classmates around him. Right away, he knew he shouldn't have.

"I didn't like Kennedy anyway."

"Maybe, he deserved it."

His classmates' responses shocked Frank. And Frank being Frank, he couldn't keep quiet.

"I can't believe you're saying that," he half-shouted over the music from The Beatles. "He died, man. He died! Killed by an assassin's bullet. Our president. And he's your president, too!"

Later that night, Frank sat on the floor of his bedroom. He felt a sense of comfort, surrounded by his blue cowboy wallpaper, his bunk beds and his model airplanes and ships hanging from his ceiling with fishing line. He knew he needed it. In his lap was the monthly calendar that showed the faces of all the presidents and the time they served.

The face he stared at was the captain of PT Boat 109. Frank couldn't believe he was gone. He kept hearing in his head the words Cronkite spoke earlier that night. Frank closed his eyes. He thought of his mom saying prayers with him and his two sisters every night. Those nightly prayers anchored him. So, as he sat on the floor, he knew he had to do this by himself.

"God, please protect our country."

Frank said it over and over.

President John F. Kennedy and his wife, Jackie, arrive that fateful day in
Dallas. Photo credit: Cecil Stoughton. White House Photographs. John F.
Kennedy Presidential Library and Museum, Boston

* * *

Throughout his teenage years, Frank leaned on God a lot. He learned
that from his family. His mom read the Bible to him and his sisters
every night, and his dad was the Sunday School superintendent at First
Presbyterian, their home church. Frank would find himself there every
Sunday, sitting two thirds of the way back in the sanctuary. His dad
sat on one end of the pew and his mom on the other. He sat beside
his dad; his sisters sat to his right. And there they'd be, every Sunday,
his dad passing peppermint lifesavers to him and his sisters during the
sermon to keep them quiet. Frank began to think about his next step
in life. He knew why.

It was because of that Friday in November 1963, his mom's
birthday. And that Tuesday in November 1968; Cronkite's editorial.
Those were moments in his life that hit him like the bombing of Pearl

Harbor had hit his dad.

His dad went into the Army. Frank went toward God. Frank believed God would show him how to fight for what he believed in and what route he could take. And Frank only thought of two routes — either work in politics or wear the white collar of a minister. Even living in his hometown of Lumberton, a cocoon of a place that protected him and showed him love, Frank felt an earthquake of bigotry and racism, hate and callous indifference rippling toward him, and he was going to do something about it.

But what?

Frank knew God would help show him the way.

Or would He?

Frank on Frank

"Seeing Is Not Always Believing"

My earliest memory of prayer goes back to my mom and my sisters, Phyl and Sara.

We prayed together almost every night, around 8 o'clock. We'd all go up to my sisters' room, I would sit on one bed, and my mom would be on the opposite bed, and she would read from a children's devotional Bible for about 15 minutes.

By the way, Sara still has that book.

Back then, those nightly sessions reminded me that God is real and personal and that He cared about our circumstances, and even at a young age, prayer taught me that I could go to God with my concerns, whatever they might be.

Given my upbringing, it was a natural thing for me to do that, especially in a time of crisis. I looked toward a power that was greater than myself. So, when John F. Kennedy was killed, and I was sitting on the floor of my bedroom holding that calendar with a picture of him on it, I knew we all needed that loving, caring, providential power to guide and protect our country.

One of the things I've learned from the 12-step folks is that two of the most important prayers are 'Help' and 'Thank you.' I often like to say that when you hear people talking about prayer in schools, I always said that as long as you have math in schools, you'll have prayer in schools. You know what I mean? We all need help in math, don't we?

One of the unique things about Christianity is this whole idea of the incarnation, the enfleshment of God. He is real. I've had people ask, 'What is God?' And the simple and profound answer is God is like Jesus. So, while we can't see God, what we know about God most clearly is that we see Him in the life of Jesus.

That tells us a ton, don't you think?

God is not a fill-in-the-blank God. God has filled in the blanks with Jesus. We can look to Him in times of joy and celebration, gratitude and thanksgiving, and you can trust Him even in a moment of uncertainty. I've always believed that.

I remember one time in my early 40s when I called a friend in Lumberton, and I wanted him to help me find a Chevrolet Blazer to buy. My dad had bought cars from him, I trusted him, and I figured I'd trade in my car for the Blazer. So, I called him up, and he said, 'Oh, I can get that for you. I'll have one of my guys drive it up to Southern Pines, and we'll meet you there. You can give us your car, and you can take this one.'

It was the color of silver champagne, a beautiful car. I bought it without seeing it, and it turned out to be a great car. But my dad, he simply couldn't understand why I did that. He was like, 'Are you going to buy a car you've never seen before?' And I told him, 'Dad, I do things every day that I have not seen before. Seeing is not always believing.'

People ask me all the time, 'What is prayer?' And to me, it's the awareness of being in the presence of God. Prayer is deeper than words. Paul talks about praying constantly. So, it's not always about saying something. Sometimes, it's more about listening and awareness.

You hear this term a lot today. Mindfulness. To me, that is what prayer is. It's your mindful connection with God, and when you think of prayer that way, all of life becomes a prayer. Here's what I mean.

I can walk outside and see the beauty, the sunshine, and all the leaves that have fallen over the grass around my house. The beauty of that is like a painter's palette. But you have to be aware of that and connect with that. It's not always about giving God a to-do list. It can simply be all about listening. You never know what you'll hear.

Carolina Theater. Photo credit: NC State University Libraries

Chapter 3
Planting The Seed

"I saw the need for change all around me in Robeson County. My county was wrestling with all sorts of race issues. All I had to do was look at the Carolina Theatre in downtown Lumberton and be reminded of the racism around me. Or really, I simply had to stand on North Chestnut and look for the three separate doors — one for Blacks, one for Lumbees, one for people who looked like me."

The Rev. Frank Dew

Frank knows that baseball field.

It sits beside the National Guard Armory in Lumberton, and when he was 10, he went to see the great Leroy Paige pitch.

Yes, that's Satchel Paige.

As a youngster growing up in Mobile, Alabama, Paige earned his nickname by carrying luggage for businessmen at the local train station and hearing one of his co-workers say, "You look like a walking satchel tree." The nickname stuck. But he earned his legend by throwing a whistling fastball that hovered just above your knees. He stood 6-feet-4, thin as a rail, and when he pitched, he'd kick his foot high in the air, bring his right arm from behind his body and hurl it forward like a whip. And he learned that in reform school in Alabama, sent there at age 12 for petty theft and truancy.

"You might say," he once said, "I traded five years of freedom to learn how to pitch."

Satchel was a baseball legend, a walking symbol of segregation when the major leagues didn't allow Blacks to play. And yet, at 42, he entered the majors for the first time. At 59, he continued to play. At 65, he was inducted into the Baseball Hall of Fame, a talented showman from the Deep South who used baseball and an eye-catching delivery to dismantle a country's color barrier that made no sense to Frank Dew.

Frank remembers that baseball field, the one that sits next to Bethany Presbyterian Church, the only other Presbyterian church in town. It was the Black church, built out of cinder blocks by the descendants of freed slaves.

Bethany Presbyterian was founded in 1875 in the homes of former slaves. By 1932, a time when one out of every three Americans was unemployed, parishioners built Bethany Presbyterian on the land where it stands today. A church elder named William Hooper Jr. drew up the architectural plans, parishioners used cinder blocks made on the property, and they began building their dream church. They provided the muscle and expertise, and for six years, they worked. By 1938, they stepped into a church that looked like a small castle at the corner of Willow Street and Elizabethtown Road. With two stained glass windows and a cascading stairway, Bethany Presbyterian became, as the Apostle Paul once wrote, "God's household."

Frank thought he could fight the lunacy of segregation he saw around him by working with Bethany Presbyterian in some way. But how? At just 16, he was trying to figure out the how. He simply knew the why. In the summer of 1968, he knew he needed to do something,

He saw his country beginning to unravel. An assassin's bullet had taken down two of his heroes — presidential candidate Robert F. Kennedy and civil rights leader Martin Luther King Jr. — and he felt helpless. He felt a need to bring people together in his hometown.

For years, he cringed how racism stained his city, and he wanted to do something about it, something that could bring people together, both Black and white. He had an idea. He wanted to carry out a ritual as old as the New Testament, a ritual both Blacks and whites embraced. Frank wanted to host Communion at his home church and invite parishioners from Bethany Presbyterian. Frank brought the idea to the elders of First Presbyterian, and they encouraged Frank to do it. But being 16, an idealistic junior at Lumberton High with big ideas, Frank knew he needed help. So, he turned to his best friend, his fishing buddy and fellow hunter, Spencer Clark. He knew Spencer felt the same way he did.

Like Frank, Spencer saw racism up-close.

* * *

Spencer lived a 10-minute bike ride from Frank. From his home in the neighborhood known as Tanglewood, Frank could hop on his blue Schwinn from his house on West 28th Street, pedal south two blocks and take a left onto West 26th Street. Three blocks later, he'd arrive at Spencer's house. There, they'd work on school projects together and shoot hoops on Spencer's backyard basketball goal. Or Frank would simply look at the car parked in the driveway of Spencer's neighbor next door.

Spencer lived next to Charles Robert Minges, the co-owner of a Pepsi Cola Bottling franchise in Lumberton. Minges' Pepsi Cola plant bottled Mountain Dew and made the soft drink a commercial success. And who could forget the image on that green glass bottle? A gun-toting hillbilly.

Anyway, Frank liked Mountain Dew and all. But what Frank really liked was what he saw in the Minges' driveway — a navy-blue Ford Mustang with a white convertible top and wire wheels. Frank was around 14 when he saw it. He had never seen one before, and when he did in the Minges' driveway, he just stared. Then, he began to dream.

"I want me one of them," he told himself.

He would — in due time. But at 16, he had more important things to do, and he knew Spencer would help him pull it off.

Spencer was one of four, the second oldest child of Douglas Hendon and Carolyn Huntington Jordan Clark. His dad was a doctor; his mom, a homemaker and a member of the first class of several notable Presbyterian women selected by the congregation as Elders at First Presbyterian.

The Clark family used to eat at about three or four restaurants in Lumberton. The one Spencer remembers was on the corner across the street from the Confederate memorial in front of the courthouse. Spencer was no older than 10 when his family left the restaurant, and his dad told him they would never eat there again.

"Why not?" Spencer asked.

"They have a sign in the front door that says, 'Whites Only,'" his dad told him. "We won't be going anymore because of the sign 'Whites Only.'"

Dr. Clark was the chairman of the school board, a man who helped integrate Lumberton's public schools. Carolyn Clark was the wise sage, the woman who believed Sunday mornings shouldn't be the most segregated hour of the week. She talked to Spencer about that during their afternoons together after school.

Spencer sat on the kitchen counter and listened. From those discussions, Spencer believed that the church should be more involved in helping right the wrongs in a segregated society.

And what was Spencer's society? His church. First Presbyterian Church.

Frank felt the same way. And like Spencer, Frank's idea of racism had a place.

* * *

The Carolina Civic Center was a box of a building in downtown Lumberton. Opened in 1928 as the Carolina Theatre, the showplace was one of a handful of theaters built across North Carolina that showed silent movies and vaudeville performances. These theaters were always stately structures. They anchored historic sections of Charlotte and Winston-Salem, Durham and Greensboro.

They also were a brick-and-mortar metaphor, an overt sign of segregation. Blacks and whites had separate entrances, separate bathrooms, and separate sections in which to sit.

The Carolina Theatre in Lumberton was no exception.

As a kid, the Carolina Theatre was the place where Frank's imagination roared. He'd go there on Saturdays with his Aunt Sally or his mom. He, Spencer and his two cousins, Alex and James Donald, would sink into the seats downstairs and take in Disney movies about talking dogs and frontier legends played by actor Fess Parker. But every time he went, he'd look above him and wonder, "What's up there?"

He never went upstairs. But he knew. All he had to do was stand on North Chestnut and see where he entered — through a door in the front. But not patrons who were Black or members of the Lumbee Tribe of North Carolina. They'd enter through doors on the side, walk up to the balcony and sit in a section separated by a wall. The Blacks sat on one side; the Lumbees on the other.

Historians believe the Lumbees, the largest Native American tribe in North Carolina, descended from several Native American tribes as well as the English settlers of the Lost Colony in Eastern North Carolina in the 16th century. Lumbees adopted the English language and Christianity and made Robeson as well as surrounding counties in southeastern North Carolina their home. Nearly a third of Robeson County's residents were Lumbees. Yet, like the Blacks, Lumbees couldn't escape the shame of discrimination. All they had to do was see the separate door at the Carolina, attend the separate schools reserved for them and find the separate bathrooms with the one initial on the door — I for Indian.

Frank could never understand any of that. It didn't make sense to him, even when he was as young as 6. He was raised in a house where the New Testament prevailed. It was the idea of loving your neighbor, like you loved yourself, no matter the color of your skin, the background of your family, the gender you claimed, or the church you attended.

And yet, like Spencer, Frank saw the "Whites Only" signs in places like the downtown restaurant across from the courthouse and the separate bathrooms for Blacks and whites and Lumbees and the separate waiting rooms at the bus station and the separate water fountains at the courthouse. That separation without explanation bothered him even when his boyhood universe involved baseball cards and a parakeet named Zipper.

It bothered him because of two Black women named Hattie and Dee Dee.

* * *

Hattie was a short, slender woman, with narrow shoulders and kind eyes. She worked in the Dew house for at least six years, and Frank loved her like family. Frank rode with his mom to pick her up at her house on the south side of the Lumber River, where many Blacks in Lumberton lived. They lived, as Frank always heard, "across the river."

That separation didn't exist in the Dews' house or in the Dews' station wagon.

"Frank, you need to sit in the back seat," his mother would tell him every time she picked up Hattie.

Frank always slipped into the back of the family station wagon. But with Frank being Frank, he asked why. The question first came when he was at Tanglewood Elementary. His mom had an answer.

"Why does Hattie always sit in the front seat when we pick her up?" he asked one day.

"Well, Frank," his mom responded. "Hattie is older than you, and we should respect her as an adult. And remember, when she tells you to do something, you do it. You have to respect her."

He also saw his mom loan Hattie money when she needed something or someone in her family needed something. But he didn't ask a question about that. His mom — the former Miss Robeson County, the woman who lost her mom when she was in elementary school — knew heartache and struggle firsthand. Hattie knew it, too. Frank began to understand that compassion had no color line, no sign that exclaimed for "Whites Only." Nope. So, he absorbed what he saw, especially when he sat in the back going across the Lumber to Hattie's house.

He'd listen to his mom and Hattie chatting like neighbors across a backyard fence. At the Dew house, Hattie did a little of everything. She ironed and washed clothes and did a lot of what Frank calls "straightening up." She also gave Frank a front-row seat in understanding the impact of grief. That was the day John F. Kennedy was assassinated. Frank saw her ironing, watching the news reports on the Dews' black-and-white TV with tears streaming down her face.

Then there was Bessie Moore. Everyone called her Dee Dee. She was the Black maid for the McLeods, Frank's cousins. She was the ever-present figure during their trips to Holden Beach. And Frank loved those trips.

His Aunt Sally was the fun aunt who took Frank and her sons, Alex and James Donald, to the Carolina Theatre for Saturday matinees. She became their storyteller on trips to the beach in their family's white Ford station wagon. She would sit in the front seat, and the boys sat in the back. Aunt Sally would read "Swiss Family Robinson" or "Robinson Crusoe" or "Treasure Island" on their way toward the coast. Like those Saturdays in a darkened theater in downtown Lumberton, Frank's imagination took off. He was surrounded by people he loved, even more so when he got to the beach.

Dee Dee was a part of that.

She'd already be at the McLeod's beach house, in her dark blue dress and blue apron trimmed in white. Dee Dee became their chaperone, their playmate, their friend.

She walked down to the pier with the boys and she'd be with them catching crabs with fish heads and chicken necks. Or she'd be an arm's length away, supervising them as they caught croakers and spots off the pier using shrimp as bait. Then, back at the house, she'd boil the crabs and fry up the fish the boys caught. Dee Dee would toss the croakers and spots in flour, fry up the day's catch and serve it up alongside her cornbread, the signature dish she cooked in a cast iron skillet.

Frank and his cousins loved that cornbread for its crunchy buttery taste. But as Frank got older, Frank started to pay more attention to Dee Dee. She'd slip snuff into her lower lip, and as she cooked or did anything around the beach house, she'd be humming. It was this low hum, deep and melodious. As church became more of a cornerstone of his life, Frank recognized what Dee Dee was humming. Hymns. These were the hymns she learned in church. But he also recognized the authoritative firmness she held over him and his cousins during their stays at the beach. She worked hard for the McLeod family and Frank respected that firmness. She also looked out for James Donald, known today by the nickname his brother, Alex, gave him decades ago.

Brownie. That's the name of Alex's sock monkey.

Brownie was the youngest of the three cousins, and he had to endure the tricks Frank and Alex played on him. There were a few. One involved black mud along the coast.

Frank and Alex told Brownie he'd get a $1 million from their neighbor, Mr. Shambley, if he jumped off the pier near their house, into the black mud of the Intracoastal Waterway. Brownie did it. He figured he could use the $1 million. So, he jumped and walked up to Mr. Shambley's house, caked in black mud that often smelled like rotten eggs. He knocked on the front door and out came Mr. Shambley.

"Mr. Shambley?" Brownie asked. "I want my million dollars!"

Brownie walked back, long faced. Alex and Frank laughed until they saw the look on Dee Dee's face. And she could give them a look. She'd cock her head, show a slight smile, and begin with her index finger raised.

"Now, boys," she told them in her sternest voice. "You know you did Brownie wrong. You can laugh and all. But you need to stop teasing him. That just ain't right. Now, Brownie, you go get cleaned up. And Alex and Frank, I got one thing to say to you. Stop." And so Brownie, covered in black mud and humiliation, was christened.

The boys always listened to Dee Dee. The McLeods thought of her like extended family, an aunt they trusted with their family life.

On their beach trips, she and Brownie shared a room. And behind the McLeod's home in the country just outside Lumberton, they built a small house for Dee Dee.

Frank and his cousins played football in the goat pasture to the left of their house, using the goats as blockers and thinking they were Lumberton's version of Charlie "Choo-Choo" Justice. After the games, they'd sometimes go see Dee Dee.

Inside her house were portraits Frank knew. Dee Dee had them hanging on the wall, pictures of Martin Luther King Jr., John F. Kennedy and the handsome Jesus seen in many a church fellowship hall. For a young boy, that house symbolized what was good about his world —Dee Dee humming under her breath, serving her buttery sweet cornbread and keeping them in line with a smile and wag of her finger.

But Frank grew up in a world where he heard whites degrade the civil rights movement by calling the Blacks involved the six-letter word that cut deep. Frank heard other words, too. Blacks involved in civil rights were seen as "uppity" and whites who got involved were "outside agitators" and "troublemakers." As he grew older, those words hit Frank like a punch in the gut, and he always felt helpless. He wanted to change the South that he loved and show them why the lessons he learned from the New Testament applied to all people, not just white people who attended First Presbyterian. By the time of his junior year at Lumberton High, he believed communion with Bethany Presbyterian was the way to go. But as he and Spencer spent months making this happen, Frank had one question bouncing constantly in his head.

Would this work?

* * *

Anti-war demonstrators gather opposite the Lincoln Memorial in Washington, D.C., Oct. 21, 1967. Photo credit: The Associated Press.

Spencer and Frank sat side by side in the fellowship hall of First Presbyterian. And they were just giddy.

They saw members of two Presbyterian churches, Black and white, holding individual cups and individual wafers and sharing communion together. It was months in the making, full of compromises where the setting went from a sanctuary to the fellowship hall, from a common cup and common loaf to individual servings. But the big thing was this: It happened. Blacks and whites came together and shared what they have in common, and it happened during the summer of 1968 after an assassin's bullet extinguished hope in an America that needed hope. Frank felt this one act in his hometown was a good beginning. And with that sense of strength came a sense of activism with Spencer and Frank. That summer brought their other big move. And it started with the new ministry intern at First Presbyterian, Ken Crews.

Ken made being a minister look cool. He played quarterback and played tennis for Davidson College, he had a pretty girlfriend, and he wasn't afraid to talk about God. Spencer and Frank gravitated toward Ken. As the church's intern, Ken was responsible for leading its youth group, and he came to First Presbyterian as a college junior who was thinking of going to seminary. His thoughts got Frank thinking about going to seminary. Frank had only seen older, more stodgy men becoming ministers. And here was Ken, a quarterback and tennis player with a pretty girlfriend, thinking about wearing the white collar. That summer, Frank and Ken played tennis together, and they worked together at a Presbyterian summer camp in Scotland County known as Operation Fun. Later that summer on a whim, Frank and Spencer went to Holden Beach with Ken right before Ken gave his last sermon. There, they talked about God. Frank and Spencer also talked to Ken about the Vietnam War.

They were sitting on the beach on a Saturday afternoon, watching the waves roll when Frank broke the silence.

"Ken, I know you're preaching tomorrow before you go back to Davidson. What are you going to preach about?"

"I don't know," Ken responded.

"I got an idea," Frank said. "You ought to preach about the Vietnam War."

"Well, I already have something planned," Ken said.

"Oh, c'mon, Ken," Spencer chimed in. "This war is what's dividing us as a nation. I mean, what's a church supposed to do except raise questions about what is moral and what is right?"

"Hmm, I don't know," Ken said.

"Listen," Spencer responded. "Frank and I actually know former students from Lumberton High who have died in the war. And people your age and just a year or two older than me and Frank are going to war. And why? Why are we going?"

As Spencer talked, he thought of Joseph Sandlin. He was a banker in town, the Sunday School teacher who encouraged them to explore their values about race, sexuality and kindness. Spencer also thought about Jimmy Tisdale. He was the local postal carrier, the Scoutmaster who picked him up every Tuesday and took him to Boy Scouts for six years. For Spencer, both these men emulated what being Christian meant — follow the footsteps of Jesus, stand up for what you believe in and ask tough questions to yourself and the community where you live.

"What do you think?" Spencer asked.

"Yeah," Frank responded. "What do you think, Ken? You should do this, Ken. After all, it's your last sermon anyway."

"Yeah, I'll think about it," Ken responded, looking toward the Atlantic.

Their conversation ended, and Spencer and Frank didn't think Ken would do it. But next Sunday, Ken did. He preached about the Vietnam War and raised big questions about the morality of the war. He shared his concerns about the war and asked why America was involved in a strategy that destroyed villages in order to save them.

Frank was sitting halfway back in the sanctuary, in his usual spot in church with his family, and he couldn't believe it. It was the first time he remembered a sermon at First Presbyterian that connected faith and politics, and he and Spencer had a part in it. And it was coming from a guy a few years older than them who made ministry seem not only cool but relevant.

As he sat there, Frank grew energized. He didn't feel helpless. He had helped raise important questions that faced his hometown and the rest of America. Finally, Frank saw that he could make an impact. He and Spencer made an impact, and they were just 17.

Ken's sermon did hit the congregation hard. First Presbyterian had its share of military veterans like his dad. They had fought in World War II and the Korean War, and they saw war as someone's patriotic duty. But Ken raised the question that someone could still be patriotic and not support the war. Several men walked out during Ken's sermon, and afterward, Frank figured Ken would be a bit shook up by what he saw from the pulpit. So, after the sermon, Frank made a beeline to Ken. He had something to say. "Thank you, Ken," Frank said. "I'm proud of what you did. It took guts."

Frank didn't talk to his dad about the sermon afterward. That came later during one of their spirited dinner-table discussions. As he and his dad went back and forth, Frank kept thinking, "Heck, this didn't hurt Ken. He spoke his mind."

That fall, Ken invited Spencer and Frank to a Davidson College football game. As a thank you to his older friend, Frank gave him a cherished gift he'd gotten from his father — a tie tack/lapel pin of a PT Boat 109, JFK's boat. Frank recognized Ken's courage at the pulpit, courage like JFK had, and Frank wanted to honor that.

Spencer still remembers that gift.

A few decades later, after he moved to Maryland just outside Washington, DC, Spencer spotted the tie tack/lapel pin of the PT-109 available at the store at the Smithsonian Museum, and he sent it to Frank as a gift. Spencer wanted to remind Frank of his selfless generosity in giving away one of his most cherished possessions to Ken, their mentor. He also wanted to remind both of them of that historic period in their young lives. That year changed Frank. He broke bread with Bethany Presbyterian, helped convince Ken to question the Vietnam War, and he saw firsthand the importance of social justice and the role he could play in it. The question was how.

He found his answer in Winston-Salem.

Frank on Frank
Give It To God

It goes back to one of my sayings, 'Give God something to work with.'

It's that idea of feeding the 5,000. All you've got are five loaves and two fish, and you don't know what you're going to do. So, Give it to God. That's where faith comes in. In the summer of 1968, I began to understand that concept. That's when I gave God something to work with.

And I gave Him a lot.

That year was a real coming-of-age time for me, a time when my desire for social justice really first took root. I was about to enter my senior year at Lumberton High, and I felt it was perfectly appropriate for a church to connect faith with politics and talk about what is right, what is wrong and how we — you and I and everyone else — can change it.

I saw the need for change all around me in Robeson County. My county was wrestling with all sorts of race issues. All I had to do was look at the Carolina Theatre in downtown Lumberton and be reminded of the racism around me. Or really, I simply had to stand on North Chestnut and look for the three separate doors — one for Blacks, one for Lumbees, one for people who looked like me.

Or I could sit in my den with my dad and listen to what I heard almost every night. Walter Cronkite brought into our house scenes from the war in Vietnam, and with everything I saw and heard, I knew I couldn't support a war that felt morally wrong.

Yet, I felt helpless.

In the early '60s, when I was a seventh-grader, dealing with the unspeakable sadness of John F. Kennedy's assassination, I didn't know what to do except pray. But by the time 1968 rolled around, I felt I could make an impact. I could change what I saw around me.

Now, I admit, I don't know if I was confident or just delusional. But I truly believed I could do it. You have to remember what it was like back then. Change was in the air. Think about what was on the radio. You had The Drifters and The Beach Boys and The Supremes. But you also had Joan Baez and Pete Seeger, just all sorts of music that questioned the war and segregation and pushed for change and civil rights. That was big time.

Then, think of the biggest movies back then, 'The Graduate.' It was pivotal for me. 'The Graduate' came out right before Christmas in 1967, and Dustin Hoffman was playing a college graduate who had no idea what he was going to do with his life. Man, I could identify with his character. In the film, he gets asked, 'What are you going to do with your life?' And what does he hear?

Plastics.

'The Graduate' was emblematic of the emptiness my generation felt in the 1960s. But my generation felt we could change our country's future — our future — and it had nothing to do with plastics and everything to do with us.

I think back to what we did with Bethany Presbyterian. The communion brought Blacks and whites together in our fellowship hall at First Presbyterian and showed them that we had more similarities than differences.

Then, there's the sermon by Ken Crews, our church's intern. I'll always remember it. It showed a congregation that you *can* be patriotic and be against the Vietnam War. Sure, I did see a couple of people walk out, people my dad's age, men who had fought in World War II. They felt Ken was unpatriotic. I sure didn't think so. Ken's sermon was the first time I had heard anyone in my church connect faith and politics from the pulpit. But that's what I think a church needs to do. That's what a church *has* to do.

Over the years, I've heard people say, 'You can't politic in church!' When I hear that, I'll respond with, 'Life is political. Who does the dishes is political. Who gets the promotion at work is political. The failure of politics leads to war, violence and insurrection.'

When we use the word, 'politics,' people hear 'partisan.' But church is not partisan, and as the Rev. William Barber says, the Kingdom of God is bigger than red or blue or purple. It's not about left or right. It's about right and wrong.

That is what the Kingdom of God is all about. I've had people ask, 'What difference can I make? Why go to Washington? Why go to Raleigh? You're just spitting in the wind.' When I hear people say that, I remind them of two things.

One is the speech by Ted Kennedy at the 1980 Democratic Convention at Madison Square Garden. He had just ended his presidential campaign and Jimmy Carter was the party's nominee. Well, what he said at the end of his speech is something that we need to remember today. And remember always when you're fighting for justice.

'For all those whose cares have been our concern, the work goes on, the cause endures, the hope still lives, and the dream shall never die.'

The dream shall never die. I love that.

I also remind people of Jesus and his parable of the mustard seed. Jesus talks about how the mustard seed, the smallest seed, can grow into a huge plant.

So, something that seems so insignificant like a mustard seed *can* make a difference. That is, if we give it to God. Now, you don't give it to God because you know it's going to be successful. You give it to God because it's the right and faithful thing to do. Therefore, if we give it to God, it will make a difference.

God requires human hands — and feet — in order to accomplish God's work in this world. It's what I always say, 'We can't do it without God, and God won't do it without us.'

Every fall, Frank and Michie Dew never miss Wake Forest football game at home.

Chapter 4

"Which Side Am I On Here?"

"God always has a plan and a purpose for all of us. That's why we call it faith, right?"
The Rev. Frank Dew

Like many kids of his generation, Frank discovered Wake Forest in the most ordinary of ways — on a Saturday afternoon, hanging out on his couch and watching drama unfold from baseline to baseline. Frank discovered Wake Forest the North Carolina way. Through basketball.

A few hours before kickoff on a late Saturday morning, Frank is decked head to toe in black and gold.

He sees his longtime friend, Burt Higgins, walk through the front door, and Frank frowns. He doesn't say a word. He immediately heads to a hallway closet and begins rummaging through it for something, anything that Burt can wear. Frank pulls out a ballcap, all black.

"Does it say Wake Forest?" Burt asks.

"Of course," Frank deadpans, pointing to the "WF" above the bill. "I don't buy crap."

"How did you ever get ordained?" Burt says, laughing, reaching for the hat.

"Hold on, I have to adjust this," Frank responds, holding the ballcap. "I didn't know your head was so small."

"That's what we call humility," Burt says.

"That's because of MY humility," Frank responds.

Since he first enrolled as a freshman in the fall of 1969, Frank has watched Wake Forest University play football in the old Groves Stadium, now known as Allegacy Stadium. And like any true fan, he has watched games in the pouring rain, freezing temperatures, even snow. Frank would huddle in the stands surrounded in layers of black and gold, and he'd watch the game until the very end.

Win or lose.

Year after year after year.

"This could be the year," Frank would tell everybody.

On this particular Saturday, the day before Halloween 2021, this is the year.

Wake Forest Football came into the game against Duke undefeated and ranked No. 13 in the country. That's pretty incredible for a school of 5,000 students, the smallest school in the ACC and one of the smallest Division 1 schools in the country. In the fall of 2021, Wake Forest came up big because of a talented quarterback and his cadre of talented receivers. Their 8-0 start is the best ever in the school's gridiron history. That's saying something for a school that started playing football in 1888.

"This IS the year," Frank tells everybody.

He says that a lot in the fall of 2021. When he does, he'll hear his nickname. He hears it every football season. Nope, not Buzzard. That's from his sisters, Sara and Phyl. No, this nickname comes from his wife.

The Right Reverend Hotdog, the Super Fan of Wake Forest.

"If he could say 'Jesus' in six syllables," she says, 'he'd *really* be successful."

He's close. Frank does stretch the word "Jesus" like a rubber band sometimes in his sermons. But his love for Wake Forest is strong because of what the school helped him become. For example, he had never played tennis for Lumberton High. His school didn't even have a tennis team. He just played for years with his dad and others. But when he got to Wake Forest, he was confident enough and felt he was good enough to walk up to the Wake Forest tennis coach in his freshman year and say, "I'd like to come out for the team." Frank did

— and he made the team.

And to think, he almost didn't make Wake Forest in the first place.

When he initially applied, Frank was wait-listed. That crushed him. He longed to be a Demon Deacon, but they said no, and he began looking for other colleges to attend. Just someplace close. Any place close. In the spring of 1969, while on a senior trip to New York City with his classmates from Lumberton High, he got a call from his parents, and he talked to them on a hotel phone. They told him he had gotten a letter from Wake Forest, and he asked them to read it. He couldn't believe it. He got off the phone and immediately blurted out to his classmates seated nearby.

"I got in! I got in!" he shouted.

Today, whenever Frank talks about Wake Forest, he'll mention his wife — and his luck: "She graduated in three years, Phi Beta Kappa and cum laude. And I graduated in four years and 'Oh, lawdy!' " But whenever he thinks about Wake Forest's impact on him, he first mentions the graduate known as "Wake Forest's favorite son."

That's golfing legend Arnold Palmer.

"He speaks my mind," Frank says.

In 1947, Palmer came to Wake Forest on a golfing scholarship from his hometown of Latrobe, Pennsylvania. He came on a bus, carrying only his suitcase and his golf clubs. He did well. He eventually left Wake Forest before he graduated, turned pro, won 62 PGA Titles, and became one of the greatest golfers of all time.

"What other people find in poetry, I find in the flight of a good drive," he once said.

In October 2013, Wake Forest dedicated a nine-foot statue of Palmer on campus, honoring him for what he did for his alma mater. Of anything he ever accomplished and received in life, Palmer said Wake Forest was the most memorable.

"You can do things in your life, and you can watch what happens in your life, and you can go back to the things that meant the most to you," Palmer said during the ceremony. "Wake Forest meant the most. It's the greatest, nicest thing that has ever happened to me."

Frank understands what Palmer means. Frank loves Wake Forest with an intensity beyond any football or basketball game. Wake Forest gave him the self-confidence and focus to stand up for what he believed in for the rest of his life. You find evidence of that today a half century later in Frank's house in an upstairs bedroom.

On the wall is a poster he made when he was a student at Wake Forest. He cut out photos from magazines and created a collage of images, quotes and phrases that represented who he was. That really hasn't changed. Lean in close. Look. Read. And see.

There's the Kennedy brothers, John and Robert, as well as Martin Luther King Jr.

There's the famous photo of a 14-year-old girl kneeling over the body of a Kent State University student shot dead by the National Guard in 1970.

There's the headline "He Had a Dream" published after the assassination of King.

There's the view of the Earth from space, college students staging a sit-in, and a shot of Arthur Ashe playing tennis. Frank did like Arthur Ashe.

Then there is a quote. It's torn and water-stained, something said by a guy named David Moss in Dallas, Texas. It's right there in the middle of the collage. The guy named David says, "A person must tell the government to change. I intend to state my case, and even when they spite me, I mean to stand th …"

You figure the last word is "there." But you get the idea. A guy named David was standing in defiance more than a half century ago over what he saw around him.

Wake Forest gave Frank the confidence to do the same thing. So, he'll forever support his alma mater. At any football game or any basketball game, he never leaves until the final second. Sure, he wants to see the whole game. But there is something else. Something much more meaningful and reverential to him than the final score.

That happened at the Duke game. With less than a minute left and Wake Forest winning 45-7, Frank turned to everyone he came with. That included Burt, his friend in the borrowed black Wake

Forest ballcap. They were getting ready to leave. But not Frank.

"Let's not leave yet," he told them. "We have to sing the alma mater one more time."

A minute or so later, with his head and shoulders back, Frank started to sing.

Dear Old Wake Forest,
Thine is a Noble Name;
Thine is a Glorious Fame,
Constant and True. We Give Thee of Our Praise,
Adore Thine Ancient Days,
Sing Thee Our Humble Lays,

MOTHER, SO DEAR

Frank hollered the last line. Seconds later, the entire stadium hollered with him.

Let's go Deacs.

Like many kids of his generation, Frank discovered Wake Forest in the most ordinary of ways — on a Saturday afternoon, hanging out on his couch and watching drama unfold from baseline to baseline.

Frank discovered Wake Forest the North Carolina way.

Through basketball.

Growing up, Frank spent many Saturday afternoons in his den in Lumberton tuning in to Channel 4 and watching a team from the Atlantic Coast Conference play basketball. Often, he watched UNC-Chapel Hill. He became a Tar Heel fan, and he watched every game with no sound.

He and his dad relied on the radio.

Frank would be on the couch; his dad in his favorite chair; their eyes would dart back and forth from the TV to the radio and back to the TV. They'd see the score in the upper right corner and listen to the play by play from the radio perched on a nearby table. Sometimes, when there was a break in an intense game, Frank's dad would share one of his favorite UNC stories. It was the story of a rarity in sports:

watching the televised game between UNC and Kansas when they played for the NCAA national championship on a Friday night in March 1957.

"Frank, I promised God that night I'd quit drinking if Carolina won," Luther told his son.

And UNC won. The Tar Heels beat the Jayhawks in triple overtime 54-53.

"Frank, I can quit drinking anytime, and I have," Luther continued. "But that was one heckuva game. We beat Wilt Chamberlain. Who would believe that?"

Luther had always figured his oldest child would end up at UNC-Chapel Hill. But the summer before his senior year at Lumberton High, Frank stayed at Wake Forest for a week to attend Boys State. That's a big deal for any teenager interested in politics and leadership. High schools picked a few of their young leaders to attend Boys State so they could better understand how local, state, and national government works. And Frank was one of Lumberton High's young leaders. He was the school's sergeant of arms and the president of its High-Y Club, the social club spearheaded by the YMCA. And the summer of 1968, when he was breaking bread with Blacks from Bethany Presbyterian and helping convince his church's intern from Davidson to question the Vietnam War in his last sermon, Frank was looking for his next step after Lumberton High. Being Presbyterian, he figured something Presbyterian. But St. Andrews Presbyterian College in nearby Laurinburg didn't win him over, and he barely knew *anything* about Presbyterian College in South Carolina. But he was a die-hard ACC fan. And when he attended Boys State at Wake Forest, Frank found he liked the campus and the small-school feel. And the Demon Deacons played in the ACC.

But mainly, Frank wanted to do his own thing, blaze his own path. So, after he came back that summer from Boys State, he approached his dad and talked about college. His dad thought his son would always become a Tar Heel. He expected it, even with his questions about college.

He was wrong.

"So, you want to go to Carolina?" his dad asked.

"No, I want to go to Wake Forest," Frank responded.

His dad went mom??, raising his eyebrows and looking quizzically at his son. Frank winced. He wondered if their discussion was bound for something more emotional, something more like their dinner table debates after Walter Cronkite.

Frank was wrong, too.

"OK, we'll send you wherever you want to go," his dad told him after his long pause.

His response amazed Frank. He figured his dad would be dead-set against Wake Forest. His dad wasn't. So, in August of 1969, Frank stepped on campus as a freshman at Wake Forest, two years after it became designated as a university.

Frank, a Presbyterian, came to a school created by the Baptist State Convention of North Carolina in 1834. But that wasn't the biggest thing. He came wearing a uniform.

An Army uniform.

At the height of the Vietnam War, with more than a half million U.S. troops fighting in a conflict that had already claimed more than 33,000 lives, Frank came to Wake Forest as a member of the Army ROTC.

When Frank told his dad of his decision to join ROTC, he watched his dad look away and grimace. Frank knew why. It's one thing to support the government's policy, Frank figured; it's another thing to be willing to commit your son to that fight.

After years of debates at dinner, Luther Dew knew he couldn't change Frank's mind. Plus, Frank's viewpoint on Vietnam made him start to question what he saw — and felt. Frank opposed the U.S. involvement in the Vietnam War because he saw it as an immoral fight fueled more by power than righteousness. And as a member of the Reserve Officer Training Corps at Wake Forest, Frank knew he could avoid the voluntary draft because he already was in the service. In that sense, by becoming an ROTC cadet, Frank became a conscientious objector to the war. Luther Dew supported that. He sure didn't want to see his only son with a rifle in his hands on a battlefield halfway around the world.

Frank felt like many his age. Antiwar protests started to take root on campuses nationwide, and ROTC enrollment dropped 25 percent from 1968 to 1969 when the draft lottery started. It was the biggest percentage drop since ROTC started in 1916. College students nationwide were leery of joining something they didn't trust.

Frank felt the same away. Yet, his Army uniform helped him protest the Vietnam War in his own way. He wore it one day a week and practiced maneuvers in the woods near campus. Still, the battlefield seemed so far away. But that disappeared one night during his freshman year at Wake Forest in a dorm named after a guy nicknamed Dr. Billy.

* * *

Dr. William Poteat

Dr. William Poteat, better known as Dr. Billy, served as president of Wake Forest from 1905 to 1927. Like Frank, he knew how to shake the cage of the establishment.

Dr. Poteat was a devout Baptist. Yet, he taught evolution at Wake Forest at the beginning of the 20th century. When fundamentalist Baptists got all distraught and tried to discredit him, they failed because Wake Forest's influential alumni defended him vehemently.

"Wake Forest had opened for us the wonderful world of the mind," they said, "and we don't intend to see that door slammed shut in the faces of our children."

Wake Forest named Poteat Hall after Dr. Billy, and on a Monday in December 1969, Frank stood in the lounge of Poteat Hall huddling with other students around a color TV. It was like they were watching a big basketball game. They weren't. They were watching men in suits pull blue capsules from a glass jar two feet high and 16 inches wide. Those blue capsules contained a date, and those dates were stuck on a big board behind the big jar. The first 195 dates drawn signified grim news for millions of young men between the ages of 19 to 26. The date meant a young man's date of birth, and they'd hear in their heads, "Welcome to the Army, son, you're going to Vietnam."

For the first time since 1942, the U.S. had instituted a draft to correct the deficit left by the lack of young men volunteering for the military. And standing inside Poteat Hall, Frank couldn't get over how surreal it felt. He wasn't even eligible. He was only 18. But others around him were. So, for 90 minutes, they watched. One moment was as raucous as a Saturday night; the next moment, as silent as a Sunday morning. The lives of the young men in that lounge felt so precarious because of a number. A simple number. The lower the number, the more likely they knew they would be bound for Vietnam. Frank knew he wouldn't be eligible for the draft until the following year. Still, here he was walking around campus wearing an Army ROTC uniform one day a week, and here was someone he didn't even know in Poteat Hall being ordered to go halfway around the world to grab a rifle and fight.

"Some of these guys might not live to come back," he told

himself.

Frank and the other residents all put in a dollar, and the guy who got the lowest number that night got all the cash. Frank's dorm residents backslapped and congratulated him. But Frank couldn't understand why. The winner of the money was really the loser. But he didn't say anything. Nor could anyone. As Frank and others walked back to their rooms, they all heard the mournful tone of a trumpet.

Someone was playing "Taps."

The Vietnam War had come to North Carolina.

All because of a number drawn from a jar.

* * *

That spring, Frank marched. He carried out his ROTC drills near the cross-country track or carried out battle simulations near campus. It felt so make believe for him. Except when he was sitting in the ROTC classroom and cleaning his rifle, surplus from World War II. Or when he thought about the grassy hill near Wait Chapel and the lines of white crosses commemorating the young men and women killed in Vietnam.

But the biggest impact of all happened six hours north in northeast Ohio. And it happened in just 13 seconds at a place known as Blanket Hill.

On May 4, 1970, troops from the Ohio National Guard opened fire on a crowd who had gathered at Kent State University to protest the Vietnam War. Twenty-eight Guardsmen stood atop Blanket Hill on the Kent State campus and fired nearly 70 rounds into the crowd below. Four students were killed, nine others were injured. All in 13 seconds.

Frank wrestled with the contradiction. He was a ROTC cadet, in a uniform, and college students just like him lost their lives because they were standing up for what they believe in. In his mind, he kept thinking of the song he first heard in "The Graduate." It was the Simon and Garfunkel tune, "The Sounds of Silence." But really, it was one verse that he kept rewinding in his mind.

And the people bowed and prayed
To the neon god they made
And the sign flashed out its warning
In the words that it was forming
Then the sign said, "The words of the prophets are written on the subway walls
In tenement halls
And whispered in the sound of silence

Frank couldn't shake it. He saw his own "subway walls" as the public places around him that showed him this constant need for justice and peace.

Like the three doors at the Carolina Theater or the "Whites Only" sign at the Sanitary Café.

Or the grassy hill outside Wait Chapel.

Or the bottom of Blanket Hill where four students took their last breath.

He hated how he felt.

"Which side am I on here?" he kept asking himself.

Frank turned 19 in August 1970, and when the draft lottery cranked up again, the number that fell on his birth date was 252. Frank still remembers that number to this day. His number was high enough that he knew he wouldn't be drafted for combat. That fall, when he went back to Wake Forest, he still wrestled with the contradiction of his life — wearing an Army uniform, going through drills and battle simulations yet siding with college students and knowing that in no way he could support the Vietnam War.

By the end of his sophomore year, Frank dropped out of Army ROTC. He then turned his attention to politics. He saw it as a way to stabilize an unstable world.

Or so he thought.

Frank as WFU student. Frank Dew, WFU senior.

* * *

Frank had always liked politics.

He saw John F. Kennedy and his brother, Robert, as mentors, and he believed politicians were good, moral people who through elections could become leaders with the capacity to change their country, their state and their community. All for the better. As a junior at Lumberton High, Frank first tested the waters of politics when he ran to be the school's sergeant of arms. In his election speech in Lumberton High's auditorium, Frank tried to showcase his leadership skills in a different kind of way.

"Alright," he said. "I want everyone to slide to the left of your seat."

He paused.

"Now I want you to slide to the right of your seat."

He paused again.

"Now, sit forward."

His classmates did.

"I've now demonstrated my leadership skills and the ability to get things done. We have now dusted all the seats in the auditorium."

Frank won.

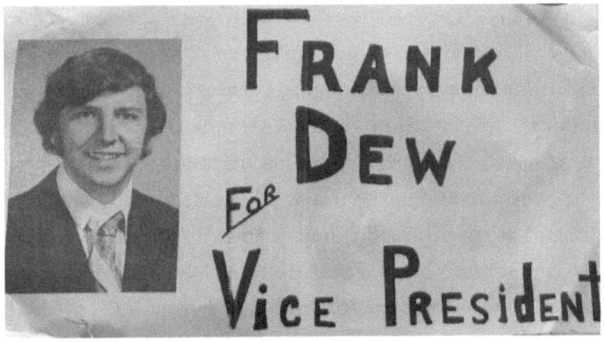

The poster Frank used in running for vice president of Wake Forest's student body when he was a junior.

As a junior at Wake Forest, he supported a black pastor named E.B. Turner to be the chair of Robeson County's Democratic Party. Frank believed in Turner. But Turner lost. A white attorney won. Frank still put his name in to become a potential delegate at the Democratic Convention in the summer of 1972 in Miami. Frank didn't get picked, and that loss became his first lesson in the consequences of politics. You pick wrong, and you lose. Frank remained undeterred, though. At the end of his junior year, he ran for vice president of Wake Forest's student body. He won. Then came a stroke of luck. One of his political science professors needed a few of his students to interview the North Carolina delegates at the Democratic Convention in Miami, and he picked Frank. That was a dream come true. In 1968, he sat on his couch in the den and watched the Democratic Convention in Chicago. He knew then he always wanted to go. Now, he had the chance.

He, his professor and two other students piled into his professor's station wagon and drove to Miami. Once there, Frank walked into the big arena and saw a can't miss metaphor of grassroots politics in action. Signs. Just lots of signs. He saw signs for California, Texas, North Carolina. He saw them everywhere. He saw recognizable faces from the TV, and he felt the electricity of change, too. George McGovern was selected as the Democratic candidate for president, and back in their hotel room in Coral Gables, Frank stood around a TV with students once again.

This time, there was no anguish of possibilities. It was only the excitement for the future. His future. And the country. It was because of what he heard McGovern say in his acceptance speech.

"In Scripture and in the music of our children we are told: "To everything there is a season, and a time to every purpose under heaven," McGovern told the crowd. "And for America, the time has come at last. This is the time for truth, not falsehood."

As applause rippled through the arena, McGovern continued with what he wanted to do.

"Join with me in this campaign, lend me your strength and your support, give me your voice—and together, we will call America home to the founding ideals that nourished us in the beginning.

"From secrecy and deception in high places, come home, America.

"From a conflict in Indochina which maims our ideals as well as our soldiers, come home, America.

"From military spending so wasteful that it weakens our nation, come home, America. From the entrenchment of special privilege and tax favoritism, come home, America.

"From the waste of idle hands to the joy of useful labor, come home, America.

"From the prejudice of race and sex, come home, America. From the loneliness of the aging poor and the despair of the neglected sick, come home, America.

"Come home to the affirmation that we have a dream. Come

home to the conviction that we can move our country forward. Come home to the belief that we can seek a newer world. And let us be joyful in that homecoming.

"For this land is your land, this land is my land, From California to the New York Island, From the Redwood Forest to the Gulfstream waters, This land was made for you and me.

"May God grant us the wisdom to cherish this good land and to meet the great challenge that beckons us home."

Come home, Frank heard. *Come home.*

"McGovern," Frank thought. "He's gotta win."

He didn't.

The only state he won was Massachusetts. President Richard Nixon, the Republican incumbent, trounced him during the presidential election in November 1972. Frank walked away from that election as disillusioned as ever. He only got more disillusioned when a burglary a few months before the election became public. In July 1972, at the complex of offices and luxury apartments known as Watergate, prowlers broke into the office of the Democratic National Committee. The crime revealed to Frank the seedy side of politics. The criminals arrested were connected to Nixon's re-election campaign. Evidence later became public of how Nixon's supporters stole documents and wiretapped phones. Nixon tried to cover it up, he got caught, and in August 1974, Nixon resigned.

Frank felt resigned, too.

Politics, he realized, couldn't solve the root causes of society's ills. No way. In the spring of 1972, after campaigning to be vice president of Wake Forest the end of his junior year, his once burning interest in politics began to wane. Politics wasn't for him. Neither was law school. He really thought that was where he was going. But not now. He kept thinking about Robert Frost and a line from one of his favorite poems he learned back at Lumberton High.

> *Two roads diverged in a wood, and I—*
> *I took the one less traveled by,*
> *And that has made all the difference.*

Frank started thinking about a less familiar path, about going to divinity school to become a minister. But who was he going to tell?

He had an idea, and his conversation took place in a gold Oldsmobile.

State Senator Luther Britt lived two blocks from Frank, and Britt's wife, Sarah, knew Frank from tennis. She recommended to her husband that he should bring Frank on as an intern. Britt agreed.

For three straight summers, Frank interned for Britt. He sat beside him in court and watched him try cases. But a lot of times, he drove Britt from Lumberton to Raleigh and back. Like any teenager with political dreams, Frank was awed by Britt. He had served as the city attorney of Lumberton as well as many positions with the Jaycees, a social organization that prepared young men for leadership. Britt had been president of the Lumberton Jaycees, vice president and president of the North Carolina Jaycees as well as president of the Robeson County Bar Association. Now, as state senator and chair of the Senate Judiciary II Committee, Britt found himself constantly busy, going from one place to another. His personal motto backed up the need for his frenetic lifestyle: Make things happen. He did. But Britt needed help. And that help came from Frank.

After a day in Raleigh, Frank and his boss stopped at the Arby's off Hillsborough Street for a late lunch. Britt would be in his gray or beige business suit; Frank, in his blue blazer, light blue shirt, khakis and a tie. They'd order — always a roast beef sandwich, potato cakes and sweet tea – and then Frank would drive back to Lumberton in Britt's gold Oldsmobile. Britt sat in the front seat, jacket off, loosened tie, a sheaf of papers in his lap. He knew he could get some work done before he'd hit his hometown, go to his law office, and see a few clients before he went home to see Sarah and their four kids.

One day was no different in the summer of 1972. But this time, Frank had a question for his boss, and he wanted his advice. But he knew it would be a bit tricky. He needed to share with a prominent politician and a prominent lawyer — his boss — a brutal truth. His boss' professional path wasn't his path, and Frank couched his question by saying what he thought was right for him.

He said a quick prayer — "God, give me words that'll work" — — and a few minutes out of the Arby's parking lot, Frank began.

"Mr. Britt, you got a minute?" Frank asked.

"Sure, Frank," Britt responded, not looking up from the papers in his lap. "What's up?"

"I've been thinking about what I'm going to be doing after college, and I've always wrestled with politics and the ministry," Frank said. "And I've always felt that as a Christian and as a follower of Jesus that we are all called to ministry. The question for me is what form will that ministry take?"

He stole a glance at Britt and saw he wasn't looking down. He was looking at him. Frank continued.

"Well, Mr. Britt, I've decided for me that the right path at this point is not law school or politics. That's your path, and you're good at it, believe me. But the right path for me is to go into full-time ministry. I've decided to go to divinity school."

Silence.

Frank began kneading the steering wheel. He didn't look over anymore. No stolen glances. He waited. He didn't have to wait long.

"I understand, Frank," Britt responded. "Law has been good to me. Politics, too. I felt I was led to do both because I felt led. And I believe you when you feel you're being led, that is what you should do. And you feel you're being led to the ministry, then so be it."

"Thank you, Mr. Britt," Frank responded. "That means a lot you saying that. You don't think it's stupid, do you?"

"Of course not, Frank," Britt said, laughing. "You need to follow your heart. Think about that communion you helped pull off with Bethany Presbyterian. And didn't you tell me you helped convince your church intern to stand up and question the morality of the Vietnam War? And he did it in front of more than a few World War II veterans. And your dad.

"Frank, what is it I always say? 'Make it happen.' Well, you made it happen. So, I think you'd be a fine minister. Really. You do have my support. And thanks for telling me. Means a lot to me, too. You'll make it happen."

Britt went back to studying his papers, and Frank kept quiet for the rest of the drive. But he could barely contain his excitement. He still had to talk to his dad and the Rev. Sloop at First Presbyterian. But he felt better.

Well, almost.

As he drove home, he kept thinking about that moment the summer before. He was in the fellowship hall of First Presbyterian with his youth group, and he was wearing his favorite suede jacket. They booked a singer-songwriter to perform and invited the youth group from Chestnut Street United Methodist to join them.

Only a few people came because of the pouring rain. But she came. She had moved to Lumberton with her family two years before, and she was getting ready to start her senior year at Lumberton High.

Right there in the fellowship hall, he knew. Or at least he thought he knew. He had never really been smitten by a girl before. They had been dating a year, and there was something about her that just hit him. Maybe it was her directness, her smarts, her beauty, her confidence, just something.

He didn't want to lose her. In his letters he wrote to her, he did talk about his plans for divinity school. But now, he was going to do it for real. If he went to divinity school, what would happen to them?

Would she stay? Or would she go?

Frank on Frank

"Who Do I Follow?"

I've had people ask me, 'Why did you go into the ministry?' and my answer has always been, 'I didn't realize that ministry was optional,' As Christians, we're all called to ministry. The question is this: What form will my ministry take?

As Christians, we are all called to live out our ministry through the lives we lead, and that could be in a church, at a hospital, in a school or even behind the cash register at Wendy's. We all can live out our ministry in so many different ways, and that could be at any stage of your life.

Here's a perfect example. Or really two.

There was a woman who used to work the cash register at the drive-through window at the Wendy's just up from my house, and that cash register was her pulpit. I don't mean she was quoting Scripture and using overly religious language. Nothing like that. But every time I'd pull up and pay for my order, she'd reply, "Be blessed!" or 'Have a blessed day!' That was always her exchange with every customer she met. I remember when she said that to me once, I told her, 'Thank you, I can always use that.'

Then, there was another time when a woman came to my office, and she told me, 'My kids are grown, and they have moved away, and I feel like I am ready to do what God is ready for me to do.' And when she told me that, I got really excited. I told her, 'What you have been doing is God's work. Now, you're ready to enter a new chapter in your life.'

And you know what she said to me? 'I have never really thought about it that way.'

When I first started thinking about going into the ministry as a student at Wake, I wrestled with all the Watergate stuff. Remember, I'd been involved in politics at Wake, and I was interning with a state senator. I also was still smarting over not getting elected to be a delegate for the Democratic Convention back in '72 because I supported a black minister running to be the chair of the Democratic Party in Robeson County. That was my first brush with hardball politics. That stung, let me tell you. But when I saw what was happening on a national level, I kept thinking, 'Is this for me?'

A political career, I realized, could bring out the best in me. Or it could bring out the worst in me. I sure didn't want that. I had grown up thinking politicians were good moral people who tackled the root causes of inequality and strife in our country. But as I got older, especially when I got to Wake, I realized that wasn't the case. Watergate showed me that. And I worried about what kind of compromises I'd have to make and what demands would be made of me if I became a politician. And of course, I worried how that would impact my family life.

That's when I asked myself the big question: Who do I really want to follow?

It was a real adjustment for me to see myself as a minister rather than this person who has a political career in mind. But at Wake, it became clearer to me. It's because of this idea of stewardship.

When something is given to you, it's not really yours. It's really a gift. And therefore, you have to honor that gift by the way you see it. And for me, I felt I was given a gift of feeling what other people are feeling, of being able to empathize with what other people were going through. That has been my gift.

I've always believed one of the most important things clergy can do is to help people see their gifts and claim their gifts. Like the mother who came to see me years ago in my office. Unfortunately, too many clergy don't see ministry in the broad sense. They see ministry needs to be done by only people of the cloth. Not me. I see it in a much broader sense. I'm like Andy Griffith. I'll deputize everybody.

The question we all have to ask ourselves is what form will our ministry take?

For some people, it could be standing at the cash register at Wendy's and saying, 'Have a blessed day!' Her saying that can lift up so many people and help them have a better day. And maybe even think about God. You don't have to be behind a pulpit to do that. But we all have to ask ourselves that question: Who am I going to follow?

Do that and your faith gets practical, and it can lead to some tangible results.

For example, you can't just tell somebody you hope they have a place to stay. No, you have to figure out how to *get* them a place to stay. And if somebody is hungry, you have to find out how to feed them, how to get them food. Faith has to be practical to get things done. Like for me at Wake. I joined ROTC to avoid going to Vietnam because I didn't support the war. I saw it as immoral, and I had to live out my faith. My faith became practical.

The worst thing we can do is find ourselves way down the road in life and discover we're empty inside because we've given up our values and our dreams. That is not the way to live. As Robert Frost put it, you have to take the road less traveled and hold onto those values and dreams and see where it takes you.

My good friend, Robin Britt, has a great way of illustrating that. He says, 'Life is like driving down a two-lane highway at night. You can only see so far down the road.'

True. But God always has a plan and a purpose for all of us. That's why we call it faith, right? In Hebrews, Chapter 11, verse 1, it says: 'Faith is the assurance of things hoped for, the conviction of things not seen.' That is where you say, 'OK, God, this is what I believe, and this is the best way I can see it. I'm trusting you to do the rest.'

That's what I did back at Wake when I asked myself that big question.

And that has made all the difference.

Michie and Frank Dew were married on a hot Sunday afternoon in August 1975 inside Chestnut Street United Methodist. The temperatures reached 100 degrees outside, and the packed sanctuary felt like one big oven because of an air conditioning system that just didn't work.

Chapter 5

Day By Day

"Being in love is that emotional connection, and that bond is all about physical attraction and infatuation. All that is necessary and important. I won't deny that. But for any long-term relationship to survive, there has got to be more. There has to be a shared direction in life."
The Rev. Frank Dew

Frank stood outside the fellowship hall at First Presbyterian, pulling his black Wake Forest windbreaker tight as if by instinct. Rain peppered the asphalt just beyond the front door, and he watched only a few people trickling in through the front door that Monday in July 1971.

"Is this really going to work?" he asked himself.

For years, he had been a youth leader at First Presbyterian, and even when he went off to Wake Forest for college, he kept in close contact with the church because he saw First Presbyterian as his second home.

But not really this night.

"It's just horrible outside," he whispered to himself.

The youth group from Chestnut Street United Methodist were coming over to hear a singer-songwriter in the fellowship hall. But as Frank stood in the hallway outside the fellowship hall, he couldn't help but think that this classic summer rainstorm would stop everyone from coming. Too sticky. Too humid. Too miserable. No one's going to come.

But she did. And she was standing a few feet away.

Frank didn't recognize her. As a guy who grew up in Lumberton, he thought he knew everybody. But not this girl. Her brown hair, parted in the middle, fell to the middle of her back, and she was talking to the circle of teenagers around her. He figured she must be from Chestnut Street Methodist. But he looked away. He got lost in his thoughts about his summer, his upcoming junior year at Wake Forest and his gopher work with Sen. Britt. That's when he heard the question. It came from her. And she was standing right in front of him.

"Tell me about Wake Forest."

It wasn't really a question. It was a declarative sentence, and this girl with the long brown hair pointed to the WF insignia over his heart.

"You go to Wake, right?" she continued. "Tell me about Wake Forest."

For a few seconds, Frank was flustered. But really, he was surprised. Someone in his hometown was interested in Wake Forest, and it was a someone he didn't know. Talking about Wake Forest was one of Frank's favorite subjects. But who is this girl? Anyway, he gathered his thoughts and began.

"Well, it's great," he said. "Really. Small school with big-time opportunities. That's a rare combination. And I like it. You go to Lumberton High?"

"I do," she responded.

"You know, I didn't play tennis at Lumberton because you know we don't have a team. Well, Wake does. I talked to the tennis coach. He let me try out, and I got on it, and I got a letter. So, yeah. Lots of opportunities. You just got to take advantage of them."

He stopped. She was listening. Who *is* this girl?

"I'll be a junior there next fall, and I'm majoring in political science," he said. "And what year are you?"

"I'll be a senior next year," she said.

"So, where are you looking?"

"Hollins," she said.

"Where's that?" Frank asked.

"Oh, in Virginia," she said. "It's an all-girls' school. But I've always heard good things about Wake, and when I saw you standing over here by yourself, wearing that Wake Forest jacket, I figured you had to know *something*."

"I do," Frank said, smiling. "I'm sorry. I didn't get your name."

"Michie," she said. "Michie Harriss. And you?"

"I'm Frank," he said. "Frank Dew. Like Mountain."

"Mountain?" Michie asked, sounding incredulous.

"Mountain Dew," Frank responded, embarrassed. "You know, the drink with the hillbilly on the bottle? Michie. That's an interesting name."

"I'm named after my grandmother, and that's M-I-C-H-I-E. It's Scottish."

"We're Scottish, too," Frank said enthusiastically.

"Well, whadda know," Michie said. "By the way, that's not the only odd spelling about my name. I'm a Harriss with two s's. You can't miss us in the telephone book. Not too many Harriss' in Lumberton with two s's."

Frank and Michie talked for a few minutes before going into the fellowship hall and listening to a singer-songwriter perform for a small crowd. Frank tried to listen, but he kept thinking about Michie, the self-assured girl with the long brown hair.

When the concert ended, he found her afterward.

"Listen," Frank said. "Great to meet you. Hope to see you again."

"That'd be great," Michie responded.

Then, she walked away. Frank just stood there. He kept thinking, "Who is this girl?"

Immediately, Frank found his sisters, Phyl and Sara, and all three climbed into the family's maroon station wagon. Frank drove, Sara slipped beside him in the front seat and Phyl climbed in the back. Before they pulled out of the church parking lot, Frank popped the question. He had to know.

"Hey, Phyl, Sara? Who was that girl from the Methodist church? I've never seen her before."

"Oh, that's Michie, Buzzard," Sara said. "She's the new girl. She moved here after you went to Wake. I think her dad works at the bank or something. Isn't that right, Phyl?"

"That's right," said Phyl. "She's sharp, Buzzard. Pretty, too, don't you think?"

"Yeah," Frank responded.

"I met her with Von," Phyl said. "Anyway, I went with her to her youth group once a year or so ago, and that's when I met Michie."

Phyl had scooched forward in the back seat, resting her hands on the front seat between Frank and Sara. Frank had never asked her and Sara about a girl before. Ever.

"I saw y'all talking," Sara said, ribbing her brother a bit.

"Oh, she wanted to know about Wake Forest," Frank responded. "She's looking at it."

"Really?" Sara said. "She's gonna go?"

"Heck if I know," Frank responded. "She said something about a college named Hollins. I have no idea where that is."

Frank laughed; their conversation ended. By now, the rain had stopped. But not Frank's thoughts.

Who is this girl anyway?

* * *

Michie is a child of North Carolina, reared in Sanford, a small town 70 miles north of Lumberton. She moved to Lumberton at the end of her freshman year in high school because of her dad's job as a corporate trust officer. When National Bank merged with Southern National Bank, her dad moved their family to Robeson County.

Michie did miss Sanford because of Beulah Harriss, the woman she called "Grandmother." Beulah lived right past St. Clair Elementary, Michie's school, and Michie used to walk to her house all the time for conversation, cookies and games. Beulah made sugar, chocolate chip and oatmeal cookies and kept them in the freezer for when her grandchildren, Michie and Michie's older brother, Lee, came over. They'd play Old Maid or Canasta, or a board game Beulah created out of spare cardboard and buttons. She called it The Fox and The Geese. They would play for hours.

"If we ever get arrested, you know who to call?" Lee told Michie.

"You call Grandmother. She'd get you out of jail. Our parents wouldn't."

Today, Michie keeps a jar of her grandmother's buttons on a shelf in her den. When people see it, she tells them what she and her brother used to say. But beyond playing card games and hopscotching buttons across cardboard, Michie learned about the empathetic side of life. Bealuh told her grandchildren anyone is always someone to love. Those lessons came in handy in a household shadowed by grief.

Michie had a brother named John Gregory, and he was born 16 months before Michie. He was born in April; he died in July. Michie was born a year later in July 1954. As she grew older, she became aware how that loss helped her family appreciate their time spent together as well as time spent with others.

That came naturally to Michie. She was an extrovert who thought nothing of striking up a conversation with someone she didn't know. She learned that from her parents. Her father, Meader, nicknamed "Red," knew no strangers; her mother, Blanna, knew no organization she wouldn't join.

Blanna dove into anything she ever did. During World War II, she went to Duke School of Law and finished first in her class. When she married Red, a World War II veteran, she became a homemaker and got involved with almost every organization in town — League of Women Voters, the American Red Cross, Girl Scouts, the local hospital auxiliary, PTA, and head elder at Chestnut Street Methodist Church.

Like many white families of the time, the Harriss family employed a Black maid when they lived in Sanford. Her name was Annie. Like Frank's mom, Blanna helped Annie with clothes, food, and money. Just whatever Annie needed. Blanna's compassionate spirit was honed by her own heartache.

It wasn't just the loss of her son, John Gregory. She lost her mom when she was 6. She named Michie after her mom and shared with Michie her open-armed view of life.

But Lumberton was different. It was no Sanford. When she moved to Lumberton, Michie noticed that immediately. She saw the three entrances at the Carolina Theatre downtown and the three separate schools in the county — one for whites, one for Blacks, one for Lumbee Indians. She heard her white classmates use the six-letter N-word to describe the people of color. That always upset her. But there is one instance she still remembers. It was a front-yard conversation that showed her how those small moments in life can reveal to you something bigger than any book.

She had been in Lumberton maybe three months or so, when she struck up a conversation with her neighbor, a white teenager. He lived across the street. They were talking about where they both came from, what they liked to do, and who they knew when her neighbor dropped his take on race and class.

"You know," he said, "God made Blacks inferior to whites and didn't want them to have access to life's privileges."

After their conversation ended, she stayed in her front yard. She couldn't shake what her neighbor said.

"Why didn't I say anything?"

"What could I say?"

"I've NEVER heard someone say that!"

"Why did we move here?"

"Is this what Lumberton is all about?"

The following year when she was a sophomore, Michie was sitting in her social studies class when she heard students yelling in the halls and pounding on lockers.

"What is THAT?" she asked herself.

She knew Lumberton High was in its first year of integration, of having Blacks and Lumbee Indians attend their school. But she naively thought that decision wouldn't cause conflict. So, she just sat there. The school's public address system crackled awake, and Lumberton High's principal, Bill Gay, spoke. He was crying.

"Y'all, we have to learn how to get along," he told the students. "We have to learn to live in peace."

As she wrestled with what she saw and heard in her new town, Michie dove into her church. She saw it as her sanctuary, a place where love wasn't relegated to skin color or someone's station in life. Church was her safe place. She could be who she wanted to be. Her family encouraged that. A man named Mr. Hood did, too.

Back in Sanford, Mr. Hood taught her Sunday School, and he encouraged Michie and the rest of his class to question what they read in the Bible. That included the red-letter words spoken by Jesus. He challenged his class intellectually and asked such questions as "Do you believe in the virgin birth?" Michie was in seventh grade, and those questions encouraged her not to be afraid to question what she didn't understand. Mr. Hood encouraged her to talk about race, class, and social justice. Then, when she moved to Lumberton and her family joined Chestnut Street United Methodist, her search in answering such thorny questions continued.

Once, when she was a rising junior at Lumberton High, her youth group went to Washington that summer on a field trip. On that trip, she joined teenagers from all over the country to talk about world hunger. They visited the United Nations Information Center and did a 24-hour simulation to understand what it was like to be hungry.

They received cards that informed them how much money they could live on for a day. It varied from $50 to 19 cents a day. Michie lived on 38 cents a day. For 24 hours, she and the other teenagers in her group lived on stale bread and a jar of peanut butter. That is all they could afford.

By the time she was a senior at Lumberton High, Michie became president of the youth group. One weekend, she joined a conference with another Methodist church in the county. A black Methodist church. She found herself the only white person there. When she arrived, Black teenagers walked up to her immediately.

"We're glad you're here," one of them told her.

Michie never shied away from standing up for what she believed in. And like her father, she had no problem walking up to someone she wanted to get to know. So, on that rainy Monday night in July 1971, she saw a guy in a black Wake Forest windbreaker, and she wanted to find out what it was like to be a Demon Deacon. But when she left First Presbyterian, she felt a bit taken by the Wake Forest junior. He was cute, smart. But there was something else.

"He's the nicest human being I've met in Lumberton," she told herself. "And I know this guy's gonna call me and ask me for a date. I know he will."

But he didn't. At least not at first.

*　*　*

It had been almost a month before Frank decided to pick up the phone.

He went up to his parents' bedroom to use their phone. He didn't want to use the one in the kitchen. He didn't want his sisters to hear because he was nervous about calling a high school senior he barely knew and asking her to a dance at the Lumberton Country Club on a Saturday night.

Frank had always dated older girls in high school. Not younger girls. At least not a lot. But here was this girl, a cute girl with long brown hair who was three years younger than him. He walked up the stairs, sat on his mom's side of the bed and stared at the turquoise rotary phone on her bedside table.

"OK, Frank, call her," he said to himself. "You can do this. You don't have to entertain her. You can just talk about Wake. That's a plus. But what if I call and she says no? That would be really embarrassing."

His mind was a blur. What would he say? What could he say? Can he really do this?

"Oh, what the heck. I'm going back to school anyway, and I betcha I'll never see her again. I'm gonna call her up."

He picked up the phone book on his mom's bedside table and looked up "Harriss." Michie was right. Not many Harrisses with two S's. He ran his finger down the page. OK, there it is. The Harriss on 33rd Street. He dialed, her mom answered, and Michie came to the phone.

"Hey, it was good to run into you at First Presbyterian the other night," he said.

The other night, Michie thought. That was July 9. It's now August 9. Whatever.

"Hey, Frank," she said. "That was fun."

"Um, I was really glad to hear your interest in Wake," he said. "If I can help in any way, let me know."

Really glad to hear your interest. That sounds stupid, Frank thought.

Pause.

"Thanks," she said.

Pause.

Here goes nothing, Frank thought.

"Well, I wanted to call and see if you wanted to go out," he said. "There is a dance at the Country Club Saturday night, and I wanted to see if you'd like to go."

Michie didn't hesitate.

"Frank, that would be fun," she said.

"Great!" Frank responded.

Oh, a little too enthusiastic.

"I'll pick you up at 7?" Frank asked.

"That'll be great," Michie said. "You know where I live right? I'm five blocks from you. On 33rd Street."

"My sisters told me," Frank said. "Can't wait."

"Me neither," Michie said.

He hung up the phone.

"Yes!" Frank said in a stage whisper. "Glad I did that."

Four days later, Frank drove up to the Harriss' house in the family's maroon station wagon. He walked up to the door in his grey plaid suit and knocked. He worried he was overdressed or looked too grown up or was working too hard to impress Michie's parents.

The door opened. Michie's dad invited him in. They shook hands, exchanged small talk, and up walked Michie's mom. More small talk. They walked into the den, and Frank sat down, on the edge of the couch, hands on knees, back straight, looking at both Blanna and Meader Harriss. Don't sound stupid, he thought.

He concentrated on the conversation, hoping he wouldn't say anything stupid when he heard steps echoing in the stairwell.

Michie walked into the den.

She had rifled through her closet and picked out one of the few dresses she owned. It was ankle-length with a red bodice and little red apples on the sleeves. Very coffee house, she thought. Michie simply hoped it would work for a Country Club dance.

Frank stood up. He didn't say anything.

"Oh, she's better looking than I remember," he said to himself.

They both walked toward the door, with Michie's parents walking a few feet behind them.

"Hope you'll come back," Michie's dad said.

"I'm planning on it," Frank responded.

Like any typical August night in Lumberton, the country club was a rock 'n' roll sauna. Lots of dancing bodies. Lots of loud music. Frank and Michie danced. But mostly, they talked. They walked outside to the tennis courts where Frank played often and walked over to the maroon station wagon. Frank leaned on the hood, and they talked about lots.

The three doors at the Carolina Theater.

The tearful reply from Lumberton High's principal Bill Gay.

Michie's unsettling conversation with her neighbor.

The night at Wake when Frank stared at a TV in the Poteat Hall lounge and watched someone in a suit pull a blue capsule from a big jar that held a number that would send someone halfway around the world to fight in Vietnam.

Then there were the white crosses near Wait Chapel.

And "Taps."

So much.

Frank and Michie didn't go back inside. Frank talked about Ken Crews, the Davidson College quarterback who questioned the morality of the Vietnam War. Michie talked about Mr. Hood, the Sunday School teacher who encouraged her to ask big questions about touchy subjects. They stayed parked beside the station wagon, losing track of time until Frank looked at his watch.

Time to take Michie home.

Frank walked Michie to the front door and didn't hesitate. He kissed her because he wanted Michie to know he was serious, that he was interested in her, that those conversations showed him she was more than just a pretty face.

"I'd like to see you again," Frank said.

"I'd like that, too," Michie responded.

He walked back to the car, his mind swimming with "What ifs."

"We are so much alike," he kept saying to himself. "That was more fun than I thought."

Frank looked up. He was home. That's weird, he thought, I don't even remember driving five blocks. Frank leaned his chin on the steering wheel of his family's maroon station wagon. That brown-haired girl. In a dress covered in apples.

What to do next?

* * *

Frank was nervous enough when the phone rang in the kitchen. His mom picked it up.

"Frank, are you having a meeting at the church?"

"Mom," Frank said, "Don't worry about it."

"What?"

"Don't worry about it!" he shouted back.

Frank was sitting in the den, with the ring he bought burning a hole in his pocket. He was thinking about what he was going to say. Now, it seems his plan began to unravel before it even started.

"They wanted to know if you needed chairs set up," his mom shouted.

"Mom," he responded. "I got it."

"What?"

"Mom," Frank shouted back. "I got it!"

But did he?

His plan: Pick up Michie for dinner at the Peddler's Steakhouse, detour by First Presbyterian, walk together into the hallway, turn around. And ask. A good plan, he thought. Now, the church called. His mom hollered. And he was sitting in the den, drumming up the courage to pop the biggest question in his young life.

It was August 1974. Frank was 23, in his first year at Duke Divinity School, and Michie was a rising senior at Hollins College. They had dated for three years. With long-distance phone calls so expensive, they wrote letters to one another on lined notebook paper. They had visited one another at college whenever they could because a two-hour drive separated Wake from Hollins in Roanoke, Virginia. But mainly, they wrote. A lot. In Lumberton, they had posted McGovern For President signs across Robeson County and joked, "Well, we have to get married. We are the only two liberals in Robeson County."

They had survived some danger, too. Kinda.

One weekend, Frank and Michie wanted to head to the beach. They stopped at a restaurant in Shallotte for lunch, and when Frank stopped the car, the engine in the Dews' maroon family station wagon caught fire. He pulled off the windbreaker he borrowed from Michie's dad and beat the fire out. He let the car rest, cranked it, and he and Michie ditched their beach plans and drove home. Frank didn't freak. But Michie, she was a bit anxious. As they drove home, she watched the road. The station wagon's floorboards were a crossword puzzle of rust, and Michie could see the lines in the road passing inches beneath her feet. She kept tightlipped and prayed.

"Please don't let this car explode on the way home."

It didn't. Frank got her home and handed back the windbreaker to Michie's dad. He looked at Frank, shook his head and asked, "What did you do?"

Frank and Michie had talked several times about marriage, and Michie knew he had bought a ring. Frank told her over the phone. But now came the moment. He wanted to ask her to marry him at the very place where they first met — right outside the fellowship hall at First Presbyterian when she walked up to him and said, "Tell me about Wake Forest."

Michie knew about Wake. She had been to campus for football and basketball games. She even had endured her worst stomach bug ever when she went to visit Frank for the first time. Michie barely left a girl's dorm room where she was staying. And Frank stayed with her, nursing her with cups of chicken-noodle soup poured from a can.

"I am at my grossest," Michie kept saying to herself, curled up on her side.

Then there was the time in the fall of Frank's senior year at Wake. They were both home for the weekend, and Frank picked her up in his gold Nova. On that Saturday night, when they were parked in Michie's driveway, he shared for the first time what he wanted to do with his life.

It wasn't politics.

"Michie, I can't," he told her, a touch of disappointment in his voice. "I remember staring at that calendar on my wall as a kid and seeing all those presidents, and I looked at John and Bobby Kennedy like they were saints. I remember going into Dee Dee's house when Brownie, Alec and I were playing football with the goats. And when I walked in there, there was a photo of John Kennedy on the wall right there with Jesus and Martin Luther King.

"But Michie, look what politics gave us? A war in Vietnam. And that doesn't help us. Doesn't help us at all. And politics, there's a level of ruthlessness to it all. You know, win at all costs. I can't do that. What kind of person would I be? But with ministry, I'd feel like I'd be the better person. I KNOW I'd be the better person. What's that verse in Jeremiah? You know, 'There is a fire shut up in my bones, and I am weary with holding it in, and I cannot.'

"That's the way I feel about the ministry. That is where you can change people's minds and people's hearts. And you can't change things without changing people's hearts."

Frank looked at Michie, wondering what she'd say and how the decision would affect their relationship. He didn't have to wait long.

"Frank, you know I will support you in anything you do," she said, her hand on his knee. "You've got a good heart. You've always had a good heart. And if going to divinity school is what you feel called to do, I say follow that. So, where are you thinking of going?"

"Duke," he said.

"Duke!" Michie responded. "I didn't know you liked the Blue Devils."

"Well," Frank said, smiling. "I'm still in the ACC, Michie. Going into the ministry was a big enough change for me. There is religion. And there is RELIGION."

Frank's worry over Michie's reaction evaporated. She supported him, and to Frank, she sounded relieved. That was huge.

He just wished the Rev. Sloop and his dad felt the same way.

* * *

Sloop had known Frank since he was 3, and Frank thought his longtime minister would be ecstatic with his decision. So, that day when he walked into his office, he thought his longtime minister would be excited about his news. Nope. He listened, leaning back in his chair behind his desk, his face masking any kind of emotion. Just like when he heard Frank's first sermon and called him a "social gospeler." Frank was flummoxed then. And he was flummoxed now. At the end of their conversation, Sloop had some advice for Frank.

"Well, don't do it if you can be satisfied in doing anything else," he said.

"Rev. Sloop, what do you mean?" Frank asked.

"Just be darn sure that is what you want to do," Sloop responded. "Being a minister is no walk in the park, Frank."

When Frank told his parents, they were sitting at the dining room table. He, too, thought they would be excited about his plans. His mom was. But she would be excited with everything Frank did. She made sure she had his favorite ice cream — Breyer's vanilla — every time he came home from Wake. But his dad was more circumspect.

He knew the politics of running a church. He had been on various boards and held various duties in the church, and he knew what Frank faced.

"This is no picnic you're talking about," he said.

"I know," Frank said. "This is what I want to do, Dad. I feel called to do this."

His dad leaned forward, lacing his fingers together. He looked Frank straight in the eye. Frank recognized that look. He had seen it many times during their discussions over dinner after watching Walter Cronkite.

"You sure you want to do this?"

Frank didn't hesitate.

"Yes. I do."

The following spring, Frank drove to Highland Presbyterian to talk to the committee of ministers from the Central Carolina Presbytery, the administrative body that represents Robeson County. Frank had to go before them as part of an age-old process that felt more byzantine than practical. He needed their blessing on his decision.

During dinner, one of the ministers asked Frank where he was going. When Frank said Duke, the minister almost spit out his food He knew the minister's reaction had nothing to do with basketball or collegiate allegiance along what's known as Tobacco Road. Duke Divinity was a seminary founded and supported by the United Methodist Church. So, the minister balked over a divinity school he felt was in no way suitable for Frank's walk of faith. Not a good sign, Frank thought.

When he went before the committee, Frank went second. A guy named Bobby went first. Bobby's plans included attending Union Presbyterian Seminary in Richmond, Virginia. That was the seminary where many would-be Presbyterian ministers went. Bobby told the committee that he felt the call when he was sitting up late with his elderly grandmother. He was quite specific; Frank … was not. He was all over the place on the why behind his plan on attending Duke.

After the presentations, the ministers announced their decisions.

"Bobby, we give you our full blessing," one of the ministers said. "And Frank, we give you our half blessing."

Frank took a deep breath.

"Fortunately, that's all I need," he said to himself.

Frank white-knuckled the steering wheel when he set his plan in motion.

"Let's go by the church."

Michie looked at him.

"What for?"

"Oh," Frank responded, trying to sound nonchalant. "I need to go by and check something. It'll only take a minute. Really. You can come in with me if you want. Then, we'll be able to get out of there quicker."

"No, you don't need me to go in with you," Michie said, exasperated.

"No, no, no," Frank responded. "It'll only take a minute."

"I don't know why," Michie said, resigned.

Frank pulled into the parking lot. They both walked toward the white columns, up the steps, through the door and took a left toward the fellowship hall. Once inside, Frank turned around in the hallway and faced Michie. He took her hands in his hands, remembering what he rehearsed in his mind in his den. He was ready for the words to come.

"The only way I would have courage enough to do this is to come to the exact place where we first met," he said. "But Michie, I feel God has meant for us to be together. We're like two puzzle pieces. We match. I mean, I feel we are a match. We've always been a match. We're like soulmates."

Wait a minute, Frank thought. Like?

"No, we ARE soulmates. I really do think that. That's right, we're soulmates. Oh, Michie, I feel like I'm talking too much. I mean, I have a question. I've got a question."

He took a deep breath.

"Will you marry me?"

Day by day
Day by day
Oh Dear Lord
Three things I pray

Cynthia Hale, doing the popular dance known as "The Bump" after the wedding, sang "Day by Day" at Frank and Michie's wedding.

Frank listened as Michie's college friend, Cynthia Hale, sang their favorite song from "Godspell" that hot Sunday afternoon in August 1975 inside Chestnut Street United Methodist. The temperatures reached 100 degrees outside, and the packed sanctuary felt like one big oven because of an air conditioning system that just didn't work.

Frank felt it. So did his sisters, Sara and Phyl. They stood to the left of Michie as bridesmaids. They wore ocean blue dresses and clutched bouquets of daisies. As they stood, trying to remain composed in a stifling hot sanctuary, they both felt sweat rolling down to the small of their backs. Still, they were happy. There was a time

when they weren't. They were jealous of Michie. They would say to
Frank, "Please come home this week!" When he did, he spent all his
time with Michie, not them. They realized they were no longer the
most important girls in his life. But they had come to terms with it.
They liked Michie, and they liked Michie and Frank together. Sara was
a rising sophomore at Meredith College; Phyl was getting ready to
follow Frank's footsteps and attend Wake Forest; and as they stood
in Michie's church, sweat rolled down their backs. It was the first
wedding they had ever been in, but they were happy because Frank
was happy.

Phyl and Sara could see Frank's face. It glistened with a sheen
of sweat. But Frank was sweaty all over. Sweat pooled underneath his
black tuxedo and on the back of his neck. Still, he knew he didn't want
to be in any other place.

He stood beside Michie, with his dad, his best man, an elbow
away on his right. He found himself twisting his new wedding ring,
trying to get used to the new band on his finger. The band held three
words. On the inside was the inscription, "Day By Day." To him,
those three words represented the importance of making a marriage
work one day at a time.

One day at a time, he thought. Me and Michie. One day at a
time.

> *To see thee more clearly*
> *Love thee more dearly*
> *Follow thee more nearly*
> *Day by day*

That morning at 7, Frank and Michie had completed a sunrise
communion service in Michie's backyard for anyone in the wedding
party who wanted to come. And they came in their shorts and sun
dresses, drank grape juice from a big goblet and pulled a piece of bread
from a loaf on a plate.

Frank and Michie had written their vows together. Michie didn't
use the word "obey" when it came to their marriage. She saw herself

and Frank as a team, as partners, as soulmates. She also saw Frank as her launching pad.

She had just graduated from Hollins College in three years with a degree in psychology. She graduated Phi Beta Kappa, and she was getting ready to be a youth director for a Methodist church in Raleigh. Michie did love her mother. But she didn't want to follow her path. She knew she wanted to go for her doctorate in psychology, possibly at UNC-Chapel Hill. And like she had done for Frank when he approached her about his own dream, Frank had done the same for her.

"I want you to keep going and get that degree," he told her. "You need to do whatever it is you want to do."

Frank had one more year at Duke Divinity School. He didn't know what he would do after that. How could he? Would-be Presbyterian ministers like Frank had no idea. It was a free market, and Frank could end up ministering a congregation or bagging groceries.

Still, he knew he took the right road. And he felt it on that hot Sunday afternoon in August 1975.

He and Michie would soon walk down the aisle and off to a reception at the Lumberton Country Club, the site of their first date. Then, they'd drive to their apartment in Raleigh for one night before traveling west to their honeymoon at Beech Mountain in western North Carolina. They'd get there in Michie's UNC blue Ford Pinto, a car whose engine sounded like a washing machine.

Frank gave Spencer Clark and his seven other groomsmen a copy of his favorite book, "The Old Man and the Sea" by Ernest Hemingway. He saw the book's old fisherman named Santiago as a Christ-like figure in his battle with the huge marlin way off the coast of Cuba. But what he loved about the book was its sense of freedom. Frank felt that freedom in Santiago's dreams. Santiago dreamed of lions. In one of Frank's favorite passages, Hemingway wrote:

"After that he began to dream of the long yellow beach and he saw the first of the lions come down onto it in the early dark and then the other lions came and he rested his chin on the wood of the bows where the ship lay anchored with the evening off-shore breeze and he wanted to see if there would be more lions and he was happy."

Through those very words, Frank felt he could see that Santiago, the old fisherman, was at peace as he journeyed alone into the deep sea. And Frank, the young minister, knew he could be at peace on his own kind of journey.

But he wasn't alone.

No way.

Frank on Frank

How to Love, How to Be

When you call someone your soulmate, it's an intuitive feeling we all have. But it's also a recognition of a shared world view.

We all know there has got to be that spark, that physical attraction. That is what I call being in love. But being in love is not the same as loving that person.

Being in love is that emotional connection, and that bond is all about physical attraction and infatuation. All that is necessary and important. I won't deny that. But for any long-term relationship to survive, there has got to be more. There has to be a shared direction in life.

From the very beginning with Michie and I, we were like two pieces of a puzzle. We fit. We were together side by side putting up McGovern signs at polling places around Lumberton before the 1972 election, and we were having so much fun. I know Michie likes to say, 'We had to get married. We were the only two liberals in Robeson County!' That's not totally true. But Good Lord, when we were putting up those McGovern signs, we had to make sure no one would shoot at us.

But that's what I mean when I say a shared direction in life. When it comes to marrying someone, you have to think of it as a journey. You've got to figure out where each of you is coming from. What are you bringing with you in terms of life experiences and life perspective and where do you want to go? You have to ask yourself, 'What are our goals? What are our hopes? What are our dreams?'

People don't give that much thought. I've seen it in pre-marital counseling. They'll talk about what kind of china patterns they want or what color the bridesmaids' dresses are going to be. But I urge the couples I've talked to over the years to think deeper than that. We all will grow and change, but you need to have a basic shared vision of where you're going.

I married both of my sisters in First Presbyterian in Lumberton, and I remember standing there, in my white cotton stole made by Michie's mom and reciting the well-known verse from 1 Corinthians: "Love is patient, love is kind. It does not envy, it does not boast, it is not proud. It does not dishonor others, it is not self-seeking, it is not easily angered, it keeps no record of wrongs."

True. But remember, love is more than just an emotion. Love is about choosing each day to be loving.

People talk about how a relationship has to be 50-50. To me, it's more 100-100. We have to do more than our half in order to meet the other person where they are. We all know we're going to screw up and fall short and not live up to your end of the bargain, and whatever happens, you know your partner will go that extra mile for you, no questions asked. And they love you anyway.

I remember hearing what writer Mitch Albom told Oprah Winfrey when he was talking about the 20th anniversary of his bestseller, "Tuesdays with Morrie." Oprah asked him what's the best advice he's ever gotten and followed. He said: 'You're only going to have a few really good, really true friends in your life. And if you're really smart, you'll marry the best one. And I did.'

I did, too.

The decision of who you marry is the most important single decision in your life. That person will share so much of you going forward. Your life with children. Your life vocationally. Your life together. Just everything. We don't say, 'In sickness and in health' for nothing. You have to share what's coming along so you can reap the benefits of a stable relationship no matter what life throws you. Then, you get to enjoy seeing your kids grown, seeing them thrive, and you get to play with your grandkids and wonder what they will call you today.

They call Michie 'Mimi.' As for me, they call me 'Beak.' They couldn't pronounce "Deacon." But I don't mind. Michie calls me the Right Reverend Hotdog. I don't mind that either. I mean, she doesn't complain when I want to stay to the very end of a Wake Forest football game so I can sing the alma mater.

I have to do that.

The photo comes from the booklet Durham's Trinity Presbyterian put together after they hired Frank as its associate minister following his graduation from Duke Divinity.

Chapter 6
Answering God's Call

"Faith can be a struggle, no doubt. But when that happens, that is when we learn. We see it as a lesson that can guide us. That's when faith becomes a gift."

The Rev. Frank Dew

Frank felt lucky. After graduating from Duke Divinity School, he landed a job that put his ministerial education to work.

He became the associate pastor at Trinity Avenue Presbyterian, a church near Duke's East Campus. He got the job tip from one of his professors, and Trinity hired him. He was relieved. He didn't have to head home to Lumberton to find a job. He got his first job in Durham, and it seemed almost providential. Two years into his marriage to Michie, they both looked toward their future rather than revisiting their past. They moved into a small apartment in Raleigh and began the first chapter of their lives together. Michie wanted to become a high school guidance counselor and enrolled at UNC-Chapel Hill to obtain her master's degree in educational counseling, and Frank slipped into the black robe he received as a gift from his parents after graduating from Duke Divinity School. Now began the rest of his life. He started learning the ins and outs of being a minister from Trinity's senior pastor, the Rev. Bill Bennett. All the responsibilities. The many responsibilities. All as tricky as trying to maneuver through a minefield.

How to conduct a wedding.

How to conduct a funeral.

How to run a youth group.

All that. And more.

Then, once a month, he would step up to the pulpit and preach. He thought he had that. He'd been doing that since he was a high school senior. This time, though, he had a wealth of knowledge and wisdom from his mentors and courses at Duke. There, his faith really took wings. But two years into his work at Trinity Presbyterian, maneuvering well through his minefield of responsibilities, Frank felt his wings got clipped.

It happened on a Monday, and he didn't know what to do.

* * *

"Can I talk to you for a minute?"

The question from Rev. Bennett surprised Frank. Yet, Bennett's knitted brow told him he needed to listen. They walked into Bennett's office, and Frank felt he was stepping back into a? memory, back into his senior year at Lumberton High, sitting in front of the Rev. Sloop's desk at First Presbyterian and hearing the man who had known him since he was 3 tell him he was a "social gospeler."

That seemed so long ago for Frank. But not the feeling of getting ushered into what felt like the principal's office for doing something wrong. Frank didn't feel like he did anything wrong. At all.

Bennett, though, begged to differ.

He slipped into his seat behind his desk and motioned for Frank to sit in the chair in front. Bennett leaned forward, head down, hands in his lap, like he was praying or grasping for what words to say. Then, he began.

"Do you realize all the trouble you got me into?"

"What do you mean?" Frank asked.

"Your sermon yesterday," Bennett responded. "You got up in front of our whole congregation, a congregation full of business owners, and you told them we need to boycott a business. Boycott Nestle. Not buy their products because they were selling baby formula to mothers in Third World countries."

"But Dr. Bennett," Frank began, "they are. And that's what I believe the church is called to do."

"By telling people not to buy Cheerios because of something they have no control over?"

Frank could tell by Bennett's voice he wasn't pleased. He spoke in a sharp, staccato tone, and Frank could sense he overstepped some line he never knew existed. Frank had created a list of Nestle products in the church bulletin and wrote that parishioners shouldn't buy them. Don't, he wrote. Nestle is encouraging women in Africa and other Third World countries to buy baby formula rather than rely on their own breast milk to keep their babies healthy. And this move was happening in countries where poverty exists, and people starve.

And babies starve, too, Frank told himself. Babies.

As he sat in front of Bennett, Frank thought about charging headlong into that argument. But he stopped himself when he saw Bennett's knitted brow and pursed lips. Be more contrite, Frank told himself. Don't. Lose. Your. Job.

"I'm sorry that happened," Frank said, his voice conciliatory. "But I think it's important that the church speak out about issues like this on behalf of the poor and the vulnerable. And I feel like this is what I'm here to do."

Bennett, who had been at Trinity Presbyterian for 20 years, listened. He pulled his hands from his lap and steepled his fingers, sitting his elbows on the table. Frank felt his stomach jumping to his throat.

Don't. Lose. Your. Job.

Frank continued. Once he finished, Bennett let the silence between them hang in his office.

"All that might be true," Bennett responded. "But I have to deal with the people who are upset."

Frank walked out feeling dejected. He didn't want his boss to be upset with him or to upset anyone in his new congregation. But he felt he had a responsibility. He knew that. What to do. He didn't know. As he wrestled with how to remedy this new religious minefield of his, a verse from Romans, Chapter 12 popped into his mind.

Do not conform to the pattern of this world but be transformed by the renewing of your mind. Then you will be able to test and approve what God's will is—his good, pleasing, and perfect will.

Yes, Frank told himself, do not conform. You have a job to do. He knew where to go next.

He needed to see the woman he called "Pal" or "Boog" or "Moser," as in "We love each other the most-est!"

He needed to see Michie.

At their apartment in Raleigh, Frank and Michie sat on the couch. She listened as Frank relayed to her what happened that morning at church. Michie could tell he was upset. But she knew Frank. He'll do what he thinks is right, and she knew this was right. And what happened didn't surprise her. Southerners, she knew, hate controversy, and they would rather be civil and say, "Bless your heart!" than confront what angered them head on. Bless their heart, she thought. But as a minister's wife, she knew this came with the job.

As she listened, she kept her concern in check.

"Bones," she told her husband, calling him by his nickname because of his skinny frame. "Remember when we put all those McGovern signs all over Robeson County?"

"What do you mean?" Frank asked.

"You know what we worried about?"

Frank laughed.

"Afraid we were going to get shot."

"And did we?" Michie asked.

"No, we didn't, Pal," Frank responded.

"And we kept doing what we thought was important," she said. "And you need to do that here. Do what you think is important."

"You're right," he said. "You know, sometimes ministers have an over-exaggerated view of them changing others. My greater fear is others changing you."

"What is it you tell me about the ministry?" Michie asked.

"Oh that?" Frank responded. "It's something I heard at Duke. The ministry is a little like peeing in your pants when you're wearing a dark suit. It'll give you a warm feeling, but most people won't even notice."

"Do you want that?" Michie asked.

"Oh, heck no!" Frank said.

Frank shared with Michie his concern over what he saw and felt at Trinity Avenue Presbyterian. He knew after this exchange in Bennett's office that he should begin looking for a new place to preach, a new place to land. He told Michie about this, and Michie being Michie — the Phi Beta Kappa grad from Hollins — took it all in stride. They'd be moving, she knew. But what did she expect from the guy she called Bones?

"This is just another day in the life of Frank Dew," she told herself. "There will be a lot more of these."

And why? It's not just what she saw firsthand in Lumberton. It's what she saw happen in Durham. As she worked as the director of Christian education at Hayes Barton United Methodist in Raleigh, she saw what happened to Frank as he studied at Duke.

He found his happy place. He found people of faith just like him.

* * *

Frank spotted the flier on campus, tacked to the bulletin board in the Gothic building housing the Duke Divinity School.

Arthur Simon, Frank read, will be speaking on campus. About the Bread for the World. An advocacy group dealing with hunger. A new advocacy group.

"Wow," Frank told himself. "This sounds like a way to bridge the gap between faith and politics. This is exactly what I'm looking for."

In his second year at Duke, Frank needed to see that flier. He was still struggling, full of questions about his future. He didn't know what he was going to do after graduation. Work at a church and minister to a congregation? But what if they didn't want to do anything past Sunday morning? Or maybe I should work for an organization handling some social issue. Something like Bread for the World.

But would that align with my faith? Would that work for me and Michie? Would I really be happy?

Frank didn't have any answers. But he knew what he read on the flier, about Arthur Simon speaking on campus, was something he needed to hear.

He found Simon in a student lounge, a slender man in professor glasses surrounded by fewer than 15 students. No matter, Frank couldn't help but think he was in the right place. Simon was talking his language.

Simon was an ordained Lutheran minister, the founder of Bread for the World and the brother of Paul Simon, the politician from Illinois. His parents were missionaries, and when he became a minister, he sent his friends a two-page mimeographed letter in which he asked, "Do you think we could start a movement to persuade our public officials to devote more of our resources to the poor and hungry?"

From that came Bread for the World, an organization Simon saw as a "cloud of witnesses" brought together by He who is the Bread of Life and He who calls all of us to be, in Simon's words, the "bread for the world."

Frank couldn't get over it. He left the student lounge in the Duke Divinity Building just buzzing over what he heard. There was never a lot of talk about liberation theology in Lumberton, and he always felt like a ringmaster in an empty arena. No one listened, save his best friend, Spencer. But at Duke, Frank's intellectual journey excited him by the people he met.

People like Arthur Simon. He was far from the only one.

At an organizing meeting for Bread for the World, Frank saw her up front. She had sandy blonde hair and a quick smile. He listened to her talk, and even from where he sat, he saw that her faith just radiated from her. Afterward, he walked up and introduced himself.

"Hi," he said, "I'm Frank."

"I'm Sister Evelyn," she said, smiling.

So began Frank's friendship with Sister Evelyn Mattern. She was the first Catholic nun he ever met. She didn't wear a habit, and she lived in a log home just north of Raleigh in a rural stretch of land she called Peace Hill. And Sister Evelyn, a native of Philadelphia, saw peace and justice as her spiritual North Star. She had earned her doctorate in literature at the University of Pennsylvania in 1969 and came south a few years later to teach English at St. Augustine's University, an historically black college in Raleigh.

Sister Evelyn Mattern

She taught at St. Augustine's for just a year. She then left to start the Office of Peace and Justice at the Roman Catholic Diocese in Raleigh and began working with the North Carolina Council of Churches, an organization headquartered on Duke's campus.

Sister Evelyn focused her energy on helping the vulnerable and spurring the powerful and influential to act. She'd be in the fields talking to migrant farm workers about what they need, and then, she'd head to the halls of power in Raleigh to lobby state legislators to act. She worked to bring justice to farm workers. She also worked to heal racial divisions, stop the death penalty, alleviate poverty, and improve healthcare for children. Once, she snuck into the gallery of the N.C. House chamber, and she along with two of her friends unfurled above the heads of the legislators a banner that read, "Health Care For

Children, Not More Welfare for the Rich."

That was Sister Evelyn's idea. And it was illegal. But she knew it was so needed because of her charge in life.

"Jesus," she liked to say, "was a man of action."

Frank began working with her when he interned in Durham for the interfaith hunger education and fundraising event known as the CROP Walk. The event had outgrown its acronym — Christian Rural Overseas Program — and became an inclusive event that helped Church World Service raise money to fight hunger worldwide. He also worked alongside Sister Evelyn as a volunteer at the N.C. Council of Churches and Bread for the World. She also energized Frank's efforts to protest the death penalty, an issue Frank began lobbying against when he wrote a paper about it in high school.

"Those without capital," Frank liked to say, "get the punishment."

Frank saw his faith taking shape. He found mentors in people like Sister Evelyn. He discovered other like-minded individuals through the N.C. Council of Churches, people like the Revs. Sam Wiley and Collins Kilburn. He realized through Duke what he longed to find. He discovered allies.

Frank felt God was putting these people in his life, helping him find his way. And the more he thought about the chance encounters that evolved into friendships, the more he thought about a rug. That is, turn over a rug and you see the knots and tangles that don't make sense. But flip it back over, and you see a beautiful, eye-catching pattern. Those knots and tangles then make sense.

Just like those chance encounters.

"Hold a little piece of truth up to the light," Sister Evelyn used to say, "and you hope a few people see it."

Frank saw it. And it did burn bright, thanks to Sister Evelyn and a Duke professor named Dr. Moody Smith.

Frank called him Moody. But not until he graduated from Duke Divinity School. He called him Dr. Smith while in divinity school at Duke. Moody was a respected New Testament scholar, an expert on the Book of John. Frank took his class. Frank also took his advice.

They became fast friends for 40 years. Moody became Frank's tennis playing partner. He also became his spiritual sounding board and one of the biggest mentors of his life.

And what sparked that lifelong friendship? A signup sheet on a bulletin board.

* * *

Frank played tennis for Lumberton High and was good enough to make the tennis team at Wake Forest. (left) Frank is on the front row on the far right. (right)

Frank loved tennis. Matter of fact, that's how he got to Duke Divinity School. The Rev. Jim Bailey, a Methodist minister, was one of Frank's playing partners in Lumberton, and when Bailey heard Frank was interested in going into the ministry, he had a suggestion.

"Frank, let me take you up for a tour of Duke."

He did, and Frank was sold. He wanted to go to Duke — and he wanted to stay in North Carolina and be close to the action of the ACC. Moreover, he knew he would have freedom to explore at a divinity school where 60 percent of its students were Methodist and

40 percent were everything else.

So, as he stared at the bulletin board and saw the deadline: Divinity School Tennis League, he knew. Sign up. That's how he met Moody, a father of four from South Carolina who loved pulling for the Atlanta Braves and playing tennis.

He and Frank played almost every Friday. They started first on campus and later moved their games to the Hollow Rock Swim and Racquet Club in Durham. As he was in class, Moody was just as methodical on the court. He'd lay his car keys and spare change on a nearby bench, walk onto the court and volley back and forth. He was competitive, but he sure wasn't a man to cuss over a missed shot. He'd swing, see his ball go wide and holler some theological phrase plucked from his storied academic career.

"Holy Peter!" he'd holler.

By the end of the game, after yelling "Holy Peter!" more than once, Moody would look at Frank, shake his head and mention the woman he married in Spartanburg, S.C., in 1954.

"Jane Allen Smith," he'd say, "would not be happy with me today."

What always struck Frank was how humble and approachable Moody was. He was a giant in the study of the New Testament. In 1965, after earning his doctorate at Yale Divinity School, he became a professor at Duke Divinity School. He stayed in the classroom for 37 years until he retired in 2002. Throughout that time, he became a favorite among students. He and his wife hosted graduate students in their home. Like Frank. And Frank needed someone like Moody to help him understand the social justice implications of Jesus. The more Frank learned, the more his faith grew, and the more he saw the church as a vehicle to help convince a community to help the least, the last, and the left out.

Moody reaffirmed that drive in Frank. It backed up what Frank saw in five verses from Matthew, Chapter 25.

For I was hungry, and you gave me something to eat, I was thirsty, and you gave me something to drink, 'I was a stranger and you invited me in, I needed clothes and you clothed me, I was sick and you looked after me, I was in prison and you came to visit me.'

Then the righteous will answer him, 'Lord, when did we see you hungry and feed you, or thirsty and give you something to drink? When did we see you a stranger and invite you in, or needing clothes and clothe you? When did we see you sick or in prison and go to visit you?'

"The King will reply, 'I tell you the truth, whatever you did for one of the least of these brothers of mine, you did for me.'"

Frank needed that support. Duke Divinity, as Frank found out, was no walk in the park.

* * *

Frank couldn't help but fidget.

He had to take five oral exams before he could be ordained. Tack onto that work five written exams and a sermon in front of the entire Presbytery, and he saw his route toward ordination more like a marathon than a sprint. And on this particular day, as he sat in front of several Presbyterian faculty members testing his Biblical knowledge on yet another oral exam, he could feel his nervousness crawl up his back.

He joined two doctorate students at Duke. As he listened to their answers, Frank kept quiet and started thinking about baseball. Minor league baseball. They were Triple A; Frank was Double A.

"What do you think of the theme of freedom in Paul's Letter to Galatians?"

They answered, Frank listened. He learned this from his experience in student politics at Wake as well as listening to Sen. Luther Britt. Wait for the other people to answer first. Then, respond. Fools rush in, Frank thought, where angels fear to tread. And Frank, by far, was no fool. He was Buzzard, Bones, the son of Luther and Louise Dew. Wait it out, he told himself, wait it out.

"Mr. Dew," one of the professors asked him, "we notice you seem to answer last every time."

"That just shows you my wisdom in listening to my scholarly brothers," Frank responded.

Frank smiled. The committee members did not. Afterward,

Frank got what he called a "gentleman's C" after his oral exam, and he assured the committee members his graduation from the seminary was the beginning of his own study of the Gospel, not the end. And his work was far from over. He had to preach a sermon in front of the Presbytery meeting, and that meeting happened in a city he equated more with basketball than religion.

Frank came to Greensboro on a Saturday in August 1976, and he preached in one of the biggest churches in the city.

First Presbyterian Church.

Standing in the pulpit in the sanctuary of First Presbyterian can be intimidating. It's big. Like arena big. And when Frank stepped up to the pulpit to preach that Sunday morning, he looked out onto an audience of at least 300 people. He had never preached in front of 300 people before. And what was worse? His sermon had to count.

When he pulled up, he thought the outside of the building looked more like a fortress than a church. When he stepped inside, he didn't know anybody. Not a soul. He looked at the high ceilings and the long center aisle and tried to keep his nervousness in check.

"God of the Universe must be in here somewhere," he told himself.

After he preached, he knew he'd be asked questions just like the questions he fielded from the committee members during his oral exams. He'd be right there on the floor, and in front of "God of the Universe" and everybody else, they would take a vote whether they approved — or not. And they would vote by raising their hands right in front of Frank.

Like with every sermon he gave, Frank wrote down his thoughts on a legal pad. And his thoughts were simply phrases, a Bible verse, or a few words scribbled on one page. Frank would go over it, time and again, so he wouldn't have to look at his legal pad. He always wanted to make eye contact with everyone in front of him. And this time, at First Presbyterian Church, a place called "First Church" in Greensboro, he had a lot of people in front of him.

He stepped up to the pulpit, saw the crowd in front of him and thought first not of God making a way, but God helping people laugh.

"Man, this is a big place," Frank told himself as he looked at the many faces in front of him. "And boy, do I feel like I'm in a cockpit of a huge plane. That's it. Do that! Say that!"

Frank smiled and began.

"I guess this is what it feels like when you're flying a 747," Frank said.

Laughter rippled through the sanctuary.

"Good," Frank told himself. "You got this."

Frank preached about we all need to build a personal relationship with God and he talked about how the cross, the universal symbol of Christianity, is really our bridge between us and God. He titled his sermon "Crossing the Bridge."

Afterward, Frank answered questions and listened some more. Then came the voice vote and showing of hands in the huge sanctuary. Frank passed.

"Thank God," he said to himself.

Four months later, wearing the black robe his parents gave him and the green cotton stole Michie's mom made for him, Frank stood in a pulpit in a much smaller sanctuary. He was back at Trinity Presbyterian for the most important service of his young life.

He was 25, getting ready to begin his ministry. But he almost didn't even make the service. The night before, he found himself the sickest he's ever been.

Frank thought it was the flu. Or something flu-like. Or something. He hovered over his commode in his apartment, throwing up everything he ate. Michie was there, right beside him, helping and hoping he could make it to his ordination the next day. Everyone was going to be there. Frank's parents. Her parents. The Presbytery. Everybody. All to see Frank cross the proverbial threshold to become a minister. A heady service, indeed. Still, could Frank make it?

"What are we going to do if you're not better?" Michie asked.

"I'll be fine, Moser," Frank croaked.

"Really? OK, Frank."

Another day in the life, Michie thought.

The next day, Frank surprisingly felt fine. At Trinity Avenue

Presbyterian, Frank's ordination unfolded without him doubling over. At the end of it all came the ceremony he'd only dreamed about during those fog-like days and nights studying for three years at Duke Divinity.

It was the laying of the hands.

The ceremony symbolized the transfer of authority from those who had authority to someone new in authority. In this case, that someone new was Frank. He walked down in front from the pulpit where he was encircled by members of his Presbytery. And his dad, an elder at First Presbyterian in Lumberton. Frank lowered his head and knelt down. His emotions somersaulted from joy to humility. It reminded him of his wedding day to Michie. That day, he was so happy. He was marrying his soulmate. He had no idea of where they were going or what they were getting into. But he knew wherever he was going they would go together. His entry into the ministry felt just like that.

"You are on the right track," Frank told himself. "This is what God is calling you to do."

He kept thinking about the classes he took with Dr. Smith. Well, since his graduation from Duke Divinity, Frank now called him Moody. Still, he had much respect for the man who introduced him to the passage that resonated with him about his own faith walk.

It came from the Book of John, Chapter 15, verse 16.

You did not choose me, but I chose you and appointed you so that you might go and bear fruit—fruit that will last—and so that whatever you ask in my name the Father will give you.

Really, it's the first nine words that anchored Frank — "You did not choose me, but I chose you." For Frank, it was personal, Jesus' analogy of the vines and the branches. Through that analogy, Jesus encouraged His disciples to stay with Him so they could spread His message when He was gone.

The work of the disciples, Jesus said, would bear fruit. They did just that. And so will Frank.

He's been thinking about it since the summer of 1969. It was right before he started at Wake Forest when he interned for his home church, First Presbyterian Church. On a Sunday morning, he stood in a mission church of white cinder blocks and clear glass windows and talked about taking your faith from your heart to your hands and working toward making the world better for the least, the last and the left out.

You did not choose me, but I chose you.

But now, it was a Sunday in 1976. He was a husband, a graduate of Duke Divinity, a man lucky enough to get a job after graduation at a church right off Duke's East Campus. He got the job because one of his professors recommended him to the Dr. Bill Bennett, Trinity's senior pastor. There was no way Frank would have gotten that job without that recommendation. Frank saw that one instance as the experience of grace in his life. He and Michie got to stay in Durham, and Michie got to start her doctorate in psychology at UNC-Chapel Hill. And just like Michie had encouraged Frank, he encouraged her to go after what she wanted to do.

Except this time, their conversation didn't happen in a driveway in Lumberton. It happened on the couch in their apartment in Raleigh, when Michie realized her master's in guidance counseling equaled a lifetime of pushing papers rather than changing lives.

"You need to go ahead and get your PhD," Frank told Michie.

Michie looked at him, as she often does, in that quizzical way of saying through the expression on her face, "Are you sure?"

"I don't know if I can do that," she responded.

"Yeah," Frank said, "you can go and do that."

Michie did, and she and Frank were now looking forward to the rest of their life together. Their lives became a partnership, and they began discussing things like settling down, having children, and starting a family. Still, some things remained the same. For Frank, it was his love for tennis, his love for Wake Forest, and his love for his home state embodied in the State Toast his parents kept on the dining room wall. And those same nine words from the Book of John. They still moved his heart and stirred his soul.

You did not choose me, but I chose you.

He knew he was doing the right thing on a Christmas Eve at

Trinity Avenue Presbyterian. He was conducting a funeral. He kept asking himself, "How did I get into this?" He remembered what Rev. Sloop told him a few years back, "Don't do it if you can do anything else." He knew he could do something else, but on Christmas Eve at Trinity Avenue conducting a funeral for someone he barely knew, he knew this was it.

He had the gift of an empathetic ear and a demeanor that could calm anyone in a time of stress and pain. And as he held his Bible, reciting passages before a family at one of the most painful times of their life, Frank had an epiphany that settled any nervousness he had about his chosen path in life.

"Frank," he told himself, ""This is what you are called to do."

After his sermon on boycotting Nestle, Frank had another epiphany: He had to leave Trinity Avenue Presbyterian. His sermon convinced him he needed to find his own church rather than cave to a congregation whose values about right and wrong steered a bit different from his.

But before he would leave Trinity Avenue, he got a call in July 1978 from Sarah Britt, Luther's wife.

She wanted Frank to know that Luther had died. And she had a request.

Will you speak at his memorial service? Will you speak for our family?

Frank said yes.

* * *

On his left sat Jim Hunt, North Carolina's governor. On his right sat the Rev. E.B. Turner, the member of the Lumberton City Council and the pastor he supported to be the chair of Robeson County's Democratic Party when he was a junior at Wake Forest. Turner lost; Frank remembered. But Frank didn't lose his drive, and as he sat in Lumberton's First Baptist Church, he saw his past colliding with his present.

He was 27, two years out of Duke Divinity, two years into being the associate pastor at Trinity Avenue Presbyterian, and two years into thinking constantly about his future. But this time, he was thinking about what he saw in the front row: Sarah, Luther's wife, with her family — her daughter, Sarah Beta; and her sons, Luther, Hewitt, and Lee. In the back sat Michie with his parents. He looked out onto a packed congregation, a tell-tale sign of a well-lived life that touched many. And Luther touched many.

A father. A husband. An attorney. A Wake Forest grad. A graduate of the Wake Forest School of Law. The city attorney of Lumberton, his hometown A state senator. A chairman of the Senate Judiciary Committee. A former president of the North Carolina Jaycees. A man who exemplified his own personal motto: "Make things happen."

Frank had not experienced losing many people close to him. He remembered the death of Benjie Witt, his classmate in kindergarten who died in a car accident while they were classmates at Lumberton High.

Benjie Witt was the first; his grandfather, Luther Dew Sr., and Luther Britt were the second.

His death shocked Frank. But he wasn't surprised. From driving Britt back and forth to Raleigh, Frank saw Britt as a man incredibly driven, maybe driven too much. He was constantly rushing from the floor of the General Assembly in Raleigh to his law office in Lumberton. Back and forth. Back and forth. For seven years. That frenetic life, Frank thought, could have led to a life cut short. Sen. Britt died, Frank knew, of something heart related. That's all he knew. But Sen. Britt was only 46 when he died.

Forty-six. Too young, Frank thought. Just too young.

But as he sat in his black pastoral robe between E.B. Turner and Gov. Hunt, holding his eulogy he wrote on a legal pad inside a leather binder, he knew he had to come up with words that would impact the people present. He particularly wanted to impact those in the front row, Sarah and her children. Sarah had asked Frank to speak for the family, and Frank hoped his words would be eloquent enough to ease the heartache he saw and felt in the front row.

The service began.

Said Gov. Hunt:

"Tenacious in his love of the law and the legislative process, but even more tenacious in his dedication that the law and the legislative process deal fairly with men and women. He was a quiet man in the Senate, not given to long speeches or frequent comment … his words were carefully chosen and carefully offered, and the Senate of this State listened when he spoke. A real leader of the Legislature. A true friend of the people."

Said Turner:

"His philosophy in government was as a servant. His purpose in government was to make life better. His will in government was to be open, accessible, and a voice for that which was right."

And Frank.

"He was the kind of man who always made every one of us feel special when we were in his presence. If you knew him, you felt a part of his family. He made me feel like a part of his family. That was his gift. He had a gift of making other people feel important and valued."

Frank saw Sen. Britt as a mentor. He was one of the most organized people Frank had ever met. He admired that, and he took to heart the advice Britt gave him: "Frank, you know you don't have to fight every fight. You have a certain number of arrows in your quiver so save them for the battles that are most important."

Less than a year after Britt's memorial service, Frank found himself in the city where he saw the ACC Men's Basketball Tournament, thanks to tickets he'd received from Britt. The world does work in mysterious ways, Frank said to himself.

In April 1979, when he was 29, Frank became the pastor of Vandalia Presbyterian in Greensboro, and Britt's advice about keeping enough arrows in your quiver came in handy sooner rather than later for Frank.

Frank realized that when he was conducting, of all things, a children's sermon on a Sunday morning at his new church. Frank was talking to a circle of kids, no older than 7. One of those kids was a Black boy, the son of a police sergeant with the Greensboro Police Department. Frank was talking about Jesus and the Bible. He asked a question, and the young Black boy responded with an acronym every

Southerner, every American, knew.

"The KKK!" the boy blurted out.

The church gasped. Frank, right then, didn't know what to do.

Frank on Frank

Finding My Faucet

Always remember this.

Be the person God created you to be. That is what we're here to do. You'll know. It's an intuitive feeling that tells you you're on the right path, and that is confirmed by the people that God puts in your path. They're like signposts along a highway, and when I was at Duke, I saw those signposts in people like Art Simon, Evelyn Mattern, and Moody Smith.

They all helped show me I belonged at Duke. Now, I'm not saying there weren't some conflicts along the way. Duke was far from easy. But I discovered kindred spirits there who encouraged me and mentored me, and they helped me feel I was in the right place doing what God called me to do.

In our lives, we all need mentors. I mean, it's one thing to read about something. It's quite another thing to see people do it. So, I felt God gave me a gift by the people I met. Like Bill Bennett at Trinity Avenue Presbyterian. I've often said about Bill that I learned a number of things I wanted to do — and a number of things I didn't want to do.

For example, after his reaction to my sermon about boycotting Nestle, I learned I didn't want to be pigeonholed by influential people in the church. I wanted to carry out what I felt called to do, and one of the best gifts you can ever have is when you are shown what you *don't* want to do. I knew I didn't want to feel constrained, and at that point in my life, being 27 and just out of Duke Divinity School, I knew I didn't want to be changed more than I wanted to. I knew I needed to find a place where I could be free to be myself, and I wouldn't be compromised in what I believe.

We all have those kinds of moments in our lives. It's that moment when you feel you're at a crossroads, particularly when you have a crisis of faith. You realize people are trying to change you and what you believe. When you see that, you know it's time to go. We all need to stand up for what we believe in and what we believe is right. That is part of our calling, too.

Faith can be a struggle, no doubt. But when that happens, that is when we learn. We see it as a lesson that can guide us. That's when faith becomes a gift. We often think we are doing all the work. We aren't. We need to recognize God has been with us all along.

It's like one of my favorite verses: You did not choose me; I chose you.

One of my favorite stories in the Bible is the feeding of the 5,000. That is such a great story. It's one of the most inspiring stories in the entire Bible, because it shows what we can do when we have faith.

Disciples brought to Jesus five loaves and two fish to feed 5,000 people who came to hear Him preach. Just five loaves and two fish. That's all they had, and Jesus told his disciples, "Bring them here to me." Jesus received five loaves and two fish from a young boy, and everyone was fed — and there were baskets of leftovers.

Such a beautiful story, isn't it? It's the only miracle you'll find in the Gospel of John, Mark, Matthew, and Luke. It shows you nothing we face is too big for God. It also reminds us of Jesus' compassion for others and how our compassion can connect us to justice in addressing hunger.

There is no better example of that than the feeding of the 5,000. What that story really means to me is the importance of advocacy, about speaking out for those who aren't being heard and don't have bread on the table.

Now, I want you to imagine that you find water flooding the floor of your kitchen. You rush to get a mop and a bucket to clean up the water. But you forget to turn off the faucet. You see the problem?

That is what we often do in the church. We address the immediate need and fail to address the root cause. When we think about addressing hunger, we manage the problem by feeding people who are hungry *today*. But guess what? *Tomorrow* they will be hungry again. So, we have to make that connection between compassion and justice so we can address issues of public policy to get to those root causes and fix them.

I really discovered the importance of advocacy at Duke, through people like Sister Evelyn and Arthur Simon, and of course, my good friend Moody Smith. I knew the church needed to advocate for those who had no voice. Even at 27, I knew I needed to find a church — even start a church — where I could take seriously what you'll find in Proverbs 31: 8-9:

> *Speak up for those who cannot speak for themselves,*
> *for the rights of all who are destitute.*
> *Speak up and judge fairly;*
> *defend the rights of the poor and needy.*

I knew I couldn't do that with just a mop and a bucket. I needed to find a place that would help me turn off the faucet.

So, I looked toward Greensboro. And I never left.

On November 3, 1979, a Saturday, local members of the Communist Workers
Party were holding a "Death to the Klan" rally in east Greensboro at
Morningside Homes, a federal housing community. As they began to march
singing and yelling "Death to the Klan!", 40 neo-Nazis and members of the Ku
Klux Klan rolled up in nine cars and stopped. They pulled rifles from the trunks
of cars and jumped out onto the street with knives and pistols in their hands.
After 88 seconds, five Communist Workers Party members — four white men,
one black woman — were killed and 10 people were wounded. WFMY, the
city's CBS affiliate, had captured the entire melee on camera, and those images
raced around the world. Photo credit: Courtesy of the News & Record.

Chapter 7

"I Think He's Been Infected"

In our lifetime, we will all take leaps of faith that can change the direction of our lives and even transform who we are. And that can be fearful. None of us really like change. But think about what happens when we take that leap. We land on the other side. We experience the true feeling of faith, and we recognize faith is a gift that you can't make happen no matter how hard you try. You have to thank God.

The Rev. Frank Dew

That Sunday morning, a few weeks before Thanksgiving, Frank became the student, not the teacher.

He had gathered around him a handful of children to help them understand that not *everyone* recognized Jesus as the Messiah. Frank had been at Vandalia Presbyterian for about eight months or so, and he and Michie were getting used to Greensboro. Frank saw it as the place to see ACC basketball. He never saw it as a city to set down roots. Yet, he liked Greensboro, and he enjoyed the idea of being THE pastor for a congregation of 250 people. He especially liked plucking some wisdom from the Bible and sharing it with children. It always reminded him of his own Sunday mornings just beyond the white columns of First Presbyterian in Lumberton. So, on that second Sunday morning in November 1979, he turned the steps beneath the pulpit at Vandalia Presbyterian into a spiritual version of "Sesame Street." He asked the 10 children around him about some images that he *knew* they'd get.

"When you think about someone who wears a whistle and a shirt with black and white stripes," he asked, "you think of who?"

"A referee!" one of them yelled.

"That's right," Frank said, nodding. "Now, think about someone who wears all white. Who comes to mind?"

Frank knew what came to his mind. A nurse. But that's not the answer he got on Sunday morning.

"The KKK!"

The shout came from the Black boy seated to Frank's right. He was no older than 6. But even at that tender age, he already knew the ugly side of the South.

Frank figured he heard about it from his dad, the police sergeant at the Greensboro Police Department. But really, the boy could've heard it anywhere. Because in Greensboro, a city that prided itself as a bastion of nonviolence, what happened a few miles from Vandalia Presbyterian had shocked everyone around the world.

Especially Frank.

It happened on November 3, a Saturday, just eight days before Frank's spiritual sit-down with children. Local members of the Communist Workers Party were holding a "Death to the Klan" rally in east Greensboro at Morningside Homes, a federal housing community where struggle was a way of life. As they began to march singing and yelling "Death to the Klan!", 40 neo-Nazis and members of the Ku Klux Klan rolled up in nine cars and stopped. They pulled rifles from the trunks of cars and jumped out onto the street with knives and pistols in their hands. Rally participants and onlookers fled. Others dove underneath cars, just anywhere they could find cover. After 88 seconds, five Communist Workers Party members — four white men, one black woman — were killed and 10 people were wounded. WFMY, the city's CBS affiliate, had captured the entire melee on camera, and those images raced around the world. Everyone saw it.

That included a Black boy seated near Frank.

Someone who wears all white, Frank asked.

The KKK, the Black boy blurted out.

"Well, that wasn't exactly what I had in mind," Frank said. "I was thinking of a nurse."

Michie was sitting halfway back in the sanctuary when she heard Frank's response. Several church members around her chuckled nervously. Michie, though, sat silent. She kept thinking of the incredulity of it all, of hearing on a Sunday morning what first came to mind to a young Black boy when asked about someone wearing all white. Not someone like a nurse who helps people. No, the boy thought of someone who hides beneath a white sheet. Someone who uses hate as a cudgel. Someone who epitomizes the legacy of lynching, of rounding up Blacks and hanging them from a tree. Like strange fruit, a grisly image made memorable by Billie Holiday.

> *Southern trees bear a strange fruit*
> *Blood on the leaves and blood at the root*
> *Black bodies swingin' in the Southern breeze*
> *Strange fruit hangin' from the poplar trees*

"Wow," Michie told herself. "That's not the first thing that comes to mind for most white people."

But for Black people — a young Black boy no older than 6 — yes.

In that one instance, inside the sanctuary of his new church, Frank realized once again the different world Blacks see — and fear. He thought back to the Black maids of his childhood, the women who helped raise him. They were his tour guides into the Black World of Lumberton. He remembers seeing Hattie cry as she watched the reports of John F. Kennedy's assassination on the TV screen. He also remembers walking into the home of Bessie Moore, the woman he called "Dee Dee" and seeing the framed photo of Martin Luther King Jr. and John F. Kennedy right there on the wall beside the Protestant portrait of the handsome, blue-eyed, hippie Jesus.

The white Jesus.

Frank knew he had work to do. But how?

* * *

The leaders of Vandalia Presbyterian discovered Frank when he was the associate pastor at Durham's Trinity Avenue Presbyterian. Immediately, Frank liked what he heard and saw. And it had nothing to do with ACC basketball.

Well, kinda. First, about the church.

Vandalia Presbyterian sat a two-minute drive from Vandalia Elementary, ensconced in the middle-class integrated neighborhood known as Woodlea. Frank saw much potential inside the contemporary-looking building, which looked like a pyramid from the street. He discovered a growing church full of young families, about 250 people strong, and the people he talked to illustrated through their conversations a commitment to hard work, discipline and building community. Frank met plumbers and teachers, police officers and school maintenance workers, restaurant owners and construction superintendents. Because of the church's location in a neighborhood diverse in class and color, Frank had this vision of looking out onto a congregation of white and Black and brown members. He could just see it — him in the pulpit, preaching in his let's-get-serious voice massaged by an accent of his Southern upbringing in small-town North Carolina. He'd preach to them about being faithful to the Gospel of Jesus and taking to heart the verse from the Book of Mark, Chapter 12, verse 31: "The second most important command is this: Love your neighbor the same as you love yourself. These two commands are the most important."

Frank had been approached by a Presbyterian church in Aberdeen. It just didn't feel right for Frank. But Vandalia Presbyterian felt right. Really, it felt providential. One of the first people he met from the church was Jack Baldwin, a Wake Forest grad. Moreover, Jack was THE first Demon Deacon mascot. He dressed in a top hat and tails and cheered on the Demon Deacons courtside at basketball games and on the sidelines during football season many Saturdays in the fall.

"God must be at work," Frank told himself. "He's showing me a sign. Greensboro must be the place to be."

But really, Frank figured Vandalia Presbyterian would be a great

place to continue his ministerial career. Michie, who was finishing up
her doctorate work in psychology at UNC-Chapel Hill, had a year-
long internship at the VA Hospital in Salisbury, and Greensboro was
much closer to her job than Durham. Meanwhile, Frank found signs
in Greensboro that showed him the city was a good fit. The city was
home to the N.C. Tennis Hall of Fame as well as the zip code for
someone Frank long admired — L. Richardson Preyer, the World War
II Navy veteran and Congressman who chaired the House Committee
on the Assassination of President Kennedy and Martin Luther King
Jr. In 1957, as a Superior Court judge, Preyer upheld a ruling that
enabled five Black children to attend the previously all-white Gillespie
Park School in Greensboro. Gillespie Park became the first integrated
school in the city of Greensboro.

For Frank, Greensboro became the place to be. And yet, how
he got there was, well, memorable, too. And like much of Frank's life,
it happened on a Sunday morning.

* * *

A few minutes before he was slated to preach, Frank saw the
commotion in the back.

A large woman sitting in the last pew at Trinity Avenue
Presbyterian had fainted and a clutch of people surrounded her
immediately. The service stopped, Dr. Bennett walked up to the pulpit
and craned his neck to see the backs of parishioners huddling around
her. He knew all of them well. All doctors. All from Duke. He looked
over the congregation, knowing he needed to settle the anxiousness
he felt rippling through the sanctuary.

"Let's pray for her," he said.

He nodded to the church's organist, and she began to play.

"What a day for the search committee to come," Frank told
himself.

Members of the minister search committee from Vandalia
Presbyterian were somewhere in the sanctuary. Frank didn't know
where. But he knew he had to do well and deliver what he hoped
would work. His sermon was a job interview, and in the middle of his
job interview, a woman fainted. Yet, unlike those times he stood in

front of his Duke professors for his oral exams in divinity school, he wasn't nervous. He felt comfortable. And when the doctors moved the woman from the back pew to the narthex, Frank sensed a calm envelop the sanctuary. The service continued, the organist stopped playing, and Frank walked up to the pulpit. It was time.

"It seems appropriate we're focusing on prayer," Frank said, "because today, I'll talk about prayer."

With his voice rising and falling like musical notes on a scale, Frank began.

"Do you remember the section in the Lord's Prayer that begins 'Thy will be done on earth as it is in heaven?" Think of how we pray for things. But ultimately, we give our will over for God's will. We desire what God desires, and we change in the process."

As Frank got deeper into the sermon, he knew the ambulance had arrived. It wasn't because of the siren. The ambulance arrived in silence. But when he looked over the congregation, he noticed the red lights flashing through the stained-glass windows like a strobe. It was a bit distracting. But Frank got through it. The service ended, the woman was taken away in an ambulance, and Frank met the members of the minister search committee.

"Well, that was a different kind of service," said one member of the search committee.

"It sure was," added a second member.

"But you did well," said a third, looking at Frank.

"We were sure impressed how you kept your wits about you," said the first.

"That's right," said the second. "With all those red lights coming through those stained-glass windows, I thought I was in a disco."

Frank laughed.

"Well, if it looked like a disco," Frank said. "I guess I was dancing with God."

They all laughed and shook hands. A month later, right after Easter 1979, Michie and Frank found themselves in Greensboro.

Their new home.

* * *

Frank had his first full-time job as minister at Vandalia Presbyterian in Greensboro.

Frank and Michie arrived in Greensboro at a time when the city always shakes off the chill of winter for the short-sleeve warmth of spring. Azaleas and cherry blossoms bloomed along Battleground Avenue, and Stamey's scented the winding curve of East Lee with vinegar-kissed barbecue that attracted many to a booth along the wall of windows. Later that month, Greensboro would host the Beach Boys in the biggest room between Atlanta and Washington, DC — the Greensboro Coliseum. A month before in that big room, UNC beat Duke 71-63 in Greensboro's version of Mardi Gras, the ACC Men's Basketball Tournament. Frank's Wake Forest? Didn't get past the first round. Lost in a squeaker to Duke 58-56. As Frank would say, no God miracle that day.

Every March in Greensboro, the city becomes awash in the colors of the ACC — red and gold, black and orange, and two shades of blue. School kids roll TVs into classrooms, scores of people call in sick at work to watch the game somewhere, and churches let out early so parishioners could watch the championship on an early Sunday afternoon. And everywhere, fans hang on every word from the play-by-play crew — broadcaster Jim Thacker and analysts Billy Packer and Bones McKinney, both former basketball players from Frank's Wake Forest. Basketball crazy, Greensboro is. That was fine by Frank and

Michie. They liked what they saw — and felt — about the city.

When they stepped into the church's manse in Greensboro's Woodlea neighborhood, Michie did feel a bit overwhelmed. She'd been buried in her dissertation work, and she had gotten used to moving from one tiny two-bedroom apartment to another. She and Frank now found themselves in a spacious home with a living room and dining room.

Michie walked from room to room, contemplating the next chapter in their young lives. She was 25; Frank, 28. As she entered each bedroom, she replayed in her mind her own conversation with the search committee members at the church.

"What can we expect from you?" one member asked.

"Absolutely nothing," Michie replied.

Stark silence.

Michie never minced words with anyone, and she knew many churches saw minister's wives as unpaid staff members. That wasn't her. She knew she couldn't devote hours upon hours to church work. Every weekday, she drove from Greensboro to Salisbury and back for her work at the VA Hospital where she worked with veterans dealing with physical pain and the visions of war playing out in their minds. She wouldn't have buckets of time for Vandalia Presbyterian. But she knew she could work with the church's youth. She did it as a paid youth director for a year at Hayes Barton United Methodist Church in Raleigh before she enrolled at UNC. But when she answered, "Absolutely nothing," she saw the blank looks on the men's faces. She knew she had to break the silence before the silence broke Frank's chances for his first full-time job as a senior pastor.

"Let me explain," she said. "Frank can expect from me to be a loving, supportive wife, and you can expect me to be a church member who will contribute to the work of the church. As a minister's wife, though, you can't expect anything else."

The members nodded.

"Thank you, Michie," one member said. "We appreciate your honesty."

Michie pondered that conversation as she walked from the

second bedroom to the third bedroom and into the fourth.

Big house, she thought. Big, big house.

"Frank?" Michie yelled.

"Yeah, Boog?" Frank answered.

"We're going to need more furniture," Michie said.

* * *

It was a Sunday in January 1980 when Frank stepped up to the pulpit, a grin spreading across his face.

His Demon Deacons had a good week on the hardwood. On Wednesday, they beat Duke in Cameron Indoor Stadium 76-73. Three days later, they beat N.C. State 60-52. Wake Forest had won 11 straight to reach No. 5 in the latest basketball poll. And here came UNC on the following Thursday.

"God's miracles are still occurring," he told his congregation at Vandalia Presbyterian.

Frank never passed up a chance to pitch hard for his alma mater, especially in a city where ACC rivalries mattered. And his parishioners, especially those loyal to a lighter shade of blue, never passed up a chance to poke Frank back. He saw it one weekday morning right there in front of the church's big A-frame window. A light blue sheet hung from the rafters with two numbers and two schools written in black.

Except one school was misspelled.

Frank's school.

Weak Forest 9

Carolina 27

By the fall of 1980, UNC had beaten Wake Forest in football for the fourth time in five years. On Oct. 12, 1980, Wake Forest lost to UNC in Chapel Hill 27-9. The following Sunday, a few days after spying the light blue bed sheet in the back of the church, Frank stepped up to the podium for his moment of truth about the longtime rivalry. When he did, he broke out into a grin.

"God didn't smile on us Demon Deacons this go-round," he said. "But He did smile on those Tar Heels, especially the folks who owned that light-blue sheet. Thank you for that reminder, even the misspelling. But I would bet the Baptists wouldn't take too kindly to that. We Presbyterians are much more forgiving. "

His parishioners laughed. Yeah, Frank said to himself, this is my kind of place.

Frank grew to really enjoy Vandalia Presbyterian. He took what he learned from Dr. Bennett at Trinity Avenue Presbyterian and applied it to helping run Vandalia Presbyterian. He never cottoned to the administrative duties of running a church. He'd rather choose a way to reach the poor than choose the color of an altar cloth. Still, he knew administrative duties were the burden every minister must bear, and he used a technique he had mastered in his hometown of Lumberton, especially during his dinner-table discussions with his dad. He relied on humor, and it helped diffuse some of the toughest administrative situations known to any minister. And those tough situations were much thornier than a light-blue sheet hanging in the back of church.

Frank still remembers one. And this one involved Frankenstein.

One weeknight, Frank was helping lead a meeting focused on whether Vandalia would allow fundraising events to raise money for the church. Some thought it was a good idea, putting together something like a spaghetti dinner to help beef up the budget of the church. Others, though, wanted to raise money the old-fashioned way through tithes and passing the plate every Sunday.

The night of the meeting, Vandalia held an event for the church's youth, and people came wearing costumes. And with it being close to Halloween, people came in as ghouls and vampires, cowboys and ACC fans wearing almost every color of the rainbow. And yes, there was a Frankenstein. A parent. An elder in the church. He came to Frank's meeting. And as the people around the table edged nearer to taking a vote, Frankenstein raised his hand.

"Before we continue, let me recognize the elder from Transylvania," Frank said.

That one comment broke the tension in the room, and like he does on Sunday mornings, Frank used humor to shepherd the congregation through something tough. Vandalia ended up voting yes to car washes, spaghetti events and other fundraising ideas.

With the help of Frankenstein.

As Frank worked with the church, Michie worked with the church's teenagers. She got involved with them in all sorts of activities. When she brought them over to the manse, they walked in and looked a bit dumbfounded by what they saw.

"When's the rest of the furniture coming?" one asked.

Michie laughed.

"That's it, y'all," she replied. "That's all we got."

She needed the relief she found in the good-natured demeanor of Vandalia's teenagers. It's because of her internship at the VA Hospital. It wasn't really the hour-long drive. It's what she discovered along the hallways of the hospital.

Her coursework for her doctorate was done at UNC-Chapel Hill. All she had left was writing her dissertation and finishing her year-long internship. At the VA, she saw mostly World War II veterans who were dealing with illnesses that wracked both their bodies and their minds. She talked to them individually and in group therapy sessions, and what she discovered angered her.

She felt the doctors and nurses lacked the empathy needed in dealing with veterans wrestling with all kinds of ailments. She saw them simply "putting in your eight," which basically meant putting in your eight hours at work and going home. Meanwhile, Michie never saw the director of the VA Hospital talk to any patients. But she did see him interact with one. The patient barked at the director. He'd be walking down the hall, and the patient would be inches from his ear, barking like a dog as loud as he could.

Michie learned who to rely on — and who not. And during her year at the hospital, she learned to rely on the Black aides. She saw they cared. So, when she needed to know something about a patient, she never went to a doctor, and she never went to a nurse. She went to the Black aides, and they were always accurate, straight to the point.

She never really told Luther, Frank's dad, about what she saw. She simply gave him advice.

"If you ever need care, go to the VA in Durham, not in

Salisbury."

After a year of seeing firsthand "putting in your eight," Michie was ready to leave the VA. After a few years stepping up to the pulpit every Sunday, Frank was ready to leave Vandalia Presbyterian, too.

He had wanted to steer Vandalia toward his own vision of what a church should be. But when he tried, he remembered a story he heard at Duke about pastors trying to change a church's direction. It involved a turtle. Changing a church, someone told him, was like peeing on a turtle. Mostly, you got it all on yourself.

That turtle story became real for Frank at Vandalia.

Frank was steering his first church retreat when he sat down with a handful of his parishioners in the church's fellowship hall and began talking about long-range planning. That's when he brought up the two banks down the street.

"We have two banks one long block away from us," Frank said. "Right there at the corner of Vandalia and Randleman Road is First Union and Wachovia. And you know, it strikes me that both First Union and Wachovia would be more than upset if they didn't have any Black customers. So, shouldn't we as a church be concerned about that as well? Banks would see this as a problem. But for us, it's not a problem. This, I believe, is an opportunity. Does that make sense?"

Discussion started around the tables in the fellowship hall. Frank brought up that the church's Boy Scout troop had some Black members, and the church's pre-school had some Black kids, too. Meanwhile, the church's after-school program had some Black children bussed from Vandalia Elementary situated less than a mile west of the church. Parishioners talked back and forth about the need to witness, the need to reach out. Then came a comment from a mother in the church.

"Our children have to go to school with them," she said. "But they don't have to worship with them."

"Well, thank you for that perspective," Frank responded. "But I think we are called to a higher standard than First Union or Wachovia."

Discussion continued, and comments volleyed back and forth.

After the meeting, Frank walked to the manse next door and met Michie in the kitchen.

"So, how did it go?" she asked.

"It went pretty well," Frank responded. "But we did have this weird thing happen. I was suggesting we should be concerned that we don't have any Black folks coming to worship, and I compared us to the banks up the street. You know, Wachovia and First Union and how they would be some kind of upset if they didn't have any Black customers.

And someone said, 'Well, our kids have to go to school with them, but they don't have to worship with them.' Fortunately, that wasn't the only thing said. But man, that was hard to hear."

"Wow, *that* was something you didn't expect to hear," Michie said.

"Yeah, Boog," Frank responded. "After I heard that, I kept thinking, 'I've got a lot of work to do.'"

Frank put in the work, and after six years at Vandalia, two Black families and one Indian-American family joined the church. But Frank wanted to do more. He wanted to start his own church, one that would be more diverse, more inclusive, more inviting to everyone, not just people of a certain skin color from a certain side of the city. His local Presbytery, one of six Presbyterian boards in North Carolina, had not seen a new church formed in 20 years in central North Carolina. But Frank really believed he could do it, and he believed in himself. His dad? Not so much.

"You sure you want to create something out of nothing?" he asked his son.

"Dad, you don't become outstanding," Frank said, "when you do what everybody else does."

But why did Frank want to start a church? It came from a book, and that book changed everything.

Frank has always been a reader.

When he got married on one of the hottest days he ever endured in Lumberton, he gave his groomsmen copies of "The Old Man and the Sea" by Ernest Hemingway. But when he picked up Elizabeth

O'Connor's "Call to Commitment," a book published in 1963 about
the creation of the Church of the Saviour in Washington, DC, he
discovered a blueprint of what he wanted to do.

He couldn't believe he had never heard about the Church of the
Saviour at Duke Divinity School. But in those pages, he saw a way to
turn what the book called "mild Christianity" into a revolution of faith
that stirred people to pray, witness and serve. All anyone had to do
was look at the church's brochure and realize the faith of the Church
of the Saviour wasn't just for Sunday mornings. It was a life, a
movement, a way to see Jesus in the faces of the people they helped.
In the church's brochure, O'Connor wrote:

"This is a dangerous book about a demanding way of life and a
vigorous institution that would propagate it, It is dangerous because
you may find yourself digging with a shovel, or tracing current
theologies, or reading the Bible, or changing your job, or explaining
what the word "ecumenism" means or praying as you've never prayed
before. It is indeed dangerous, for if one becomes committed to this
way, all life will be different and every sphere of one's existence
involved in the change."

As Frank pored through the book, he found sentences and
entire paragraphs that invigorated him about his future and his own
calling.

"The Church of the Saviour is an attempt to recover in one local
expression of the Church University something of the vitality and life,
vigor and power of the early Christian community."

"Redemption and salvation are more than high-sounding
ecclesiastical words when we live them out on the streets and alleys
where we dwell."

"We still believe in intentional evangelism, but not as completely
as we once did. Many of us are past that time when we are sure that
we know what is good for a person and who can best be his minister.
We now know that God calls his own and that he sometimes uses the
most unlikely people."

Frank felt that call. He was one of those "unlikely people." And
the longer he stayed at Vandalia Presbyterian, the more he realized

that the church was changing him rather than the other way around. That realization came into sharp focus as he sat in his office on a weekday morning during his fifth year at Vandalia Presbyterian. He was writing his Sunday sermon on a legal pad like he always does, and he came face to face on the page with something he always hated to think about.

"If I say this, I'll lose two-thirds of my congregation," he told himself. "What am I going to do?"

He decided to say it. But deep inside, he felt something familiar. It was that very same feeling he had when he preached about boycotting Nestle during one of his sermons at Trinity Avenue Presbyterian. As he sat in his office at Vandalia Presbyterian, with a picture of Michie near his elbow, he knew it was time to move on.

And what stirred him? It was a quote by Martin Luther King Jr. from the letter he wrote from a jail cell in Birmingham, Alabama. And King wrote that letter in the same year "Call to Commitment" was published — 1963.

It was Good Friday when King and hundreds of others participated in a mass demonstration to protest Alabama's racism and racial segregation. A judge had issued a blanket injunction to stop any demonstration of any kind. But King and hundreds of others defied that injunction. In a nonviolent demonstration organized by the Alabama Christian Movement for Human Rights and King's own organization, Southern Christian Leadership Conference, King marched from the Sixth Avenue Baptist Church and into a waiting police wagon. The day of his arrest, eight white clergymen from Alabama criticized King and his actions in a piece published in Birmingham's newspaper, the Birmingham News. They called King's method "unwise and untimely" and urged him to pursue a more common-sense approach that would be more lawful.

When King read their response, King began to write in his jail cell. First on newspaper, then on pieces of paper and later on a pad supplied by his attorneys. King chastised the response from the eight white clergyman and questioned the role of white moderates in the fight for social reform nationwide. He wanted them to do more, say more, act more rather than sit idly by. So, in his sermon, Frank rang out King's charge like a bell on Sunday morning.

"Martin Luther King often said the church too often resembles brake lights instead of highlights," Frank told his congregation. "The church is putting the brakes on things instead of showing the way."

Afterward, Frank's parishioners smiled, shook his hand, and walked out. As he stood in the narthex shaking hands, Frank remembered something he read: "If you think you're saying to people they're going to change the world, you need to reevaluate how much they're listening." Frank wondered how much his parishioners were listening, and he worried if they were changing him rather than the other way around. The passages he found in "Call to Commitment" showed him what he needed to do. He needed to follow his head and his heart. But at 33, in his first full-time job as a senior Presbyterian minister, he looked for guidance.

He found it in one of the most unlikely places – on a running route with a man called Z.

* * *

Like Frank, the Rev. Dr. Zeb Holler spent 40 years in Greensboro, his hometown, as a soft-spoken fighter for social justice. Here, he stands in the center of religion majors from High Point University. Holler gave his book collection to HPU's libraries so students could use them.

The Rev. Dr. Zeb Holler was as slender as a fence rail. Like Frank, he spoke in a soft Southern drawl, and he never shied away from writing a whip-smart sermon or calling out the broader community to help the most vulnerable among us. He saw the Parables of Jesus as the blueprint of his life, and he believed those New Testament stories held important lessons that help make the community he served a better place to live. And for nearly 40 years, the community he served was the community of his childhood.

Z grew up in Greensboro's Westerwood neighborhood, attended Presbyterian Church of the Covenant every Sunday with his family and listened to every word the minister said — so much so that at age 10 the minister told him, "Z, you need to be a preacher."

He graduated from Greensboro Senior High and Davidson College. He taught high school English, coached high school football, flew planes for the Navy and fell in love with a spirited teenage girl from Florida. He met his wife, Charlene, at a church party during flight training school in Pensacola, Fla. She was 16; Z was 22. They got married two years later, started a family and became a couple who pushed for racial equality and social justice at every stop along his ministerial path.

After his four years in the Navy, Z enrolled at Union Theological Seminary in Richmond, Va., and heard one of his professors exclaim, "The problem with Holler is that he's too much like Jesus!"

Z wanted to be. He went on to get his doctorate at the University of Aberdeen in Scotland and titled his dissertation, "Jesus and The Suffering Servant." After that, he went on to fight the injustices of the world with fierce honesty and undeniable love.

In 1960 in Anderson, S.C., he hosted civil rights activists known as the Freedom Riders. While they were there, he got a call from the Ku Klux Klan. They told him to stop. Z said no. Six years later in Atlanta, following the assassination of civil rights leader Martin Luther King Jr., Z and his church fed more than 5,000 people and housed in the church's gym more than 100 who came to the city to mourn.

He later became a campus minister at N.C. State during the

Vietnam War and a pastor at a Presbyterian church in Clemson, S.C. Then, in 1979, he came back home. He came back to be the pastor at his home church, Presbyterian Church of the Covenant.

Around that time, Z met Frank and they became running partners.

Z reminded Frank a lot of Moody Smith. Both Moody and Z graduated from Davidson, both had doctorates, and both were New Testament scholars. They were athletes, 20 years older than Frank, and they both saw exercise as a crucial part of their lives.

Frank played tennis with Moody for 40 years; Frank ran with Z for almost 20 before Z's knees gave out. As he shared exercise, Frank shared his life with two men who became his best friends. They both had their share of verbal quirks. Whereas Moody would miss a shot playing tennis and yell, "Holy Peter!" Z would listen intently to anyone, cock his head ever so slightly, break out into a grin as thin as a pencil and say, "Press on, brother."

Both men mentored Frank until their deaths. Frank spoke at both of their memorial services. In each eulogy, he used the same quote from "The Quest of the Historical Jesus," the book by German theologian Albert Schweitzer. The quote fit both men. From Schweitzer's book, Frank read this:

"He comes to us as One unknown, without a name, as of old, by the lakeside, He came to those men who knew Him not. He speaks to us the same words: "Follow thou me!" and sets us to the tasks which He has to fulfill for our time.

"He commands. And to those who obey Him, whether they be wise or simple, He will reveal himself in the toils, the conflicts, the sufferings which they shall pass through in His fellowship, and, as an ineffable mystery, they shall learn in their own experience who He is."

Through Moody and Z, Frank did learn who He is.

* * *

Frank met Z several times a week at the YMCA downtown, then at the corner of West Market and Tate. They'd run out Market, down Greenway, cut over to Benjamin Parkway, run through Z's childhood neighborhood of Westerwood and up Mendenhall back to the Y.

During one of their runs in 1984, Frank ran an idea by Z. It was an idea that had been pinging in Frank's head for a few months. On one of their runs, Frank knew it was time. He needed some Z advice.

"I've been reading about this church up in Washington called the Church of the Saviour," Frank said between strides. "Have you heard of it?"

"I think I have," Z replied.

"Well, when I first started reading about it," Frank continued, "I thought this is the kind of church I've always wanted to be a part of."

"Tell me more about it," Z said.

"I've been thinking about how we do church the same ol' way, like we're in some cookie cutter mold, and we need to have some congregation doing some research and development," Frank said.

"What are you talking about?" Z asked.

"Well, I'm talking about starting a new church," Frank replied.

"Wow, that's big!" Z said. "Press on, brother."

Frank paused. Then came the kicker.

"I was hoping you might help me," Frank said. "I was thinking about using some space at the Church of the Covenant. To me, that's a really ripe area close to UNCG and downtown."

"Well, you know we could use your help with our church," Z responded, "Because we need to create a new ring of growth there."

"I'd be interested in that," Frank said, "if you'd be interested in helping me with that."

In mid-stride, Z cocked his head toward Frank and cracked a smile that wrinkled his eyes.

"Well, Frank," he said, "I think I am."

Frank felt so moved by what he read in Elizabeth O'Connor's "Call To Commitment," he knew he had to see for himself. So, one weekend, he drove up to Washington, DC, into the city's Dupont Circle neighborhood to visit the Church of the Saviour. When he arrived, he stepped into a 19th century 12,000-square-foot Romanesque mansion the church had bought in 1950. The walnut paneling was painted apple green, and the white chapel was simply an empty room with straight rows of ladder-back chairs in front of a handmade altar and a large wooden cross. That was it. There was no, as Z liked to say, "any gilding of the lily." Frank loved what he saw. It wasn't the building, though. It was the building's spirit and what the members did with that.

He saw the church's after-school program, their child-care program, their job-readiness program, their medical clinic and their bookstore and coffee house they called the Potter's House. He found people who talked his language, about reaching out to the poor and destitute. They weren't concerned with finding Presbyterians, as Frank saw in his own denomination. Frank saw Church of the Saviour was concerned about finding followers of Jesus. As he talked to his tour guide that day, Frank couldn't help but think about a verse from Jeremiah, one of his favorite Bible verses: "His word is in my heart like a fire, a fire shut up in my bones. I am weary of holding it in; indeed, I cannot."

As he stood in the Potter's House talking to his tour guide, up walked Gordon Cosby. He was the former Army chaplain from World War II who started the church with his wife Mary and five others. Frank began talking to Gordon about what he saw and how impressed he was. Gordon laughed.

"We really don't know what we're doing," Gordon told him.

"What?" Frank asked.

Gordon then explained how it all came about. They were simply doing what they believed Jesus would do. They really didn't know what they were doing. But what they did know was that they were so different from how other churches approached their mission. There was no feasibility study, no fundraising campaign. When compared to other mainstream faiths, Church of the Saviour was counterculture. They required members to study for two years, attend silent retreats, tithe 10 percent of their income, and pray an hour a day. They weren't playing church, Frank found. They were being church.

Frank explained to Gordon what he had hoped to do in North Carolina. Gordon listened before turning to Frank's tour guide.

"I think he's been infected," Gordon said.

For Frank, the idea of starting a church had been an evolving process over at least a year. Like he did with much in his life, Frank was meticulous in his research. Ever since he heard about Elizabeth O'Connor's book "Call To Commitment" in an article he read in the Sojourners magazine, he started digging into everything about Church of the Saviour. He listened to the church's cassettes, went on their retreats, talked to people like Z as well as the four ministers he met with every Monday. They always talked about the lectionary scriptures in the fellowship hall at Vandalia Presbyterian, and like Z, the ministers were all older than Frank by at least a decade. They urged Frank to take the ministerial leap. And it all happened because of one article in a magazine.

From that one article, Frank began to dream.

Of course, he talked to Michie. A month after meeting Gordon Cosby, he and Michie drove up to DC to visit the church in Dupont Circle. Michie liked the church. Then, she looked around Dupont Circle, the neighborhood created in the 1870s. Named after Civil War hero Samuel Francis Du Pont, the neighborhood had an eye-catching detail: a fountain designed by the same architects who designed the Lincoln Memorial. Presidents like William Taft, Calvin Coolidge and Franklin Delano Roosevelt had lived in Dupont Circle. But that was a long time ago, a time when millionaires walked the sidewalks. But when Michie walked the sidewalks in the early 1980s in DC's Adams Morgan neighborhood, she found a dog-eared neighborhood that showed the tell-tale signs of drug addiction.

"Bones, I'm fine with the church," she said, "but I'm not thrilled about raising kids with needles in the front yard."

Michie had only recently talked about starting a family. It had never been a make-or-break detail for Frank and Michie. Even when they got married, people would ask Michie, "So, when are you going to start a family?" Michie's response? "IF we start a family," she'd say.

Michie began talking to Frank about starting a family because she saw herself edging deeper into her 30s. If she wanted children, she knew it had to be sooner rather than later. So, when she mentioned children to Frank during their walk through the neighborhood, he knew he had to face the idea of becoming a father at some point. But not right then. He was preoccupied with starting his own church. But before he could even start, he knew he needed to have a tough conversation.

That came on a Sunday night in the parlor of Vandalia Presbyterian. He broke the news to the church's elders. They sat silent for a few seconds. Then, the questions came.

* * *

"Couldn't we do those things here?" one of them asked.

"I don't think it would be fair to the church," Frank told them. "People who have joined the church came with one set of expectations. Then, I impose a whole new level of expectations? That would be like marrying someone, and after the ceremony, you change everything in what you expected from your spouse. It wouldn't be fair. Does that make sense?"

It did to Frank. And to the elders, too. But the meeting turned bittersweet. People cried. They hugged, and Frank hugged them. Frank found it hard to leave friends, his connections, and the joy he found in that A-frame church. Michie felt the same way. But she supported Frank, and Frank knew this was what God was calling him to do.

He took up Z's offer of becoming the associate pastor at Church of the Covenant, a large church a block from UNC-Greensboro in the city's College Hill neighborhood, and he began pursuing in earnest the creation of his own church. And Z would help. He sat on the Presbytery, the denomination's local administrative board, and he could help shepherd his request. Frank's new move did make good fiscal sense. The Church of the Covenant paid half his salary, and with him starting a new church, the Presbytery paid the other half. With his new job at Church of the Covenant, Frank began meeting with people in their living rooms about creating a new church. And one of the first people he met were Fran and Margaret Young, husband and wife.

The Youngs were their 40s, two people who came of age during the Vietnam War. They both looked at religion as a way to change lives and help the most vulnerable. Fran worked as a purchasing agent for Western Electric, and Margaret stayed at home raising their three sons. They were attending a Lutheran church in Greensboro when their minister moved to another church in North Carolina and a new minister came in. That minister saw communion much different than the Youngs did.

The minister said members had to see the bread served as the body of Christ. But Margaret told him she saw it as just bread. That's it. When she told him that, the minister refused to serve her communion. That angered Margaret, and the Youngs went looking for a new church. They heard about Frank from a friend and stepped into their living room to hear Frank speak about what he wanted to do.

Margaret, who was raised in Scotland, was leery at first. She and Fran had belonged to a nondenominational church in New Jersey that they didn't enjoy, and they worried that Frank was doing the same thing. They also saw what was happening an hour south of them in Charlotte with televangelist Jim Bakker hosting the program "The PTL Club," and running a theme park called Heritage USA. Bakker was nondenominational, too. So, Margaret had some questions. And Margaret, never one to mince words, asked.

"So, Frank, what umbrella denomination are we going to be under?"

"Presbyterian," he responded.

"OK," she said, nodding.

That satisfied her. Then came another question.

"Now, Frank," she continued. "If I came to your church and said something you don't agree with, you're not going to throw me out, are you? I'm going to be honest."

"Absolutely not!" Frank said.

That was enough for Margaret and Fran. They joined Frank's church. So did Virginia Driscoll.

She was a Quaker, a single mother shattered by her recent divorce and raising two children she had recently adopted. With Frank's interest in feeding the hungry and helping the homeless, she felt his faith walk matched her faith talk, and she liked how he attached faith with action. So, as she attended New Garden Friends Meeting in Greensboro, she gathered in various living rooms with Frank and a handful of others. She wanted to help structure the church.

She remembers one influential night. It was the night the new church found its name. They were sitting in Frank and Michie's new home in Greensboro's Lindley Park neighborhood and listing potential church names on sheets of blank newsprint. Someone — she doesn't remember who — read verse 17 from 2 Corinthians, Chapter 5.

Therefore, if anyone is in Christ, the new creation has come: The old has gone, the new is here!

New Creation.

"Write that down!" someone said.

"What about the word 'community?' Frank asked.

"Let's write that down, too!" someone else said.

New Creation Community.

New Creation Community Presbyterian Church.

The once raucous living room, where people threw out name after name, grew quiet. They stared at the name, written in black marker on newsprint.

"That's it," someone said.

"Yes, that's it," Frank said. "That's who we are."

The church now had a name that everyone embraced. So, Frank got busy. But he soon found out he and Michie would get even busier. It had a lot to do with faith — their own. It wasn't just starting a new church, buying a new house and Michie starting a new job when she opened her own private psychological practice in Greensboro.

No, their life took on a new focus, a more emotional focus. His name was David. Her name was Christie. They were brother and sister, and Frank and Michie became their parents.

For Frank and Michie, another journey began.

Frank On Frank

Take That Leap

When I was 6, we lived on 14th Street in the Godwin Heights neighborhood in Lumberton. It was a year before we moved a dozen blocks or so to the Tanglewood neighborhood. If you stood in front of our house on 14th Street and looked to the right, you'd see this ditch. It wasn't a very deep ditch. But it was a ditch, and it acted as the border to our house.

Well, as soon as I saw it, I wanted to jump over it.

I know you're going to ask why, and I'll tell you the same thing Sir Edmund Hillary said when asked about why he wanted to climb Mount Everest? 'Because it's there!' he said. I felt the same way about that ditch.

So, there I was as a 6-year-old, a big fan of the Lone Ranger. I summoned up enough courage, backed far enough up and ran toward that ditch. Then, I leaped. Oh, I was scared. No doubt about it. But you know what? I got to the other side.

We all have to do that sometimes in our lives. We see something we want to do, that we've dreamed about, that makes us scared, and we have to take that leap. Or we face looking back years later, we get all discouraged because we didn't do what we thought was really important.

It reminds me of this quote from Soren Kierkegaard, the Danish theologian. He talks about taking what he called a 'leap of faith.' It's that idea of accepting something outside the boundaries of reason or believing in something and going forward without all the facts.

That's how we started New Creation. We took a leap of faith.

I knew it was risky. But my vision and fear for *not* doing it were so much greater. I didn't want to turn 65, wake up one morning and say, 'Oh, crap, I didn't pursue my dream!' And just like when I jumped over that ditch when I was 6, I knew I had to take that leap when I was 34.

In our lifetime, we will all take leaps of faith that can change the direction of our lives and even transform who we are. And that can be fearful. None of us really like change. But think about what happens when we take that leap. We land on the other side. We experience the true feeling of faith, and we recognize faith is a gift that you *can't* make happen no matter how hard you try. You have to thank God.

With what I saw with the Church of the Saviour, I saw a membership that shared in the ministry of the church. It wasn't that they came and observed what the minister was doing. They took part in what the church did, and I saw it as the perfect intersection of spiritual growth and social activism.

But I knew it wouldn't be a perfect intersection for Vandalia Presbyterian. It wouldn't be fair for me to impose my beliefs on people who joined the church for a totally different set of expectations. I knew I had to be true to Vandalia. But I also knew I had to be true to me.

It's like when I quoted that line from Martin Luther King Jr. in one of my sermons at Vandalia. When I started to worry that I would turn off members of our congregation, I knew then that the church was changing me. I sure didn't want that. But I knew I had to honor my true calling.

We'll all face those kinds of crossroads in our lives. King did. In 1963, he sat in his jail cell in Birmingham, Alabama, after being arrested for marching against Alabama's law against mass public demonstrations over the state's racist policies. He was angry over what he read that the white religious leadership said about the march. They called his strategy 'unwise and untimely.' That's why he felt he had to get his message out. He had to honor his own calling of standing up for the oppressed and marching for change and praying with his feet.

In 1968, in one of his last sermons, King said he wanted to be a drum major for justice, peace and righteousness. And that is what I believed a church should be and needs to be. That's what I saw with the Church of the New Saviour in Washington, DC. And that's what I wanted to happen with New Creation.

I did face some skepticism over what I wanted to do. Like with my dad. He wasn't too thrilled with me leaving an established church to take my own leap of faith. Matter of fact, when I started New Creation, it was hard for my parents to explain to their friends what I was doing. Before that, I was on what they saw as the career ladder for what they had expected. You know, going from one established Presbyterian church to another established Presbyterian church and preaching to bigger and bigger congregations.

I remember when Z told me what he heard when he became the campus minister at N.C. State. His mom asked him, 'Is this a promotion?'

I experienced a similar thing. My dad asked me one time, 'You sure you want to create something out of nothing?" I respected what he said, but again, he looked at life so much differently than I did. He was like, 'You get out of the Army, you finish school, you get married, and you have kids.' It was the predictable suburban pattern, and I knew that wasn't for me. I wanted to plow my own field, so to speak. I felt that all was a part of my calling. I wanted to do something different.

I did feel a little bit of guilt about all that because I felt like I was taking away some of my parents' pleasure in me. Being the oldest child, I felt they no longer were basking in the glow of what I was doing because it really didn't compute for them or their peers.

But I knew I had to keep going with what I wanted to do. In retrospect, I see it as a gift God gave me. It wasn't like him saying, 'Hey, you got the gifts! Now, go out and do what you think you want to do!' No, it was more like, 'You have the gifts. Now, go out there and do what is *expected* of you.'

It's like verse 2 from Romans, Chapter 12: Do not conform to the pattern of this world but be transformed by the renewing of your mind. Then you will be able to test and approve what God's will is—his good, pleasing, and perfect will.

I have tried to follow that verse my whole life. It never let me down.

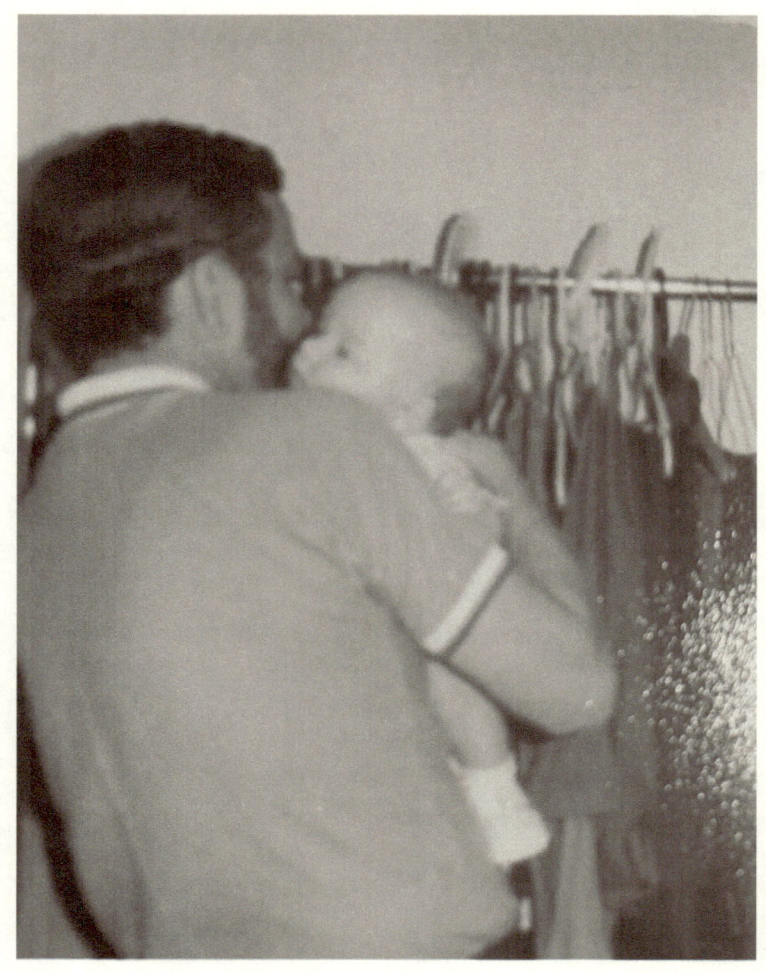

Frank picked up David for the first time and walked to the back room and begin slowly pacing in a small circle to keep David — and himself — calm.

Chapter 8

'New Beginnings All Around'

"We human beings don't know what our purpose is until we look back on things. Our hindsight is like flying in an airplane and looking down from 30,000 feet at the ground below. Flying that high gives us perspective on the lay of the land. Our hindsight gives us perspective on our life.

It's like when I look back at holding David in my arms in Olathe, Kansas — a place I had never been before. Right there, in that room, I had faith Michie and I were doing the right thing. We put one foot in front of the other. It reminds me of that saying that speaks to God's role in our lives: "When I saw a single set of footprints, I realize You were carrying me.""

The Rev. Frank Dew

It's a Tuesday in August 1985 when Frank drives a rental car through a part of the country he has never seen before.

"Where is this place, Michie?" he asks. "And what are we looking for? It's a building, right?"

"That's what they told me," Michie says, her head on a swivel and looking at every building they pass. "They told me there's nothing impressive about the office. It's like in a strip mall or something. But they gave me an address. I'm looking for numbers, and the name on the door."

"Alright," Frank says. "Just let me know."

"I just want to get there," Michie says. "I know we'll have to go over loads of paperwork, and that's going to be complicated. I just want to say, 'Bring me my baby.'"

"Yeah," Frank responds, "Our son."

"Yeah, our son," Michie says, looking out the window.

Michie let her response hang in the air. She dreams, for just a few seconds, on what could be. Then, Michie transforms back to Dr. Dew.

"Now," she says, looking at Frank. "Let's find that address."

Michie and Frank fly to Kansas City, rent a car and drive northeast through the flatlands of Kansas toward Olathe, a sprawling city of more than 140,000 people. Olathe is known for making cowboy boots and manufacturing electronic devices for aircraft, as well as helping kindergarteners through 12th-graders find their futures and themselves at a school known around Olathe as KSD, or the Kansas School of the Deaf.

The city grew up beside the Great Prairie Highway, the 19th century route known as the Santa Fe Trail. To speak the city's name is to speak Shawnee. Say Olathe — as in Oh-LAY-tha — and you're saying the Shawnee Indian word for "beautiful."

And that morning, for Frank and Michie, the word "beautiful" doesn't feel abstract. At all.

"Frank, there it is!" Michie says, pointing to the office door.

She sees the sign — The Gentle Shepherd Child Placement Services. It's an adoption agency run by Gaye and Ron Runberg, a husband and wife who are adoptive parents as well. Frank pulls into a parking lot, stops the car and looks at Michie.

"Well, here we go," he says.

Michie smiles. "Yes, here we go," she says.

It's been a long time coming, a long painful time coming. For both of them.

Michie and Frank go through nearly two years of infertility treatments, and the process strains their marriage. Despite all the treatments, all the work, Michie doesn't get pregnant. Michie often wants to talk about it. Frank does not. Despite the differences in how they cope, they both grieve. Michie had just completed her doctorate in psychology from UNC-Chapel Hill, and her background made it easier for her to understand what she was going through as well as Frank. She recognizes the stages of grief immediately, but that doesn't ease her rollercoaster of emotions. She analyzes her grief from every angle and talks to Frank about it. Every time, she can see it in his face. His eyes downcast, his face long, Frank listens. He always was a good listener. But she is never used to the silent Frank. She is used to the ever-positive Frank, a man afflicted with what she likes to call "Dewitus." Frank is always positive about everything. But in their conversations about all things having kids, Frank says only two or three sentences. Michie understands. From her years of study and psychology work, she knows the importance of giving people grace. And she knows this is a time to give Frank grace.

She also knows she needed to give herself grace, too.

Since their marriage, she has always fielded questions about children. They'd be visiting family in Lumberton, and she and Frank would hear the questions that always put her on edge.

"So, when are you going to start a family?"

"How many kids you want?"

Michie is always civil. It's not in her nature to lash out. But she responds with each question the same way.

"If we have children," she says.

At the time, Michie was going after her doctorate in psychology, and she always felt like she was walking through a fog of work. She spent a year writing her dissertation and poring over her research – – countless days of her and Frank punching holes into cards as big as a business envelope so she could feed them into a computer to get the data she needed.

But once she received her doctorate and opened a practice in Greensboro, Michie feels something she can hardly describe. It feels so *real* for her. She wants to start a family, and she feels ready. Plus, she has a good role model to follow. Her own mom, Blanna Brower Harriss.

Her mom was the Duke Law grad, the effective leader, the professional volunteer, the woman who always told her, "You can be anything you want to be." Michie didn't discuss her longing for motherhood with anyone but Frank. When she did, like she does always, she never minced any words.

"Frank, I just feel the timing is right," she says. "I don't know how to describe it, but I feel it deep in my bones. And really, it feels actually in every way, it's more important than my career.

"I mean, think about it. Having a kid in your arms and cheering them on at some sporting event. It just feels so right. And you know, a career doesn't keep you warm at night, and it sure doesn't love you back. And Frank, I hope we'll be good parents!

"When people ask me today, I'm not going to say what I did before — 'If we have kids.' Oh, it's now 'When.' It's a question I used to hate — 'When are you going to start a family?' Not anymore. When people ask me that, I'm going to say, 'Soon.' Soon. Soon.

"Listen to the sound of that, Frank. I just think it will complete our lives. Without kids, I just feel like I'll have a hole in my heart. A hole that will never go away."

Frank listens. But unlike Michie, he never feels the urge to become a father. He has never really held a baby before, let alone babysat for any neighborhood kid back in Lumberton. But he can see Michie really wants to start a family, and he loves Michie, and he knows they need to begin their journey together.

But heartache does come. From the trying. From the infertility treatments. From the times he sits by himself, his hands clasped, eyes closed.

"God, please help us through this process," Frank prays. "We both want it, Michie and me. So, please help us find an answer. We hope that answer will be a biological child."

Frank continues to pray. So does Michie. She, though, is more direct.

"God, why are you not answering my prayers? We want children. Please bring us children!"

That never happens.

* * *

One day, as Frank and Michie head out of Greensboro to see relatives in Lumberton, they pull up to a stop sign outside Greensboro. Frank looks at the stop sign and thinks about the nearly two years of infertility treatments, the two years of frustration, the two years of constant prayers and constant conversations with Michie where he hardly says no more than a few sentences. That, he believes, has to stop.

Yeah, stop.

The stop sign.

Stop.

"Wait a minute," Frank says to himself.

He turns to Michie and begins.

"Michie, maybe this is a sign," he says, pointing at the stop sign. "I think we need to stop pursuing this treatment path and follow the path of adoption."

Soon, Michie begins poring over the lists of adoption agencies, and with every office they visit and every office she calls, Michie hears pretty much the same thing: It will take years before you're able to adopt a child. The paperwork is daunting. Then, even the office visits hit them in the heart. It's because of the questions they hear.

Can you provide a good home?

Why do you think you could be a good parent?

Do you think you can handle it?

On and on it goes.

Same questions. Just in a different office.

Michie and Frank leave every interview feeling like they're auditioning for a role in a play — and they feel they'll never make the cut. But Gentle Shepherd is different.

It's an adoption agency in Olathe, Kansas. Michie finds the agency through one of her lists, and when she contacts them, she immediately feels they are more empathetic, more understanding – – and more importantly, the wait will be months instead of years. She and Frank write a short profile of themselves and send it to the agency. Gentle Shepherd distributes their profiles to potential fits. Frank, the minister; Michie, the psychologist. Frank is 34, Michie, 31. They long for an answer. Soon, they get one. Parents who made the hard decision to give up their child have picked Frank and Michie. They want Frank and Michie to adopt their newborn son. It's May 1985. Michie gets the call from Gentle Shepherd on a Thursday.

"Are you ready?"

Michie was breathless.

"Yes!"

"You'll hear from us the first of next week."

But Michie doesn't. She calls a week later to get an update. The update she hears breaks her heart.

"The parents who wanted you to have their newborn son have changed their mind. They want to keep the baby."

Michie hangs up the phone. She can't speak until she gets home and talks to Frank.

"You know what it feels like?" says Michie, her voice thick with emotion. "It feels like that feeling you get when you walk out of the hospital after seeing someone you love and hearing that they're going to die. That's what it feels like, Frank. I'm just numb. Just numb!"

She looks up and sees a face she hates to recognize. Sad eyes. Long face. Frank, the hardly ever silent Frank. He is numb, too.

Michie soldiers on. She sets up her new practice, Carolina Psychological Associates, on Battleground Avenue in Greensboro, and begins seeing patients. She starts her life's work and helps people cope with the heartache in their

own lives as she tries to cope with the heartache of her own. Three months later, as Michie takes some quiet time between clients, she gets another phone call from Gentle Shepherd. It's Gaye Runberg. And once again, she calls on a Thursday.

"We have a baby for you! The parents who picked you have changed their minds again. Are you still interested?"

"Yes!" Michie half-shouts on the phone.

"Well, why don't you come on Monday?"

Michie hangs up the phone and immediately calls Frank.

"You won't *believe* who called," she exclaims. "Gentle Shepherd. They said, 'We have a baby for you!' And we can come as soon as Monday. Monday! Like four days from now. But Frank, I'm ready to hop on that plane right now! Look up flights we can take right now!"

"Michie," Frank says. "I can't do that. I have a funeral this afternoon."

"Frank," Michie snaps back. "People die every day! We have to do this. It's for our baby!"

"Michie, I can't. Not today. But let's do Monday. That's just four days away."

Michie reluctantly agrees. They board a plane, fly to Kansas City and search for a hard-to-find office in a blink-and-miss strip mall in Olathe, Kansas, a city 22 miles south of Kansas City. This place is as familiar as the moon to Frank and Michie. But this place, they know, will change their lives forever.

All with the help of the profiles they wrote themselves.

Two pages, chock-full of hope, love, and longing. Those two pages would change their lives.

From Frank:

"My relationship with Michie has continued to grow and develop and change over the 10 years of our marriage. Our marriage began on a firm foundation of shared interests, values, and backgrounds. We have learned what it means to sacrifice for each other and for shared goals as we have put each other through graduate school. Our experience in dealing with our infertility has been a most painful and growing experience. Through this, we have both come to a more mature appreciation of the fact that we can not always meet the other person's needs, but that we can still love each other. We are both excited about the idea of adopting a child, and we look forward to that part of our life together."

From Michie:

"Fortunately, and joyously for us, life is now moving on. I feel like I've been through a terrible winter and the joy and beauty of spring are here and coming. Or to use a religious analogy, I feel like I've been through the death, tragedy, and pain of Maundy Thursday and Good Friday, but now the joy and hope of Easter have dawned. Our biological children are dead, but we have grieved the loss and are overjoyed at the prospect of adoption. We have so much new and fresh in our lives — new beginnings all around. Frank's new church, a new house, my full-time private practice is relatively new, and soon, a new baby in our family. With all the changes, I'm not quite sure where our new directions will take us, but I am excited about them. I don't feel the naïve excitement of someone who walks blindly

into changes, but rather the joy and excitement of someone who knows that new directions and challenges are joyous and exciting, especially after the winter."

In the parking lot outside the Gentle Shepherd office, Frank turns to Michie. She sees it immediately. Frank is smiling through his beard.

"You ready?" he asks.

"You betcha!" she says. "Let's go meet our baby!"

Frank and Michie sit in a small office with cream-colored walls. Scads of paperwork lie in neat stacks in front of them, and they have to read and sign, read and sign every single sheet. When they do, they can adopt their son and take him back to North Carolina the following day. Michie is all expectant. She wants to get it over with as soon as she can so she can hold her son. As for Frank, he is all nerves. This is so new for him. He's always calm under pressure, especially when he helps his parishioners in times of stress. But now, he's stressed, and in this small office in an unfamiliar city, Frank doesn't feel in control at all. He knows he's going to hold a little boy for the first time, a little boy he's going to call his son. But Frank can't get his head around that idea quite yet. His mind is a jumble of questions.

So, he sits. And waits. And searches for answers. Those answers, though, don't come. Just loads of "What ifs."

"What if I see him and go, 'Ooooo. This is not what I had imagined it to be.' What do I do?"

"What if he gets in my arms and just cries, and I can't help him?"

"What if I have to change his diaper? I have *never* changed a diaper!"

"What if he gets hungry? Do I give him a bottle? How do I do that?"

"And does this feel right? Oh, my goodness, what if this doesn't feel right? What do we do?"

After about 45 minutes, Michie and Frank go to a conference room down the hall for the big meet-up. The foster mom who has been taking care of the boy brings him in. He's three months old, with blue eyes and a full head of light brown hair. He's wearing a pale blue sailor suit. A Carolina blue sailor suit.

Frank smiles. Another sign, he thinks.

What has been so theoretical for years becomes so real because of a Carolina blue sailor suit. The questions swirling in his mind evaporate, and Frank looks at the boy with the dimpled chin, and he begins to feel what Michie had been talking about for months. It feels right.

"May I hold him?" Michie asks.

"Of course," responds the foster mom.

Michie gingerly takes the boy from the arms of the foster mom and begins walking him around the room. In a sing-song voice, she whispers one word over and over, Hello."

Frank watches from the other side of the room and marvels at how relaxed Michie has become. It's a different side of Michie that Frank had never seen before. The teenage girl he fell in love with years ago seems so natural with a baby in her arms. As Michie walks, the boy begins to cry. The foster mom steps in.

"Mrs. Dew, let me take him," she says. "He does get like that at this time of day."

The foster mom begins to rock him in her arms, but his fussiness doesn't dissipate. Like Michie, the foster mom walks around the room to calm him down. It doesn't work. On the other side of the conference table, the foster mom stops and looks at Frank.

"Rev. Dew, you want to hold him?" she asks. "Maybe you have the magic touch."

"Uh, sure," Frank stammers.

He takes the boy from the arms of the foster mom, and like Michie and the foster mom, he begins to rock him. But he spies a room in the back, full of clothes for expectant mothers. Instead of walking around the table, he walks to the back room and begins slowly pacing in a small circle. As he walks, the questions he wrestled with earlier come back.

"What if he gets in my arms and just cries?"

"And if he cries, what do we do?"

"Do I rock him more? Do I sing to him? Do I say … what?"

As questions race through Frank's mind, he looks down at the boy's face. His eyes are closed. He's sleeping.

The foster mom peeks in from the door.

"Rev. Dew, seems you have the touch," she says.

Over her shoulder, Frank sees Michie. She's beaming.

"Look at you, Frank," she says. "You're a natural!"

"I don't know about that, Michie," Frank responds. "But oh my goodness, look! He's responding to me."

Right then, in a back room in Olathe, Kansas, Frank's ambivalence about becoming a father vanishes. A warmth Frank can't describe envelopes him. But he feels it, from his toes to his fingers because of the little boy he holds in his arms. He finds himself looking down at the boy. He can't take his eyes off him. Frank looks up and sees Michie standing a few feet away.

"He is beautiful, isn't he?" Michie whispers.

"Yes, Michie," Frank responds. "He is beautiful. *This* is beautiful."

"It is," she says.

"You know, Michie," Frank says. "You were right. This does feel like it fills a hole in my heart."

Frank and Michie spend six hours at the office with the little boy. Frank and Michie play with him, he eats his lunch in Michie's arms, and he falls asleep once again in Frank's arms. By the time they get back into their rental car and head back to the hotel, Frank and Michie feel like they're floating. Like they do with every perspective adoptive parent, Gentle Shepherd wants Frank and Michie to sleep on it to make sure they're making the right decision. But really, they don't need to sleep on it. They already have an answer.

They will adopt that little boy, that three-month-old boy with the dimpled chin and a head full of brown hair. They name him David. David Franklin Dew. David, after the giant slayer in the Bible. And

Franklin after the common name in Frank's family. David Franklin Dew. Both Frank and Michie like the alliteration of it, how it rolls off their tongue.

David Dew. David Dew. Their son.

When they get to the airport, the questions come quick.

"Oh, what a cute baby. How old is he?"

Michie hears it time and again, and she begins to tell strangers her story in conversational shorthand: His name is David, she says, we've adopted him. That's right. We just adopted him. Yes, his name is David.

After the third question, Michie realizes she doesn't need to tell everyone David's story. Or their story for that matter.

More questions come, and Michie simply says, "Thank you."

Finally, though, she gets a new question. From a woman.

"For someone who gave birth, you look really good," she says.

Michie laughs.

"You know," Michie says in a stage whisper. "Those Jane Fonda exercises really work wonders."

The woman laughs, too.

"Where you all going?" she asks.

"Greensboro, North Carolina," Michie says. "That's home."

* * *

Frank and Michie see the signs and balloons first.

They're walking up the concourse at Piedmont Triad International Airport, and they see a crowd of parishioners from New Creation Community Presbyterian Church, Frank's new church, as well as from Vandalia Presbyterian, Frank's old church. The parishioners look like fans at a Saturday afternoon football game, yelling and waving and holding up handmade signs. The closer they get to the gate the more faces they recognize. At least a dozen parishioners come out to the airport to welcome them home. By the time Frank and Michie get within earshot, they hear the shouts.

"Congratulations!"

"Let's see that boy!"

"You'll turn him into a Demon Deacon, won't you, Frank!"

Frank and Michie get through the gate, and they're immediately engulfed by a crowd of well-wishers. Frank's head is spinning from their emotional journey to and from Kansas. But like Michie, he feels a sense of calm, of affirmation. He knows he and Michie made the right decision, and the greeting at the airport confirms what he always believed what(delete) a church can do — create a community that will help them through thick and thin. And he and Michie had gone through the thick of it.

"How do you feel Frank?" one of his parishioners shouts.

"Oh, I feel great!" he responds.

When Frank and Michie pull up to their house in Greensboro's Lindley Park neighborhood, they see blue bows everywhere. On the porch. On trees. Just everywhere. And right there, in the middle of their front yard, is a big sign with Carolina blue letters shouting, "It's a Boy!" At least 15 friends stand on their front porch when they pull up. After a few minutes of loud conversations and shouted greetings, Michie and Frank pass David from parishioner to parent. From the melee at the airport and now at the house, it's a bit too much for young David. He vomits.

Frank plucks David from the arms of a parishioner and whisks David to a bedroom to change him. He later smells the tell-tale sign every parent learns to know well. He finds Michie. He doesn't know. He figures she'll know.

"Should we wake him up and change him?" he asks.

Before she answers, Frank answers his own question.

"Oh, we should let sleeping dogs lie, don't you think?" he says.

Michie sidles up to Frank and looks at the boy in his arms.

"He is our Little Mr. Special, Frank," she says, looking at David and then her husband.

She has noticed the change. No long face. No sad eyes. No longer the ever-silent Frank.

"Frank, you good?"

Frank smiles.

"Never better!"

So far.

* * *

Frank's idea of fatherhood sprang from the monster TV console in his family's den in Lumberton.

Growing up, he'd watch "Leave it to Beaver" or "Father Knows Best" and his idea of a dad was coming home from work in a coat and tie, catching up with the family and then relaxing in your favorite chair in the den with the TV on and a newspaper across your lap.

That's exactly what Frank's dad did. He'd come home from working real estate all day, hang up his coat and take off his tie. He'd then go to the den to watch TV until supper was ready or pull a "Reader's Digest" compilation from a bookshelf and read in the living room.

When Frank becomes a father, his dad doesn't offer any advice. But that doesn't surprise Frank. When he broke the news to his parents about getting married, his dad hugged Michie and shouted, "Thank you, Girl!" See, in the Dew household, it went like this: When you get married, you are on your own, and you pay your own bills.

So, when Frank becomes a dad, he knows he has to figure out everything on the fly. He makes the baby bottles in advance, numbers them and puts them in the refrigerator in proper order. Give David this one first, Frank thinks. Then, this one and this one.

Michie is a bit incredulous over Frank's bottle-numbering process. But Frank feels he needs to number the bottles because he needs some predictability in a process that feels so unpredictable. Michie knows he doesn't need to do it, but she doesn't say anything – – until one day.

"Frank, just grab one!"

"I'm a father now, Michie," Frank responds, emphatically. "And I need to know what I'm doing."

On the two-page worksheet Frank filled out for Gentle Shephard, in the question that asked what a good parent-child relationship means, Frank wrote: "a two-way giving and taking, which enables the child to grow and mature and the parent to find fulfillment in that growth."

Frank is definitely feeling that. The first few months with David are idyllic. David is sleeping through the night, he is sleeping late and the whole back-and-forth of what bottle to get when works itself out. When parishioners or friends or anyone asks how everything is going — dad, kid, Michie — Frank gives the same answer: "It's great!"

Some would chalk up that response to Dew-itus, the Dew family's ever-present positivity. Frank is positive about most everything, even with his alma mater every football season.

"This could be Wake Forest's year," he likes to say.

But really, Frank is finding the rhythm of fatherhood to his liking, and he and Michie begin talking about adopting with Gentle Shepherd again. Maybe in two or three years. Or something like that. They both feel at ease with their transition into parenthood, and they're surrounded by a sea of support. They find like-minded parents at New Creation. Frank's parishioner parents have adopted children from India and elsewhere, and their circle-of-chairs service on Sunday afternoons at Presbyterian Church of the Covenant is filled with eight children, all adopted, all but two older than David.

"All those beautiful, adopted children are in our little church," Frank says to Michie one day. "They're not delivered by Lamaze. They're delivered by Delta Airlines."

In April 1986, Frank and Michie decide to fly out to Kansas City once again. Gaye Runberg from Gentle Shepherd had called them to come and fill out the paperwork needed to adopt another child. This time, they fly out there with Sam and Susan Bays, another couple from New Creation who are interested in adopting a child. Both Frank and Michie feel this trip is simply to get things started. And they both think it'll be fun.

When they walk in, Gaye asks about David immediately. Then, she pauses for a second and looks at them both.

"Can you two come back to the office?" she asks.

"Sure," says Frank, his voice bouncy and light.

Michie gives Frank a side look. She senses something immediately. Frank? Not so much. They sit down across from Gaye, and another important question-and-answer begins.

"What are your thoughts about the timing of your second

child?" Gaye asks them.

"Oh, we'd like for them to be two or three years apart," Frank replies.

Michie kicks Frank's shin under the table.

Once.

Twice.

Three times.

Frank looks at her, puzzled. Michie shoots him a look and jumps into the conversation.

"We're looking for the right situation, not the right time," she blurts out.

Gaye takes a deep breath. She looks at Frank, then to Michie before responding. Again, Michie senses something is up. She is right.

"David's parents ended up staying together, and they have gotten pregnant again," Gaye says.

She pauses and adds, "And they want to place their new baby with you."

Michie's heart jumps to her throat. Before she can even think, she responds.

"Absolutely," Michie says. "They need to be together."

Frank and Michie are both stunned. They talk a little more and emerge from the office a bit numb by what they heard. But they now know that their two- to three-year wait for another child is moot. It will happen soon.

Very soon.

"Frank, I can't believe it," says Michie in a quivering voice barely above a whisper. "After all this time! All this time! I ... I'm just walking on air!"

"Me, too, Michie," Frank says, wrapping his arm around her. "Me, too."

By September, Frank and Michie can barely sleep. Michie talks to Gentle Shepherd almost every day and keeps tabs on the pending birth. They don't know much, only that it's a girl. A baby girl. Then, on a Friday afternoon, Michie receives a message at the office that Gentle Shepherd had called. When Michie calls them back, their office had closed for the weekend, and Michie figures their baby must've been born early. Immediately, she calls Frank.

"I just got a message from Gentle Shepherd," Michie says, breathlessly. "Our little girl. She must've come earlier than expected."

"So, what do we do?" he asks.

"Well, we have to wait," Michie says. "Gaye says we have to give them a week to make sure they don't change their mind. Remember what the social worker told us on the home visit."

"Oh, I remember," Frank responds. "'If it's a girl, I bet they'll change their minds.'"

"When I heard that, I thought, 'Oh, shit!'" Michie says. "But you know me, Frank. I can be a big worrier. But ever since she told us that, I've tried to live in the present and not let my mind go that way."

"Sure," Frank says. "I bet everything will be fine."

"I sure hope so, Frank," she responds, exhaling audibly into the phone. "You've always been the positive one. May that be so."

Michie has always seen Frank as her launching pad, her support to help her do what she wanted to do — become the first in her family to earn a doctorate and open her own private practice to help others help themselves.

But 14 months after the happiness of adopting David, she feels the ache in her heart. She and Frank hear about David. Then, they hear the parents want to keep David. Three months later, David's parents change their mind. Michie doesn't want to go through that again, the back and forth of "Will they, or won't they?" And after nearly two years of going through infertility treatments, when she dealt with a maelstrom of emotions that had her getting angry at God, Michie longs for some peace of mind. And that peace of mind will come from Gentle Shepherd. Michie knows it.

That peace of mind comes the following Thursday.

"I have good news," says Gaye Runberg. "That little girl. She is yours."

"Oh, thank you, Gaye," Michie gushes. "Thank you."

By Monday morning, Frank and Michie are back in Olathe, Kansas, back in the office of Gentle Shepherd. And there, they meet their little girl, David's little sister. She's wearing a pink dress with a pink bow in her hair. Her eyes are blue; her hair is black and brown with a hint of a curl. Standing in the conference room are two people Frank and Michie don't recognize. Gaye smiles and brings him forward.

"Frank, Michie," Gaye says. "I want you to meet the parents of your two children. They wanted to meet you."

Michie steps forward right away. Her face is open, her smile wide.

"Thank you for the beautiful gift," she says, taking the mother's hand in both of her hands and smiling at the father.

Their conversation lasts 15 minutes or so. With the parents' 3-year-old bustling around them, the father doesn't say much. Neither does the mom. They only know Frank and Michie from the words they read on a page, and they chose Frank and Michie from those very words. And that Monday morning, more than 1,000 miles west of their home in Greensboro, Frank and Michie meet the parents of their children for the first — and only — time.

An extraordinary meeting in an ordinary office with beige walls.

The meeting comes at a time when the couple are giving away the second of their three children. Then, they will walk out and never see their daughter again. The weight of the moment is not lost on Frank and Michie.

From the look on the father's face, Michie perceives he's relieved. She doesn't ask about what led to the decision. Neither does Frank. Everything in the Gentle Shepherd office is left unsaid. But the reason why feels as ominous as an approaching storm. Frank and Michie sense that. They also see it in the father's face. The mother's face, too. It's a look of pain and resignation as well as relief. So, in an ever-so-subtle way, Michie and Frank try to settle the suspected fears and emotions they see and feel.

Michie speaks first

"We are so grateful to you two."

"I can imagine this was not an easy decision," Frank says.

"And we want you to know," Michie says, "we'll do our absolute best."

"Amen," Frank adds.

The parents leave with their 3-year-old son in tow. Frank and Michie stay. They can't get over the sadness they feel. They watch them leave with their little boy, and they know their children will never have a chance to interact with their big brother. Within minutes, though, the awkwardness gives way to unadulterated joy. Frank and Michie focus on the little girl cradled in Michie's arms. Neither Frank nor Michie can get over how tiny she is. David was a chunk at three months old. At least 13 pounds. But his sister, she's no more than seven pounds, and she's all slender fingers, slender arms, slender legs, and a slender face framed in brown curls.

"Frank" Michie says, "She's so little! I feel like she'll fall through the cracks of my elbow!"

Frank stands at Michie's right elbow. By the time Michie hands their little girl to Frank, he just gushes.

"Michie," Frank says, "she feels as light as balsa wood!"

Michie laughs.

"Don't break her, Frank!"

According to Gentle Shepherd's regulations, the agency usually requires the parents to come back the next day to pick up the child they adopt. But because of what Frank and Michie have experienced — already adopting one sibling from the same birth parents — Gentle Shepherd allows Frank and Michie to take their little girl back to the hotel.

They turn a drawer from the hotel's dresser into a bassinet and lay a blanket on the bottom. Michie places the drawer on her side of the bed. Meanwhile, in a need for normalcy on such an emotional day, Frank turns on Monday Night Football. The Chicago Bears are playing the Green Bay Packers. Frank tunes into the game. Michie tunes into her daughter, the little girl with the vivid blue eyes, swaddled in a blanket in a drawer by the bed.

She turns to Frank.

"How in the world, Frank?" she says. "How in the world? Who has ever *heard* of Olathe, Kansas? And who has ever *heard* of the

Gentle Shepherd Child Placement Services? A cosmic higher power has put this all together."

Frank mutes the game and turns to Michie.

"How in the world," he says. "The biggest thing for me in all this is how we talk about love. We know God loves us. But where does the love for our child come from? Little kids, they don't give much feedback. They eat, sleep, and poop. Now, if they're telling me, 'I have three tickets to the ACC Tournament,' I'd love that. But they don't.

"And yet, I feel that love coming up from within me, and it really gives me an insight into how God loves us. That experience is a gift beyond ourselves, Michie."

"Frank, that's faith," Michie responds. "It's always been there. But it's stronger. This is a confirmation in our lives that God directs our lives in ways we don't understand."

Frank and Michie soon go back and forth on names. They ponder the name Christian. Nope. That's won't work. Don't name her after our faith, Frank and Michie say. Kathleen? That's Michie's grandmother's name and Michie's first name. That doesn't work either. What about a woman's name from the Bible? Michie and Frank say no. Finally, they decide upon Christie. It's feminine, perky and … her.

Christie Harriss Dew. That sticks.

Frank and Michie both wonder how David will react to Christie. They still remember what happened right before they left.

"David, guess what?" Michie tells him. "You're going to have a new baby sister."

Christian Harriss Dew.

David begins shaking his head.

"No! No! No!" he cries.

So, when Frank and Michie fly home, they're full of questions that revolve around "What's next?" They walk in and see Frank's parents who drive up from Lumberton to watch David. Then, they see David. And David sees them. He spots Michie holding Christie, and he starts crying.

"David, David," Frank says as he tries to comfort his son. "She is your new sister."

"Yes, David," Michie responds. "We love her just like we love you."

David's crying only gets louder. Like open-your-mouth-squeezing-your-eyes-shut crying. David turns and runs out of the room.

"Oh my," Frank says. "Don't like to see that."

Michie doesn't say a word. She hates what she sees, and she worries if she's seeing a glimpse of things to come. But both she and Frank find out later David has an ear infection. A few days later, David goes from sad to curious. When Michie or Frank is sitting and holding Christie, David rotates around them like a satellite. He can't take his eyes off Christie. He simply stares at the tiny baby in his parents' arms. Soon, he gets up enough courage to pat her on the head. He pats her like how someone pets a cat — very carefully.

"It looks like everything will be alright," says Frank, ever the optimist.

"Sure hope so," says Michie, ever the realist.

As weeks turn to months, Frank and Michie find the rhythm of raising two children 16 months apart. Michie stays home a lot to take care of David and Christie, while Frank stays as focused as he can on getting his new church off the ground. They realize quick they need to rely on a system, a routine that helps keep everything in their lives from falling into disarray.

"If one domino falls," Frank says to Michie often, "our whole system falls apart."

Now, about the system. The Dew System.

If David or Christie cries at night on Monday, Wednesday or Friday, Michie gets up. On Tuesday, Thursday and Saturday, Frank gets up. That schedule leads to a strict sense of boundaries for them both. Say, it's a Monday night at 11:30, and Christie lets out a wail. Frank and Michie wake up, and Frank turns to Michie and says, "It's still your night."

Frank and Michie learn how to juggle. They also learn how to love. Parishioners and friends come around to see David and Christie, and Frank says the same thing when people dote on their two children.

"You can tell they're adopted," he says, "because they both look better than we do."

Michie realizes the divine intervention involved in adopting David and Christie. The realization comes in a phone call.

Right when David and Christie are adopted, the Dews' extended family take part in a medical study spearheaded by Duke University. The study involves researching the family connection to genetic disorders, and Frank and his sisters get involved after Charlie, Sara's son, was born with cystic fibrosis.

A decade or so later, a staff member from Duke calls with what they have discovered. Michie gets the call at work. Frank, the staff member says to Michie, is a carrier, and he urges both Frank and Michie to come in for genetic counseling. But Michie declines.

"Trust me, there's no reason for us to come in," she tells him.

"You don't understand," responds the staff member, a touch of exasperation in his voice.

"Oh, I do understand," Michie says emphatically. "Frank and I are both infertile. We went through treatments for nearly two years, and we've now adopted two kids. So, there is no reason to be concerned."

"But ..." the staff member injects.

"Really, there is no reason to be concerned," Michie says. "But one thing's for sure. My life now makes sense."

Michie hangs up the phone and begins her conversation with God.

"So that's why God," she says. "That's why You said no. I prayed to have children, pleaded with You to help me have children, and I felt You never answered my prayers. But You knew. You knew the whole time! You were protecting us, and You took a difficult situation we faced, and the difficult situation David and Christie's parents faced, and You helped both of us. What the heck. You knew!"

After she comes home, she's in the den when she hears Frank come through the door. She hollers.

"Hey, Frank."

"Yeah, Michie."

"I got the most interesting news today."

"What's that?"

"News from God. Seems like he's been looking out for us the whole time."

* * *

On a Friday night in 2015, Frank doesn't know what he's going to say.

He looks out onto the Atlantic, hoping some words will come. They don't. But he has a great view of one of his favorite places in

North Carolina, one of his favorite places on the Earth — Ocean Isle Beach. Frank sits in a dining room framed on three sides by windows, and he's surrounded by 50 people, many of whom are his son's best friends.

They all come to Ocean Isle for the wedding of David Dew and Lauren Walker, a fellow Grimsley High grad David met years later in Greensboro when she was walking her dog. David proposes to Lauren in 2014 over Labor Day weekend at Ocean Isle on its long, iconic wooden pier built in 1957.

Ocean Isle is a dime-sized town beside the Atlantic an hour south of Wilmington. It's known as the "Gem of the Brunswick Islands." Ocean Isle does seem appropriate for this big event in the life of the Dews. Ocean Isle is the very place where Michie's grandmother, Beulah Harriss, had a cottage and taught a young Michie how to play canasta, gin rummy and Old Maid. So, on this Friday night in an oceanfront dining room at the Isles Restaurant and Tiki Bar, David and Lauren celebrate with their closest friends.

Meanwhile, the man who will marry them the next day struggles for words. He has to make a toast. It has to mean something. It's a big day in his son's life. And Frank's, too.

"Michie," Frank whispers to his wife sitting beside him. "I don't know what I'm going to say."

"Frank, oh, you'll come up with something," she responds. "You always do."

Frank begins to think, and like turning the pages of a family scrapbook, Frank begins to remember.

Of taking the training wheels off David's bike in the backyard. Frank watches David wobble away on two wheels on the grass. Still, Frank wishes his arms were 10 feet long to catch David if he falls.

Of reading to David and Christie a picture book about adoption. He and Michie tell them both, "Even though we didn't have you like other parents do, you are still our son, and you are still our daughter. For us, there is no difference." David was 5.

Of watching David walk across the stage at Wake Forest and graduate from his alma mater. Frank tells him, "David, you may not believe in prayer, but you are an answer to a prayer." David graduated in 2013 with a degree in political science. All those moments surface like sepia-toned snapshots in Frank's mind. What to say?

"Wait a minute," he tells myself. "Olathe, Kansas. The sailor suit. That's it!"

When the time comes, Frank looks at Michie and smiles. He then looks over at David and Lauren and stands up. He begins.

"Like most of the guys from my generation, I had zero experience with little kids. Zero. Matter of fact, the first time I held David might have been the first time I ever held a baby, I think. And for me, that was a huge revelation.

"That all happened in Olathe, Kansas. That's a city near Kansas City. I mean, who has ever heard of Olathe, Kansas? Michie and I hadn't. But we flew out there to an adoption agency called Gentle Shepherd to meet David and fly him home, back to North Carolina.

"Well, the first day I met David, he was wearing sort of a light blue sailor suit. I guess we could call it a Carolina blue sailor suit. Not a stitch of black and gold on him."

A few people laugh.

"Anyway, David started fretting, and several people tried to calm him down. When they couldn't do it, I thought I'd give it a try.

"So, I walk back to this room in the back of this office where they store clothes for expectant mothers, and I held him and rocked him and walked around with him. And he fell asleep. At that moment, I felt he responded to me. I even hollered back to Michie, 'Oh my goodness, look! He's responding to me.'"

He looks over at his son, and as he feels that lump in his throat turn into a baseball, Frank continues.

"That was the initial bonding, David. And from that moment until now, you have been teaching me what it means to be a father."

Frank's toast silences the room of 50. David looks at his father, and with tears welling up in the corners of his eyes, he looks down. He squeezes Lauren's hand and remembers.

His parents' bedroom.

The picture book.

His dad telling him he was adopted.

His dad saying, 'You are still our son."

David looks up. His dad is 10 feet away. He gives him a tight-lipped smile. Frank nods, sits down and bows his head.

"God," Frank says. "Thank you."

It's Sunday in late September 2022, and Frank is preaching once again at Sedgefield Presbyterian. Michie sits nine rows back when she sees a familiar face slip in behind her.

"Come up," she says, smiling. "Sit with me."

Cindy Washington slips into the pew beside Michie. She comes to see Frank preach because he asked. She also comes because she wanted to.

Cindy has known Frank and Michie since 1985. Cindy worked for 18 years as a pre-school teacher at the College Hill Child Care Co-op at the Presbyterian Church of the Covenant. She came in 1985 when David and Christie were adopted, and she came to a parent-run business full of kids whose parents were doctors and lawyers, college professors and psychologists.

And ministers like Frank.

Cindy is the lone Black woman surrounded by a sea of white faces. But soon, she gets comfortable. They treat her well, they pay her well, and they help her buy a red Ford Escort so she can get to and from work. Cindy calls her car "Pony."

Soon after she arrives, Cindy meets David and Christie.

The Dew kids start going to the College Hill Co-op, and parents are required to volunteer in the Co-Op one day a week. Frank volunteers in the Co-Op. He changes diapers. He plays with kids. And he gets to know Cindy, a mother to three young children.

She babysits David and Christie when they're young. And she fields phone calls from a young Christie at night when she can't find her favorite Care Bear, the pink bear with the rainbow on its chest.

"Have you seen Happy Bear?" Christie asks.

Cindy gets into her car Pony and drives 10 minutes from her apartment near UNC-Greensboro to the Co-Op. She unlocks the door, goes into the pre-school room and calls Christie.

"Christie, I see Happy Bear right here in your basket."

Cindy is particularly close with Christie. She also is particularly close to Frank. When she needs someone to co-sign her apartment lease, she first calls her son in Atlanta. He's a pastor. He says no. She then calls Frank. He says yes.

"He reminds me of Moses," Cindy says today. "There is an aura around him, and you feel it. I mean, there is nobody like him. Nobody. I think that's the way God wants people to be. To be humble. To look after the poor. To take care of the sick. And talk to them when they need help. That's Frank. And I wasn't used to nobody like that. Not in my family."

So, on that Sunday morning in late September, Cindy comes to Sedgefield Presbyterian. Coincidentally, she comes on what Michie and Frank call their Joy Day. It's the day they picked up Christie at Gentle Shepherd and swaddled her in a blanket, tucked her into a hotel room's dresser drawer and placed her on Michie's side of the bed.

Cindy sits shoulder to shoulder with Michie. They've been good friends for years, Cindy and Michie. They've laughed together, joked together, and sang together. On that Sunday, Michie and Cindy sing together once again. This time, it's the hymn, "God Leads Us Along."

In shady, green pastures, so rich and so sweet,
God leads His dear children along.
Where the water's cool flow bathes the weary one's feet,
God leads His dear children along.

Coincidence? Or divine intervention? However you see it, the hymn comes on a poignant day for the Dews. It's a day where they think about how their heartbreak turned into happiness in a city they never knew existed on the plains of Kansas.

What Frank and Michie discover after leaving Gentle Shepherd with their second child is reminiscent of the last four lines of "Joy," a poem written by Donna Ashworth.

Like the hymn, those last four lines seem to fit.

You cannot invite her, you can only be ready when she appears.
And hug her with meaning,
because in this very moment,
joy chose you.

David Dew and Christie Dew Hartman.

Frank on Frank

Love & Faith & Fatherhood

We Presbyterians do believe in the providence of God. It's that idea of believing what we can't see and understanding that we're not always in control. Maybe you've seen that in your life. I know I have.

For me, I've seen God's hand throughout my life. It's like when I met Michie or when Michie and I adopted David and Christie. Those are two of the biggest moments in my life. Sure, if you ask me, I would say I was doing the choosing in both those situations. But now, as I look back on it, it also feels like I was participating in God's choosing, God's plan.

That, for me, has always been very reassuring.

When I think of God's plan, I think of two things that really show me how He is guiding my life. It's David's response to me back in the clothes closet at Gentle Shepherd and the fact that Christie, the little girl we adopted 14 months later, is his biological sibling. Those were all signs that David and Christie were meant to be with us and meant to be together.

We all have moments in our lives like that. Here's what I mean:

You always hear people talk about athletes being in the 'zone' or 'in the flow.' I would say we all have moments in our lives like that.

Imagine yourself in a river, in a kayak or in an inner tube, and you're just floating downstream. You're going with the flow. You don't know where you're going, but you stick with it because you *know* you're going in the right direction. It just feels … right.

That's what I call faith. And trust!

Unfortunately, in today's church, we have translated the word 'faith' as something we see as knowledge. If you just have faith, you will know the answer. Well, faith is not the answer so much as it is what you do when you *don't* have the answer. If I have the answer, I don't need faith. If I don't have the answer, I have to trust something. That's faith, and you're trusting in God to help you find the answer.

So, when you put your trust in something you can't see — let alone touch or talk to — you realize faith is a gift.

Hebrews, Chapter 11, is often called the faith chapter. You see why right there in the first verse: 'Now faith is confidence in what we hope for and assurance about what we do not see." What we do not see. That is trust. That is being in the zone.' And it's OK if we don't see it. God is saying, 'I'm going to believe *for* you.'

There's a great story that illustrates that in the New Testament.

It's the time when a group of men brought their paralyzed friend to Jesus. But they couldn't get in to see Him. There were just so many people gathered around the house where Jesus was. So, these men had an idea. They were going to go through the roof and lower their friend down to see Jesus.

Now, back then, roofs aren't what we think of roofs today. Back then, houses were built with flat roofs made of clay and straw, and houses usually had stairs on the outside so people could climb on top of the roof to sleep or get some fresh air.

That's how the men got to the roof, and what did they do? They dug. They dug through the clay and straw and lowered their paralyzed friend to Jesus. Now, Jesus told the paralyzed man, "(use single quote marks throughout this graf)Son, your sins are forgiven." He later said, "Get up, take your mat and go home." The man did.

That's one of Jesus' miracles that you'll find in the Book of Luke, Chapter 5, and that story is a classic example of faith — but not in the way you may think. See, what impressed Jesus so was *not* the faith of the paralyzed man. But of(delete) the faith of his friends. They believed in Him.

See what I mean? Faith is having trust that there is purpose and meaning in what you're doing even when you don't know what it is at that particular time in whatever circumstance you face. You simply put one foot in front of the other because you'll know what the purpose is, what the meaning is — when you get there. Really, we human beings don't know what our purpose is until we look back on things. Our hindsight is like flying in an airplane and looking down from 30,000 feet at the ground below. Flying that high gives us perspective on the lay of the land. Our hindsight gives us perspective on our life. It's like when I look back at holding David in my arms in Olathe, Kansas — a place I had never been before. Right there, in that room, I had faith Michie and I were doing the right thing. We put one foot in front of the other. It reminds me of that saying that speaks to God's role in our lives: 'When I saw a single set of footprints, I realize You were carrying me."

I didn't know what being a father was, but I had faith I would find out, and I first felt it when I held David. And meeting Christie and holding Christie — such a tiny thing, she was — right then, I felt the same thing again. I had faith that I would figure out what this whole fatherhood thing meant. I did. And when I did, it helped me understand what true love is.

The only other time I felt that was when I met Michie. The thing about love is that it makes you vulnerable. That's a good thing.

I remember hearing someone say one time when talking about romantic relationships: 'I want to be in a relationship, but I don't want to get hurt." But that's not possible. And so, what I've learned about being a father is that parenting makes you vulnerable. You'll get sad, you'll get disappointed, even angry. I mean, we're human. But you will love, and when you love, you feel the love of another.

If you love, you are going to be hurt. That's what makes love so powerful. Think about Jesus on the cross. Isn't that what love really looks like? And to some extent, that is what parenting is. To be that vulnerable gives meaning and purpose to your love because you love someone *that* much.

Love means that we care deeply enough to be hurt. And that is a big part of what grief is. When someone dies, you have a sense of loss. And the depth of that loss creates a sense of grief. It also shows you the depth of love you have for that special person in your life.

To understand that, look at your own family. I know I look at my own. My mom and dad weren't always the closest. They didn't always see eye to eye. But weeks after my dad passed, I was eating lunch with my mom, and she said, 'You know, I must've loved him because I sure do miss him "

Because I miss him.

That is grief. That also is love.

A month after starting New Creation Community Presbyterian Church, Frank and a other church members travel to Washington DC to join an anti-apartheid protest in front of the South African embassy.

Photo credit: Courtesy of Ginny Hullquist

Chapter 9

"Community Is Not Microwavable"

"So many times, we ask ourselves, 'Do I have the time? Do I have the money? Do I have ... whatever?' But that's not the question to ask. The question to ask is, 'What is God calling me to do?' We may not know the answer right away, but just asking the question can help us move in the right direction. We're moving from our night to the light of our day."
The Rev. Frank Dew

As he stands on the sidewalk along Massachusetts Avenue in Washington, DC, Frank remembers.

It's that same feeling he had when he stood in a dimly lit closet in Kansas with an infant in his arms. Back then, Frank was awash with emotion, and he knew he made the right move.

He feels the same way along Massachusetts Avenue on that beautiful fall day in 1985.

He's standing outside the South African Embassy with nine other members from New Creation Community Presbyterian Church, the church he helped create in his living room in Greensboro's Lindley Park neighborhood.

"This," Frank keeps telling himself, "is our first step."

Frank and his parishioners come to protest South Africa's own version of Jim Crow. That legislation enacted by the country's all-white government is really an invisible prison. It separates whites, or Afrikaners, from people of color in everything from where they can live to what they can do. Afrikaners know it as "apartness." Frank and everyone else in the world know it by a more gruesome name.

Apartheid.

So, in the fall of 1985, on a day when the temperatures warrant more short sleeves than sweaters, Frank stands in solidarity with his new parishioners. New Creation had been only a month or two old when his small congregation of no more than 25 people decide to join others in DC. It's New Creation's first official move, and Frank can't be any prouder of what he sees around him. They all stand in a semicircle on a sidewalk holding signs outside the South African Embassy. Frank holds a sign, too. It proclaims three words that say so much to him.

Presbyterians Against Apartheid.

New Creation joins parishioners primarily from churches in North Carolina. Initiated by Presbyterian Church USA, the protest draws at least 80 people to the sidewalk that day. But New Creation is the only church from Greensboro that came. It disappoints Frank. In a city where a lunch counter sit-in in 1960 revived America's civil rights movement, he figures more churches would step up because he believes activism is part of the city's consciousness. But the only church that steps up is his. With his three-word sign in his hands, a quote from Martin Luther King Jr. rings in his ears.

"Why are churches always a taillight rather than a headlight?"

Frank doesn't have an answer. But he does know what he wants his church to be.

Be a headlight, New Creation. Let's be a headlight.

Their day in DC becomes their first step.

The day before, they all pile into a van, drive to DC and sleep in the basement of the Church of the Pilgrims, the century-old Gothic Revival church in downtown DC. The next day, they gather with the other protesters. They worship together, pray together, and steady themselves in scripture to help them with their day ahead. Yet, Frank can tell some in his congregation are worried about getting arrested or stepping out into something that makes them feel too uncomfortable. It's not anything they say. It's what he sees and feels — the furrowed brow, the tight-lipped smile, the nonreaction to the excitement around them. Before they leave the next morning for the South African

Embassy, he circles up his parishioners.

"We are putting our words and deeds together," he tells them, knitting his fingers together and stressing the last word. "We are not just talking about it. We're doing something about it. We are here together as New Creation. We are where we should be, doing what we should be doing. This is living out our calling as Christians, as a congregation. Amen?"

"Amen," a few respond.

Frank looks at the circle of faces.

"Oh, I've got work to do," Frank tells himself.

He has to work on himself, too.

Like his parishioners, Frank grew up comfortable, far from the injustices of a world where race and class had separated everyone around him into the haves and have-nots. And like his parishioners, those injustices nagged at him even before he gave his first sermon as a high school senior. All he has to do is remember going to the Carolina Theatre in downtown Lumberton to see a Saturday matinee and spotting those three doors — one for Blacks, one for whites and one for members of the Lumbee Tribe. That day in the fall of 1985, Frank reminds his parishioners of those three doors. He also reminds them of what they want to remember as they stand outside the embassy, with signs in their hands.

"We always want to hold onto what is comfortable in our world and being comfortable enables us to stay in a certain cocoon of privilege," he tells them. "But you know what the problem is? When you stay in a cocoon, we can never become a butterfly, right? That is the image of a new creation. Amen?"

"Amen!" his parishioners said.

They respond more enthusiastically this time. Still, Frank has questions he can't answer.

Could this get out of hand?

Might any of us get unintentionally arrested?

Could this get violent?

Frank hadn't joined a protest since his undergraduate days at Wake Forest University when he and others gathered to rail against the Vietnam War. That was 12 years ago. Yet, he remembers how that protest strengthened his faith, and he figures the protest outside the South African Embassy will do the same for his parishioners. But will it? Can it? Frank doesn't know. So, he prays. When he does, he remembers another story about a butterfly. This one is about a little boy and his grandfather.

The little boy finds a butterfly struggling to get out of a cocoon. He brings the cocoon into his house, uses a pair of scissors, and slits the cocoon to help the butterfly emerge. But as the butterfly emerges from the cocoon, its wings crumple. The butterfly dies. Crying, the little boy shows his grandfather the dead butterfly and asks why.

"You can't help the butterfly because you have to let the butterfly help himself," he tells his grandson. "You have to let the butterfly struggle. It's the struggle that helps the butterfly get stronger. That same goes for you, too. The struggle you're facing today will make you stronger for what you face tomorrow."

"Lord, let's be that butterfly," Frank prays.

But will they?

Members from New Creation Community Presbyterian Church join a crowd in front of the South African Embassy to protest apartheid in 1985.

Photo credit: Courtesy of Ginny Hullquist

* * *

Ginny Hultquist joins New Creation right after her son, Erik, is born. She's one of the first members, the ones who turn the living room of Frank and Michie into a tiny church. As they all pray and as she listens, Erik is a few steps away in a playpen.

So, when Frank tells her and others about the DC protest, she jumps at the chance — and she takes Erik. He's no more than 4, but she feels he's old enough. Ginny wants her son to be like a sponge and absorb what he sees. She also wants him to see what his mother does to help the community — and to help him. So, mother and father and son stand outside the South African Embassy. Erik sits on his dad's shoulders, and Ginny stands beside him with their fellow church members and dozens of others who feel the same way she does.

"These people," she tells herself. "They're people I trust."

Ginny grew up in West Fargo, North Dakota, the oldest of five. Her mom worked as a paralegal; her dad managed a Ford dealership. When she was a high school sophomore taking a sociology class, she saw photos of abused children burned by cigarettes. Those images stuck with her, and right then, in a city where Ginny felt protected, social justice became a part of her DNA.

Ginny majored in sociology at North Dakota State, and in 1977, two years after the Vietnam War ended, she began helping Vietnamese resettle in the United States. A year later, she moved to North Carolina with her husband for his job. She became a social worker with the local Department of Social Services in Greensboro and continued her resettlement work. This time, she began helping Cambodians resettle in North Carolina after fleeing Pol Pot's deadly Khmer Rouge regime.

Ginny later became the director of what was then known as the Lutheran Immigration and Refugee Services. In 1983, six months pregnant with her daughter, Siri, she visited refugee camps in Thailand where Cambodians lived. She carried with her a plastic box 15 inches long and five inches high. The box contained the ashes of a Cambodian named Ben Vuong. He was in his 80s when he arrived in North Carolina from Cambodia. He died six months later. Ginny carried Ben's ashes with her on the plane and walked across the border to the refugee camp in Thailand into Cambodia and buried his ashes under a tree at a Buddhist temple.

Ginny always has had a service-driven heart, but she is no Bible thumper. She considered herself agnostic. But when she finds out about New Creation, she joins. It feels right because Frank feels right. He's a man whose heart she believes matches the vision of what the church can be and will be.

So, when she stands outside the South African Embassy, two years after carrying the ashes of Ben Vuong across the globe, she feels she's following what Jesus teaches her to do.

"You can sit in your home and stew, but unless you put yourself out there, there is no chance you can make a difference," Ginny said decades later, recalling that DC protest. "You have to show up."

Her son, Erik, is now in his 40s, and he's a lot like his mom. He joined the Army after terrorists turned planes into bombs on Sept. 11, 2001. After he was discharged several years later, he went to the U.S. Coast Guard Academy. He now finds himself in Seattle, Washington, married for the second time and a father to a combined family of five kids. He and his wife live on a boat in Seattle where he is the transportation manager for a business where members can rent boats for pleasure. Away from work, he helps with food drives and volunteers through his church. On his LinkedIn page, in his About section, he writes: "I work hard and make things happen, but nothing is worth doing if your goal is not to enjoy it."

For his sixth birthday, Ginny Hultquist's grandson Toren collected canned food for the nonprofit Bread For The World.

Photo credit: Courtesy of Ginny Hullquist

Ginny is now in her 70s, a grandmother to 11 grandchildren. They call her Grandma Ginny. She took Toren, Erik's son, to a national meeting in Washington, DC, of the nonprofit Bread for the World. At the time, he was 6. Just like she did with Erik in 1985, she wanted Toren to understand. He does. For his sixth birthday, he didn't want presents. He wanted his friends to bring canned food to feed people who are hungry.

Ginny still has a photo from her 1985 protest in DC. She and other parishioners are standing together in two rows. Erik sits on her husband's shoulder, and she's smiling in the second row with Frank standing in front. Frank's beard is brown, a few years before it turns Ernest Hemingway gray. He's smiling, too. Ask her about that day, and Ginny remembers she wasn't afraid about getting arrested, and she didn't think any of them were doing anything dangerous. But she felt what she and the others were doing was right.

So right.

"We were a young church at that point, and we all had the same view of the world and the same view of apartheid," she says. "I just hoped that we were making a difference because it was the only thing we could do. But it affirmed with what I saw with New Creation. We all have a role to play. We can't just worship on Sundays."

Frank does believe in that.

* * *

To be a member of New Creation Community Presbyterian Church, you can't just show up on Sundays and think, "OK, that's it."

Nope.

Every year, on the first Sunday in Advent, a New Creation member has to sign a Covenant of Membership. Members not only come to church, but their goal is to tithe at least 10 percent of their income. They also have to get involved with a fellowship group, does a deep intellectual dive into the Bible and serves others. And that can be everything from fixing up a home to preparing a meal for those without a home.

Members have to review a two-page document, front and back. It's what Frank calls "My Personal Calling." Members volunteer to lead worship or coordinate food for retreats. They also can run a Bible study group, give their time and talent to help fight hunger, and lobby for peace and justice beyond the church.

At the top of the second page is a verse from the Book of Romans, Chapter 12: "I appeal to you therefore, my brothers and sisters, by the mercies of God, to present your bodies as a living sacrifice, holy and acceptable to God, which is your spiritual worship … Be transformed by the renewing of your mind, so that you may discern what is the will of God."

Frank sees the benefit as clear as the beard on his face. His new members? They're not so sure.

"Frank," one friend tells him, "This is the first church that's made it hard for me to join."

"You're exactly right," Frank responds. "That's *exactly* the kind of church I want to be a pastor of."

Frank wants that kind of church because he's exasperated by what he sees around him. People simply show up for Sunday morning service. That's it. Yet, despite their lackluster involvement, they still long for that sense of belonging and rootedness brought on by supporting others and being supported. They want instant gratification, a quick jolt of spiritual dopamine. They want the "grace gifts" that the church provides. That's a Frank phrase. The way Frank sees it, they want the church to be like microwavable popcorn. That's a Frank phrase, too.

"Community," he tells his new parishioners, "is not microwavable."

Frank uses the microwavable phrase a lot when people ask him to explain New Creation's Covenant of Membership. When his response draws more quizzical looks than knowing nods, he brings up an analogy that anyone in North Carolina will understand, particularly those who equate the jingle "Sail with the pilot all the way ..." to Saturday afternoons glued to the TV. That's what Frank did. He grew up watching North Carolina's recognizable colors of winter — red, black, and gold and two different shades of blue — run up and down 94 feet of varnished wood.

"A pastor," Frank says, "is like a coach. Think about it this way. If I was a basketball coach, I'd want my players to work on everything. Shooting. Rebounding. Dribbling. Defense. Just everything. I wouldn't tell some player, 'Oh, just send in a check to my basketball camp.' What kind of coach would do that? So, like any good basketball player does, you have to put in the work. How *else* are you going to grow your faith?

"So, that's what we do here at New Creation. I'm the coach, and our players will work on everything. And they are *gooood*. I have to tell you, I have a bunch of first-round draft picks!"

But after Frank leaves Vandalia Presbyterian and begins the church in his living room, his first-round draft picks couldn't fill a church fellowship hall, let alone a sanctuary. Yet, with its small size, Frank believes New Creation can pivot easily and tackle thorny issues rather than spend too much time on what Frank hates. That's the bureaucracy of church. He has seen too many churches enamored by what he calls the "edifice complex." Church members circle a table and worry about how big the building is or how many members they have or how many of those members are tithing enough to keep the lights on and the copy machine working.

"Churches need to be run like a business."

Before New Creation, Frank had sat in meetings and heard that phrase so many times. He hates it.

So, with New Creation, he looks to its spiritual cousin in Washington, DC, for guidance. That's the Church of the Saviour in Washington, DC. Frank believes he and New Creation members can follow Church of the Saviour's roll-up-the-sleeves-and-be-Jesus blueprint in Greensboro. So, Frank encourages his members to experience their Christianity not just with their heads and their hearts, but also with their hands and feet.

"You won't just know Jesus," he tells them. "You'll *follow* Jesus."

Frank works to make that happen.

Frank joins John Fisher, George Arnold, Norman Graham and Bob Kelly and helps start the first Habitat for Humanity chapter. Then, with a hammer and saw in hand, he and his parishioners help build houses for those in need. He helps develop the Presbyterian Pilgrimage Retreat Program, patterned after the Cursillo movement in Spain, and creates an opportunity where church members can spend a weekend learning how to deepen their faith. He creates a weekly gathering in downtown Greensboro to protest the death penalty. He and his parishioners do that for years.

Those efforts all help build a sense of community inside New Creation. But the biggest community builder happens every Sunday. New Creation has communion. Walk in and you step into what looks like a family reunion. People sing, play the piano, and sit across from one another on tables lined end to end and placed perpendicular. That is the New Creation Way, the Frank Way. Just look at the tables.

They are in the shape of a cross.

In First Presbyterian Church in Lumberton, where Frank's faith first took root, one of the first verses he recognized came from Chapter 11 in 1 Corinthians. Just three verses. Yet, before he reached the age of 10, Frank knew those three verses by heart because they become more than just words one Sunday of the month. These words became three dimensional. They became Communion Sunday.

And when he had given thanks, he broke it and said, "This is my body, which is for you; do this in remembrance of me."
In the same way, after supper he took the cup, saying, "This cup is the new covenant in my blood; do this, whenever you drink it, in remembrance of me."
For whenever you eat this bread and drink this cup, you proclaim the Lord's death until he comes.

At age 34, those three verses turn into Frank's foundation of building community in a church fellowship hall less than two blocks from UNC-Greensboro. He feels having communion every Sunday afternoon at Presbyterian Church of the Covenant will create a more unshakeable bond. Members, he believes, will get to know more about one another beyond where they sit and how they sing for Sunday afternoon service.

The communion looks like any communion in any church. Wine and later grape juice symbolize the body of Christ and homemade bread kneaded and baked by member Margaret Young symbolizes Jesus' body. Afterward, members turn their symbolically sacred service into a celebration created by the food the members cook, bake and create. There is spaghetti night. And a taco night. And a baked potato night. And a chili night. It's really one big potluck. A table becomes a family reunion familiar with an array of mismatched dishes of casseroles and desserts and every kind of salad you can name. But that's not what made New Creation's communion different than any other communion in Greensboro — or probably anywhere else. It's the people who come. They come for worship. But really, they come for the food. At least at first.

They live at Greensboro's first night shelter, an old grocery store off Asheboro Street, now known as Martin Luther King Jr. Drive in downtown Greensboro. The night shelter is run by Greensboro Urban Ministry, the nonprofit helping feed, clothe, and house those without homes or those battling all kinds of personal struggles.

Frank knows them like he knows his neighbors. They are Vince Sims, Joseph Rankin, and Rick Tatum. Everyone calls Rick "Goose."

They really don't have an address, just a location. They are homeless or have been homeless.

"Can I sing during worship?" Joseph asks.

"Sure, Joseph," Frank responds.

Joseph Rankin is a short, wiry guy with skin the color of charcoal. He fancies himself as a singer. He is a bit off-key, but Frank doesn't mind too much. If anyone questions Joseph's singing, Frank has a response ready.

"It's not great, sure, but it's real," he'll say. "And I would much rather have something that is real than something that is polished and not real. And you know, we all can learn something from Joseph don't you think? Everyone has a gift to give, and there's something special about people feeling like they can offer their gift."

Joseph only knows three songs. But before he sings a note, he'll offer a brief testimony about what God is doing in his life. Just three or four sentences. Then, he'll sing. Frank meets Joseph at the night shelter in a former grocery store off Asheboro Street in downtown Greensboro. Once a month, Frank and other parishioners worship and serve breakfast. That's when Frank invites Joseph to come to church. Joseph comes. He comes for worship and stays afterward to help set up the folding chairs and situate the tables in the shape of a cross.

Vince Sims comes, too. He starts helping out in the kitchen washing dishes. He later gets more involved. He's a tall, slender guy whose skin is as dark as midnight. Once Vince gets on his feet and finds an apartment, Frank goes with him to negotiate with Vince's landlord. They park near the St. Benedict Catholic Church, Greensboro's oldest Catholic church. Frank senses Vince's nervousness and sees a sign near the parking lot. It's a sign about the St. Vincent de Paul Society, a non-profit made up of church members that serves the poor.

Frank nods at Vince and points.

"See that sign?" Frank tells Vince. "We'll just tell him what your name is."

"You right, Frank!" Vince says, laughing.

Rick Tatum is a tall, slender guy with milk chocolate skin. He always needs a ride to church. So, Frank picks him up every Sunday. In return, Rick sets up the folding chairs in a semi-circle for church and later in the shape of a cross for communion. Rick carries out that task every Sunday, setting up chairs and putting them away.

One Sunday, as he puts up chairs for the umpteenth time, Rick shares with Frank something he's wanted to tell him for weeks.

"You know, Frank, I first started coming for the food, too," he says. "Just like Joseph and Vince. But you know what keeps me coming back? It's you and this church. You all welcomed me."

"Of course, you are welcome," Frank responds. "Always will be. You have become a part of things."

Frank makes sure Rick and Joseph and Vince get involved. He wants them to feel like they belong. But Frank does that with all of his members.

Like Ginnie Tate.

In and around Greensboro, particularly at the Farmer's Market near War Memorial Stadium off Yanceyville Street, Ginnie is known by another name.

She's The Goat Lady.

Ginnie Tate.

Ginnie spends 40 years as a nurse before she retired at age 65. But as she works to nurse people back to health in Greensboro, she works at beginning one of North Carolina's first goat-cheese diaries 30 minutes south of city. In 1984, she buys an abandoned 45-acre tobacco farm beside a corkscrew of a road in Randolph County. Ginnie lives in a 18ᵗʰ century log cabin that takes her and her hired help five years to refurbish. When she moves in, the log cabin has no running water and little electricity. So, she sleeps under blankets, cooks on a wood stove, and relieves herself out the back door, if need be. Before going to work at Moses Cone Hospital, where she works as a nursing administrator, she showers at the then-Greensboro YMCA off West Market Street. When she sees familiar faces, they often ask the same thing.

"Ginnie, how was your workout?"

"Oh, it was good," she'll respond. "Really good."

Ginnie first starts making goat cheese as a hobby in her kitchen. She then takes her goat cheese to local farmers markets, puts on a straw hat, and sells her cheese. Word of mouth helps her find customers, and her business begins to take off. Or as Ginnie says, in her own Ginnie way, she turns "yuckers" into "gushers."

Steve Tate. (left) Lee Tate. (right)

Ginnie becomes known in and around Greensboro as The Goat Lady, and in 1994, she turns her hobby into a business. She convinces her younger brother, Steve, and his wife, Lee, to move down from Minnesota, and together, they start Goat Lady Diary. She gets the name from the locals. They'd be hanging out at a store near the farm, jawing about current events near the counter and someone would say, "Hey, guess who I saw this weekend? That short, odd Yankee woman with the goats. You know, the Goat Lady." Or they'd see her and her brother, Steve, walk into a supermarket test marketing their goat cheese, and Ginnie and Steve would hear someone holler from the back of the store and wave saying "Hey, it's the Goat Lady!"

The name sticks, and her business grows. Her farm eventually grosses $300,000 a year and sells as much as 35,000 pounds of goat cheese a year, with the help of a herd that grows to 130 goats.

Ginnie is drawn to New Creation because of Frank. She sees Frank as a rebel because she sees herself as a rebel.

Ginnie is born in 1939 on a corn farm in rural Illinois. She comes of age at a time when women's options were as narrow as the roads near her Randolph County farm. Women could either be a teacher or a nurse, secretary or a mother and a wife. Ginnie chooses to be a nurse. She earns a nursing degree at Southern Illinois University, moves to Chicago, and lives and works as a nurse in its inner city. She loves being a nurse, but she hates what she sees — the sexism and misogyny of healthcare. She gets involved with nursing organizations that help empower the women she works with, and she doesn't think twice about telling other nurses what she believes.

"Don't let doctors treat you like shit," she'll tell them.

After getting a master's degree in nursing administration at Boston University and after moving to North Carolina to work for hospitals first in Greenville and later Greensboro, she buys the abandoned tobacco farm in 1984 in a tiny community known as Grays Chapel's in Randolph County. She then moves into an unheated 200-year-old log cabin with her goat, Nubie.

Around that time, she hears about New Creation. She likes the diversity of its congregation. She visits the church during a Sunday afternoon service and sees homeless people, Blacks and whites, young and old. She likes that, and she believes in that. Like Frank, she attracts people perceived as outcasts like a mother hen. Frank draws them to his congregation; Ginnie draws them to her farm and into her new business. She gives them jobs. So, she's comfortable with attending New Creation — so comfortable she'll walk into a church service with kids, baby goats, under each arm and think it's as normal as a sunrise. Like with anything she joins, she gets involved. With New Creation, she recruits Frank and others from the congregation and coaxes them to get dirty, dirty all the way up to their elbows.

They tend a quarter-acre garden near Guilford College. They plant all kinds of vegetables — squash, kale, zucchini, tomatoes, bell peppers, and broccoli. Their vegetables are shared among the church members and grow in a garden beside The Grange, a well-known venue in Greensboro that's used for contra dancing.

On most Saturdays, church members tend the garden. Frank, too. Frank uses the garden spearheaded by Ginnie as another lesson of stewardship for New Creation.

"To me, it helps us be rooted if you will," he tells his church members during one Sunday sermon. "It's that understanding that our life really comes from the earth and that caring for the earth is part of maintaining our life as well as acknowledging what God has given us to do.

"That is to be good stewards of what we have been given. Working in the garden helps us stay rooted in that knowledge that our life is dependent on the earth. We are blessed by that."

A few efforts New Creation starts spring up out of the blue. Frank just happens to be in the right place at the right time.

The right place, one time, is at the church office one Sunday when Frank stands at the copy machine running off the church bulletins for the worship service that afternoon. He looks up and sees a woman standing a few feet away.

"I have spent all my money on crack, and I have no place to go and nothing to eat," she tells Frank.

Frank can tell she's in trouble. She's fidgeting from foot to foot, her eyes dancing with fear.

"Why don't you come and worship with us and afterward, we're going to have supper together," Frank tells her. "You can eat with us, and we can talk about what might be possible."

From their conversation, Frank learns there is no halfway house for homeless women recovering from substance abuse. And if those women are single mothers, they have to bring with them not only their addictions, but their children as well.

Frank and others in New Creation help start one of the few programs in the United States that allow women to raise their children while they are in treatment for addiction issues. They name the program Mary's House after Mary Magdalene, the woman who Jesus healed and befriended. All that is initiated by a Sunday afternoon conversation beside a copy machine.

Frank experiences so many moments like that at New Creation. Those moments change him, educate him, and show him how the most ordinary of moments can become incredibly sacred.

That is, if you pay attention. And Frank pays attention because he knows those moments will come. And they do come.

Here are three.

* * *

Frank and Michie sit in a large circle with other members in the fellowship hall at Presbyterian Church of the Covenant, the place where New Creation meets every Sunday afternoon. They're holding hands, eyes closed, saying the Lord's Prayer, when they hear these tiny voices from a few feet away. Frank squints his eyes open and looks over his shoulder.

"Well, I'll be," he tells himself.

He sees David and Christie, heads bowed, hands clasped together, eyes shut tight — and they are reciting the Lord's Prayer. They're no more than 4 or 5. He and Michie have not drilled that memorization lesson into their children. They haven't even rehearsed it with them. But David and Christie learn it by sitting in church, surrounded by Frank's first-round draft picks.

Another time, Frank finds himself in the kitchen cleaning up when he hears someone playing "Amazing Grace" on the upright piano in the church's fellowship hall. Frank walks out and sees David. He is 6, a boy who had never had a music lesson.

"I didn't know you could play that," Frank tells his son, surprised. "How did you learn that?"

"I just picked it out," David responds.

Frank immediately thinks of Olathe, Kansas, a back closet and a little boy in the Carolina blue sailor suit. And now, that little boy sits at an upright piano playing a tune he learned by ear.

"David," Frank says, "That is just beautiful."

Frank forgets what he needs to finish in the kitchen. He simply stands there, soaking in the moment. He knows he'd tell Michie. But right then, he just listens.

"That boy," Frank tells himself. "He is something."

There was a time when Frank felt ambivalent about being a parent. He and Michie talked about it. She was really excited; Frank … was not. Then, they fly to Kansas, find the office of the Gentle Shepherd in a blink-and-miss strip mall, and as soon as he rocks David in his arms, Frank's feelings change. He feels like a father. He wants to be a father. And those moments on a Sunday afternoon, brief snapshots in any family's life, solidify that he knew he did the right thing.

Then comes another Sunday afternoon. That's the third moment, another incredibly sacred moment when his beliefs first formed during his halcyon childhood in Lumberton are turned upside down.

It's because of Gayle Wulk.

Gayle is the daughter of a career Marine, and she never lived anyplace with her family for more than three years. Gayle goes on to earn three degrees and moves to Greensboro in 1972 to earn her doctorate in physical education at UNC-Greensboro. But unlike her nomadic childhood, Gayle decides to settle in Greensboro. She stays to teach. But she also stays because she finds a community where she feels welcome for really the first time in her life. She meets people who don't see her lifestyle as a sin. Gayle is a lesbian, and in Greensboro, she finds a comforting circle of friends. She also finds Sheri Bonner.

They meet on a blind date in 1989. At first, they don't feel drawn to one another but over time, they grow close and become a couple. When Gayle first came to Greensboro, she sought out a church to attend. The first church she goes to she hears a minister ranting about the evils of homosexuality. Gayle gets up and leaves. The next church she visits she arrives early. She finds her seat in a nearly empty sanctuary, sits down, and feels a tap on her shoulder.

"Would you mind moving?" the man told her. "This is someone's seat."

Instead, she leaves and quits her search for a church. That search doesn't resume until after she and Sheri became life-partners.

She hears about New Creation through a friend, and she and Sheri visit because they're in the process of adopting a little girl from Guatemala, and they both want to raise their daughter in a church and give their family that church experience. But Gayle is skeptical. Church has never done much for her.

Still, she and Sheri visit New Creation, and right away, she feels this church is different. Everyone is dressed more like Saturday afternoon than Sunday morning, and no one bats an eye when she and Sheri walk in together. Then, she listens to Frank.

She feels his sermons make sense, and he zeroes in on issues that are going on in the world and in Greensboro. Meanwhile, he uses theological language to address issues like abortion and racism, homelessness and hunger. Gayle has never heard a church discuss these issues on a Sunday morning. But New Creation does. So, she and Sheri come back Sunday after Sunday. She sits in the fellowship hall at Presbyterian Church of the Covenant, and with every sermon Frank gives, she begins to see church — or really New Creation — in a whole new light.

"Frank may sometimes sound like a good ol' boy, but he definitely isn't," she says decades later. "I've lived in the South most of my life, I grew up in a Southern household where my dad from Wisconsin liked grits better than my momma from Tennessee. But the informality and laid-backness I found, I really liked.

"I don't like uppityness, you know, people who are more impressed by themselves and more concerned about how they present themselves rather than how they look at humanity. You find that in academia, and I never bought into that.

"But at New Creation, I found people who were very accepting and very thoughtful. They were sharing their theological ideas, and they were thoughtful about how they interacted with other people."

After attending New Creation for three years, Gayle and Sheri join. But their decision to join convinces three families to leave. They leave because, they say, they love the sinner, but they hate the sin. So, when one family decides to leave, Frank acts. He asks one of the families leaving if they're up to having what's known as a commissioning ceremony to bless them as they continue their own journey of faith. They agree.

Frank sees the service as a way to be honest with the sense of pain and loss on both sides as well as build community from that experience so they all – the people in New Creation and the family leaving — can grow.

As he prepares for that service, though, Frank realizes he has grown himself.

Like with everything, it all starts with his hometown.

* * *

In Lumberton, whenever the issue about homosexuality came up, people would bring up verses in the Old Testament and tell the young Frank Dew, "Oh, the Bible says it's wrong, Frank." Young Frank accepted that because he didn't know any gay people growing up. And if he did, he didn't know it. Back then, anyone who was gay kept their lifestyle a secret to avoid any kind of persecution. So, Frank went about his life. He dove into his faith, became committed to being a preacher and went from Wake Forest to Duke and finally to Greensboro where his childhood perceptions about homosexuality were somehow part of his spiritual DNA.

Then, he meets Gayle. And Sheri.

He gets to know them, he likes them, and he can see that their love for each other comes from a genuine, authentic place. Just like the love he has for Michie. As Gayle and Sheri get more involved in the church, Frank becomes a student; they become his teacher. His viewpoints change, and he begins to look at what he knows in the Bible through a different lens.

He sees how the church is wrestling with the gay issue — and how he is wrestling with the gay issue — is just like the early church when Jews worried about Gentiles joining their congregation. Jews saw the lifestyle of the Gentiles — or anyone who was not Jewish at the time — as an abomination. Then came Peter as well as Paul who preached the importance of including everyone as part of their spiritual flock.

Throughout his life, Frank has used the Bible as a tool to right his moral compass. As the issue of homosexuality takes on names and families, and with his education from his new teachers, Gayle and Sheri, three verses Frank knows from the Book of Acts help. Those three verses come from Chapter 15. It reads:

And after there had been much debate, Peter stood up and said to them, "Brothers, you know that in the early days God made a choice among you, that by my mouth the Gentiles should hear the word of the gospel and believe.

And God, who knows the heart, bore witness to them, by giving them the Holy Spirit just as he did to us, and he made no distinction between us and them, having cleansed their hearts by faith.

Cleansed their hearts by faith. Frank takes that to heart.

He sees how the early church accepted Gentiles without requiring them to convert to Judaism, and he can see parallels with how the church came around to accepting Blacks and women. Frank knows such people. He loves such people. And he loves Gayle and Sheri. They're adopting a girl from Guatemala in a church filled with families who have adopted children.

Just like Frank and Michie.

Frank knows his viewpoints on gays have changed. He wants to make clear to this family — and any family who decides to leave — that they are glad for them and want them to stay. But at the same time, he wants to emphasize New Creation was not going to change its stance on homosexuality. Just like Peter in the Book of Acts, Frank stands his ground. He thinks back to the conversation he had with the father and husband of that one family involved in the commissioning service. That husband is an elder until the day he leaves.

"Frank, we don't agree with their lifestyle, and we feel that should be the message of the church," he tells Frank. "That was in the Bible."

Frank pauses, gathering what he hopes are the right words to say.

"Well, I look at it a little differently," Frank responds finally. "To me, that is taking a very small portion of the Bible literally, and not taking the whole Bible seriously. The Bible says we do have to love and accept one another."

New Creation had talked about the issue in its session meetings, and Frank knew the stance the church had taken. Plus, with a congregation of only 50 members, Frank knows you don't need a Gallop poll to tell you what a church believes or how it thinks. New Creation wants to be an affirming church.

But for four families, that stance is a deal breaker. Three families simply stop coming. One family wants to say good-bye because the church was a big part of their life. So, on a Sunday afternoon in the fellowship hall at Presbyterian Church of the Covenant, Frank schedules the commissioning service.

To understand the impact, think of the size of New Creation. When people leave, it's a big deal. New Creation is so small that people notice when someone is not there. The parishioners who remain feel the effect firsthand. There are just fewer people to do the many things the church wants to do. Usually, when people leave New Creation, it's positive. They're moving away from Greensboro to a new city, a new job or a new opportunity. Frank always schedules a commissioning service because he doesn't want his church to be one where parishioners see an empty pew, look at one another and say, "Where is Bill?" or "What happened to Jane?" He sees the commissioning service as a way to mark a family's commitment to the church and give everyone in the congregation a chance to say goodbye.

But on this particular Sunday, this is a different kind of goodbye. Frank knows tension will fill the fellowship hall because everyone knows why this one family is leaving. It'll be uncomfortable for everyone, including him. But he knows it has to happen.

"It's part of being real," Frank tells himself. "We can't be a church that says, 'Oh, how are you? Oh, I'm fine.' But no one is really fine. That's a pretend church, and that's not what we're aiming for."

The day comes one Sunday in the mid-1990s. Tears come. People cry. Frank begins.

"We are thanking God for all this family has meant to our congregation, and we need to acknowledge the sense of loss and pain we're all wrestling with, and we pray that they will be faithful in following Jesus as they move into the future. And we pray for our church as we move into our future."

Afterward, people hug. People cry some more. And the family leaves New Creation for the last time.

Gayle was there. And she remembers.

"They were friends, and there was no friction between us

personally," she says today. "It was like a rejection on a theoretical level. But I didn't feel rejected as a person. I felt it was my lifestyle that was rejected, but everything (in the service) was done very lovingly. Frank modeled that and demanded that. If anyone started to get hurtful, he would draw us back. He never let an elephant sit in the middle of the room."

A few years later, Gayle feels the call to become an elder in the church. But there is a catch. An elder has to be an ordained lay person, and according to the Presbytery — the governing body of Presbyterian Church USA – an ordained lay person could not be gay. But she hears that an individual church can make their own decision about who an elder can be.

Gayle doesn't like that at all. Why can't the Presbyterian Church be more affirming? It doesn't make sense to her. But what does make sense is talking to Frank. She catches him after a Sunday afternoon church service to discuss her newfound sense of service and ask for guidance in what to do. Frank doesn't mince words.

"Gayle, I think you'd be a great elder, and I would encourage you to pursue it," Frank tells her.

Gayle, though, decides to wait. If she becomes an elder, she worries she'll put Frank's retirement in jeopardy in some way. A few weeks later, Frank stops her after church. She tells him her decision and why.

"Gayle," Frank says. "Don't let that be a deciding factor. If you feel the call, you go for it."

The Presbyterian Church wrestled with the "gay issue" for years before a decision is made that an individual church can make their own decision about who an elder can be. With that decision made, Gayle feels she can listen to Frank's encouragement, and she puts her name in as an elder. The congregation votes, and it must be unanimous. With Gayle, it is. She becomes an elder. She becomes an elder twice. She serves six years, two three-year terms, in which she becomes a worship leader, and she trains worship leaders.

And with everything she is as an elder, she thinks of Frank and his approach to her sense of calling, the need to do more.

"He's selfless, and he's had my back," she says. "He didn't try to protect his retirement. He didn't see that as a hurdle. His attitude was 'If it's going to happen, it's going to happen.' He was going to do it from his perspective and do what he thought was right."

The year before the commissioning ceremony, Frank is scheduled to speak in front of the Greensboro City Council. When he does, he sees a familiar face in the gallery. It's the husband, the father, the church elder who leaves the church with his family the following year. They both come to address the City Council on the same issue — except from different sides. Frank is anti-death penalty; the church elder … is not.

When the meeting ends, Frank offers the man a ride home. They go home together. Frank wants the man to know their differences on some fundamental issues will not undermine their friendship.

Ask Frank about that today, and he brings up Clarence Jordan, a Georgia farmer and New Testament scholar who was instrumental in creating Habitat for Humanity. As Frank tells it, Jordan sees Jesus as an excellent mediator when it comes to group dynamics. His one disciple, Simon the Zealot, is sworn to kill people like the disciple, Matthew, the tax collector. That doesn't happen. Of course.

"I imagine Jesus had to sleep between these two people on occasion, but Jesus gets them to love each other," Frank says. "That's real. I mean, look what you see today. We have red churches and blue churches and purple churches. Just churches whose congregations are bonded to one another by politics. But churches, I think, lose sight of what really matters. It's about Jesus. It's not about right or left or in between.

"The Jesus I understand requires that we love. He doesn't say love the people who love you. He says love your enemies. That's always hard. But to love. Just love. That is what we need to be all about."

* * *

On a beautiful summer day in 2009, underneath a big walnut tree in Randolph County, Frank and many others say goodbye to The Goat Lady. They say goodbye to Ginnie.

Three years before, Ginnie was diagnosed with a death sentence of a disease. Steve and others first noticed that Ginnie started slurring her speech. Ginnie later noticed that she was dragging her feet, and she couldn't get mucus out of the back of her throat. All this happened over the span of a few months. Ginnie then went to Duke and got the diagnosis. She had a neurodegenerative disease better known by its dreaded acronym: ALS. It's a disease that took baseball legend Lou Gehrig. And decades later, it took Ginnie. She was 69.

When her doctors at Duke told her they wanted to insert a breathing tube to help her breathe, she says no. Her brother, Steve, asks why. Ginnie picks up a pad and writes: "I've had a good life. I'm not afraid to die."

A reporter from the News & Record, the daily newspaper in Greensboro, later asks Ginnie about what she wrote. As she stands in the barn kitchen, stirring marinara sauce for the lunchtime spaghetti she'll share with her employees, she has an answer ready.

"What else are you going to do? Two years ago, I was milking goats five mornings a week. Plus doing other stuff. Now, I do what I can. Something's always going to kill you. I just hope I die when I'm walking. That means I wasn't in the bed."

Ginnie wants to die on her own terms, on her farm where the church-like chime of a pottery bowl is the only sound anyone hears, even in the slightest wind. So, she plans her memorial service. She wants it to have a theme: "The Garden."

Steve acts as the emcee, the husband-and-wife duo of Don and Kristy Milholin sing, and Frank is a primary participant. When he gets up to speak underneath the black walnut tree, he talks about service, about gardens, about goats and about dreams.

"Ginnie was so important to the life of our church, and it's not just because of the goats she brought to church under each arm.

"She started the garden out near The Grange that showed us that we have to be good stewards with what God has given us, and she helped us see that we could live out our calling and live out our dreams. Her dream wasn't my dream, but when you see someone living out their dream, it gives you the courage that you can live out your own.

"That is what Ginnie did for us. That was the most important thing she gave us. God had a plan and a purpose for her life, and she took hold of that and lived the way she wanted to live to the very end. There is a lot of satisfaction in that, and we can learn much from Ginnie. And today, in a sense, Ginnie finished the race. She kept the faith."

Soon, everyone who came turned into one big choir. They looked in the program, saw the lyrics and began to sing Pete Seeger's "The Garden Song."

Plant your rows straight and long
Season with a prayer and song
Mother Earth will make you strong
If you give her loving care
Inch by inch, row by row
Gonna make this garden grow
Gonna mulch it deep and low
Gonna make it fertile ground

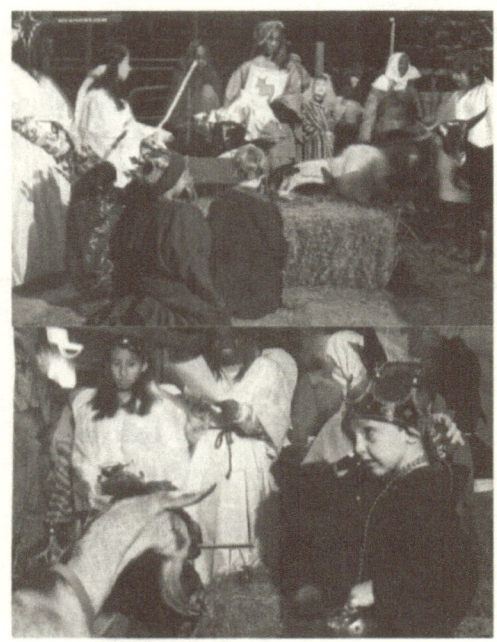

New Creation held its annual Christmas pageant for more than 10 years in the barn at Goat Lady Diary.

Photo credit: Courtesy of Divinity, Duke University's magazine

The Goat Lady Diary Farm remains as fertile ground for New Creation. For years, parishioners drive out there every Christmas to stage a live Nativity around the goats. They sing carols, hear the Christmas story and watch 8-year-olds as shepherds stand beside a homeless man who is a shepherd, too. Some parishioners have been on a farm. Some parishioners have no idea what a farm is. No matter, the live Nativity becomes akin to a family reunion. New Creation parishioners come for a meal and a message. They hear the message inside the barn or on the big porch of the dairy under a wide-open sky in Randolph County. And every year, the ordinary becomes surreal, and the moments become sacred.

Like this one.

"For to you is born this day in the city of David, a Savior, who is Christ the Lord, and the Angel of the Lord said, 'Be not afraid,' an adult says reading the Christmas story from the Bible.

A little boy, dressed in a sheet and acting as a shepherd, listens. He has something to say about that.

"I'm not afraid!" he yells from the porch.

Or this one.

Following the live Nativity, parishioner Vince Sims totes bags of garbage to the Dumpster. He can't see well. It's dark in the country where there are no streetlights. Steve points to where Vince needs to go. A minute or so later, Steve hears Vince holler. He'd fallen into a pond, and the water is freezing.

That year, Frank takes Vince and Rick Tatum and Joseph Rankin home. All three men have been homeless off and on for years. Conversation between all four men begins with Vince's mishap, and they laugh. As he drives up US 421, under a star-lit sky, Frank hears all three men go back and forth about everything. They don't talk about their struggles. At least not at that moment. They talk about one another and how the church and the live Nativity have become a part of their lives.

Frank listens. He never imagined he'd be in this kind of company. But it feels like such a good thing. As he drives north toward home, one thought bounces in his head.

"This is exactly where I am supposed to be."

True. But Frank also sees somewhere else he is supposed to be. And it's nowhere close to Greensboro.

It's south. Way south.

Since 1995, from a beautiful spot in the rolling hills of Randolph County, Goat Lady Dairy has produced award-winning handcrafted goat and cow milk cheeses sold throughout North Carolina and beyond. Photo credit: Courtesy of Goat Lady Dairy.

Frank On Frank
The Rabbi's Question

There's an African proverb I love. It's about an elephant — and what we can see. And can't.

Elephants are big animals, we all know. So, if you can stand in one place, you can never see the whole elephant. There's no way. But what if you have others circle the elephant from the trunk to the tail and around the other side? Think of what happens. You'll be able to see the whole elephant so much better than what you can see just by yourself.

The point is what we see — and what we experience — determines where we stand. But if you have others helping you, you'll see a whole lot more. You see a bigger picture, and your perspective can change dramatically

I bring up the African proverb of the elephant to emphasize the importance of diversity, particularly in churches. And when I say diversity, I don't mean just Black and white. I'm thinking socio-economic, gender and sexual orientation. Think about what everyone would discover. You have PhDs in academia bumping into PhDs in life, sitting shoulder to shoulder. They get to know one another and see how their differences and their similarities bond them as brothers and sisters in Christ. They see in one another their common humanity, and that's the greatest thing we all can give one another.

One of my favorite stories is about a rabbi and a question he poses to his students. He asks, 'How can you tell that the night is over and a new day has begun?' One of his students raises his hand and says, "When you can tell a fig tree from an oak tree!" Then, another student raises his hand and says, "When you can tell a sheep from a goat!" The rabbi smiles and shakes his head. "Alright, rabbi," one of the students said, "tell us."

The rabbi looks around at his students to make sure he has their attention, and he says, 'You know you have enough light when you can see the faces of another, and you can recognize the face of another brother or sister. That's when you know the night is over, and a new day has begun.'

Perspective is like that. It shines a light and lets us see things that were once invisible to us. And when that happens, we see life from so many different perspectives. We get to see a whole lot more of the truth. In the African proverb, the elephant is a metaphor for truth, and none of us can ever see the whole truth — until we circle around it with others and share our perspectives of life and how we live.

I felt we were blessed at New Creation. We were small, sure. Our largest number during my time at New Creation was no more than 50 members. But our diversity allowed us to see different perspectives, especially when we sat down and had communion after our service every Sunday. Rich and poor. Black, white, and brown. Gay and straight. Those different perspectives helped us see the whole elephant.

A lot of churches today talk about the value of diversity but not many churches have it. It's easy to understand why. We all feel more comfortable in a congregation when people look like us and think like us. It gives us a sense of a security, yes.

But if we give that up, think about what happens if we're around people who don't look or live like us. We can discover something so much deeper. We create community, and at New Creation, we believed that being in community begins with being with the poor. Then, transformation can happen. That kind of community can be created in any church, not just New Creation.

In my five decades as a pastor, I've learned the best place to learn gratitude is a homeless shelter. You're doing something for someone else, and you realize you're being blessed by them. That's the best kind of ministry. Together, you learn what it looks like to follow Jesus.

I remember sitting in a session meeting of another church, and they were talking about the need to raise money for the budget. I heard someone say, 'The church is a business, and it has to be run like a business.' That church, like so many other churches I see today, saw they needed to follow the big box model of religion. They believed bigger is better.

That reminds me of a story about a church elder who was asked about someone in their congregation. He looked puzzled, and he didn't even recognize their name. Then, he figured it out, 'They must go to the other service." That cracks me up, but the more I think about it, the sadder I get. Churches today see families as line items on a budget. They wonder how many families they need to make a $150,000 budget. The better question is how many people they need to throw a good party and remember the names of *everyone* who comes.

You don't create community by singing the right kind of music or having the right bumper sticker or having the best video on your Facebook page. That is just gimmicky and doesn't lead people to seek the deeper meaning of what their faith means to them and others around them. Instead, I worry that it leads them to ask, 'What do I need God for?'

I see that happening more and more today because of the growing secularization of our society. People think they don't need church at all. And what do we lose? It's that idea of a having a big, thriving church. But look at what we can gain. We can have churches that are smaller, more intentional, more deeply committed. I see that happening more and more. It reminds me of the monastic communities of the Dark Ages. Now, I'm not saying people should live like a monk or a nun. But I think smaller communities of faith can help keep the light of Christianity alive and show those involved the fundamental issue of why we're here.

We are given this blessing of life each day, and the point is to be here and do what God intends us to *be* and to *do*. We can imagine that or dream that. But at some point, it has to become a reality for us. At New Creation, with rich and poor, gay and straight, black and white,

I felt we were really living that out with the help of all those different perspectives of life. We were surrounded by people who had PhDs in life, and that helped us see the whole elephant. We were seeing the whole truth. We were willing to get into the river, even when the water was choppy, because we knew God had a plan and a purpose for us.

God has a plan and a purpose for *all* of us. So many times, we ask ourselves, 'Do I have the time? Do I have the money? Do I have ... whatever?' But that's not the question to ask. The question to ask is, 'What is God calling me to do?'

We may not know the answer right away, but just asking the question can help us move in the right direction. We're moving from our night to the light of our day. Then, as the rabbi told his own students, we can begin to see the faces of others. They may not look like us or think like us or even love like us, but we can embrace them. Not just because of our differences. But also because of our similarities.

We're all brothers and sisters in Christ.

Buck Cochran took this photo of a little boy during his first trip to Nicaragua. The photo now hangs in the hallway in his Greensboro home, a reminder of that transformative trip in November 1993.

Chapter 10
"God, You're in Charge!"

"There is so much in our everyday life that we fail to see. It's because of familiarity. We think we already know stuff, and we see what we expect to see and ignore what else surrounds us. That's why we need new eyes. That helps us gain a new perspective on our lives. When we do, we realize what we didn't see was there all along."
The Rev. Frank Dew

It's late afternoon, and Frank is in the middle of a corn field far from home.

The corn has been harvested, and acres of beaten down dirt stretch toward the horizon beside a dirt road in the middle of nowhere. But Frank feels right at home. For him, the field feels more like a classroom. He's taking notes and listening to a man sitting in front of him in a chair. The man speaks no English, and a translator interprets everything the farmer says. It's not exciting really. The farmer speaks, the translator interprets, and Frank scribbles down a few more notes before asking another question. That's it. But the more Frank listens, the more he feels he's back in North Carolina, back at Duke Divinity School, listening to a professor shed light on what Frank doesn't understand. But this time, his professor is a peasant corn farmer, and his books are etched in the lines on his ruddy face and calloused hands. And right there, in a field at least 3,200 miles from Greensboro, Frank realizes once again he is the student; this farmer, his teacher. He shares with Frank and everyone around him what he has gained from a sore back, weathered hands, and long days.

As Frank listens, it hits him.

"This farmer," Frank tells himself. "He's got a PhD in life."

The farmer helps Frank see the value of a dirt-under-the-fingernails existence in one of the poorest countries in the world. That's not appreciated in Frank's world. Not really with Frank either — until he meets the farmer. There, in the middle of a corn field, Frank has an epiphany about life and his faith. He realizes being close to those subsisting on the bottom rung of society's ladder can help anyone see what Frank likes to call the "whole elephant," the whole truth.

Frank always thought he did. Not quite.

Since his days in Lumberton, he'd read or hear someone repeat the words of Jesus from verse 26 in Chapter 11 in the Book of Matthew: "For you always have the poor with you, but you will not always have me." Frank always had interpreted that verse this way: We'll always have the poor around us, so we need to get used to it. But the corn farmer reframes that verse in a transformative way. Frank sees how wrong he was for years about that verse. He scribbles his new interpretation of that verse in his notes and reads it when he walks out of the corn field. He wants to make sure he remembers it well, so it'll be ready for his next date with a legal pad when he bullet-points his next sermon and his many sermons to come.

As Frank puts away his notebook and steps into a van, his mind is swimming over his new lesson in life.

"I learned this so far from home," he tells himself. "In Nicaragua of all places. If I'm following Jesus the way I need to follow Him, the poor will always be with me. And I learned this from a peasant farmer. He delivered a Sermon in the Corn Field."

A familiar voice shakes Frank from his thoughts.

"Hey, Frank," says Buck Cochran, a fellow member of New Creation. "That was something wasn't it?"

"Yes, it was, Buck," Frank responds. "It's definitely got me thinking."

More than Frank really knew.

The idea of going to Nicaragua in November 1993 came about

in a very Frank way.

Gary and Chess Campbell, two missionaries in Nicaragua, visited New Creation one Sunday afternoon the year before. They were on a public education speaking tour through the United States to raise awareness for their work with the Council of Protestant Churches of Nicaragua, known simply by the confusingacronym CEPAD. Founded in 1972, CEPAD works with the many families living in rural communities speckled across Nicaragua and helps them with what they need. Gary, an ordained minister, preaches about CEPAD's work in a country buffeted by war, political corruption, and poverty. After his sermon, he stops Frank and offers what he sees as a jewel of an idea.

"You all should come down and visit us," he says.

"That's a great idea!" Frank responds.

A year later, Frank, Buck and four others from New Creation and Presbyterian Church of the Covenant fly from Greensboro to Houston. From the country's fourth largest city, Frank and Buck and their friends board a two-engine jet bound for Managua, the capital of Nicaragua, the country of 3.5 million people considered the second-poorest country in Central America. Haiti is the first.

After a three-hour flight, Frank looks out the window and sees below him a tiny airport, much tinier that Piedmont Triad International Airport in Greensboro. The land below is one big, lush expanse of green. Yet, that natural beauty belies how dangerous Nicaragua was and how dangerous it still can be. More than 30,000 Nicaraguans died in the Contra War, a conflict that had become a bloody metaphor of the Cold War in Central America. The US backed the Contras; the Soviet Union supported the Sandinista National Liberation Front. The war began in 1981; it ended nine years later. Yet, three years after the war ended, Frank and his friends land in Nicaragua, and the country is still a powder keg. It's gut-punched by one political crisis after another.

According to the United Nations' Human Rights Watch, government figures placed the unemployment and underemployment rates at 50 percent. In July 1993, armed rebels take over the city of

Esteli 92 miles north of Managua. Only after an intense battle that rages for 24 hours do the government troops take back the city. It's the worst fighting since the Contra War ended. More than 150 people are dead and wounded, and according to the Los Angeles Times, a local hospital becomes the epicenter of chaos. Tracy Wilkinson, a LA Times reporter, discovers a grim scene: The wounded lie stacked on gurneys, blood covers everything, and a woman sobs in the corner of a room.

"Bullets everywhere!" she wails. "Let them just kill us. How can they do this, take a place like a hospital? A hospital is for saving lives, not for a massacre."

This is the country Frank and Buck fly into. As they get ready to land, their minds wander. They think of home.

Frank sits by the window in his favorite chair. For weeks, he's thought about the trip to Nicaragua and his burning need to go. But he has yet to talk to Michie about it. He knows he will. But he knows the time has to be right. On this particular weeknight, it is. Dinner is over, the dishes are done, and David and Christie are in bed. Frank and Michie are sitting together in their wood-paneled den. Family photos line every shelf in their new home in Greensboro's Sunset Hills neighborhood. Frank looks at Michie on the couch a few feet away. It's time. Frank breaks the quiet.

"Michie, I'm thinking about going to Nicaragua."

Michie just looks at him.

"Here he goes again," she tells herself. "Frank, the risk taker."

After their bout of infertility, Frank and Michie have both learned how to communicate better, and as a psychologist, Michie has come to see their emotional journey has helped them become closer. They lift each other up. Frank supported her when she pursued her doctorate at UNC-Chapel Hill, and she supported him through Duke, Trinity Avenue Presbyterian, Vandalia Presbyterian and his ambitious venture in starting New Creation.

But Nicaragua?

"Are you sure this is a good idea?" she asks.

"I do," Frank says.

He explains how he believes such a trip will help the congregation become more empathetic and more aware of the poor they see, feed, talk to and help. But really, Michie doesn't need an explanation. She believes what Frank believes: As Christians, you are called to continue the good work of Jesus, despite the risk. Then, she remembers that time at Ocean Isle, where they sat side by side for days cross-checking every punch card of data that represented the research in her dissertation. She and Frank cross-checked hundreds of punch cards. Frank called out every number, and Michie made sure every number was right. It was mind-numbing work, enough for Michie to exclaim, "God, it about killed me!" So, as Frank maps out the reasoning behind going to Nicaragua, she tells herself, "They'll all be alright. They'll be with the Campbells. What really could go wrong?"

When Frank flies to Nicaragua for a week, Michie stays busy. Kids. Laundry. Dishes. Work. Just everything. She doesn't think about the danger. She doesn't want to. She knows he'll be alright. She has to think that way. Has to.

As the plane prepares to land, Frank thinks about his conversation with Michie. He looks over at Buck, and he sees the former Navy officer, the new member of his congregation, looking out the window.

"Hey, Buck," Frank says. "You alright?"

"Yeah," Buck says. "I'm good, Frank."

But really, Buck is not. He's in a tug-of-war with himself over where he's going and where he's been.

* * *

Buck, the naval flight officer, married Cathy, his high school sweetheart, in 1984. Photo credit: Courtesy of Buck Cochran.

Buck spent nearly nine years as a naval flight officer after graduating from Wake Forest with a chemistry degree and going to Aviation Officer Candidate School in Pensacola, Florida. He went to Pensacola right after the film "An Officer and a Gentleman" made that whole professional foray famous. Buck loved the Navy, and he loved the friends he made. But he struggles with the stand his own country took in Nicaragua as well as other parts of the world. Buck had been stationed in Iceland, the United Kingdom, Bermuda, and the Mediterranean Sea with NATO. But he had never been sent to a war zone. And now, as the plane descends, he enters a country where his own country has blood on its hands because of the Contra War.

After reading about the violence that has erupted in Nicaragua, he worries. He worries if his military career could jeopardize him or their group if they get stopped at gunpoint or, God forbid, kidnapped and held for ransom for some inane reason. But Buck tosses it from his mind. He can't think about it. He can't. But he can't say that to Cathy, his wife.

Cathy was his high school sweetheart at West Montgomery High in Mt. Gilead, North Carolina. She was a member of the homecoming court, and she asked Buck to escort her on a fateful Friday night when she was 14. Buck was 16. They've been together ever since. Cathy knows Buck, and when she became a Navy wife, she had gotten used to their shorthand conversations before he took off for some Naval exercise he couldn't divulge. But his trip to Nicaragua is different. She can see it in his face, sense it in his demeanor. Buck is not only wrestling whether he should go, but he's also wrestling with who he is. So, when Buck brings up Nicaragua, Cathy doesn't mince any words.

"You're seeking something, Buck," she says.

"Should I be doing this?" Buck asks.

"Well, I'm used to you jetting off to some place," Cathy responds. "You'd always say something like, 'I'll be home in a little bit, and I'm taking the toothpaste and some clothes.' But this is different, I know. What did Z tell you?"

"Oh, over breakfast?" Buck asks.

"Yeah, over breakfast," Cathy responds.

Buck remembers. The Rev. Z. Holler serves as the pastor at Presbyterian Church of the Covenant. Buck had just gotten out of the Navy, and he moved Cathy and their two young children from Philadelphia to Greensboro in 1991 for his corporate sales job with a large chemical company. When they arrive, Buck and Cathy move into a home in Greensboro's Green Valley neighborhood and begin attending the Church of the Covenant and New Creation. They join and get busy with the church's outreach work. That's when Z Holler invites Buck to breakfast at Tex & Shirley's, the city's go-to breakfast spot.

"What did he tell you?" Cathy asks.

"He told me, 'I think God is messing with you,'" Buck says. "I really didn't know what Z was talking about. Then, he tells me, 'Something is going on, and you need to look for new ways to explore your faith.'"

"So, you want to go to Nicaragua," Cathy deadpans.

"Yeah," Buck responds. "I want to go to Nicaragua. I don't know why, but I need to go on this trip."

"OK," responds Cathy, feeling more fearful than she'd like to be. "But be careful. Nicaragua sure isn't Bermuda."

Seated in the plane, Buck thinks back to his conversation with Cathy. In his mind's eye, he sees Cathy with their two kids, daughter, Cameron; and son, Trey. Cameron is 4, Trey is 2. Cathy is smiling, Cameron and Trey are happy. But he's not there. So, he prays. For his safety. For his family's comfort. For his own future. Buck is a few days from turning 34. He's looking forward, not back.

Or so he tells himself.

"Seeking something," Buck says to himself. "Cathy, I believe I am."

Chess and Gary Campbell meet Frank and Buck and the four others from Greensboro at the airport. Once they all get through customs and fill out more paperwork, they climb into a van and travel 30 minutes through the countryside to where they're staying — an auto repair shop where the bays have been turned into dorm rooms with bunk beds. It's Frank's first trip to Central America, and as he looks out the van window, he sees community in action. People walking, people riding bicycles, people eating, people clustering in tight circles around roadside markets, roadside stands and flea markets. He also sees rows and rows of homes, made from cinder block with roofs made out of tin.

Frank breathes in and catches the ever-present scent of the Third World. Diesel and burning trash merge with the aromatic sizzle of food being prepared along the dirt road. Music comes from unseen corners and exclamations of Spanish come from everywhere. It's loud, living-in-the-moment loud. Even with it being in November, windows are open in every house because air conditioning is a Third World wish. With his one suitcase tucked under his seat, Frank thinks back to why he felt he needed to come and why a few of his church members needed to come, too.

It's because of the ladder. And a deep hole.

* * *

For months, Frank and members of New Creation visit the night shelter on Asheboro Street to talk to strangers who see a patch of woods or a bridge underpass as their only homes. Frank and his church members feed them breakfast every other month and give them a bit of God by reading the red-letter scriptures. Frank feels it in his bones that he and his congregation are doing the right thing.

"We're down there with the poor," he tells himself. "This is what Jesus wants us to do."

Some of those they meet at the night shelter come to worship with them on Sunday afternoons around the circle of chairs in the fellowship hall at Presbyterian Church of the Covenant. Frank can see it all coming together, the disparate faces of Greensboro gathering under one roof near UNC-Greensboro to worship, eat, sing, and fellowship.

"We are doing it!" Frank tells himself. "We are getting it right!"

Not so fast. One of his church members convinced him of that.

"Frank," she says a few days after one of their sessions at the night shelter. "I don't feel like I'm connecting with who we meet at all. I don't know who they are. I don't know their stories. I feel like I just feed them and tell them what I hope they want to hear."

At first, Frank is hurt. "Man," he tells himself. "She's raining on my parade." But the more he thinks about it, the more he realizes she's right. One Sunday afternoon, as they sit in a circle of folding chairs, Frank infuses his sermon with his new take on his church's pilgrimages downtown. As he always does, he pulls out a story to drive his point home.

"It's like we walked up to this deep hole in the ground and put a ladder down to reach all these people we have breakfast with. We worship with them down in that deep hole. We eat with them in that deep hole. Then, we climb back up that ladder, bring the ladder with us and shout, 'Hey, see you all in a couple of months!' Do you all see the problem with that?"

He looks around the circle. He sees a few faces blank of emotion. Some of the members, though, begin to nod.

"Like some of you, I didn't at first. But one of our fellow church members did. She opened my eyes, and I am thankful for that. She told me, 'I don't feel like I'm connecting with who we meet at all. I don't know who they are. I don't know their stories.' And when she told me that, I realized I had it all wrong. I didn't look at the people we met at the night shelter as people who could give something to us. It was us giving something to them.

"The point is what we were doing was just one-way, not two-way. We were bringing food and worship, and they were receiving. But that's it. We need to have peer relationships with the people we meet at the night shelter. We need to know who they are and where they come from. That is the one way we can really create community. I've said it so often 'Community is not microwavable.' So, we need to do more, be more and understand more."

He looks around the circle and sees people listening. More nod their heads. Most of all, they're listening.

"Amen?" Frank asks.

"Amen!" a few of his church members exclaim.

When Gary and Chess Campbell come to New Creation in the fall of 1992, Frank sees it as the perfect opportunity for him and his congregation to get the immersion they need. Their trip to Nicaragua will help them understand why the last need to be first. It's a mission trip, yes. But not to build homes. It's to build relationships. It's a chance for him and his congregation to learn the importance of valuing people for who they are, not for what they represent. For the first time in his life, Frank sees Central America as a theological classroom. But he needs someone in the church to help him spearhead the effort. Right away, he knows who.

A kind-faced farmer's daughter.

* * *

Barbara Clawson, who taught Sunday School at New Creation, was one of Frank's first members. And she is still with the church.

Barbara Clawson grew up on a 113-acre farm in Iowa. She was raised Presbyterian, went to church every Sunday with her parents, and learned early to care and reach out to those who are less able and more vulnerable. When she was young, she saw people in her town laugh at a man her dad hired. They saw the man as we say today developmentally disabled. But Charles Clawson saw him as a man who had value, and he and his wife, Hazel, taught his oldest child that concept of compassion. Treat others the way you want to be treated. Very New Testament. Barbara embraces that sense of spiritual responsibility. It's that idea that not only do you have to believe in something, but you have to act. And Barbara's idea of taking action takes root in 1957. She leaves her small-town life on her family's Iowa farm and lives with Japanese families for five months as part of a program created by 4-H and the Cooperative Extension Service. Twelve years after World War II, 12 years after our country dropped two atomic bombs on Japan to end the war and killed hundreds of thousands of people, Barbara learns lessons about forgiveness, hope and the need to dream big.

"What am I trying to preserve if I don't do things that are the expression of my Christian faith?" Barbara tells a reporter in 2008. "I believe the church needs to stand up for truth and justice. This is not about me, but about supporting people who are being faithful to God's call."

After Barbara graduates from Iowa State with a home economics education degree, she comes to North Carolina to attend UNC-Greensboro for graduate school. She later becomes a professor. She also begins doing mission work in all kinds of places. When she meets Frank, he comes to her church, Starmount Presbyterian, to talk about nuclear disarmament. She really likes what he says. But what he says really gets her thinking. When she hears Frank is starting a church, Barbara starts thinking even more.

"Here's a man of integrity, and he walks the walk," she tells herself. "That's two of the highest compliments I can give anybody."

Barbara enjoys Starmount, and she has a lot of friends there. But she finds that New Creation tackles issues surrounding poverty and inequity that are part of what she sees as "God's call to all of us." So, she leaves Starmount and joins New Creation. She becomes what Frank calls "one of my first-round draft picks."

When the idea of going to Nicaragua comes up, she helps arrange the trip. As she works out the details, she remembers a question Frank raises in many of his sermons. It's a question that has always been the foundation of her faith. Now, it has become the foundation of New Creation.

"What does it mean to follow Jesus?" Frank always asks.

It means building relationships in a country where bullets replace diplomacy.

* * *

It's July 1993, a month when the temperature reaches nearly 100 degrees by 12 noon. A rebel leader nicknamed Honduran Pete, a former major in the Sandinista Army, wages guerilla warfare with government troops while civilians run for cover and run to survive. In the aftermath of one of those battles, the reporter named Tracy Wilkinson from the Los Angeles Times finds a 16-year-old girl cowering in a hospital driveway. She wants to go inside to check on a friend who is wounded by a grenade. She can't. She can't even get close to the door. She tells Wilkinson, "I tried to go inside, but a man pointed his AK-47 at me."

Five months later, Barbara and Frank and Buck, along with three others from Greensboro, arrive in Managua. They learn firsthand the fallout of America's longstanding support of a patriarchal dictatorship whose leader at one time is reported to have said: "I don't want an educated population; I want oxen." Frank, Barbara, and Buck hear from people who have lost someone they love in a war the U.S. supported. And they hear those stories and see the pain in an open-air church in Managua. It's a church where parishioners sing about going on a pilgrimage to a cornfield.

Let's go to the Lord's cornfield.
Jesus Christ invites us to his harvest of love,
The corn shines in the light of the sun,
Let's go to the cornfield of communion.

Frank and the others spend a week in Nicaragua, escorted at every step by Gary and Chess Campbell. They visit a health clinic, a school, and a daycare program. They see the ruins of a cathedral, destroyed by an earthquake. They swim in the Pacific Ocean and sit around a bonfire on a beach. They see downtown Managua, and they go out into the countryside and spend the night with families whose bathrooms are outhouses, and whose only light comes from kerosene, candles, and the sun. At the end of the week, the Campbells take them to the oldest church in the country, a church that will become a spiritual cousin to New Creation in the years ahead.

St. Paul the Apostle Christian Base Community in Managua traces its roots back to the 1960s. The church split from the Catholic hierarchy because it supported the government and U.S.-backed Contras. St. Paul doesn't have a priest. It has lay people who lead Sunday mass and Bible studies. Their faith centers around liberation theology, a religious movement that aids the poor and the oppressed. St. Paul's philosophy sounds a lot like New Creation. St. Paul believes that God speaks through the poor and that the Bible can be understood only when seen through the perspective of the poor. Frank sees the potential of St. Paul's becoming a sister church to New Creation. Frank envisions that more mission trips can bring members of St. Paul's to Greensboro and members of New Creation back to Nicaragua. So, when Frank arrives at the open-air church on a Sunday, he wants to see if this communal link can work. He believes it can. But when he arrives, he immediately feels uncomfortable. He, Buck, and Barbara, along with the three others from Greensboro, join a worship service that honors one of the church's own. He was a son, a brother, and a church member. He was killed in the Contra War, killed by government troops supported by the United States.

As Frank takes it all in, he works to keep his unsettled nerves at bay. It's difficult because his mind is a storytelling rollercoaster.

"Is this what it would be like if I was a Southerner in Philadelphia attending a memorial service for a Union soldier killed in the Civil War?" he asks himself. "I don't know, but I feel like one. I mean, I feel so complicit in his death. Why would we support the Contras? But then again, why would we go into Vietnam? And why would we have three doors at the Carolina Theatre in my hometown — one for whites, one for Blacks and one for Lumbee Indians? So, we won't mingle?

"It doesn't make sense to me. But what does make sense is what I see here today. That is real."

When the service ends, Buck finds Frank.

"Gosh, that was hard," Buck says.

"I know," responds Frank, his voice barely above a whisper. "But think about what we've found here, Buck. Forgiveness. Real forgiveness. Forgiveness sets us free from harboring any resentment. And that's just impressive, the grace they have shown us. It makes me think of what Peter asked Jesus about forgiveness. Remember that? 'How many times should we forgive?' Peter asked. "Is seven enough?' And Jesus said, 'No, not seven times. But 77 times.'

"Thanks, Frank," Buck says.

Buck looks around and finds himself surrounded by members

of St. Paul's. They're smiling and offering him food. They're showing him hospitality in the wake of pain partly caused by a country he swore an oath to support. He wrestles with that thought, and he thinks back to his conversation with Cathy, of what she perceives and what he has come to believe about his search for … something.

That's when Buck sees him.

It's a little boy three feet away. He's standing with what looks like his dad and his grandmother. He looks no more than 5, maybe 6. Buck walks over to the boy, introduces himself and asks, "May I take your picture?" The father smiles, the grandmother smiles, the boy nods and Buck steps back, crouches and focuses his Nikon F3 on the stern face of a boy a little older than Trey and Cameron, Buck's two children. Buck bought his Nikon F3, his first camera, when he was a young teenager. He bought it with money he earned from his part-time job working for the U.S. Forestry Service in his home county. He maintained trails in the Uwharrie National Forest, nearly 51,000 acres of federal land established in 1961 as a national forest by President John F. Kennedy. Buck cherishes his Nikon F3. And from what he sees through his lens, he believes he'll cherish his photo of the little boy, too.

But there's much from his trip that he'll cherish. All he has to do is remember that night where he needed to pee.

* * *

Buck and Frank spend the night with a husband and wife. The husband and wife can't speak English; Buck and Frank can't speak Spanish. They gather around a rectangular table and eat a meal of rice and beans. They nod at each other a lot. They try to sing together, but that really doesn't work. Then, Frank has an idea. He pulls out his Bible; the husband pulls out his Bible; and the two trade off their favorite verses.

"Oh yes! Yes!" Frank exclaims before picking out the same Bible verse and reading his in English. That is the way they communicate.

The husband pulls out his Bible and points to a verse from the Book of John. He reads: "Porque de tal manera amó Dios al mundo, que dio a su único hijo, para que todo aquel que cree en él no se perezca, sino que tenga vida eterna."

Frank looks at the husband's Bible and smiles. He reads: "For God so loved the world, that he gave his only son, that whoever believes in him should not perish but have eternal life."

They discover what they have in common. Through English and Spanish, they discover where their hearts meet.

Frank and Buck retire to a room with a dirt floor and walls papered with newspaper to keep in the heat. They sleep on cots made of burlap from feed bags, and Frank notices through an opening in the tin roof that he can see the moon and the stars outside.

"God, you're in charge!" Frank tells himself.

After drinking lots of water, Frank figures he'd better relieve himself before he sleeps.

"Buck, you up?" Frank asks.

"Yeah."

"I'm gonna go find the outhouse," Frank says.

He goes to the door and tries the latch. It's locked.

"Hey, Buck," Frank whispers. "How 'bout you try this door. I can't get it open."

Buck tries.

"I can't get the thing open either, Frank," Buck says.

"Well, we can't wake our hosts up," Frank responds. "We just have to figure out how to open this thing."

It takes them both an hour. Finally, they figure out the latch, get the door open and scurry to the outhouse.

"Frank, you go first," Buck whispers.

Frank goes in. Buck doesn't hear a word.

"Frank, you OK?" Buck asks.

"Yeah," Frank says. "And oh man, Buck the view is amazing. Wait until you see it."

Buck laughs.

"OK," he says. "Well, hurry up. I gotta pee, Frank. I'd like to see it, too. Like soon."

* * *

On their last day in Nicaragua, Gary and Chess Campbell take the small crew from Greensboro to the Managua airport. The Campbells say their goodbyes and Frank promises they will see them again. Frank then finds a pay phone and calls Michie collect. Nicaragua is only an hour behind Greensboro's time, and Frank hopes he can get her. He hasn't talked with her all week. The phone rings and rings. Michie picks up.

"Hey," Frank says.

"I am so glad to hear from you!" Michie says. "So how was it?"

"Great!" Frank says.

Michie listens. She's used to Frank's "Dewitus," his overflowing optimism. He tells her about visiting St. Paul's and trading Bible verses with a couple who couldn't speak English and getting locked in a bedroom.

"Only you, Frank," Michie says, laughing.

"Well, at least we didn't run into what another group here had to deal with," Frank says. "It was a church group, and they got stopped by rebel soldiers who held them at gunpoint and stood them up against a wall before letting them go."

"Gunpoint?" Michie asks.

"Yeah, AK-47s, Michie," Frank responds.

"Oh, shit, Frank!" Michie says. "I'm sure not going to tell David and Christie about that. All I've said was 'Your dad is going on a trip to some country named Nicaragua.' So, you don't tell them that. I'm just glad everyone is OK."

When they all take off in a small twin-engine plane, Frank and everyone from New Creation begin trading stories. Barbara shares her conversation she had with a nurse at the healthcare clinic. They both talk about the detrimental effects of the prosperity gospel, this idea that God blesses his followers with wealth, health, and power.

"The thing that disturbs me about that is these are people of deep faith, and they believe that God is punishing them because they aren't wealthy," Barbara says.

Buck chimes in. He shares a story about meeting a young woman who watches "The Hour of Power" on TV, which is broadcast from the Crystal Cathedral in California. From a pulpit in a glass-and-steel church, the Rev. Robert Schuller preaches a positive theology that draws millions of viewers. He encourages his congregation and those tuning in that they can reach their dreams and find riches if they follow Jesus. He tells viewers to tell themselves: "I *am* somebody. I *can* do something. I *will* do something. Only when you do that is when you really bring glory to God." But the young woman Buck met worries her life of poverty shows her that she's being unfaithful.

"She told me, 'How am I not measuring up?' Buck asks. "I didn't know what to tell her."

As their conversation deepens, Frank realizes his small cadre of friends have learned much in their week in Nicaragua. So has he. He and Buck trade Bible verses with a couple he can't understand, and Barbara communicates with a couple she stayed with through sign language. Like Frank and Buck, Barbara discovers a valuable lesson. It's one she still believes today, especially with her relationship she has developed with St. Paul the Apostle Christian Base Community.

"Over the next 30 years of our relationship, my faith has only been strengthened in terms of being more willing to share and see people who have so little experience so much joy in their lives," Barbara says. "People at our sister church laugh and joke and just seem to enjoy life more than most people in the United States, and I think their dependance on God is a part of that.

"And all that has helped me rely on God more and less on myself. That, to me, is the key. In this country, we have so much, and that makes us believe we are in control of things. And in Nicaragua, at our sister church, they have so little. They know they don't have control. But they trust in God at a deeper level, deeper than I did until I had those experiences in Nicaragua."

Barbara gives that take on her faith during an interview in 2023. She is days away from turning 88, and every year, she learns how to be a better steward of what she calls "God's Earth."

Buck feels the same way. All he has to do is walk down his hallway at his house and see a framed black-and-white photo of the stoic-faced boy he met in November 1993.

That trip to Nicaragua changed his life.

It's a Saturday morning, in the first few months of 2023. Buck cradles a cup of coffee and walks down a hallway to the photo on his wall.

"It's one of my favorite pictures," Buck says. "It captures the memory of a seminal moment in my life. Spiritually, professionally, all of those things. We went back to Nicaragua in 2000, back to that church, and I went looking for that little boy. I showed someone the picture I took and asked, 'Do you know him?' And they pointed.

"There he was. Just a few feet away.

"I bet he was 13, I believe. I walked over to him and said, 'Do you remember me taking your picture?' He didn't. He was with his dad and mom. The grandmother in the photo had passed. I told him, 'I took a picture of you seven years ago, and I want to show it to you.' I showed it to him, and he was just amazed. He smiled big. His mom and dad did, too. That was a cool moment."

After he returns from Nicaragua in 1993, Buck comes home with a new outlook on his life. He knows corporate sales is not for him, and he begins asking himself, "What is God calling me to do?" But he has a sense of freedom, and tells himself, "I'm OK. We're going to be OK. I don't have to follow a set path and climb the corporate ladder."

Buck stays with his corporate sales job for another three years. By 1997, he enrolls in Duke's Divinity School. Three years later, he becomes an ordained minister and serves as an associate pastor at Greensboro's Westminster Presbyterian. By 2007, Buck takes another step in his faith. He leaves Westminster and turns a former dairy farm 25 minutes north of Greensboro into a pastoral place for adults with developmental disabilities. He creates it for adults who the world sees as broken. Those are adults with special needs. He and his friend, Susan Elliott, along with an ocean of volunteers turn 89 acres into a place where people with special needs can feel accepted, loved, and valued. They live there. They also grow their own food, make money, and deliver what extra they have to food pantries nearby.

He and Susan call it Peacehaven Community Farm, and they create it for people like their children. Buck and Susan were parents of children with special needs. Buck's son, Trey, has autism. He was diagnosed when he was 2. Buck becomes Peacehaven's executive director, one of the farm's two full-time employees. He knows a place like Peacehaven can help Trey — and others like Trey — grow.

And Peacehaven does grow. With the help of Habitat for Humanity, volunteers build a 5,000-square-foot house where adults with disabilities can live. Buck calls the house Susan's View. But Susan never sees it. In 2010, she succumbs to breast cancer. She was 44. In a shaded grove of oak and cedar, Buck builds a private columbarium for Susan. It's a low stone wall 65 feet long. It contains shells, flowers, and Susan's ashes. Buck visits Susan's columbarium every week. Ask Buck why, and he has an answer: "It's just a place to be."

In 2021, Buck steps away from Peacehaven and joins First Baptist Church, one of the largest churches in Greensboro. He becomes the church's associate pastor for missions and community.

On a Saturday morning in 2023, when he sits on his front porch cradling a cup of coffee, Buck talks about his journey from Navy airman and corporate sales rep to a divinity student, an executive director of a nonprofit and a pastor. Buck is now 63, and he has followed a life guided by his faith for more than 20 years. It's all because of his first trip to Nicaragua.

"After that trip, my faith wasn't about me and my relationship with God. It was about this context of community. It was a call for me to get outside of a circle of people. I needed to be with the poor, folks with disabilities, not with folks like me.

"When I was in the Navy, I would be with a bunch of aviators late at night, and we would toast, 'To us! And those like us!' I've realized that I can't be like that. I have to be with others not like me. I look for what they can teach me about God's presence in their lives because the way they live is so much more authentic."

Buck and Cathy Cochran with their children, Cameron and Trey. Photo credit: Courtesy of Buck. Cochran.

Cameron, their oldest, is in her 30s and works as an assistant director of a nonprofit in Wilson, North Carolina. Trey is their youngest, a college graduate in his 30s with a degree in sustainable agriculture. He is now a farmer — or as Buck likes to say an "amazing farmer" — in Millers Creek, North Carolina, a tiny community 90 minutes west of Greensboro at the doorstep of the Blue Ridge Mountains. As for Cathy, the girl Buck escorted at their high school's homecoming, she is now the chief nursing information officer at Cone Health, Greensboro's healthcare system. Buck says he's happy.

"I really am. I am happy, and I am grateful. I've lived a life no one deserves. It's because of the people in life. I've had an opportunity to serve. That's what gives me life."

Frank understands that. Like Buck, he looks for opportunities to serve. And like Buck, the year after he comes back from Nicaragua, Frank's life changes, too. He also gains a nickname.

Rabbi. And for good reason.

Frank moves from preaching to the poor to being with the poor. And like Buck, he has new eyes. He sees his life through an entirely different lens.

Frank on Frank

Finding New Vision

There is so much in our everyday life that we fail to see.

It's because of familiarity. We think we already know stuff, and we see what we expect to see and ignore what else surrounds us. That's why we need new eyes. That helps us gain a new perspective on our lives. When we do, we realize what we didn't see was there all along.

That's why I felt New Creation's trip to Nicaragua in 1993 was so important. There was a depth of need, along with the opportunity to experience a different perspective beyond Greensboro and really beyond North Carolina. I mean, think about the farmer we met in the middle of the cornfield. That was an epiphany for me. He couldn't speak English, but he had a PhD in life. It was like being at Duke, in Divinity School. His research and knowledge were as clear as lines etched on his face. And that one experience changed the way I thought about working with the homeless in Greensboro.

When we first went to the night shelter on Asheboro Street, we went there thinking we have so much to give them. In reality, they have so much to give us. But to understand what we *can* receive, we had to spend time with them and get to know one another on a deeper level. That, I believe, is where connections really form. That's where community forms. And that definitely happened after our first trip to Nicaragua.

We went four more times when I was a pastor. We also went to Mexico and South Africa. All those mission trips were meant to build relationships, to help all of us at New Creation see the world around us with new eyes. All those places gave us a different perspective on our own circumstances, and we got to see things here in Greensboro that have been here all along.

It was like the scales were lifted from our eyes.

Now, the need beyond Greensboro is more dire. We don't have to deal with war like in Nicaragua or see the depth of poverty as we found in other parts of the world. But those mission trips really helped our folks to see that our connection with the homeless population in Greensboro was an opportunity, not a burden.

The same goes for our partnership with Saint Pablo (Saint Paul the Apostle Christian Base Community), our sister church in Nicaragua. It was not only that we went down there. They began to come here. We developed a peer-to-peer relationship with them, and it's still going strong after more than 30 years. When our relationship first began, we indicated that we had things to share with them. But as our relationship grew, they also had things to share with us. I'll always remember the letters we received from them. Those letters were just so faith-driven and so real. It was like receiving a letter from Paul.

The letters dealt with significant things through a theological lens. They talked about the struggle for decent living conditions and the struggle to be faithful to the gospel. And they talked about the struggles we had the opportunity to see. It gave us a sense that the body of Christ is much larger than we thought. The body is not just our denomination and people like us. The body of Christ is with people not like us, people in the Yucatan, in South Africa, in Nicaragua, just everywhere.

It all reminds me of the elephant analogy. You remember that. None of us ever can see the whole elephant. But the point is when we have other people seeing different sides of an elephant, we all can see more. That comprehensive vision helps us understand more. It helps us create community. We trust one another, rely on one another, and see what Jesus calls us? to do. That's to follow two of the greatest commandments: Love the Lord, your God, with all your heart; and love your neighbor just like you love yourself. When you see your life that way, you see right quick that the body of Christ is much larger than we thought.

In First Corinthians, Chapter 12, Paul gives us the image of the church like a body, and every member is a part of that body, like a hand or a foot. He emphasizes that every member is necessary and important. But Paul goes on to say that the least presentable parts of our body are to be guarded with the most care. What he means by that is the people in a church — or even in a community who are thought to be the least significant — are the very ones who must be lifted up. It's that whole idea that the last will be the first.

When we work to create these sorts of connections, whether it be here in Greensboro or in Nicaragua, it requires time and energy. Yes, it can be exhausting because it can be emotional and physical. And sure, it can be really uncomfortable. But think what we can gain. We create community, we see our world with new eyes. That is how we grow, right? We learn to trust God.

I think back to what happened when Buck Cochran and I met that couple in the countryside of Nicaragua. We couldn't speak a lick of Spanish, and they sure couldn't speak a lick of English. We tried to sing. Boy, that didn't work out all that well. But when we pulled out our Bibles, we connected. We connected through what we knew about scripture. What a wonderful discovery that was. Were Buck and I in control? Don't think so. But look at what we discovered. All four of us.

When I think back to that trip, I laugh about getting locked in the bedroom. That wasn't so wonderful. But what was wonderful is what happened after coming back from that trip. Like Buck, I saw my life in a whole different light. It helped me see what God was calling me to do. It's what the 12-Step folks like to say, "I think I'll let God be in control."

I was reminded of that when Buck and I spent the night in the Nicaraguan countryside. We slept on a cot made out of burlap feed bags in a bedroom where the walls were covered with newspaper for insulation. During the night, I looked up, and through an angle in the tin roof, I could see the moon. That's right. The moon. It was beautiful. As I lay there, I said to myself, 'God, I have no idea where I am at this moment, but I know You know where I am!'

We all can find opportunities to trust in God more fully in our everyday lives. When we do, we see ourselves in a new way. We see others in a new way, too. And like the couple Buck and I met in Nicaragua, we realize how much we can share with one another. We may not speak the same language. But we speak from the same heart, and with new eyes, we realize each of us are one, connected to one another by the body of Jesus Christ. We then care for one? another, have compassion for one another, and see the people around us not as The Other, but as our neighbor. We see them as one of our own.

Buck recently loaned me 'Between the Listening and the Telling: How Stories Can Save Us.' It's from Mark Yaconelli, the founder and executive director of The Hearth Community, a nonprofit that helps cities and charitable agencies in producing personal storytelling projects. Buck didn't say anything other than, 'got a book for you to read." After the first few pages, I understood right away the why behind Buck's request. It, indeed, is a wonderful book. But what I found on page 101 reminds me of why we all need new eyes, new eyes to help us see and understand. Yaconelli writes:

"There is a reason we do not take the time to listen to those who are suffering. To listen to the stories of the vulnerable is to become vulnerable. To hear the stories of the helpless is to be reminded of our own human frailty. To listen openly to those in need is to feel responsible for their well-being. To hear the truth of another person's struggle is to make us open to pain. The only way to keep ourselves protected, safe from empathizing with another person, is by refusing to hear their story. Otherwise, we may be tempted to care, tempted to respond, tempted to change, tempted to remember. They are just like me."

They are just like me. That resonates, doesn't it?

Urban Ministry gains a minister

● The Rev. Frank Dew will become Greensboro Urban Ministry's first chaplain.

BY ANDREW BARRON
Staff Writer

The Rev. Frank Dew has supported Greensboro Urban Ministry ever since he came to Greensboro 15 years ago.

He's served on the organization's board of directors, he's worked on fund-raising efforts and he's given both his time and his money.

On Nov. 1, Dew joined the ministry's staff, becoming Greensboro Urban Ministry's first chaplain.

"Greensboro Urban Ministry has programs to provide food, medical help and shelter, yet there hasn't been an intentional spiritual component," Dew said. "We want to keep the 'ministry' in Greensboro Urban Ministry."

Dew will work as a chaplain 20 hours a week, a position funded by an anonymous donation of $30,000.

His main responsibility will be recruiting and training ministers and laity to become volunteer chaplains.

Each volunteer chaplain will pledge to work at least six hours a month, allowing Greensboro Urban Ministry to have a chaplain on duty at all times.

These chaplains will be available for clients, volunteers and staff members at the ministry.

"One person would never be able to do all that's needed," Dew said. Dew said volunteer chaplains will need about 10 hours of training in listening skills, community resources, prayer counseling, theology of being with the poor, addictive-dependent behavior and Greensboro Urban Ministry policies. He hopes to start training volunteers in January.

"I'm anxious to have a variety of people from different faiths and racial groups," Dew said. "The breadth of support of this ministry needs to be represented so we reach out to people here."

The Rev. Mike Aiken, the ministry's executive director, said the chaplains' work will be similar to the role played by hospital chaplains.

Dew, 43, has been the assistant pastor at Greensboro's Presbyterian Church of the Covenant for the last nine years. Before that, he spent six years as pastor at Vandalia Presbyterian Church.

While at Church of the Covenant, Dew spent half his working hours starting New Creation Community Presbyterian Church. This small congregation has about 40 members, meets at Church of the Covenant and combines informal worship with an emphasis on community service.

Dew will continue to work with New Creation since the chaplain's job at Greensboro Urban Ministry is only half-time.

Dew hopes having chaplains walking the halls will help bring people closer together as people of different denominations talk about their faith and reach out to people of varying socioeconomic backgrounds.

"I think that folks will begin to see that people are individuals with particular needs and concerns, and that we share many of the same needs and concerns," Dew said. "I hope we develop a sense of a common bond rather than alienation that we don't look on others as 'those people.'"

The Rev. Frank Dew teaches a lesson as children gather around in a circle during a weekly church service at Greensboro Urban Ministry.

Scott Hoffmann/News & Record

Chapter 11
An Oasis of Hope and Transformation

*"Greensboro Urban Ministry gave me a deeper insight of what it means to bring Good News to the poor, and the poor — the people the world said, 'What do **they** really have to be grateful for?" — brought the Good News to me. They enabled me to see the world from their perspective, and it enriched our relationship in so many ways. That's why I stayed at the Greensboro Urban Ministry for 22 years. I met so many people, so many "PhDs in Life."""*

The Rev. Frank Dew

Frank looks at his watch, and he knows it is time. He walks through a maze of rooms — into the kitchen, through the dining hall, through the food pantry and into the parking lot behind the building. He pops into offices and then makes a beeline to the sidewalk and the parking lot outside where he knows he will run into more than a few he knows by face and first names. Everywhere he stops, he says the same thing.

"We're getting ready to have worship in a few minutes. Come on in!"

He checks his watch again. It's 12:30. It's time. He walks back toward the room where he spends 30 minutes every Tuesday and Thursday singing, talking, reading scripture, and asking others for their names, their stories, or their takes on what they heard. Then, they circle up, and like his parishioners at New Creation, they join hands and pray.

When he rounds the corner, he sees a man standing by the door.

With his head down and his hands clasped in front of him, he looks to be in his mid-40s. He's buried inside an igloo of a big coat, and he's wearing at least three layers. Frank recognizes the look. Like many he has preached to and talked to, Frank knows this man has no zip code. His home is a tent in the woods or a hard-dirt spot under a downtown bridge.

"Come on in!" Frank says.

"Pastor, I'm not ready for worship," he tells Frank.

"You don't have to be dressed up," Frank responds, opening his arms, palms up. "Come on in! Everyone is welcome."

"No, Pastor," he says. "I'm not ready to change."

Frank nods.

"You know, part of change begins with being honest with yourself," Frank says. "You, my friend, have already taken that first step. I want you to know that you are welcome here any time."

Since becoming chaplain at Greensboro Urban Ministry in 1994, Frank has come to see what his friend, Barbara Clawson, talked about during their trip to Nicaragua in 1993. The definition of someone who is poor, she told him, is someone who has very few options in life. Frank sees that everywhere he looks at Greensboro Urban Ministry. The nonprofit off East Lee Street in Greensboro is what Frank liked to call "the Motel 6 in the desert." And the desert is the streets of Greensboro, where hospitality is a life-or-death matter for those who have no home. The world where they exist can become as cold as a freezer or as hot as a griddle, and if they can't find someone to take them in for the night and offer them food, they die. That is why Greensboro Urban Ministry becomes important to the people who often are invisible in Greensboro and every other city in America. GUM, the well-known acronym for this well-known spot, becomes the place of hospitality, the Motel 6 in the desert of despair. It also becomes the place for Frank. GUM defines his ministry and his identity with the influential and the powerful as well as the powerless and those who feel forgotten and invisible. But they aren't forgotten and invisible to Frank. He makes sure of it.

Frank remains the chaplain at Greensboro Urban Ministry until

2016. Do the math. That's 22 years. He was the guy always in his forever uniform — khakis, light blue shirt, and running shoes. During his time at GUM, his beard goes from salt-and-pepper gray to Ernest Hemingway white. Wherever he went, he'd run into those who felt invisible and forgotten. He'd recognize them, he knew their first names and their stories, and they'd talk. Or hug. Or both. But mainly, Frank listened. He'd also run into the powerful and the influential, those cozy in life, and he knew their first names as well. They too would talk. And often, their conversations would conclude this way:

"I am so glad you're working at GUM and bringing Jesus to the people down there."

Frank, always gracious, would respond in a very Frank way. He'd smile, maybe even chuckle and respond in his relaxed accent, burnished smooth from his life in the South.

"Well, I have to say, Jesus was there before I got there."

* * *

GUM started in 1967 in the basement of Grace United Methodist Church in Greensboro. It now occupies a single-story building near the corner one minister once described as the "Corner of Concern." GUM sits near the corner of Eugene Street and what is now Gate City Boulevard. More than 200 congregations citywide support GUM through donations and volunteers, and because it receives only 3 percent of its funds from the federal government, GUM relies on the giving community of Greensboro. More than 5,000 people donate to GUM, and at least 1,700 people volunteer. They help with everything from manning the front desk to helping dole out the meals in the Potter's House. They mentor, tutor, bag groceries and provide spiritual care for the working poor and those who have no homes. These volunteers take to heart these two verses from the Book of Proverbs, Chapter 31:

"Speak up for those who cannot speak for themselves; defend the rights of all those who have nothing. Speak up and judge fairly, and defend the rights of the poor and needy."

GUM is the city's oasis of hope, healing, and transformation for many who feel hopeless. GUM feeds them, provides them a bed, food from the pantry, bus passes and emergency funds to pay the rent or cover a bill. As of 2021, 17.4 percent of the city's population — or nearly 49,000 people in Greensboro — live in poverty. At GUM, those numbers become people with stories of addiction, violence, loss, or bad luck. So, they come to Gate City Boulevard near the "Corner of Concern." It's a load of folks. Every day, GUM feeds as many as 300 homeless men, women, and children in the Potter's House Community Kitchen and packs at the food pantry hundreds of bags of groceries for more than 100 households citywide. Every night, GUM provides a bed to as many as 100 men and women in its shelter, the Weaver House. Sixteen homeless families find shelter at GUM's Pathways Center, and 15 minutes away, in a working-class stretch in north Greensboro, GUM's Partnership Village provides 68 apartments to help formerly homeless men, women and families transition to permanent housing and get their lives back on track. At Partnership Village, in its community center, is a big quilt made by the volunteers and kids there. On that quilt are 13 words: "Love is what we are born with. Fear is what we have learned."

That was Frank's world. That *is* Frank's world.

It has become so much a part of who he is. But here's the thing: Frank didn't think he'd ever end up at GUM. Matter of fact, he told Michie as much. He thought he'd go one way with his ministry and end up in a wood-paneled office with a membership at the local racquet club. But God had other plans.

Frank will tell you that.

* * *

The year: 1983, or as Frank says BC, Before Children. Frank and Michie were driving through downtown Greensboro, getting used to the city they moved to four years before. At the time, Frank was the pastor at Vandalia Presbyterian, and on their way to somewhere, they drove past the old location of GUM, which today would sit just inside the fence of First National Bank Field in center field.

"They do great work," Frank says to Michie. "But I would never want to work there."

Frank's viewpoint changed when he visited the Church of the Saviour in Washington, DC. He used the Church of the Saviour as a blueprint to start his own church in his new hometown. See, Frank never thought he'd start a church from scratch. He even told himself that. But he did, and he started it in his own living room in Greensboro's Lindley Park neighborhood before moving into space at Presbyterian Church of the Covenant in 1985. And he sure didn't think he'd drive up to DC to protest in front of an embassy. But he did, and he took a few members of his own church, New Creation Community Presbyterian Church, with him. They stood in front of the South African Embassy to protest apartheid. Frank's faith expanded from the pulpit to the street, and his ministry became what he called a "ministry of presence," of moving from the sidelines into the playing field to fight for change with Jesus as your coach. You sense that in the words he used to describe New Creation for the "Church of the Week" feature in the News & Record, the daily newspaper in Greensboro.

Frank wrote:

"One of the things that is often missing in the life of the church is a place for hands-on service. Development of ourselves as mature Christians requires the opportunity for this kind of involvement in the lives of our neighbors. All too often, we let our money become a substitute for personal contact with the needs of others and fail to utilize service as a spiritual discipline for our growth in faith.

"We facilitate the experience of service through mission groups. Someone within the congregation sounds the call for the work or service which they perceive to be needed, and a mission group, composed of others in the congregation who also perceive the need and feel a call to serve, forms around that concern.

"As members of the Body of Christ, we seek to be transformed into the new creation God intends us to be as we grow into faithfulness to the way of Jesus. The more we venture out in faith, the more we do things that require faith, the more our faith will grow. Our life together is focused around our worship, study, fellowship and witness. As we do these things together, we seek to grow into a community through the work of the Holy Spirit."

So, as his church community grew, so did Frank. His mission trip to Nicaragua in 1993 changed him. So did an essay in the Christian Century magazine. A Presbyterian campus minister at the University of Michigan wrote about how we as Christians have separated our beliefs from our practice.

"We as Christians," he wrote, "believe in Jesus Christ, but we're not big on following Jesus."

It reminded Frank of what he came to really understand in Nicaragua, that the poor will always be around us. That's what led him to GUM — and an old college friend.

* * *

Frank joined the board of directors of GUM and worked beside Mike Aiken, his college friend from Wake Forest. Mike was GUM's executive director, and he and Frank had known each other since working in student government.

Like Frank, Mike was a North Carolina native. He was raised in Greenville, the only child of a homemaker mother and a father who worked as director of sports publicity at East Carolina University. Mike graduated from Wake Forest with a biology degree. But like Frank, Mike followed his faith rather than starting a career in science. And like Frank, Mike earned his divinity degree at Duke. That's where Frank and Mike became close. In Greensboro, they played tennis and went to Wake Forest football games together. And when Frank joined GUM's board of directors, they worked together helping the people of Greensboro who felt invisible and forgotten.

As a board member, Frank sees firsthand the importance of what GUM did. He also sees what it was lacking — a chaplain. Hospitals have a chaplain, the military has a chaplain, Congress has a chaplain. Why not have a chaplain at GUM?

Frank sees it as a way to complement his work at New Creation, and he can help provide spiritual support to the staff, the volunteers and residents of GUM, the people Frank calls "guests." He also sees the chaplaincy program as an opportunity to bring in divinity students to work as interns so they can see firsthand what ministry needs to be.

Mike likes the idea of starting a chaplaincy program. But to make it a reality, Mike knows he needs to find the funds to make it happen. So, he talks to Joe Mullin, a retired minister. Joe likes the idea, too. He also has a friend who possibly could help make it happen. That's Margaret Brooks, a member of Greensboro's First Presbyterian Church who lived at Wellspring, a well-heeled retirement community in Greensboro. One day, the three of them visit Margaret. Joe leads the conversation, and Mike and Frank chime in with how it all will work. Margaret listens and says yes. She agrees to offer $30,000 to fund the position. She doesn't want any fanfare. She wants to remain anonymous. But she sees her contribution as a way to help others help themselves on their own walk of faith.

As he and Mike drive home, Frank can barely contain his excitement.

"Mike, I have never been in a meeting with someone who has committed to give that much money to anything," Frank says.

"That was something." Mike says. "You could really see her enthusiasm."

"And her passion," Frank responds. "That was such a new experience for me. Not that it doesn't happen from time to time. But just to be there and hear what she had to say. I was so impressed with her generosity. You could sense that she felt it was a blessing for her to have a hand in making something like this possible. And her willingness to help? That's a huge confirmation for us, Mike. This is the right thing."

When Mike drops off Frank at his house in Greensboro's Sunset Hills neighborhood, Frank bounds through the screen door in the back and looks for Michie. He finds her on the couch, her favorite spot in the den.

"Well, you won't believe it, Michie, but Mike and I went to visit Margaret Brooks with Joe Mullin, and she was glad to give us what we needed to get the chaplaincy program started."

"That's just great, Frank," Michie says. "Congratulations. How do you feel?"

"Well, you know I did feel I was dangling out there a little bit," Frank responds. "I didn't know where my other foot was going to land. Now, I do."

Frank starts the chaplaincy job on the first Tuesday in November 1994. He sees it as an opportunity to bring good news to the poor. But in the process, the poor bring good news to him. Frank starts hearing scriptures differently. He starts to process his ministry differently. As a part-time chaplain at GUM and a full-time minister at New Creation, his professional life is some kind of hectic. He and Michie had adopted David and Christie, a brother and sister from Kansas, and Michie is an in-demand psychologist, a woman with a doctorate from UNC-Chapel Hill and an entrepreneur who is running her own business. So, Frank has less time to pull out his legal pad and sketch out the bullet points of a sermon in the quiet of an office. His life is far from quiet. Yet, while working at GUM, he finds himself surrounded by poignant material he needs for every sermon. It was far from abstract. It is real. He can touch it, see it and sense it in every corner of GUM. For Frank, his spot near the "Corner of Concern" has made one of favorite scriptures from the New Testament come alive in the best of ways.

'Come, you who are blessed by my Father, inherit the kingdom prepared for you from the foundation of the world. For I was hungry and you gave me food, I was thirsty and you gave me drink, I was a stranger and you welcomed me, I was naked and you clothed me, I was sick and you visited me, I was in prison and you came to me.'

Then the righteous will answer him, saying, 'Lord, when did we see you hungry and feed you, or thirsty and give you drink? And when did we see you a stranger and welcome you, or naked and clothe you? And when did we see you sick or in prison and visit you?'

And the King will answer them, 'Truly, I say to you, as you did it to one of the least of these my brothers, you did it to me.'

In those six verses from Chapter 25 in the Book of Matthew,

Frank sees the names and faces from GUM. He hears their stories, and during those worship services on Tuesdays and Thursdays, he asks them questions like, "How many know someone who has been shot? How many know someone who has been in prison?" He sees the hands go up, and he asks them to share. They do. It always reminds Frank of what he first learned at First Presbyterian Church in his hometown of Lumberton, of how Jesus reached out to the poor and the disenfranchised. Now, those lessons from Sunday School become more than just words. They become people Frank embraces. He sees in them what he discovered in a far-away field in Nicaragua. He met not just a farmer. He met a man who had a "PhD in life." He knew he could find "PhDs in life" in Greensboro, too.

Frank was 43 when he becomes GUM's chaplain. In an interview with the News & Record, he talks about his hope of bringing in divinity students and laity to become volunteer chaplains to make sure someone is on duty at all times to help the staff, volunteers and the guests. Frank tells Andrew Barron, the religion reporter for the News & Record: "I think that folks will begin to see that people are individuals with particular needs and concerns, and that we share many of the same needs and concerns. I hope we develop a sense of common bond rather than alienation, that we don't look at others as 'those people.'"

Those people. Frank hates that phrase.

Several years after starting at GUM, Frank begins training volunteers to be caregivers for the guests. The Stephen Ministries is an international program that trains lay people to be spiritual caregivers. Faye Ellison, who founded the food bank at GUM, mentions it to Frank.

Frank loves the idea and drives to Baltimore to take part in Stephen Ministries training with the Rev. Cindy Higgins, a good friend to him and Michie. And there, in a city where Edgar Allan Poe called home, Frank sees his future with the help of a Cleveland Indians fan. Today, he doesn't remember her name. He just remembers what she did.

Mike Sasser stands with Isaiah Mickens and Sentellis Cooper at the Thursday mentoring group at Guilford Park Presbyterian Church. "I get so much from being with these young men," Sasser says. Photo credit: Courtesy of Mike Sasser.

She's a nun, and when Frank meets her, she's wearing a Cleveland Indians jacket. Like he always does, Frank initiates a conversation and hears her story: Every homestand, she goes to the games with the people from the retirement community where she works. And every time they go, she brings a slew of chocolate chip cookies she bakes for the players. She brings the cookies to the dugout, the players gush, and she asks them to give the people with her an autographed baseball or an autographed something. For Frank, that is a spiritual epiphany of what he hopes Stephens Ministry will be for GUM.

"It won't be something as cool as that, giving chocolate chip cookies to baseball players," Frank says to himself. "But this is what it's all about. Here is this person of faith. She's interested in baseball and baking chocolate chip cookies, and that's my notice of what our Stephens Ministry can become — except without the cookies. Be a person of faith who can be as accessible as our nun."

When Frank returns from Baltimore, he begins training Stephen Ministers at GUM and Grace Community Church in Greensboro. Grace, which sits a few blocks west of GUM, has converted a cavernous old school into its church, and it has the space Frank needs. A Stephen Minister has to complete a 90-hour training program. Yet, despite that rigorous training schedule, Frank is effusive about the possibilities. If he can pull together a fleet of Stephen Ministers, GUM will become the first homeless shelter in the country with such a program. But will the people come? Frank doesn't know. He just knows what he feels deep in his bones about Greensboro. He sees it as a gracious city, a giving city, and when he starts talking to various churches about the program, the people come. They come from all over the city. They hear Frank speak or they hear about Frank speaking. Frank ends up training 75 people. One of those people is Mike Sasser.

* * *

Mike doesn't think he wants to be a Stephen Minister. At least not at first.

He hears about it when Frank visits his church, Guilford Park

Presbyterian, and tells the parishioners about the program.

Mike believes it's a good idea, but he tells himself, "Oh, that's not for me." He doesn't think he has the personality or the skills to help those in need, those who are so different from him.

He has worked his whole adult life at the Greensboro headquarters of VF Corp., a global apparel and footwear company, and he knows nothing about homelessness other than it's a complicated, emotional issue that had him asking himself, "How can I help?"

He tells his wife, Barbara, as much. Finally, he decides to check out a get-to-know session in September 1996. He drives over to GUM, sits in a conference room in a circle with 25 other people, and listens to Frank talk. Frank begins with what has become his style — talking about faith in a colloquial, easy-going way relatable to anyone, particularly North Carolinians. Sometimes, he talks about Wake Forest. But this particular time, he talks about his favorite sheriff from the fictional town of Mayberry.

"I'm from the Andy Griffith School of Sheriffing," he tells the group. "I want to deputize everybody! Think of it like you're at a pond and you throw a pebble. You see it ripple out, right? But think if you had five, 10, 15 pebbles. Think of the ripples all those pebbles can make. And think about what you can do as a Stephen Minister.

"You're not going to cure homelessness. But you can help a person heal. You have to listen. Just listen. Just be present. Help them see themselves as God sees them. They are valued by God. See, this is a ministry of laying on of the ears.

"What that means is when you're talking one-on-one with someone experiencing homelessness, you're not going to have all the answers. But what we can do is listen, care for that person and let them share their story. So, they don't feel worthless. So they feel worthy. Can I get an 'Amen?'"

Mike is sitting in the front row, and after hearing Frank talk, he knows within minutes. He wants to be a Stephen Minister. He feels God was telling him, "Mike, you can do this." Plus, he trusts Frank. He believes in Frank. As he drives home, he feels energized. Once he gets home, he walks in the door and goes looking for Barbara. What he says stunned her.

"I just signed up to be a Stephen Minister at GUM," he says.

"What?" she asks incredulously. "Do you think that's you?"

"Barbara," Mike responds. "I want to do this."

After finishing his Stephen Minister training, Sasser begins a men's support group on Thursday nights at GUM after the guests finish dinner. He and at least 15 men gather in the chapel, and they talk about finding a job, fighting an addiction, just anything that weighs on their hearts. Sasser encourages them to remain vigilant, to be positive. But mainly, he listens. He ends with a prayer, and everyone sings a verse from "Amazing Grace."

Gerry Waterhouse, a member of Sasser's church, makes a cake for every session. Waterhouse, at the time in her 80s, knows she can't go down to Urban Ministry and help. But she knows she can help Sasser. So, she bakes. She bakes chocolate cakes and lemon cakes and strawberry cakes. All for Mike's support group. And she *can* bake. Her cakes are popular with everyone in that group. But so is Sasser.

He keeps his Thursday night support group going until 2012, the year he retires from VF Corp. after 41 years with the company. He jokes that he can fill First National Bank Field, the minor-league baseball home of the Greensboro Grasshoppers, with all the people he has met on Thursday nights. He just hopes he has helped them in some small way. He got his answer at Four Seasons Mall in Greensboro.

Mike and Barbara were window shopping outside a store when a guy in his 30s, as big as a defensive tackle, comes up behind him and bear-hugs him. Barbara reaches for her pocketbook and is ready to clock the guy. But Mike looks and knows who it is right away. He doesn't remember his name. But he remembers his story from the Thursday night support group —abused as a kid, moved in with his grandmother for his own safety and has to leave her when she came in holding a gun and told him to get out. Mike listened to him for no more than an hour.

"Mr. Mike," the man says standing in the concourse of Four

Seasons Mall. "I miss you buddy."

Mike still volunteers at GUM. Ask him why, and he talks about his childhood in Sanford. Then, he mentions his grandfathers.

* * *

Wilbur Campbell, his maternal grandfather, was a farmer. He'd stick a young Mike Sasser in his red Ford pickup, put meat and vegetables from the Campbell's farm in a cardboard box, and together, he and Mike would go visit local families in need and give them food. Pete Sasser, his paternal grandfather, would take the two of them on a city bus and head to a department store in downtown Sanford. During their trip, Mike's grandfather would point to the signs on the bus and the signs over the water fountains. On the bus, Blacks had to sit in the back. At the department store, whites drank from one water fountain; Blacks drank from another.

"Son, see these signs?" Mike's grandfather would say to him. "That is just not right."

The grandson is now a grandfather himself. He and Barbara have five grandchildren. She's Grammy; he's Grampy. His grandchildren live 15 minutes from him and Barbara, and when they come over, they often ask Grammy.

"Where's Grampy?"

"Oh, he's volunteering," Grammy will say.

And more often than not, he's at GUM. Some mornings, he's working the front desk and helping people with shelter or rental assistance or emergency funds to pay a light bill. One morning a few months ago, in the middle of helping those who come in, one of the staff members tells him, "Tony's back, and he asked about you today."

Tony is a man Mike first met around 2006. Tony has a college degree from a school in Michigan. But he has battled mental health issues his whole life. So, he wanders from city to city, and he always lives outside. After Mike gets word Tony is back, Mike looks for him. He finds him in the parking lot in a long-sleeve shirt and a big winter coat with a bag over his shoulder. He has been sleeping under a trailer in the Salvation Army parking lot nearby.

"Tony, have you ever gotten any help?" Mike asks.

"No," he replies. "I don't want to do it."

"Tony," Mike says. "I am so glad I got to see you today. I am so glad you're still doing OK."

OK may be relative. But to Mike, OK is good when it comes to Tony.

Tony is reaching out and talking. That's a start.

* * *

In every divinity student who interned at GUM, Frank recognizes their spiritual eagerness. When he was their age, Frank saw ministry as a way to fix the root causes of the social ills around him. The divinity students he works with feel the same way. They choose divinity school because of how they were raised or what they discovered in college or what they realized halfway through their careers. They feel called, pulled even, by some higher power they can barely explain, and they want to help heal the hurt they see around them.

They come from various schools in North Carolina — Duke, Wake Forest, Shaw University Divinity in Raleigh, Hood Theological Seminary in Salisbury, and Union Presbyterian Seminary in Charlotte. And when they step into GUM, they walk into a real-life classroom where their faith would be tested. What they see and what they hear give resonance to what they study in seminary. The stories they hear move them to act and tug hard at their hearts. And as they intern at GUM, doing everything from leading support groups to painting fingernails, they talk with Frank. He becomes their mentor, their sounding board, their confidante. In his Andy Griffith sort of way, he deputizes all of them. He gives them the latitude they need to go wherever their faith leads them. And as he does, he helps them understand not just the philosophy of GUM, but the philosophy of understanding what they see. And no matter where they are — the Potter's House, the Weaver House, the food pantry, the sidewalk outside or his small, windowless office inside ,— Frank turns his conversation with the divinity students into how their faith will intersect with their responsibilities at GUM every day.

Class in session.

"Here at the Greensboro Urban Ministry, you'll see a very vital, a real day-to-day and hour-to-hour faith in the people that we serve, and you will be taught a lot by them. Now, we are not trying to help them, our guests, believe in God. We are trying to help our guests believe in themselves, to see themselves in the light of God and to claim their worthiness and their value.

"You see, they don't see themselves as beloved, as valuable and as children of God. Rather, they see the values of the world and how the world sees them, they feel worthless. Why? Because they're poor.

"My friend, Barbara Clawson, when we went to Nicaragua on a mission trip, she told me her definition of what poor means. She told me poor means people who have few choices, few options. I've heard it said that the church is the only army that shoots its wounded. Have you heard that? What that means is that congregations fail to care for the most vulnerable. The challenge for us here is to allow our guests to feel comfortable being vulnerable, and to allow each other to be vulnerable. What you're doing is hard work. But it's necessary work. Our job is to help our guests — and our staff, our volunteers and you and me — to see each of us as God sees us.

"And how do we do that? It starts with listening. It starts with being present. It's not the words that we *say*. But it's more about the way we *listen*. That's how we show we *care*. Do you know what I mean? We've all been with someone, and they're not looking at their watch, they are listening to what we say. And how does that make us feel? It makes us feel we are the most important person to them right now.

"That's what we can do here. We provide housing, food, clothing, emergency funds. Just everything. I see those things like bricks. But the spiritual aspect of what we all do here is like the mortar. That holds the bricks together. And each of you can do it in your own way. And that's what's really cool.

"I remember we had a student from Duke Divinity here one summer. Her name was Sarah. She led worship and offered pastoral care to the women and children in our family shelter. But she also got into doing the fingernails of the mothers she met. She gave them a manicure, and Sarah saw it as analogous to what Jesus did before the

Last Supper — washing the feet of his 12 disciples. What Sarah did was powerful because she found a way to connect and have important conversations with people so much different than her.

"So, find your own way to connect like Sarah did. You want someone to say, like one of our guests, 'Gah, why are they paying attention to me like this? Maybe, just maybe, I am not the worthless person I thought. They are seeing something in me I wasn't sure was there.'

"Now, don't go thinking you can solve everyone's problems or fix every situation, we can't. If I thought I could do that, I would've quit after two weeks. There is no way — no WAY — we can do that. So, don't try to be the fixer, the problem solver for the people you work with or the people you see.

"But if we can help people claim a new identity for themselves, think about what that can do. That will help empower them, help them to solve their own problems. In the process, they will believe that there is a power greater than them that can help them deal with the difficulties they're facing each day.

"Can I get an Amen?"

Amen.

Class is over.

* * *

Vicki McCain. Photo credit: Buck Cochran.

McCain can't help but notice the two teenage boys sitting in the back during worship right before Christmas at GUM. She isn't used to seeing a teenage boy, let alone two in the windowless room at GUM. After the 30-minute service, she stops them.

"Excuse me," Vicki says. "May I talk to you?"

"Of course," they say.

They sit down in the back. Vicki began asking them a lot of questions. One of those being, "Do you have any prayer requests?"

"I want you to pray for my family," says one.

"I want you to pray for *us,*" says the other, meaning he and his friend.

One tells Vicki he feels lost, and he's trying to figure out where to go and what to do next. The other boy tells her about his mom. She is struggling with drug addiction and living with a guy, and as a result of a confrontation the teenage boy has with his mom's boyfriend, she kicks him out of the house. Both teenagers are friends, and they both come to Weaver House to find some sort of safety. And when they hear about the worship service right after eating lunch in Potter's House, they both feel drawn to attend. As Vicki listens to their stories, she knows she needed to do something. She and her husband, Frank, are parents of two children, a daughter and a son. Vicki's son is about the same age as the boys she meets, and those boys have no place to spend Christmas.

She remembers what her mom always told her when she was a little girl back in Rocky Mount: "Treat people the way you want to be treated." She had always believed that. So, after talking with the two boys, she seeks out Frank. He always had been her reliable go-to for guidance and advice at GUM. And she realized he always told her exactly what she needed to hear. But can Frank do it this time?

* * *

Vicki first met Frank when she began as GUM's first chaplaincy intern in 2014. She liked him immediately. He is, as she says today, "a cool dude." He was a gracious cheerleader and a keen listener who supported her as a chaplain intern at GUM. And that was quite the new direction in her life. She had no idea until it happened.

She came to GUM as a married mother in her 40s. She was an accomplished accountant who changed careers when she enrolled in Union Presbyterian Seminary in Charlotte.

In 2010, Vicki started driving on Saturdays to Charlotte to study at Union Presbyterian Seminary. She left before daybreak, and she came back sometimes by dinnertime, sometimes after dark. The heaviness she felt for years vanished. What Vickie felt is what she can describe in three words: "I feel free." She felt that enthusiasm she first encountered as a young girl in Rocky Mount growing up in her spiritual home, Ebeneezer Baptist, a red-brick church in Rocky Mount that began in 1916.

Vicki did well in the corporate world. But she felt moved to do more, to show, as she says, "real love with skin on it." She became GUM's first clinical pastoral education chaplain intern, There, she discovers what "real love" looks like.

Vicki sees it when she begins helping Frank with worship service at GUM, and she sees it when she sets up a special ministry program for the women she met at GUM. But when she meets with those two homeless teenage boys with nowhere to go at Christmas, she realizes her vision of "real love" has her struggling with questions she can't answer. So, she seeks out Frank for advice. She remembers what he told her when she arrived: "I am going to help you shape and model what God is calling you to do."

Vicki *knows* she needs help with this.

"They're bright young men who are homeless, Frank," she tells him. "And they're the same age as my son. They need help, and I want to help. Their story, it just about broke my heart."

"I sense this is what God is calling you to do," Frank says.

"It is!" she responds. "It's so sad and not necessary. I want them to have the same opportunities as Mac. I want them to know love and know how it feels to have someone support them. I want them to know what it feels like when they need to call somebody that somebody will be there for them."

"Alright, go ahead," he tells Vicki. "Be careful."

Vicki gets busy. She finds out where the teenagers go to high school. She calls their counselors and helps them get their GEDs. Her family, particularly her son, Mac, gives them clothes and shoes. For Vicki, these two teenagers become her surrogate sons. She watches them grow up and move on. The teenager who was lost ends up in prison. The teenager put out of his house by his drug-addled mom ends up in the Peace Corps. He now lives in Michigan with his family. Vicki still keeps in touch with him. With the journey she had with those two boys, Vickie finds "real love with skin on it." She finds it because of Frank.

"You always remember how he made you feel," Vicki says today of Frank. "He always made every person in that worship service feel that they were the only person God was looking at and caring for. He listened to them when they had issues. He was attentive to them. He was always so open, always so open with everybody.

"Frank could be the only Caucasian man in the room, and he would feel comfortable where he is. That's the humble spirit of God in him. That is a gift. He has been gifted with that. He makes it all alright. When you see Frank, he is going to call your name. He did it to me. He'd say, 'Hey, Vicki! Let me tell you about Vicki!' He knows you. He will tell you something that will lift your spirits. He discerns his message from God, with simple words, not something that goes over anyone's head. I always pray for simple words because of Frank. He made the Word simple. And he told you the truth, the whole truth, whether you liked it or not."

And there was no better place to see that than at GUM on Tuesdays and Thursdays right after lunch. That's when Frank looks at his watch and knows it is time.

* * *

When you walk in, you see it — the Celtic cross, three feet tall, hanging on the wall. In front is a blackboard. To the right is an upright piano. The walls are painted beige; the ceiling tiles are light blue. The folding chairs are arranged in loose rows in a windowless room a little larger than a two-car garage. This is where Frank sees Jesus in the faces of the people he met.

This is Frank's church at GUM.

"Alright, hello everybody. Glad you all could make it. Welcome. Let's go around the room and say our names."

So, it begins. Frank asks everyone their first name. And no matter if eight or a few dozen are in the room, Frank goes slow with every person's introduction. He says their first name a few times so he will remember it. He wants them to feel validated and know they are welcome in this tiny church a dozen steps or so from Potter's House Community Kitchen. He asks them where they're from and what brought them here. And with every introduction, he makes eye contact with each person and says back to them details of their story that resonate with him. And them, too.

"OK, what do we want to sing? Does anybody have a favorite hymn?"

One of the guests participating picks up an old Presbyterian hymnal from a stack nearby. But sometimes, the guests remember a favorite hymn and sing it loud like a favorite song from the radio. And sitting at the piano is Betty Allen. She knows Frank from when he was the associate minister at Presbyterian Church of the Covenant. So, when he becomes the part-time chaplain at GUM, he asks her if she wouldn't mind playing.

Betty says yes.

She plays at the room's upright piano for more than 20 years. What she sees around her is always so new to her.

Betty grew up in Norfolk, Va., the middle of three, the only girl. Her dad loaded ships on the waterfront; her mom taught piano before becoming a homemaker. Betty began playing piano at age 6. She never really stopped. She and her husband, James Henry Allen, moved to Greensboro in 1967. James became the campus minister at UNCG, and he and Betty raised their five children at their home in Greensboro's Sunset Hills neighborhood. She never was exposed to anyone going hungry or escaping beat-downs from an abusive partner or dealing with addictions, mental health problems or some personal issue that crippled their life until she sits at that upright piano in GUM's worship room.

What she sees and hears still sticks with her today.

"It opened my eyes a lot onto what people are going through in the world," Betty says. "I had never faced that. I mean, they came from all areas, all races and all different situations, and what amazed me was that quite a few had mental problems. But Frank was so great in dealing with them. He'd start talking, and he knew exactly what to say to make sure one person didn't take up the whole time talking about themselves.

"And the singing I heard? It was amazing. We had some great voices in there, and they would just bust out. That part was really great. Sometimes, the people who came hadn't had much church. But often, we'd have a group of them, and they'd come in and sing really big. They'd request hymns, those old-fashioned hymns, and Frank would let them choose whatever they wanted to sing, and we'd find it in the hymnal book.

"Then, Frank would always have a short sermon. He would get right to the point of what Christianity meant and most of them who came appreciated that."

Victory is mine
Victory is mine
Victory today is mine
I told Satan
Get thee behind
Victory today is mine
Joy is mine
Life is mine
Love is mine.

That hymn makes the rounds on many Tuesday and Thursday afternoons. Then comes Frank's sermon, and he makes sure it lasts no longer than 10 minutes. But he also makes sure that whatever he says connects with whoever comes. He looks for lessons, and those lessons he wants to deliver to his small congregation revolve around hope and love and the need to feel worthy no matter their situation. Like Jesus' parable about feeding 5,000 people with five loaves and two fish. Frank talks about parables of long ago and puts them in context with the present-day lives of the people sitting in front of him.

"Jesus cares about our needs. He saw the people were hungry. He had compassion for them. So, he recognized that we as human beings have basic needs, like the need to eat. Jesus can feed all of us on a deeper level. We need to help feed each other on a deeper level. We don't live by bread alone. We live by the bread of life. So, in the midst of a situation that seems hopeless, Jesus brought hope. Jesus brings all of us hope. Can I get an Amen?"

"Amen," a few say.

"Thank you all for coming," Frank says. "Now, let's circle up and join hands. I'll begin with a prayer. Then, I invite anyone who feels moved to offer up their prayers."

Everyone joins hands and bows their heads. Frank begins.

Frank sees magic happen in this room, with the help of two men who overcame their own struggles. Those two men become Frank's friends, and they help scores of men overcome their addictions through the allure of good food and a program embodied in nine words.

I can't. God can. I think I'll let God.

Frank loves that theology.

Frank On Frank

Beyond the 'Poor Person Merit Badge'

The prayers I heard in worship service always got me.

We would circle up after my sermon, hold hands. bow our heads, and I'd say the first prayer. Then, I asked if anyone else had another prayer to offer. More often than not, I'd hear one of our guests say, 'Lord, thank you for waking me up this morning.'

When I first heard that prayer, I was surprised. But not anymore. I see it as such an expression of gratitude. It comes from someone who maybe didn't know where they would find food that day or where they would lay their head that night. But right there, at the end of our worship service, they gave thanks for being alive, for that gift of life. That was so powerful to me. It still is to this day. Why? Think about it for a minute.

That perspective of gratitude is coming from someone who the world would say, 'What do *they* have to be grateful for?' It was 180 degrees from what we would normally expect. I mean, you could see someone driving a Porsche and saying, 'Thank you, Jesus!' But you would think you would rarely hear such gratitude from someone who didn't know if they would have a meal that day or a bed that night.

But I heard that all the time at my time at the Greensboro Urban Ministry. It made me appreciate what I discovered. It gave me a deeper insight of what it means to bring Good News to the poor, and the poor — the people the world said, 'What do *they* really have to be grateful for?' — brought the Good News to me. They enabled me to see the world from their perspective, and it enriched our relationship in so many ways. That's why I stayed at the Greensboro Urban

Ministry for 22 years. I met so many people, so many "PhDs in life."

I met my first professor in 1993 on New Creation's mission trip to Nicaragua, and I found him in the middle of a field. He was a poor farmer, and he could speak only Spanish. As his lesson in life was being translated into English, I was scribbling as fast as I could like I was in a divinity class at Duke. That's when I first began to see how people with different life experiences can become our teachers. The farmer I met had a wealth of wisdom. He had a 'PhD in life,' and standing in that field, I realized what I was missing in my own ministry. I realized I wasn't having authentic relationships with people who are poor. When I say authentic, I mean peer to peer, face to face, looking eyeball to eyeball rather than the paternal attitude of reaching down to help someone and not recognizing the way they would be helping me.

I sometimes refer to that as earning the 'Poor Person Merit Badge.'

Let's say you're walking down South Elm. You cross the railroad tracks and head toward Center City Park. On the way, you befriend someone who is poor. You've earned your Poor Person Merit Badge. But after Nicaragua, I knew that wasn't what I wanted to do. But how was I going to do that? That's when I took a spiritual inventory of me.

I was happy with what we all were doing with New Creation. A handful of us flew down to Nicaragua on a mission trip and connected with a congregation that became our sister church. But I felt God wanted me to do more. I wanted to do more. What really got me thinking about all that was this article in the Christian Century magazine I read right before we went to Nicaragua. A Presbyterian minister wrote it, and above his article was this headline: 'Believing in Christ or Following Jesus.' After Nicaragua, I started asking myself, "If I'm following Jesus, why do I have so many friends among the affluent and so few among the poor?" That's when I got the idea of starting the chaplaincy program at the Greensboro Urban Ministry.

Sure, it complemented what we were doing at New Creation. Some of our guests at the Greensboro Urban Ministry came to our church and became members. But what I discovered as the chaplain at the Greensboro Urban Ministry was much more than a place to find new members. I realized I discovered a place that could expand my view of the world.

I had lots to learn, and the people who would teach me are 'the least, the last and the left out.' They, along with our staff, our volunteers and divinity students who interned with us, gave me the gift of sight. It wasn't so much I tapped into this great wisdom. It was more like the scales fell from my eyes. It was more of a revelation or an epiphany. That's a good word. Epiphany. Moments like that opened my eyes. That happened, whether during our worship service or during lunch at Potter's House.

I always made a point to go in and talk to our guests during lunch. I'd sit down, and I'd always start with two go-to questions. I would say something like, 'How's lunch today?' I mean, we all can talk about food, right? That got us talking. The next question got them thinking. At least I hoped so. I'd ask, 'Where you from?' That's when I heard about their journey, their family, and how they came to be here. That was my way to connect or really to listen.

After they told me their story, I told them about our chaplaincy program. I wanted them to know that me or one of our Stephen Ministers or one of our divinity school interns would be there if they wanted to talk about anything. If they asked, I assured them that we weren't there to convince them to believe in God. We were there to help them believe in themselves. If I said anything religious, I assured them that we want them to see themselves as how God sees them, as someone who is valuable, who is worthy, who deserves our kindness, our compassion, and love.

There's a thing I used to tell our Stephen Ministers and our interns from divinity school. I would say to them, 'You can't make a difference if you're not different.' Then, I'd remind them what Jesus said in his Sermon on the Mount to his followers: "You are the salt of the earth; you are the light of the world."

What he was saying by that was being salt, you are distinctive. You add a particular flavor to what's around you. And by being a light, you bring light to the darkness. It's like what Dr. King once said,

'Darkness can't cast out darkness. Only light can.'

And we need to be that light.

I believe we have a partnership with God to make a difference in this world. That requires us to be different to make a difference. Think about it this way: What's the difference between a thermometer and a thermostat? A thermometer reflects the environment around you, and it tells you what the temperature is. But a thermostat changes the environment around you from cold to warm and from hot to cool.

To think of it in Bible terms, go to Romans 12. Paul says, 'Don't conform to this world. Be transformed by the renewal of your mind.' We are not meant to reflect what we see in the world. We are meant to be part of God's charge to make the world as it is *supposed* to be. That's reflected in the Lord's Prayer, something we said at the end of every worship service at the Greensboro Urban Ministry: 'Thy kingdom come, thy will be done on earth as it is in heaven.'

Did I make a difference at the Greensboro Urban Ministry? I tried. But what I do know without a doubt is that the staff, the volunteers, the divinity students, and our guests made a difference in me. My relationships with them gave me a new set of eyes to see the world differently, and I am eternally grateful to them for that. So, today, when people stop me and say, 'I was so glad you were down there bringing Jesus to those people,' I know I can say with confidence: 'You know, as soon as I started, Jesus was already there.'

That's the truth.

Bernard McCoy (left) and Tony Brown (right) ran their "Making A Difference" for 17 years at the Greensboro Urban Ministry. They started in 2003 and ended in March 2020 with the pandemic. Photo credit: Buck Cochran.

Chapter 12
Step by Step by Step

"We always felt God in those meetings. The biggest way I see it was that the spirit in the room was greater than the sum of all those individuals in that chapel. When they sang, the walls would be vibrating with such joy and defiance. They were like saying, 'This addiction is not going to win! I'm surrounded by God!'"
The Rev. Frank Dew

Every Tuesday night, right after 7, Frank knows the traveling kitchen has arrived. He'll be somewhere — up front, near the chapel or back in Weaver House, where all the guests slept — and he'll breathe in the aroma of home-cooked food wafting through almost every square foot of Greensboro Urban Ministry.

Frank can't help but notice. The guests notice, too.

They'll stop whatever they're doing and see two men rolling carts loaded with big pans full of food toward the chapel. The guests who have been at GUM for a few weeks know right away what's up. They have expected them, even called them out by their first names. But the new guests? They have no idea. Their heads are on a swivel, ping-ponging back and forth, watching two men walk past them with pans nearly as big as dresser drawers. Frank will come from wherever he was and soaks in the scene. Frank loves seeing how his friends, Tony Brown and Bernard McCoy, prep the crowd. But it's more than just about the food. They long for this time on Tuesday nights to sing, pray and open up about the addiction demons they're trying to shake.

And they'll eat. They'll eat a lot.

Bernard can flat-out cook. He learned that skill from his mom. He also can spin a tale, and he knows he can have a little fun when the questions come. On this particular night, with a curious crowd moving toward him, he hears one.

"Hey, what you got there, Bernard?"

"Well, let me tell you," says Bernard, stopping the cart and turning around.

"We were on the way here, Tony and me, and Tony hit something. We didn't know what it was, but we knew we hit something. So, we turned around, and there it was. Right there in the middle of the road. It looked like a raccoon. Or maybe it was a 'possum. Oh, I really don't know. It was dark, you know. But that's what gave me the idea."

Bernard looks at all the eyes widening around him. Men and women. Old and young. Black, white, and brown. He likes to tease.

"Well, I chopped it up, and threw it on our hot engine."

"Aw, Bernard, no you didn't," says one man.

"I did!" responds Bernard.

"What did you all hit in the road?" asks another man.

"Like I said," responds Bernard. "A raccoon. A 'possum. Just something."

"A raccoon?" chimes one man.

"Eewww, a 'possum?" chimes another.

"That doesn't make sense!" chimes a third.

"It did to me," responds Bernard, smiling. "Learned that from my mom. She taught me well. So, I threw it on the hot engine, put it in this here pan and smothered it with mushroom gravy. And here we are. We are going to eat good tonight. You wanna join us?"

The curious crowd draws closer.

"Y'all, come on," says Tony(add comma here) coming out of the chapel after placing his pans on a table inside. "We got some good food. And y'all need this as much as we do."

"And you know," says Bernard, looking around the room and catching everyone's eye. "I am a mighty fine cook."

Bernard rolls his cart into the chapel and the curious crowd follows him in. So does Frank. He recognizes many of the faces around him. He's gotten to know a few of them. He's heard their stories and understood their journeys through what they see as darkness. They all want to reach the light. For many, their Tuesday nights with Tony and Bernard are crucial toward finding that light.

"Welcome everyone," Bernard says, facing the crowd sitting in the folding chairs in front of him. "We'll get to some healing tonight. But first, the chaplain here is going to open us with prayer."

Frank steps from the side and faces the group. More men and women start coming in, and with no seats left, they start lining the walls. Frank nods. A good sign, he thinks. They'll all get fed by more than just food.

"May we bow our heads?" Frank says.

With hands clasped, many in the curious crowd look down and closd their eyes. A few of the men wearing hats or ballcaps take them off. Frank looks around the room once again. A good crowd. A big crowd. Time to begin.

"Lord, thank you for waking us up this morning, and thank you for the gift of life. Thank you for the blessing of being together and praying together as we hear about Your word tonight. Give us the strength to do whatever we need to do to live a fuller life. And all of God's children said, 'Amen.'"

"Amen!" a few men shout.

Tony steps forward.

"Alright, everybody, thank you for coming. We call our Tuesday night sessions "Making A Difference,' and we hope we can help you start making a difference in your lives and help you with your own struggle with alcohol or drugs. Bernard and I have both been there. We faced our own demons. And we made it out. You can, too. We all need to look out for one another, and no one in this room is no better — or no worse — than anyone else. Know that. Also know that we want to be there for you in your struggle, and we want you to leave with a smile on your face with a little bit of? that 'audacity of hope' inside you."

"Yo, Tony, when we gonna eat?"

"Oh, we'll eat soon enough," Tony says, laughing. "We'll get to that raccoon or possum or whatever I hit. You just wait. Isn't that right, Bernard?"

"That's right, Tony," Bernard shouts.

"Well, let's get started," Tony says. "Welcome to 'Making A Difference.' First, let's go around the room and introduce yourself. Say your names and something about yourselves. And remember our rule: Don't talk about other people; talk about yourself."

As the merry-go-round of stories begin, Frank listens. He never tires of hearing their stories. They can be from Greensboro, Winston-Salem, Randleman, New York City — just anywhere — and the stories are flush with details of loss and loneliness. There was a time in Frank's life that he didn't think he'd like working with alcoholics and addicts because he thought it would be too depressing, too hopeless. He was way wrong. As GUM's first chaplain, he sees these men and women not as hopeless, but as hopeful. He sees them as heroic, as heroic as any cancer survivor. The guests at GUM battle alcoholism, drug addiction and mental illness, and they fight hard. But the secret of success Frank finds is not in the fight but in the surrender. From that comes not weakness, but strength.

It's that whole idea of embracing one of Frank's favorite phrases that he came across when he was training for a marathon: "If you want to run fast, run by yourself. If you want to run far, run together."

Every Tuesday night, he sees that togetherness among what he likes to describe as "heroes and sheroes." Then, he remembers how he discovered that togetherness. Through running — and his running partner. That partner introduced Frank to Alcoholics Anonymous and its 12-step program, and Frank felt the togetherness created by AA felt like what church *should* be. A community supporting each other, coming together several times a week to help each other get through the rough bumps of life.

That's how "Making A Difference" came together. All with the help of a guy named Bob.

* * *

Bob Foxworth turned into Mark Twain for various presentations he gave in and around Greensboro. He also took his Mark Twain on the road to Moral Monday protests in Raleigh. Photo credit: Jeri Rowe.

Bob Foxworth is Mark Twain.

When he bought a $100 white linen suit from Barry's Menswear on High Point Road, he needed one to sing in his

gospel choir at church. But afterward, he asked himself, "What can I do with a white suit other than sing on Sundays? Well, I can do Mark Twain." That's how it started. He began a deep dive into everything Twain had said and everything that had been written about him, and in 2009, he began performing everywhere as the white-haired writer.

But before he transformed into Twain, before he wielded a cigar like a conductor's baton, before he bought a few more white linen suits for his act, Bob ran every weekday with Frank.

They ran early in the morning. They ran after work. They ran from Frank's house in Greensboro's Sunset Hills neighborhood or from Bob's apartment near Latham Park. For 40 minutes, they ran. They ran in all kinds of weather, including what Bob called "face-hurting cold." For five years. Five days a week. And when they did, Frank and Bob would talk about everything. That's how Frank heard Bob's story.

Bob was a head-strong, rail-thin kid from Raleigh who received a Morehead scholarship to attend UNC-Chapel Hill. Bob was a runner, a big-time runner, and he was good enough to run cross-country and the mile and half-mile for the Tar Heels. But beyond being a talented runner and a sharp teenager smart enough to go to UNC tuition free, Bob was an alcoholic.

Bob had his first beer when he was 12. His dad gave it to him. Bob's brother, who was six years older than him, needed to gain weight, and the family doctor told Bob's dad to have his son drink beer. When Bob's brother drank beer, Bob wanted to drink beer, too. So, he pestered his dad relentlessly. Finally, his dad gave in and gave him some beer in a shot glass.

"You would argue with Jesus Christ!" his dad told him,

"Well, he ain't available. So, I'll argue with you!"

Bob didn't say that. He just thought that. But later, he did say some harsh things to his dad. When he was 16, Bob argued with his dad over something — he doesn't remember what — and his dad popped off a declaration Bob will always remember.

"I'm not your father!"

Bob later found out that his real dad left his mom when he was 3 weeks old. His mom remarried, and her husband adopted Bob. Bob never knew that until his argument with his dad when he was 16. He later found out more about his real dad. They were a lot alike. His real dad was smart. His dad was a lawyer. He also was a morphine addict and an alcoholic. Or in Bob's words, a "drunk."

Bob never knew his dad. But he knew about his dad's addiction. He had it, too.

Bob had his first drink — a gin and tonic — when he was 16. His girlfriend's mom gave it to him. When he was 17, lifting weights at a local gym and trying to fill out his 135-pound frame, he worked as an assistant lifeguard in Virginia Beach. His maternal grandmother lived there, and in the summer of 1956, Bob felt invincible. He was getting stronger, his mile time was getting better, and he had a sweet job folding up chairs, blowing up rafts and getting a tan. One day that summer, he and one of his running buddies spent some money and bought a bottle of bourbon. The next thing Bob knew, he was running through someone's backyard shirtless. And he had to lose his shirt.

He had puked all over it.

Afterward, alcohol became the fuel of Bob's life. At UNC undergrad. At his one semester at UNC's law school. During his two years in the Army. And during his first marriage, when he worked a myriad of sales jobs. He'd come home and start drinking.

"I'd be reading to my older son, Parker, he must've been 7 or 8, and I'd be as drunk as the Lord," Bob says today. "He had never smelled my breath when it didn't have alcohol on it. That's the reason I quit. I didn't want my children to remember me as an old drunk."

Bob quit drinking in 1937. He was 38, selling Safeguard business systems and dealing with a brittle marriage. His alcoholism only made everything worse. Alcohol, Bob found, brought out his dark side. He turned into, as he says, an "asshole."

Nearly five years later, when he and his wife, Nancy, were going through counseling, Bob started going to AA. His counselor recommended it. But Bob really didn't want to go. He always thought AA was for "those people." Not him. Plus, he had quit drinking. Why would he need it? But Bob finally decided to go. He went to two meetings. They were closed. He then went to a third. It was a Monday night in a room at Congregational United Church of Christ in Greensboro. And there, leading the meeting was John Kernodle, the respected Greensboro lawyer and chair of the Guilford County school board. Bob admired John and his public service work. After the meeting, he introduced himself.

"Would you have coffee with me?" Bob asked.

John agreed. Over coffee, Bob told John his story, and he said that he couldn't see any reason why he'd join AA. Why would he get involved with the 12-step program, he asked John. He didn't need a small, round token, a chip in AA language, to mark how long he'd been sober. He already *was* sober.

"See, John, I can't be an alcoholic," Bob said. "If I was, I couldn't have quit drinking."

John paused for a few seconds and asked a question that Bob says pushed his life in a new direction.

"What harm could it be to pick up a chip?"

John convinced Bob to stay. Bob started going to meetings several times a week and told his story. Every time he did, he would mention John Kernodle, the cup of coffee and his first chip.

"I still got that chip," he'd tell the group. "I *am* an alcoholic. But being an alcoholic doesn't just manifest in drinking spirits. It manifests in your personality and your attitude. Being an alcoholic is being self-centered to the extreme. And that question John posed to me over the cup of coffee? That question saved my life.

"A different side of me came out in the wash. I've gotten away from what I call 'alcoholic thinking.' I am no longer staying in trouble with myself. AA helped me do that. I became who I am, and AA helped me get rid of my dark side. We all have a dark side and drinking alcohol encourages the darkness."

After 31 years of marriage, Bob and Nancy divorced. He moved to an apartment off Grayland Street. He found Frank when he joined the Stephen Ministry program at GUM. When Z Holler, Frank's longtime running buddy, had to stop because of his ailing knees, Frank found a new running partner in Bob. He also found AA. He discovered it wasn't for, as he's heard some say, "those people." Strangers. People he didn't know. No, Frank found it was for people he liked and respected. People like Bob and John Kernodle. They sure weren't "those people." As GUM's chaplain, Frank had gotten to know a lot of people who battled what Bob called "the darkness."

But Frank kept asking himself, "What am I going to do about it?"

He didn't know. At least right then.

* * *

One day, Bob asked Frank if he'd like to join him for an AA meeting. Bob was picking up a chip to mark a milestone in his sobriety, and he wanted Frank to be there because of their friendship. Frank said yes.

The meeting took place at Temple Emmanuel, the Jewish synagogue beside First Presbyterian in downtown Greensboro. When Frank walked in, he saw seated in a circle at least 35 people. The circle immediately reminded him of his Sunday afternoons with his congregation at New Creation. But that was as far as the familiar went.

As soon as Frank sat down, everything felt so unfamiliar. Frank had stepped out of what he knew into something he had no idea about. The introductions started, and as the people went around the room introducing themselves and telling their stories, Frank felt lost.

"Gosh, what am I going to say?" Frank told himself.

One by one, people introduced themselves. When the introductions got to Bob, he described himself as a "grateful recovering alcoholic."

"I would not be the person I am today," Bob told the group, "if I hadn't been through what I've been through."

Then, the introduction time came around to Frank. He looked around the room, and it reminded him of the stress he feels sometimes when he preaches in a new church in front of a new congregation where he has no idea how they'll react. But in a pulpit, he knows what he'll say there. But here? In this circle with 35 self-described alcoholics? In a meeting where he feels as comfortable as a new father holding his newborn son?

That experience, he knew, came out alright. But this time?

Then, it hit him. Just like when he's writing one of his sermons, scribbling notes on a legal pad, struggling to find what to say and how to say it. Out of the blue, a phrase or story or a line comes to him. Frank loves when that happens. And on that Wednesday, in a room full of strangers, it happened again.

"Hello, my name is Frank, and I am a recovering sinner."

The circle of 35 people laughed. Frank felt relieved. Then, as he always does, he listened. He heard story after story, and Frank's idea about addiction and AA began to change. He saw how AA's 12-Step program had transformed the people who dealt with their alcoholism one day at a time, sometimes one hour at a time.

In their runs together, Frank had heard how AA had helped Bob relate to other people in much better ways. Its lessons helped Bob understand what he calls the "spirituality in imperfection."

"We all have to rely on a power greater than ourselves," Bob told Frank.

For Frank, that sounded a lot like God.

There's a line some preachers say: "Religion is for people who are afraid of going to hell. Spirituality is for those who have been there." Frank felt that spirituality in that circle of recovering alcoholics. Like Bob, they knew those 12 steps like lyrics to their favorite song.

Frank got to know those 12 steps as well. He saw them as lessons as powerful as any parable in the Bible.

Like Step 1: "We admit we are powerless over alcohol — that our lives had become unmanageable."

And Step 2: "We have come to believe that a Power greater than ourselves could restore us to sanity."

Fast forward to Step 10: "Continue to take personal inventory and when we were wrong promptly admit it."

Then, end with Step 12: "Having had a spiritual awakening as a result of these Steps, we try to carry this message to alcoholics, and to practice those principles in all our affairs."

Yes, Frank thought, this is God at work. Now to find a way to use these 12 Steps at GUM. He already had an idea.

And he knew who to ask.

In 1991, Frank joined a handful of other ministers and like-minded people and created the Servant Leadership School. Headquartered at Greensboro's Holy Trinity Episcopal Church, the Servant Leadership School offered classes that helped people connect their faith with their daily lives. From that work sprang ministries and nonprofits that helped low-income families, people living with AIDS, single mothers with young children and advocates working for social justice.

Now, Frank wanted to add another program to its list: help the homeless dealing with addiction by starting an AA program at GUM.

The class brought people from the community, merged them with the guests at GUM and used as a guide Keith Miller's book "A Hunger for Healing: The Twelve Steps as a Classic Model for Christian Spiritual Growth." When the class ended, Frank asked Bob to help him continue the class with guests from GUM. Bob jumped at the chance.

Frank already had gotten Bob involved with the Stephen Ministry at GUM, and Bob saw what AA had done for him. It saved him. So, he believed it could save others. Plus, beyond running every weekday in all kinds of weather, Bob trusted Frank. Whenever he was with him, Bob felt whole.

"I think Frank showed all of us what we can be if we're willing," Bob says today. "We'd be talking, and he would get that pensive look on his face, and you could just tell his brain was chewing on something, and you'd see him milking it for all it's worth. But no matter what we talked about, you always felt he valued your presence. He was there. Right *there*. He treated you with respect, and if I was selling myself short, he'd be like 'By golly, go out and do it.' I'd first think, 'Why?' But after I did it, I'd tell myself, 'What was I so afraid of?'

With "Hunger for Healing" as its blueprint, Bob and Frank started the weekly AA program at GUM because Frank knew many guests battled with alcoholism and other addictions that shredded their lives. From those weekly meetings Bob met Richard.

"Richard was my buddy," Bob says today. "He was a garbage man. He didn't have much education. He was smart, just not a lot of education, but man, he had this harangue I'll always remember. He'd tell me, 'Bob, I can't do more than I can do. I can't do more than that.' And that was so right on and why? He and I had the same affliction. We thought we could do more than we thought we could do. And Richard and I, we just bonded.

"If nothing else happens in an AA meeting, we learn that we are all unique like everybody else. That's on the bulletin board at the Unity Club over off Glenwood Street where I go for my AA meetings. Yeah, it's 'You are all unique like everybody else.' That is such a colossal statement. But you know what else? At an AA meeting, you also realize this: 'If we want to be together, we can.'"

After five years, the AA program at GUM began to peter out because people stopped coming, and Bob moved away from it. After a while, he and Frank's weekday running days became a good memory. Bob is 12 years older than Frank, and like Z Holler, Frank's first running buddy, Bob realized his knees had had enough of the constant pounding five days a week. But he discovered he had escaped "the darkness." He had remarried, he had found joy in his life, he had found a community in Faith Community Church where he is a deacon. And he found his second act in retirement as Mark Twain. His impersonation brought him purpose that, like when he was with Frank, made him feel whole.

Take one Monday in the summer of 2013.

* * *

Bob Foxworth as Mark Twain. Photo credit: Jeri Rowe.

Bob went to Raleigh as Mark Twain, and in the heat of a July afternoon, he joined other social justice advocates. Together, as part of what became known as Moral Mondays, they all carried out a non-violent protest that Martin Luther King Jr. called a "courageous confrontation of evil by the power of love." On the grounds of the General Assembly, they all protested what they saw as economic inequalities in North Carolina created by regressive legislation by the very people North Carolinians elected.

In the middle of it all was Bob. In his white-linen suit.

"Of course, I became soaked with perspiration in my white linen suit, and it slowed me down for perhaps half a step," Bob said as Mark Twain a few days later in the News & Record. "But absolutely it was worth it because I saw people choosing not to remain silent.

"It's what I've always called the 'silent lie.' When people remain silent, they think they don't lie at all. But it's the most insidious type of lie. God punished an entire nation and exiled them to Babylon because they remained silent and did nothing to counteract the evil of a few.

"So, yes, I am a cynic. But a reformed cynic. And what I see happening in Raleigh is a spiritual obligation because those that be of the spirit cannot sit back and watch his brother being abused."

Frank found a new running partner in Rick Betton, one of his neighbors. He also found two new hosts for GUM's weekly AA meeting. He knew them through the Malachi House II, a nonprofit that helps men overcome their addictions through a nine-month, faith-based residential program. Malachi House helps men with job training, mentoring, health screenings and food. Frank knew about the food. He also knew the cook, Bernard McCoy. And Bernard was good friends with Tony Brown, a longtime staff member at Malachi House. So, like he did with Bob — and like he does with many people — Frank coaxed Bernard and Tony to take over the AA program because he knew of their own personal journeys.

Like Bob, Bernard and Tony had overcome their own addictions. And like Bob, they knew their recovery road well. Along the way, after being wounded by bad choices, Bernard and Tony realized what could help them heal — redemption and hope.

The morning sun is not even an hour old when Tony Brown gathers everyone together.

They stand in a circle in one of the bays at the Malachi House Car Wash off South Elm/Eugene Street in Greensboro. Those men surrounding Tony range in age from 18 to 70, all members of Malachi House II. Tony begins with a story, a folk tale, or a parable he has committed to memory. Like some coach before a big game, Tony wants to inspire them in some way because he knows the 30 men he manages face an eight-hour day where they would earn no money.

The car wash raises money for Malachi House, not for them. But they are there not for a paycheck. They are there, Tony reminds them, to help change their lives.

"You are all getting sobriety and a place to lay your head," Tony tells them. "That's a beautiful thing. Alright, brothers, let's bow our heads."

On those weekday mornings, Tony channels the prayerful emotion of his friend, the Rev. Otis Lockett Jr., senior pastor at Evangel Fellowship Word Ministries in Greensboro. Tony's voice rises and falls, as he stresses different words for emphasis. He wants everyone to remember. He wants to help himself remember. He has a job to do.

"Heavenly Father, we thank You for helping us learn the beauty of sobriety," he says. "We are a ministry, a working ministry, and oh, it's hard. It can be hard. But we know if we don't work, we don't eat. Yet, You — You — have helped us get up in the morning and help us focus because we know who we want us to be in Your eyes.

"We all want to be better brothers, better husbands and better sons, better uncles, better people, and You, Heavenly Father, can help steer us. You can steer us away from the aspects of our lives that we're not proud of. Forgive us. Help us. And be with us on this day here at the Malachi House Car Wash. Amen."

Tony Brown served four years in the Marines. Photo credit: Courtesy of Tony Brown.

Tony grew up in Greensboro, the older of two. His dad, Raymond, was North Carolina's first Black federal revenue agent; his mom, Elizabeth, was a maker of the flat piece of document-saving film known as microfiche. Tony graduated from Smith High, earned an English degree from N.C. Central in Durham, and enlisted in the Marines. He served four years and learned the nuances of discipline and leadership. Afterward, he worked as a meter reader and a firefighter in his hometown. That's not all. Tony remembers it this way:

"I was selling drugs and hustling folks, and I tried to become this quasi-drug dealer. But that didn't last very long.

"I started using my own product — Crack cocaine and weed — because I had these losses in my life. I lost my aunt, who I loved dearly. I lost my mom the year before. My whole world was turned upside down. It really threw me for a loop.

Bernard McCoy comes from a big family in Winston-Salem. He was one of 13 kids. Photo credit: Courtesy of Paula McCoy.

"But it all taught me a lesson. This is not something I wanted to do. I have friends who are in prison and who are dead. I didn't want that to be me."

Tony enrolled in the program at Malachi House II. He found sobriety. He also found a friend in his roommate, Bernard McCoy.

Bernard grew up on the east side of Winston-Salem, the youngest of 13. His parents worked for the same furniture company. His dad, Birden, created the furniture's handles and other hardware by pouring hot liquid into molds. His mom, Lovie, created the shine by buffing the furniture until it glowed. When she got home, she worked hard to manage a house full of kids.

"Donald! Steven! Paula! Bernard!" she'd exclaim. "You know who I'm talking to!"

With all those kids, his dad needed a second job. He worked as a barber in a five-chair shop.

But not on Sundays.

Birden McCoy (left) and Lovie McCoy (right) Phorto credit: Courtesy of Paula McCoy.

Bernard's dad was a deacon and a Sunday School superintendent at Saints Home United Methodist Church in Winston-Salem. He would load up everyone in the family's station wagon and then drive around the neighborhood and pick up everyone else.

He'd put down the station wagon's tailgate, and that would be the seat for the extra kids he picked up. And there they would sit on the back of the station wagon, traveling no more than five miles until they all reached Saints Home United Methodist.

Bernard liked to sit on the tailgate, too. But there was a time or two when he didn't think he could make it to church. When his dad asked why, Bernard showed his dad the bottom of his shoes.

"It looks bad with these holes in my shoes," Bernard would say.

His dad didn't say a word. He simply walked into a backroom, grabbed some small strips of cardboard, and inserted them into Bernard's shoes.

"There you go," his dad would say, handing him his shoes. "Now go 'head and get in the car."

For years, Bernard rang the church's bell and served as an acolyte at Saints Home United Methodist. But when his mom's eyesight started to go bad, he was picked to stay home because he was the youngest. He was no older than 10 when he started spending every Sunday morning in his family's small mint-green kitchen. He helped his mom cook.

"I would have to get on a stool to get the ingredients from the cabinets in the pantry, and she would mix everything and turn on the oven to the right temperature," Bernard says today. "But after her third eye surgery when I was 14, she had me mixing and putting it together. I knew the recipes because I was always asking questions. And I was better than my sisters. And my mom, she would always watch me and tell me how much I needed."

That's how Bernard learned how to cook. He'd mix and stir and listen to his mom give him instructions. And she gave him lots of instructions that he follows every time he steps into a kitchen today.

"Look at the clock."

"Clean up after yourself."

"Don't let the dishes pile up."

"Wipe the stove off."

"Sweep up all the mess."

"Be aware of your cooking time."

For years, Bernard helped his mom cook Sunday meals and holiday dinners for the family. He graduated from Carver High and went to college briefly. He dropped out because he realized he wanted to be a chef. He enrolled in culinary school, but he dropped out when his girlfriend got pregnant. At 20, Bernard became a father.

They got married, and Bernard went through a revolving door of jobs at a university lab, a warehouse, and at a dock at a trucking company. He also became an entrepreneur. He would go to people's houses and prepare a meal through his business, 1-800-Dial-A-Cook.

Bernard kept looking for better work and better pay and more hope in his life. Along the way, his marriage broke up, and he started smoking marijuana and crack cocaine to cope and escape. He soon found himself hooked to that high. His family got concerned. He did, too. He sought help. That's how he ended up at Malachi House II.

"It was time to get off that merry-go-round of life, and I got a chance to focus on my Bible studies and get counseled by men who had the same struggle I had," Bernard says. "I could sit with them, reflect with them, and I could be apologetic to God. I felt like I blew it, but I realized He will forgive you and help you go forward in your life. And when I realized that, I began to look at things with a different view.

"It saved my life really. I just felt like I was being reckless, you know? I was living at home with old parents. I had my own family, and I had to grow up and get things into perspective and get closer to God. I realized I was purpose-driven, and there were more things that I was supposed to be doing. It was my wake-up call."

Bernard, in the middle with two of his sisters, learned how to cook from his mom and used that knowledge to start a catering business. Photo credit: Courtesy of Paula McCoy.

At Malachi House II, Bernard met Tony. They roomed together and ministered to each other during their time at Malachi House. When he graduated, Bernard began running the kitchen at Malachi

House, and every day, he fed the men Tony managed at the Malachi House Car Wash.

But Bernard wanted to do more than just cook food. So, he got involved in the Stephen Ministry at GUM. There, he met Frank.

"From the beginning, you could tell God's presence on him," Bernard says today of Frank. "I could talk to him, and man, he would listen to me. He would help things make sense."

Bernard had started a catering business, and Frank helped him find clients. Bernard needed a home, and Frank helped Bernard find a home, a townhouse in east Greensboro built by the local Habitat for Humanity chapter.

So, when the AA program petered out at GUM, Frank approached Bernard. Then, Bernard approached Tony. They both said yes in 2003. They didn't exactly know what they were getting into, but they soon found out.

> *Victory is mine*
> *Victory is mine*
> *Victory today is mine*
> *I told Satan to get thee behind,*
> *Victory today is mine*

The voices rise in GUM's chapel like some wave of sound, loud enough to rattle the walls.

After a two-hour AA meeting, of sharing stories and holding people accountable, joy spills from the room in song. Everyone belts out a familiar hymn after Frank's prayer and before they dive into Bernard's cooking. Frank enjoys those Tuesday nights, even when he's feeling spent from the day and aching that he's going to miss, maybe, Wake Forest playing basketball on TV. But then, those Tuesday night sessions invigorate him like any Sunday morning. He'll tell the AA crowd a Bible story about resilience and redemption. The story, Frank knows, will speak volumes to people who feel forgotten and invisible. It always does. That feeling of "I can do it!" make the walls shake when everyone sings. They are loud, a bit off-key. But the words they sing, even the wrong words, are incredibly heartfelt. Their lives are not hopeless, they realize. Their lives are hopeful. And they believe it. So, they sing.

> *Happiness is mine*
> *Happiness is mine*
> *Happiness today is mine*
> *When I rose this morning*
> *I didn't have no doubt,*
> *I knew that the Lord would bring me out.*

Frank sees the gratitude painted across the faces of every guest at the end of those Tuesday nights. They walk in with their shoulders drooped, heads down, as lifeless as zombies. They walk out, shoulders pulled back, heads up, the bone-and-breath epitome of a phrase they hear every Tuesday night:

"If you fall down in the snow, you don't have to wait until spring to get up."

The AA program, Frank finds, helps them get up.

* * *

When Frank walks into Potter's House to talk to guests, he sees those who attended the AA program. With their heads bowed and eyes closed, the AA attendees clasp their hands in front of them or in their laps and pray before every meal. Almost every guest at Potter's House prays before every meal. Whenever he walks in and observes the guests praying, he sees that moment as sacred. Always, he stops and listens. A chorus of stage-whispered prayers come.

"Thank you, Lord, for waking me up this morning."

"Thank you for another shot at life."

"Lord, thank you for helping me remember why we call today the 'present' because it is a gift."

Frank never sees this kind of determined reverence at any restaurant that he and Michie patronize. But he sees that reverence at Potter's House.

Every day.

I fell on my knees
Said, "Lord, help me please!"
Got up singing and shouting the victory.
Victory is mine,
Victory is mine,
Victory today is mine.

From his years of Tuesday nights at AA, Frank remembers one particular story.

A father from South Carolina who was staying at GUM wanted to bring his son up to live with him. That story is typical of the stories the AA program unearthed at GUM. Some attendees talk about doing something for someone else rather than talk about what's going on with them. Every time, Frank or Tony or Bernard, or even the guests in the chapel work to get them back on track.

Like with the father.

He wanted his son from South Carolina to stay with him in Weaver House, the homeless shelter for men and women in Greensboro. The guests didn't hesitate to dish out a bit of tough love for one of their own.

"You got no place to live, man!"

"You have to be honest with yourself!"

"If you're not honest with yourself, the biggest person you're fooling is yourself!"

"You got to take care of you!"

"That's right, you got to take care of *you* before you can begin helping anyone else!"

I told Satan
I told Satan
I told Satan to get thee behind,
Victory today is mine.

The AA program at GUM ends in March 2020 when the global pandemic shut down the world. The AA program, though, ends for

Frank four years before. In 2016, Frank retires from GUM after 22 years as the chaplain, and Tony and Bernard and their work on Tuesday nights become a good memory.

Frank will remember those moments forever, especially how Bernard and Tony began every session, turning GUM into their personal stage and becoming Greensboro's version of the comedy duo, Key & Peele.

Frank loved telling that story.

"We had everything from chicken to beef to vegetables and dessert, and it was quite the spread," Frank tells people. "But no one knew that. Bernard and Tony would bring in these big metal pans covered with tin foil, and Bernard would say, 'On the way over, we hit something. I don't know what it was, but we cooked it up, put some mushroom gravy over it, and if you like mushroom gravy, you'll love this!'

"And people's eyes would get real big. Someone would always say, 'Are you serious?'

Frank always gets someone's attention when he reaches the let's-eat-roadkill part of Bernard and Tony's routine. Then, Frank tells the rest of the story.

"We always felt God in those meetings. The biggest way I see it was that the spirit in the room was greater than the sum of all those individuals in that chapel. When they sang, the walls would be vibrating with such joy and defiance. They were like saying, 'This addiction is not going to win! I'm surrounded by God!'

"They all were really sharing from their hearts. That is something different than quoting scripture or using religious language. As Jesus points out, even the devil can quote scripture. It's just that what they said had such depth to it. There was a presence to it. I learned so much."

After leaving GUM, Frank often wondered if he would see Tony and Bernard again, even work with them again. Years later, he would. But way before that reunion happened, Frank discovered another side of his social justice self.

It came with handcuffs. And heartache.

Frank on Frank

The 'Deep Truth' of 12 Steps

A lot of people associated 12 Steps with people who were weak, who have struggled throughout their lives, who don't have their acts together. What I found was just the total opposite. Bob and Tony and Bernard, and all of our guests at the Greensboro Urban Ministry, helped me discover that. There was such a strength there in our meetings. But it wasn't a strength that came from the people themselves, but *beyond* themselves.

It came from their recognition that they didn't have to rely on just them. They had to depend on a power that was much greater, a power they called God. Now, I've heard a lot of people — not all — but a lot of people say, 'The 12 Steps helped me go back to church.' For me, what I saw every Tuesday night at Greensboro Urban Ministry was what I believed a church *ought* to be.

Church, I believe, needs to be a refuge for people who acknowledge that they can't do this thing called life by themselves. In our lives, we constantly come up against things I call the Three C's. It's these things we can't control or change or cure, and we need something greater than ourselves to help us deal with that.

I remember walking by the 12 Step Program at the Presbyterian Church of the Covenant, when New Creation worshipped there, and I'd peek in and see people with their arms around each other. They were praying. They were saying the Lord's Prayer. They were having church. Man, that *is* church.

All too often we in the church pretend everything is fine. You know, we see someone we know and ask, 'How you doing?' and we hear, 'Oh, I'm fine. We're all fine. How are you?' But things aren't fine. All too often, the church doesn't encourage us to open up to that kind of vulnerability within ourselves. But that vulnerability, that openness, helps us open up to God.

In my work as a minister, I've said often I feel like I'm selling ice to Eskimos whenever I preach. I ask myself, 'Why do I need to preach? They all know this!' Well, the why is that there is so much in our lives that we cannot deal with on our own. We need that power, that strength beyond us. And that strength comes from a community of believers, a community any 12 Step Program creates. What I see in 12 Steps is that the people involved really encourage and support one another. When someone is down and talks about falling off the wagon, they pick that person up. They lift them up and say, 'You know the great thing about 12 Steps? You can begin again! You can start over right now! One hour at a time!' That's so inspiring. And you know, we all need that because we all fall in some way in our lives.

There's a line I remember from Ernest Hemingway's book, 'A Farewell to Arms.' I read it for an English class years ago at Wake Forest, and I still remember this line from the book: "The world breaks everyone and afterward many are strong at the broken places."

It is such a great line, but can you see the paradox, the idea of how we break in certain places to become strong? Our brokenness opens us up to a strength that is beyond us. I mean, that paradox is so important because it holds together two seemingly contradictory ideas that taken together speak a fuller truth.

In the early 90s, when I went up to DC for a retreat at the Church of the Saviour, I went with folks from the Servant Leadership School. And at the Church of the Saviour, we met Henri Nouwen. He was the Dutch priest who had written dozens of books. He talked to us about servant leadership, and the material he used became part of his latest book. I remember we were all seated in a circle, and he called us up one by one. He wrapped his arms around each one of us and whispered in our ears, ' Hold on to your calling.'

Hold on to your calling. I like that.

During the retreat, we shared communion, and Nouwen talked

in the images we all know from church. He blessed the bread, broke it and gave it to us. That communion, the image from the Last Supper, is the paradox I'm talking about. We're broken; we're blessed; and we are given. That's the paradox of Jesus. That also is the paradox we need to remember in our lives.

Following the retreat, Nouwen wrote 'Life of the Beloved,' and it contained much of what he told us. In that book are so many great passages. I've underlined a bunch in my copy. Here's one:

'The deep truth is that our human suffering need not be an obstacle to the joy and peace we so desire, but can become instead, the means to it. The great secret of the spiritual life, the life of the Beloved Sons and Daughters of God, is that everything we live, be it gladness or sadness, joy or pain, health or illness, can all be part of the journey toward the full realization of our humanity.'

That's so relevant today, isn't it?

You find that same kind of relevance in 12 Steps. Their language may be different. It has such a folklore of stories and sayings. But 12 Steps is powerful in the same way as the 'deep truth' Nouwen writes about. It's that lifesaving relationship that can transform all of us. It can help us see how the word 'beloved' can be applied in our lives. So often, we tend to think 'Well, Jesus was the Beloved Son of God. He was Jesus. How in the world can that be applied to *me*?'

But that's where the experience of grace comes in.

See, that word 'beloved' belongs to all of us. Sure, we haven't earned it or deserved it. But like the love that a parent has for their child, that love was there from the very beginning.

We love because God loves us.

During the Moral Monday protests in Raleigh, Frank became an Uber driver of sorts. He would use Facebook as a way to recruit anyone who wanted to go with him from Greensboro to Raleigh and participate in the protests.

Chapter 13
Heartache & Handcuffs

"For many, Christianity is about giving a casserole dish to our neighbor. It's that act of kindness, and we as a church are really good at that. But we're not always good at linking that kind of personal kindness with structural change and justice. One doesn't have integrity without the other."

The Rev. Frank Dew

Every Thursday, as the afternoon traffic picks up in downtown Greensboro, Frank stands at the corner of West Market and Eugene streets with other fellow members from the local chapter of People Against the Death Penalty. They've used black markers they've bought at an office supply store to write bumper sticker slogans on white poster board to turn them into a personal billboard of what they believe.

No Killing In My Name
Those Without Capital Get the Punishment
Stop the Death Penalty

They stand beside the Guilford County Courthouse, silent as a cemetery holding their signs. They gather because the Supreme Court reinstated the federal death penalty in 1976, and they all begin showing their faith with their feet by standing on a street corner in downtown Greensboro. Frank is a few miles from his house. All he has to do is wend his way through Greensboro's Sunset Hills neighborhood to West Market, take a right, and he can be at his spot on the sidewalk in three minutes. That is, if he hits the traffic lights right. Frank and the others will stand there for an hour with their signs. Some drivers honk in approval and wave. Other drivers stick their arms out of their windows and give what we all recognize — the profane middle-finger sign of disagreement.

Frank knows his weekly silent vigil is like throwing a pebble into a pond. He often wonders if anyone noticed. He knows the answer: Probably not. No amount of what Michie calls "Dewitus" can change that. But Frank's weekly vigil isn't about changing things, really. It's more about living his faith rain or shine. He can blame Lumberton High for that.

Or really Ruth Sanders.

Frank took Sanders' class in 1969, his senior year at Lumberton High. Numbed by the assassination of Martin Luther King and Robert F. Kennedy the year before, Frank felt this burning need to do something. But what? He wanted to do more than just debate his dad over dinner after watching Walter Cronkite deliver the news on CBS. Lumberton High, of all things, gave him his answer, and his answer was Ruth Sanders. The name of her class caught his attention: "Problems of Democracy." He figured he could get more ammunition in dueling with his dad. But what Frank got was the spark that helped ignite his passion for social justice. And what sparked his passion was the death penalty.

As a teenager whose moral compass was shaped by the red-letter words in the New Testament, Frank couldn't get his head around the death penalty. He saw it as a cold-blooded, state-sanctioned assassination carried out by people who supposedly believed what he believed. Frank's mind rumbled with questions he couldn't answer.

Is there a better way?

Why even think this is the best way in the first place?

Doesn't No. 6 on the slab Moses brought down from Mount Sinai say, "Thou shall not kill?'

Every moral and ethical fiber that made Frank ... Frank was against the death penalty, and he wanted to make his opinion known. In Sanders' class, he wrote a paper against the death penalty. As an undergrad at Wake Forest, he wrote another paper against the death penalty. As a student at Duke Divinity, he wrote yet another paper against the death penalty. In 1973, while studying at Duke Divinity, Frank wrote a letter to the editor to the News & Observer and assailed Rufus Edmisten, then the attorney general of North Carolina, for his support of the death penalty.

"You're basically saying your job is more important than your moral conviction."

That was the tone of Frank's letter — or so he remembers. His staunch opposition to the death penalty first took root and blossomed in Sanders' class. It became his favorite class at Lumberton High and set him on a course that mirrored what he learned from the New Testament as well as from a calendar on his bedroom wall.

* * *

When Frank was growing up in Lumberton and a cat named Caesar padded into his second-floor bedroom by climbing up a tree, he had on his bedroom wall a John F. Kennedy calendar. After Kennedy's death, Frank made a point to find out all he could about Kennedy. He then discovered through Sanders' class a proclamation Kennedy had written. In one passage from his 628-word proclamation, Kennedy wrote:

> *Yet, as our power has grown, so has our peril. Today we give our thanks, most of all, for the ideals of honor and faith we inherit from our forefathers — for the decency of purpose, steadfastness of resolve and strength of will, for the courage and the humility, which they possessed and which we must seek every day to emulate. As we express our gratitude, we must never forget that the highest appreciation is not to utter words but to live by them.*

Kennedy wrote that proclamation 18 days before his assassination on Nov. 22, 1963. It was released on Thanksgiving Day, six days after he was assassinated on a Friday afternoon in downtown Dallas. Like what Frank learned in Sunday School, the sentiment he found in Kennedy's words encouraged Frank to think about the world around him and the responsibilities he shouldered. From there, Frank began to act, little by little, year after year.

That thought process eventually leads Frank, now a married father with two young kids, to stand on a sidewalk every Thursday for four years. He stands there in the hothouse of a North Carolina summer, the icebox of a North Carolina winter or in the syncopated patter of a North Carolina rain, wearing his hunting shoes and a Wake Forest baseball cap. His mind often wanders, especially when the temperatures dip below freezing. Like many Southerners, Frank is no cold-weather fan, and as his mind wanders, Frank thinks about his past. When he does, he thinks of his hometown and the Rev. Bob Sloop.

Sloop was Frank's minister when he was a teenager at Lumberton's First Presbyterian Church. After Frank graduated from Lumberton High, Sloop asked him to preach one Sunday at First Presbyterian's mission church, the Sunday home of many of Lumberton's tobacco factory workers. Frank was 18, fresh from Sanders' class. Frank wrote his first sermon on a yellow legal pad. When he finished, he read it to Sloop and waited for a reaction. Nothing, at first. Finally, Sloop spoke.

"You know, Frank, you're a social gospeler."

Yes, Frank was.

As he stands beside the Guilford County Courthouse, Frank lets the sign he holds speak for him. Because of his faith, he knows he can't support a system that executes the powerless, the voiceless, the poor. He has come to believe their chances for fairness are doomed because of the shade of their skin, the lack of money in their pockets or the origin of where they were born. As Frank liked to say, those without capital get the punishment.

To Frank, it's just not right.

"You have to give God something to work with," Frank often tells his parishioners at New Creation Community Presbyterian Church.

Frank does give God something to work with. His advocacy, though, will soon move from the empathetic cocoon of) Greensboro Urban Ministry to the stale recirculated air of a jail cell where he asks a female U.S. Marshall the time and hears in response something he always will remember.

"I'm not on your fucking agenda! This is our time, and we'll keep the time!"

Heartache and handcuffs. It all starts with K-Mart.

* * *

The deal is seen as an economic boon for Greensboro.

K-Mart decides to build one of its main distribution centers beside Wendover Avenue, one of the city's main asphalt arteries. The center is big, 35 football fields big. City and state officials chip in about $1 million worth of incentives because they want to convince K-Mart to build one of its 12 regional centers on the city's east side, a section that often feels neglected when anyone considers where to build and invest in Greensboro. On the surface, the deal looks sweet. K-Mart will employ 550 people when the center opens in the summer of 1992, and according to news reports at the time, it will be K-Mart's only distribution center where a large majority of its employees are Black. But the shine of that opportunity begins to dull when K-Mart offers its new employees, on average, more than $5 less an hour than what workers make at the company's other distribution centers. The benefits aren't as good either. The new employees look for help, and 15 months after the distribution center opens, they vote overwhelmingly in September 1993 to join UNITE, or the Union of Needletrades, Industrial and Textile Employees. Employees want a union to help them negotiate for what they believe they deserve: benefits and an hourly wage comparable to what K-Mart employees earn at other distribution centers nationwide. The vote results in the only union at any of K-Mart's dozen regional centers. Workers feel hopeful. But that hope is soon dashed.

K-Mart, a $30 billion Fortune 500 company, doesn't budge.

K-Mart releases statements to explain its decision. The company states it set the initial wage scales based on what other businesses in the area pay their employees. Meanwhile, K-Mart gets tough. It fires the union organizers. Then, K-Mart waits. The company thinks the anger and anxiety will subside. It doesn't. In 1994, K-Mart workers hold a sit-in protest at the Greater Greensboro Open, sponsored by

K-Mart, to draw attention to their fight. It does. But the local press and the local leaders diss the effort. The News & Record, the city's daily newspaper, writes the protesters are making "fools of themselves" and "attacking Greensboro." Meanwhile, city leaders claim "outside groups" are playing "the race card" in this back-and-forth battle over better benefits and better wages. As negotiations stall, members of the Greensboro Pulpit Forum, the city's association of predominantly Black ministers, get involved. That's when everything changes. In the court of public opinion, the employees' labor fight gains credibility and traction.

On a Sunday in December 1995, eight Black ministers with the Greensboro Pulpit Forum kneel in the parking lot of the K-Mart distribution center to pray. Around them are police officers in riot gear. The ministers are then led away in plastic-tie handcuffs as the crowd of supporters around them sing "Victory Is Mine." The next day, on the front page of the News & Record, is a photograph of the police surrounding the preachers kneeling on the blacktop to pray. The headline reads: "Clergy Arrested in Labor Protest."

Around the city, readers see the pastors in the front-page picture. But Frank sees friends — the Revs. Nelson Johnson, Gregory Headen, and J Herbert Nelson, and his former running buddy, Z Holler, the retired minister from Presbyterian Church of the Covenant. He knows every one of them well, and he knows their move to get arrested is a time capsule to what put Greensboro on the civil rights map. It's imbued in the city's DNA, like ACC basketball and Stamey's barbecue.

In February 1960, four freshmen at N.C. A&T walked from their campus to the Woolworth's lunch counter. The lunch counter only served white diners. But those four Black students sat down to be served. When they did, they stood up for the rights of everyone who looked like them. The Greensboro sit-in ignited the civil rights movement and similar protests rippled across the South.

Protest has always been a key part of Greensboro's history, a crucial part of its communal DNA. And on that Sunday in December 1995, the protest is just another example of what local folks do to awaken the city to what they believe is important: Bring K-Mart to the bargaining table and negotiate for better benefits and better wages for those workers who often feel overlooked by the power structure of the city.

Frank has that protest DNA, too.

As news surrounding the protest begins to heat up, Frank organizes a meeting at Presbyterian Church of the Covenant so union organizers can talk about what's happening to one of New Creation's study groups. Local clergy come. So does a Greensboro police officer and Ginny Tate, a New Creation member who owns a goat dairy farm in Randolph County. She brings with her one of her baby goats. But no one from the News & Record comes. Frank even calls the newspaper, and from what he remembers, he's told that covering the meeting is too controversial.

"Are you serious?" Frank responds.

He hangs up the phone and feels that quick exchange is an example of how the need for profits trumps the importance of public service. At the time, K-Mart is considered one of the newspaper's biggest advertisers. When Frank starts the meeting in the church's parlor, he shares what he found out.

"The paper told me they believe this meeting is too controversial to cover so they aren't coming," he tells the group. "So, feel free to say whatever you want about the meeting. But if one person tells anyone that we have a goat in the parlor, you're in trouble with me."

Laughter ripples through the room, and the meeting begins.

Afterward, Frank walks up to a member of Presbyterian Church of the Covenant. He's also a Greensboro police officer.

"What did you think of the meeting?" Frank asks.

"It wasn't half baaaad," the member says.

"Got it," Frank responds. "Thanks for your bleat of support."

Frank wants to do more than organize meetings. He wants to join his friends and protest. And if he does, he knows he would be arrested for the first time in his life.

In the year before the K-Mart protest, Frank's ministerial life deepens. In November 1994, he becomes the first chaplain at

Greensboro Urban Ministry, and even during that short period of time, he has already heard his share of stories of the powerful hurting the powerless and the powerless sliding into despair. Those stories coincide with the stories he hears from his members of New Creation Community Presbyterian Church, particularly those members who see the outside as their home. Those stories stoke the same kind of passion Frank feels when he lobbies against the death penalty. It's that same kind of passion he discovers on his trip to Nicaragua. So, after seeing his friends get arrested for what they believe in, Frank feels he needs to channel his inner Jesus and stand with them.

But before he does anything, he has to have another conversation in his family's wood-paneled den off Camden Road in Greensboro. He has to talk to Michie.

"Michie, here's the thing," Frank says. "They're all friends of mine. And friendship requires more than just a pat on the back and me saying, 'Hey, guys, good job. You all are doing good work.' Michie, if friendship means anything, it means I need to join them. This is something I need to do."

At first, Michie doesn't say anything, but she is surprised by Frank's decision. He doesn't tell her what can happen, but she knows right away what it means if he joins his minister friends. Her husband is going to get arrested. Nope. He *plans* to get arrested.

Handcuffed.

Taken to jail.

By police.

In a van, a paddy wagon or a bus.

For everyone to see. At least in the paper the next day.

Yet, as she plays that image over and over in her mind and thinks of what she'd say to anyone who asks — "Yeah," she'd tell them, "That's Frank being Frank," she remembers why she married him. So many reasons. But as Frank sits on the couch and explains to her his intention in his measured ministerial tone, she thinks of one.

Frank could've been a pastor at a Presbyterian church where his parishioners earned six figures, and his contract included a membership to a tennis and racquet club. Instead, he becomes a chaplain of a homeless shelter, a pastor of a small Presbyterian church he creates and a former chair of the city's Human Relations Commission after the infamous shootout in November 1979 on the east side of the city.

For Frank, that shootout is personal. That shootout involved his friend, the Rev. Nelson Johnson.

* * *

For years, the Rev. Nelson Johnson carried with him the resilience to stand up and draw attention in any way he could to episodes of the powerful putting the powerless under their proverbial thumbs. Photo credit: Courtesy of Triad City Beat.

Back then, Nelson was a communist, and around Greensboro, he was perceived as the angry, outspoken man in the beret. He helped organize a "Death to the Klan" rally at Morningside Homes, a federal housing community where almost all of its residents were Black and poor. The rally was intended to draw attention to the need to snuff out racism. Instead, the march drew Nazis and members of the Ku Klux Klan. They turned Morningside Homes into a shooting gallery. A TV crew from the local CBS affiliate, WFMY, caught much of it on tape. The Nazis and the KKK arrived in a caravan of cars. They stopped, pulled out guns and rifles from the trunks of their cars, and began shooting. The shootout left 10 wounded. Five people died.

Four white men. One Black woman. All members of the Communist Workers Party. It became one of the bloodiest days in Greensboro's history.

That one event has never faded in the collective memory of Greensboro, and many in the city never forgave Nelson, even though he apologized decades ago. Meanwhile, Nelson hung up his beret and donned the recognizable collar of faith. He became grandfather, a minister of Greensboro's Faith Community Church. He carried with him the indignation of what happened long ago at Morningside Homes. But like Frank, Nelson carried with him the resilience to stand up and draw attention in any way he could to episodes of the powerful putting the powerless under their proverbial thumbs. He did that until his very last breath when he died in February 2025. He was 81.

Before his death, Nelson models for many how to protest, and if it means getting arrested, Nelson will get arrested. Frank follows Nelson's lead. And in 1995, as the K-Mart protest heat up, Frank brings up the possibility to Michie. And Michie, the wife and mother, puts on on her professional hat. She becomes Dr. Michie Dew, the psychologist.

"Okay," she responds, drawing out every letter like pulling a rubberband. "If you feel like that's what you need to do, I support it. But Frank, you've got to tell the kids. And you've got to tell your parents."

Frank nods.

"You're right."

"And you have to tell David and Christie why you are doing this and what's involved in it," she says.

Frank nods again.

"True."

"And that you're getting arrested because you want to make a statement, and the statement you want to make is bigger than you," she says.

Frank falls silent. Michie continues.

"And tell them that Jesus came to help the disenfranchised, and that includes the K-Mart workers. And that if you are to be faithful, you have to be faithful to those workers as well."

"Sounds like David and Christie need a Sunday School lesson," Frank responds.

"Yes!" says Michie. "Do that. David and Christie will definitely understand that."

Frank isn't worried about telling his dad, the World War II veteran and the Sunday School superintendent when First Presbyterian Church was his first spiritual home. He can deal with that.

But his kids?

David and Christie?

Great.

David and Christie sit shoulder to shoulder, knee to knee, on the big floral couch in the living room. David is 10; Christie, 9. They have no idea what their dad wants to talk to them about. But they know it's serious. Their dad is wearing his serious face. So is their mom. So they know they have to listen. Their dad starts first.

"David and Christie, you remember Z, right?" asks Frank, leaning forward, elbows on his knees. "The Rev. Holler? He baptized you all. Well, Z and a few of our friends are supporting working people and helping them get a fair wage. You know, get the pay they deserve. Well, I feel I need to stand with them and not applaud them from a distance, you know? In order to show my solidarity with them.

"It's like what you all learned in Sunday School. When Peter was in the courtyard standing at a distance when Jesus got arrested. Peter didn't want to stand at a distance because he and Jesus were friends. He wanted to support his friends. And I have to support my friends.

"I can't in good conscience stay at arm's length from my friends who I respect and admire. I can't say, 'Hey, you guys are doing great work! But I'm not going to stand with you.' That would make me feel less than a friend. And being a true friend means standing with them literally. That is what's motivating me.

"But if I support my friends …"

Frank pauses for a few seconds.

"… I'm going to get arrested."

David and Christie don't say a word. They just stare at their dad, unblinking. Michie jumps in.

"If Dad does get arrested, that doesn't mean he's dangerous," she says. "And he's definitely not hurting someone. He is trying to help. He's trying to help these workers get paid fairly for the work they do. And he's going out there to get the word out and speak for people who can't speak for themselves."

David and Christie stare at their mom, not saying a word. Frank breaks in.

"Your mom is right," he says. "I'm standing up for other people to help them get what they deserve."

Finally, David pipes up.

"You're getting arrested on behalf of others?" he asks.

"That's right, David," Frank responds. "I am."

"That's just weird," David says.

"I don't understand," Christie interjects.

David doesn't understand either. He and his sister have been told their whole life to do what is right, follow the rules and respect authority. And now, he and Christie are being told their dad isn't going to follow the rules, and he isn't going to respect authority. And he is going to get arrested.

All David can think about is what would Bobo say. That's Frank's dad, their grandfather.

"So," asks David, "when are you going to tell Bobo?"

"In true teenager fashion," Frank says. "I'm going to tell him after it's over."

Frank laughs. David and Christie relax, and Michie looks from Frank, then to their kids and back to Frank again.

"If your dad gets arrested Sunday, he'll be home in time to take you all to school," she says. "Isn't that right, Frank?"

Michie looks at her husband, big eyed, like "You'd better say yes!"

"That's right," Frank interjects. "I've got carpool covered."

Or at least he hopes.

* * *

Frank & Mickie with their new family, David and Christie.

Frank spots the school bus as he's kneeling on the asphalt. He knows exactly why it came.

"That's how we're getting to the jail," Frank tells himself. "Can't wait to tell the kids."

He's been praying in the parking lot at the K-Mart distribution center with his minister friends and Barbara Clawson, his church member and friend who went with him to Nicaragua. He hears the murmur of the sign-carrying crowd, and he sees on either side of him police officers dressed in riot gear. That's when he recognizes a familiar face. It's Bill Ingold, a dad whose kids are part of the Dews' carpool to Greensboro Montessori School. But Bill is there for his job. Bill is a police officer, and Bill is *the* police officer who's about to put the plastic tie handcuffs on Frank's wrists. Bill makes sure Frank has his wrists in front of his waist rather than behind for comfort and bathroom support.

"Thanks, Bill," Frank says

"Sure thing, Frank," he responds.

As the police lead the crowd of arrested protesters into the bus, Frank shouts over his shoulder to get Bill's attention.

"Bill, don't worry," he says. "I've got carpool covered."

This is all so new to Frank. The arrests are so staged, like synchronized swimming at the Olympics. We do this. Cops do that. We follow. They come closer. We sit. They walk toward us. They give us a warning. We stay put. They give us another warning. We stay put some more. We get yet another warning. Nope, not moving.

Then, we get arrested. And off we go.

"It's not all that bad," Frank tells himself.

As he sits on the bus, buried in his thoughts about becoming comfortable with the uncomfortable, he hears something he recognizes.

We shall overcome (oh Lord)
We shall overcome (oh Lord)
We shall overcome, some day!
Oh, deep in my heart
I know that I do believe
We shall overcome, some day!

The Rev. Gregory Headen, the senior pastor at Greensboro's Shiloh Baptist Church, is sitting up front leading everyone in song. Immediately, Frank feels comfortable. He knows he did the right thing, made the right decision. And now, with plastic ties on his wrists, heading to the jail to get booked, he's singing. By God, he's singing.

At the police station in downtown Greensboro, Frank is charged with trespassing. Less than an hour later, he goes home. When he walks in, Michie is standing in the den, waiting for him.

"How did it go?" she asks.

"It went well," Frank says. "But guess who arrested me? Bill did.

I told him I'll have the carpool covered for tomorrow."

Michie laughs.

"Only you Frank," she replied. "Only you would get arrested by one of our carpool dads."

* * *

Sunday after Sunday, protesters converge at the K-Mart distribution center, and they are as diverse as they are passionate.

College students.

Blue-collar workers.

State legislators.

Members of the NAACP.

Local clergy.

And an aide to then-Gov. Jim Hunt.

Then, on the last Saturday in March, the Greensboro labor dispute draws support nationwide. Rallies materialize in at least seven cities that include Cleveland, Chicago and Memphis, Tenn. More than 1,000 people in Atlanta and more than 100 people in Houston march on K-Mart stores to show their support for UNITE, Greensboro and the workers at the K-Mart distribution center off East Wendover on Penry Road.

"Here we were 300 miles from Penry Road, and the support was overwhelming," UNITE's Anthony Romano, who organized the Atlanta rally, tells the News & Record. "This injustice really resonates with other people around the nation. People in huge numbers vowed to stand by the K-Mart workers until they were treated fairly."

K-Mart feels the heat. The company already has potential shoppers boycotting the six K-Mart stores in Greensboro, and both UNITE and the Greensboro Pulpit Forum have collected more than 10,000 signatures from local residents who support the workers. The spirit of that petition crystallizes into a poignant metaphor when the members of the union and Pulpit Forum hold a press conference in downtown Greensboro in front of a cherished landmark of civil rights history — Woolworth's, the site of the 1960 sit-in.

As the labor dispute drags on week after week, it become much bigger than a battle over benefits and pay. It becomes one more example of Greensboro's scrappy spirit seen time and again throughout its history. That spirit is first unveiled in March of 1781 when the city's namesake, Gen. Nathanael Greene, and his soldiers were outnumbered by the British at the Battle of Guilford Courthouse. They fought, and they lost. But that battle turned the tide of the Revolutionary War and led to the surrender of Gen. Cornwallis and the British army seven months later.

Greensboro does love a good protest.

As more people and more cities get involved with the labor dispute, it morphs into a David-and-Goliath struggle in which corporate greed is seen as not just short-changing workers but squashing a community. That perception comes about when a group of ministers use prayer and non-violent protests to shine one big spotlight on what they believe is wrong.

And it works.

K-Mart renegotiates contracts with UNITE and its distribution center workers in Greensboro. The first new contract comes after all the protests in 1996. It's then renewed three years later. The bottom line? Greensboro workers win. Hourly wages increase by 50 percent, and workers receive benefits commiserate with those offered at other K-Mart distribution centers nationwide. Workers double their yearly allowance of paid leave, and that includes getting a paid holiday for Martin Luther King Day. Greensboro becomes the only Kmart distribution center in the country to offer that.

Seems appropriate for a city unafraid to stand up and fight for what it believes is right.

Frank knows that.

All he has to do is look around.

Meet with a few governors.

Protest on the steps of the Supreme Court.

Protest in Raleigh at the General Assembly.

Become a tour guide of civil disobedience.

And get arrested a few more times.

Of course.

Frank has participated in many rallies in North Carolina to give voice who have no voice, those North Carolinians that Frank calls "the least, the last, and the left out."

Frank on Frank

'This Is What Christianity Looks Like"

I've always liked the term 'witness.'

As Christians, we need to witness so people can see what faith looks like, so they can understand how Christianity connects with social justice and evangelism. Here's what I mean.

One time, I was at an event in Greensboro. I can't remember where, but those who had been arrested for protesting in the past were invited up onstage to say something. I remember going up there and saying something like, 'It's amazing what preachers have to do to get their names in the newspaper.'

People laughed. But really, it's true.

If I say something in church on a Sunday, it will never make the newspaper. But if I get arrested for standing up for what I believe in, you know *that'll* make the newspaper. No doubt about it. Think of what happened after that one photo appeared on the front page of the News & Record right before Christmas in 1995. It helped Greensboro's larger community take notice of the K-Mart dispute. The arrests. The newspaper stories. The pictures. They all became a witness to an even larger community nationwide. People across America saw and read what our faith needs to be.

Moral Mondays was like that, too.

It started as a small protest in 2013 at the General Assembly, and it grew into this huge movement. We all were angry because it felt like our state had been hijacked. We were being pulled into the Deep South, and I felt like North Carolina got sandwiched between Alabama and Mississippi. Really. We also were being pulled back into our segregated past with what our legislators were doing in terms of voting rights, workers' rights, education funding, health care, just everything. Oh, I was angry. I didn't even recognize my home state. So, I knew I had to do something. So, I became a tour guide for Moral Monday.

I would put stuff on Facebook and ask if anyone wanted to go. And people wanted to go. People would pile into my car, and if more people wanted to go, we all would leave Greensboro in a caravan of cars. We all drove to Raleigh to protest.

Every Moral Monday, a group would get arrested, and I was part of that group once. We'd be behind the General Assembly on a large mall. The Rev. William Barber would make an inspiring speech, and then the crowd — hundreds of people — would part in the middle and we arrestees would march through the crowd into the building.

The irony of walking through that crowd was like the parting of the Red Sea in the Bible. Like the Israelites in the Old Testament, we felt we were walking toward freedom. And as we walked through the crowd, they were cheering and saying, 'Thank you!' Thank you for your witness!'

It was really humbling, and really cool to be able to experience that. I felt appreciated. But I also felt appreciated without merit. I kept telling myself, 'I don't deserve this!'

Yet, you felt you were part of something significant, something big. As we walked into the building, we heard Sam Cooke's 'A Change Is Gonna Come.'" Then, we'd gather outside the House and Senate chambers to sing, pray, and hear scripted warnings from the police. They told us we were trespassing, and we told them we weren't. Where we were standing belonged as much to us as it did them, and we told them we were exercising our constitutional rights to address our legislators with our grievances.

Fat chance that would work. After that back and forth, they put plastic tie handcuffs on us, and we all were loaded into a prison bus and taken to Wake County Jail.

As we drove to the jail, we started singing more songs. Like 'This Little Light of Mine' and 'We Shall Overcome.' The whole time, I couldn't get over the idea that this must've been what the early days of the civil rights movement felt like. But now, we were part of our own civil rights movement.

There was a chant we used a lot during the Moral Monday protests in Raleigh. Crowds of people would gather and shout, 'This is what democracy looks like!' That's true. But to me, I kept thinking, 'This is what Christianity looks like.'

For many, Christianity is about giving a casserole dish to our neighbor. It's that act of kindness, and we as a church are really good at that. But we're not always good at linking that kind of personal kindness with structural change and justice. One doesn't have integrity without the other. What I mean by that goes back to growing up in the segregated South.

Back then, we'd all want to talk about how kind we were to the Black people in our community, and we white folks would say things like, 'Oh, they're just like family.' Really? Yet, they never ate with us in the dining room. They always ate in the kitchen. They never sat with us in the front seat. They always sat in the back seat. That's because of kind feelings. That kindness had not been translated into justice.

But why is that?

Well, it's hard and costly to change the structure of society. It rocks the boat, and when people feel that boat rocking, people get upset. The church is not accustomed to rocking the boat. But when the church does, look what can happen. Look what happened to the K-Mart protests when ministers got involved. It brought a level of equality and justice that wasn't there before.

That's what called me to ministry. I wanted to make these kinds of connections between kindness and justice, and I wanted others to participate in that so the church — the white church — could be cleansed of its complicity in the racist power structure.

I don't want to give the impression that I was doing anything important. But I was a participant in what *was* important. It was a movement to call out the church and move it to its rightful place of doing justice, loving kindness, and following God.

So, I wasn't leading. I was being led.

I'm not a rabble rouser or ringleader. People who know me will tell you that. But I see myself as a person who reaches out and brings along people who do not always see things from the point of view of the bottom, the point of view shared by the least and the left out.

So, in that sense, I'm like that mustard seed or the leaven in the lump of dough. I'm the ingredient God uses, and I become part of what God is doing. So, my role? I just give God something to work with.

One of my favorite passages comes from the Book of Romans, Chapter 12, Verse 2. It says that we can't conform to the way of this world, but we can be transformed by God. The church is constantly being co-opted by the culture, and the culture uses the power of the church to legitimize what the culture wants. It's almost like resisting gravity. It can be *that* powerful. So, we in the church have to constantly be on guard. Look what has happened with evangelical Christianity. They smelled the sweet scent of power, and they prostituted the church for the sake of power and influence.

That's not what Christianity looks like.

As Christians, we have an obligation to stand up against injustice and stand up for the poor and the oppressed. We see it not just with Jesus in the New Testament, but also with the prophets in the Old Testament.

This brings me to one of my other favorite passages, Micah 6:8. It asks the question: What does God require us to do? To act justly, to love mercy and to walk humbly with your God. It's like pairing the two wings of a dove or the two feet of a person. It's that crucial. To do justice, we must have mercy and compassion in our hearts.

That's what Christianity looks like.

*Charlie Gane heard from his grandfather that the oil from the skin of a
Chihuahua could help anyone with asthma. He then uses his birthday money to
buy a Chihuahua from a breeder in Shelby. Charlie names her "Sweetie."
Charlie battled cystic fibrosis his whole life, and he died a week after his 13th
birthday due to complications that occurred during surgery.*

Chapter 14

"I Love You Forever, My Little Boy"

*"We all will face losing people we love at some point in our lives. It will be hard. It **always** will be hard. But the people we love who have died will continue to be present with us, and we always will be able to experience that. You've heard about the idea of 'thin places,' right? It's where the distance between heaven and earth is very thin. It's a term that comes from Celtic Christianity, and it refers to those sacred moments when the separation between us here on Earth and those in heaven is so minimal, so thin that we can sense the presence of God.*

We also can sense the presence of those we love as well. We can find those 'thin places' everywhere — in a church, in a cemetery, in nature, and in your own hometown. We can hear something or smell something or see something, and it will take us back to one of those moments, those memories, that we cherish. Those moments are almost always unexpected. They come out of the blue. And what a gift that is."

The Rev. Frank Dew

The sun begins to dip below I-40 when Frank leaves Raleigh.

He has spent almost an hour talking with Gov. Jim Hunt about why he should stay the execution of a man on North Carolina's death row. Frank sits a few feet from Hunt in the governor's impressive office, and as he talks in a room surrounded by heavy curtains and dark-wood furniture, Frank feels listened to, understood, and he believes he has made a difference with a man who is a Democrat.

Just like Frank.

Politics, though, has nothing to do with Frank's fight against the death penalty. It has everything to do with principle. Hunt is a Presbyterian.

Just like Frank.

Frank believes faith binds us to the same common values we hear on Sundays, and it acts as the needle on our own personal compass we follow every day. Those common values help Presbyterians — and people of faith — understand one another. They speak the same language because they were raised in the same kind of pew.

Or so Frank hopes.

But Frank hardly gets out of Raleigh when he realizes he was way wrong. Frank turns his radio to WPTF (680 AM) and hears the man he had lobbied to save has just been executed. Hunt had passed on saving the man's life.

The circumstances make Frank think about the stone he keeps on the edge of his desk at Greensboro Urban Ministry. That stone, no bigger than the palm of Frank's hand, reminds him of what Jesus said — and what he wants people like Hunt to remember: "Let anyone among you who is without sin be the first to throw a stone against her."

But thoughts of the stone on his desk don't lessen Frank's grief.

"I am so naïve," Frank tells himself. "I should've *known* better."

Maybe.

With all his work fighting the death penalty, Frank has realized how the influential wield their power. They appease those whose faith is like theirs. They invite them in, sit with them, smile at what they say and nod their heads in agreement at just the right moments.

But once their faith company leaves, they do an about face. Why? They want to keep their jobs and hold onto their power. They assuage their conscience by telling themselves that they are doing what's right. Frank has seen that happen time and again. In his sermons, he has a go-to line that speaks to that very thing: "Those without the capital get the punishment, and those with the gold make the rules."

During his silent vigil every Thursday beside the Guilford County Courthouse, Frank has scribbled those phrases on a poster board. For four years in the 1990s, he and other members of Greensboro's chapter of People Against the Death Penalty stood for an hour on the sidewalk as a silent witness to what they believed was wrong.

Frank had now moved from the sidewalk to the power center of North Carolina — the governor's office off Hillsborough Street in downtown Raleigh. There, Frank has a front-row seat to the arbitrary maliciousness of North Carolina's death penalty.

Politics over principle. Grace and mercy be damned.

Frank felt that with Gov. Hunt, North Carolina's longest serving governor. Hunt served as governor twice, from 1977 to 1985 and from 1993 to 2001. Frank talked to Hunt during his second term. But that wasn't Frank's first visit to a North Carolina governor about the death penalty.

Gov. Jim Martin was the first.

Martin, a Republican, served as North Carolina's governor from 1985 to 1993. When the North Carolina Council of Churches approached Frank about speaking to Martin, Frank jumped at the chance. He had longed to speak to someone who had some pull with a policy he abhorred, and being the governor, Martin had the biggest pull. Plus, Frank thought he could reach Martin.

Like Hunt, Martin was a Presbyterian. But it was bigger than that. Martin was raised Presbyterian, and his dad was a Presbyterian minister in South Carolina. During their meeting, Frank appealed to Martin's faith and reason as he tried to convince him to stop the execution of another man on North Carolina's death row.

Frank couldn't. After talking with Martin, the man Frank lobbied to save was killed a few hours later by lethal injection. Like Hunt, Martin listened; he nodded; he gave Frank his time; and he said good-bye. Today, Frank doesn't remember the men's names or the circumstances surrounding their crimes when he talked with Hunt and Martin. But he does remember his despair over what happened. That never goes away.

"There was something so surreal about it," Frank says today. "You want to be solicitous and make the best argument. Yet, the absurdity of it all — of sitting three miles from where this guy was in a jail cell wondering whether he would live or die.

"So, on one hand, I wanted to make a convincing argument. On the other hand, I wanted to hop onto the governor's desk and say, 'I can't believe we're even talking about this!'"

By the time he visited the governors, Frank had heard so many stories about people feeling like an old toy — forgotten and tucked away never to be used again. He first heard those stories from his own members in his church, New Creation Community Presbyterian. He later heard more stories at Greensboro Urban Ministry where he was the chaplain. When he visited with Hunt and Martin, Frank told them the stories he'd heard and about the faith compass Christians follow. Each time he left, he felt optimistic. A few hours later, his optimism vanished. What got him through? He remembers.

"You have to still trust in God even when things don't turn out the way we hope they would," he says. "We have to remember that the ultimate issue in terms of our relationship with God is not whether we get what we want, but whether we can hold onto God even when we don't."

Ask Frank to explain what he means, and he tells the story of his nephew, a daredevil of a boy named Stephen Charles Gane Jr.

Frank called him Charlie.

* * *

Charlie (right) loved playing Davey Crockett with his first cousin, Luke Justice
Photo Credit: Courtesy of Sara Gane.

The first thing you need to know about Charlie is this: He loved Davey Crockett.

Charlie read books about Crockett, he watched the Disney film about Crockett, he had a coonskin hat like Crockett, and he had an outfit like Crockett, complete with fringe under his arms and across his chest that looked like cooked spaghetti. One of his mom's friends made it for him. Charlie even visited the David Crockett Birthplace State Park in Limestone, Tennessee. He must've been no older than 4, and in a photo taken during that visit, you can tell he is some kind of excited.

There he is with his first cousin, Luke. They're standing in front of an obelisk bearing the nuts-and-bolts details of Crockett's life: Pioneer. Patriot. Soldier. Trapper. Explorer. State Legislator.

Congressman. Martyred at The Alamo. 1786-1836.

Luke is wearing his red high-top Converses and red cowboy hat, squinting like a sharpshooter and pointing his toy musket at the camera. Luke plays Georgie Russell, Crockett's friend from the 1955 film, "Davey Crockett: King of the Wild Frontier." Luke always had to play Georgie. Why? Charlie was Davey Crockett. And in that photo, Charlie is all Davey Crockett. He's wearing his fringed tunic, with his patched pants pooling at his ankles and the coonskin cap perched atop his bangs. Charlie is in a pure patriot pose. He's holding in his right hand his toy musket above his head. Charlie called his toy musket "Old Betsy."

Charlie is the first of eight grandchildren in the Dew family. He's the leader, the big brother to his little sister, Katie, the round-faced boy with short hair as dark as shoe polish. His mom, Sara, Frank's middle sister, is an elementary school teacher; his dad, Steve, the president of a business furniture company. They both encourage Charlie to play, explore, and live wide-open. Charlie does. Like Davey Crockett, Charlie sees life as one big adventure.

He water skies. Matter of fact, he goes to a water-skiing school in Florida with his dad, and he learns how to slalom. He later learns how to barefoot, and by the time he's a fourth-grader living with his family on a lake at King's Mountain, North Carolina, he water skis before going to school and drives the boat so his dad could ski.

If Charlie finds a finger of water, he always grabs his skis. And he knows they're good skis because he always researched to make sure he and his dad have the best skis. Charlie is a genuine water bug. Any lake becomes Charlie's second home, and his dad is his constant companion.

"Let's talk and spend some time together," Charlie tells his dad.

Charlie plays soccer, he plays basketball, he gets involved in Boy Scouts, he rides a skateboard, and he takes karate lessons. And he bikes. He loves his bike. He even gives his first set of wheels a name: "Speedy Blue."

If he has a free morning or a free afternoon, Charlie jumps on "Speedy Bike" and convinces one of his buddies who lives nearby to get out of their house and join him. Together, they bolt through their neighborhood. Charlie pops wheelies and thinks nothing of it. Once, his chin hit the handlebars, and he ends up in the emergency room getting stitches. The next day, he ends up back in the emergency room to get his chin re-stitched. When the doctor asks him what happened, Charlie tells him he was riding his skateboard, and he wrecked.

"Charlie," the doctor says, shaking his head and laughing. "You are something. Let's get you stitched up."

Charlie's hobbies and sports help him feel like a normal kid. Yet, he knows his life is far from normal. He is diagnosed with a genetic disorder, an incurable disease that could attack his organs and make breathing difficult.

He has cystic fibrosis, or CF. Charlie is 6 months old.

After getting the diagnosis at the Duke Medical Center in Durham, Sara and Steve drive straight to see the man who married them.

Her big brother.

"We drove straight to Frank's house," Sara says today. "We went there for hope, and that's what we got. Frank hugged us, loved on us, and helped us process it. It's not like Charlie was going to die the next day, but Steve and I knew we had to shift our thinking and look at everything in a different light, and we needed that reassurance. Frank gave us that. That's where your faith comes in. You have to lean on it."

After his diagnosis, Charlie has to do breathing treatments every day and take medication with every meal so his food won't go right through him. As Charlie gets older, exercise becomes a part of his daily regimen. It's good for his lungs. He also takes part in a Duke study that looks into how exercise helps kids with respiratory problems.

Beyond playing sports, Charlie looks for other ways to help with his breathing. He gets one idea from his grandfather. He tells Charlie that the oil in the skin of a Chihuahua helps anyone with asthma. So, Charlie being Charlie turns that advice into action. He's in third grade, and he convinces his parents to let him buy a Chihuahua. They find a breeder in Shelby, and Charlie uses his birthday money to buy a dog. He names her "Sweetie."

As a student at Shelby's Jefferson Elementary, Charlie is hospitalized twice — once for five days when he was a kindergartener and another for two weeks when he was in second grade. But he never uses sickness as an excuse. He turns his sickness into a challenge. He challenges himself to keep his CF in check.

His mom teaches kindergarten and later second grade at Jefferson Elementary, and when her students aren't there, Charlies stops by his mom's classroom, lies down and completes his breathing treatments. If her students are there, Charlie finishes his breathing treatments in the school's supply room. Most everyone at school knows of Charlie's ailment. And everyone there looks out for Charlie.

He is Mrs. Gane's son, sure. But really, he's Charlie. And Charlie has learned how to take care of himself.

By middle school, though, Charlie wants to remain anonymous and be a student in the crowd.

By seventh grade, Charlie and his family move from Shelby to Hickory, a town 40 miles north, for Steve's job. Charlie is now the new kid in a new school. He's shorter than everybody else, and he longs to be taller. At one point, his stomach is distended because of his enlarged spleen, and his cheeks are full because of the medicine he is taking. Despite all that, he has a message for his mom: Don't let anyone know about my CF.

Charlie just wants to fit in.

But it's hard to fit in when your body is a warrior fighting an enemy attacking your lungs and your digestive system. One organ hit hard is Charlie's liver. The fall of his seventh-grade year, his liver begins to fail, and doctors suggest putting Charlie on the transplant list. All that worries Charlie. So, he tells his parents he wants to see his pediatrician in Shelby. When he does, Charlie asks him a question that has been bugging him ever since he heard about getting on the transplant list.

"Why does someone have to die so I can live?" he asks.

In December, Charlie is put on the transplant list, and Sara and

Steve think they will be waiting for years on a liver.

They're wrong.

Two months later, at 3 in the morning on a Friday, Sara and Steve get the phone call. A liver is available, they hear. A little girl no more than 4 years old was killed in a car accident caused by a drunken driver, and she's an organ donor. Doctors on the other end of the line ask if Sara and Steve are ready.

"Do we have to take it?" Steve asks Sara.

"Yes, we have to take it," Sara responds. "He's healthy. He's good."

On Thursday night, hours before Sara and Steve get the early-morning phone call, Charlie plays a soccer game. On Friday morning, he gets up and see his sister, Katie, the second-grader, before she goes to school.

Charlie with his little sister Katie.

"Katie," her mom tells her, "You'd better give Charlie a hug."

After lunch, the Ganes — Sara and Steve and Charlie — drive

to Chapel Hill. Charlie is off to UNC Children's Hospital to get a new liver and a new lease on life. Everyone else soon follows.

Phyllis Justus, Sara's younger sister, and her husband, Steve, come from Charlotte. But no one calls her Phyllis. Everyone calls her Phyl, her childhood nickname. Phyl is a nurse, and Steve is an emergency room doctor. They are the family's medical team, and they're far from alone in Chapel Hill.

Steve's parents, Lacey and Allene Gane, come from Lumberton.

Steve Gane's brother, Jim, and his wife, Amanda, come from High Point.

Steve's sister, Natalie Cook, comes from Lumberton.

Donna Suttle, Sara's good friend and walking companion, comes from Shelby.

Michie and Frank come from Greensboro.

Ten people. Quite the crew. When everyone arrives, they assemble.

"We've got the whole team here," says Frank, looking at everyone around him. "We've got the medical team with Phyl and Steve; we've got the psychological team with Michie, and well, you've got me. I make up the spiritual team. That is, me and Mom's cat, Leroy, Sara."

The wait begins. Prayers begin, too.

* * *

It was hard enough sitting in the waiting room for reports from Charlie's doctors. What makes it even harder was being in a waiting room with a TV constantly tuned into a local channel where the newscast led with the story about a how little girl died in a car accident nearby.

"Well, that's where Charlie's liver is coming from," he tells himself.

By lunchtime, the wait turns into worry. Doctors inform Sara and Steve that their son has to go back into surgery because one of the arteries is twisted and needs to be reconfigured for better blood flow.

The afternoon inches into night. Sara and Steve stay at the

hospital, and everyone spends the night in Chapel Hill. The next morning, everyone comes back to the hospital, back to what they don't want to hear.

Charlie is unconscious, they hear, and he's on dialysis.

Charlie's dad, Steve, tells the doctors he'd donate 20 percent of his liver to save his son. Doctors continue working to keep Charlie alive. Meanwhile, Frank and everyone else turn to God.

They find the hospital's tiny chapel. Frank circles everyone up. They hold hands, like at New Creation, and Frank leads them in prayer.

He prays for hope, for healing, for trust in God. He prays for Sara and Steve. He prays for the Dews' extended family. He prays for the water skier, the soccer player, the Boy Scout who can ski barefoot. He prays for Charlie. He prays for a miracle.

Yet, the miracle never comes.

Charlie doesn't regain consciousness. On Monday, though, his condition gets better. By Tuesday, Charlie's condition gets worse. The hospital's waiting room becomes their home, and Steve and Sara wrestle with a question they've worried about since Charlie was 6 months old.

"What if?"

Sara and Steve don't have an answer. Neither does Frank. All they can do is wait and pray and pray some more.

As Charlie's condition continues to decline, Sara meets a family whose daughter is dying from injuries sustained in an accident. They are all huddled together in the same small waiting room, having short conversations saddled with emotion. Sara finds out the family doesn't want to donate any of the daughter's organs. When she hears that, Sara wants to approach them, talk to them, try to convince them, even beg them to change their minds.

But she can't. What she can do is crawl into bed with Charlie. She puts her arms around him and doesn't let go. She thinks about what she used to read to him when he was little. It's the book, "Love You Forever" by Robert Munsch and Sheila McGraw. As she lays beside Charlie, a scene from the book plays over and over in her mind.

But at night time, when that teenager was asleep,
The mother opened the door to his room,
Crawled across the floor and looked up over the side of the bed.
If he really was asleep, she picked up that great big boy
and rocked him back and forth, back and forth.
While she rocked him, she sang:
I love you forever,
I'll love you for always,
As long as I'm living
My baby you will be.

Sara remembers that scene from the book as she rocks Charlie back and forth. The words on the page become real.

"I love you forever, my little boy," she tells him.

* * *

Charlie dies next day. It's a Wednesday. Charlie had just turned 13 a dozen days before. Sara and Steve drive to Charlotte to see her parents, who are keeping Katie and the rest of their grandkids. Sara and Steve tell everyone the devastating news. Surrounded by her cousins, Katie begins grappling with the loss of her brother, knowing she'll never get another hug or another Davey Crockett moment. She just looks at her feet.

"Now I'm an only child," Katie says..

Luke, Charlie's first cousin, can't understand why their prayers aren't answered. Like his cousins, Luke just wants an answer. Any answer. But it's an answer no one can give.

So many people — friends, acquaintances, strangers — had so many questions.

Charlie was just playing soccer Thursday night, and six days later, he died?

He was just 13.

He was just a kid.

He had his whole life in front of him.

Where's the justice in *that*?

What's the reason for *this*?

And where is God in that?

God. You listening?

You even *there?*

You got an *answer?*

C'mon. *Why?*

* * *

When news spreads of Charlie's death, an entire community who loved and cared for Charlie grieves in their own ways.

They can't understand how a boy who goes into the hospital a week after his 13th birthday has died. It reminds everyone how fragile life can be and how the unimaginable can become real.

Sara and Steve, accompanied by Phyl's husband, Steve, meet with one of the surgeons to discuss what had happened during surgery. They find out o of Charlie's doctors made a tragic mistake during the operation. They settle out of court with UNC Hospitals. They feel the need to stand up for their son. They also want Charlie to be more than a hospital's fatal statistic. They want to make sure Charlie's life mattered.

So, Sara and Steve get busy.

They donate Charlie's eyes and heart. Charlie's heart saves a little girl's life.

They start a scholarship in his name at Shelby High, the school Charlie would have attended with his friends if he and his family stayed in Shelby. The scholarship is awarded to a soccer player who exemplifies excellence on the field and in the classroom.

And they donate money to UNC Children's Hospital and request that it honor Charlie in some way. The hospital honors Charlie by naming a heavily used activity area on the main floor after him. It's called the Charlie Gane Performance Stage.

Charlie's best friend in Shelby, Alex Goforth, inherits the BMX bike Charlie got for Christmas in 1996. Alex never really rides it. He keeps the BMX bike in his bedroom as a memorial to Charlie. Alex is now married, living in New York, and working in the clothing industry. He still has Charlie's bike. It's in his childhood bedroom at his parents' house in Shelby.

Every year since Charlie's death, his junior high in Hickory honors a student who has exemplified courage in overcoming some kind of adversity in their life. College Park Junior High calls it the Charlie Gane Award, and the student selected has their name added to a plaque.

The plaque sits in the school's trophy case. The award was started by Charlie's friends at College Park right after his death. Patrick Phillips, Charlie's best friend in Hickory, was one. Patrick rode bikes with Charlie the morning he left for his liver transplant in Chapel Hill.

"Charlie's death had a huge impact on my life," Patrick wrote at the time. "He knew he would only live to be in his twenties, and he accepted it. Never once did I hear him complain that life was not fair. He taught me to live life one day at a time, and when you look in the mirror, be proud of who you are."

Patrick Phillips is now married, and he has a son who was born in 2015. Patrick named him Charlie.

Three days after Charlie's death, one of Steve's college friends wrote about Charlie. Donnie Douglas was the editor of the Robesonian newspaper in Lumberton, and he wrote a column that revolved around Charlie's life from when he was first diagnosed with cystic fibrosis to the day he died, March 5, 1997.

The column's headline: "Charlie's full life of 13 years." Here is an excerpt:

Charlie was 13 when he died Wednesday. But Charlie, young as he was, died a man, facing a killer disease with poise and dignity, giving strength to others who needed it more than he did.

There is nothing that can soften the fate of losing a child, but it can be said that Steve and Sara — who have a healthy 7-year-old, Katie — were not blindsided. They began preparing for the rest of Charlie's life on that sad September day 13 years ago.

"The doctor told me the best advice he could give me was to treat Charlie like a normal kid," Steve said. "I knew that every moment with Charlie was going to be precious."

Charlie wanted to be treated as any other child. He bought a Chihuahua, "Sweetie." When his family moved from Shelby to Hickory last year, Charlie insisted that new friends not be told of his disease.

Charlie was not normal, however. He was extraordinary. He made sure that while the disease might rob him of years, it could not deny him of a full life.

How many children, given the sentence of a shorter life, would seldom complain and admonish others for offering prayers on their behalf?

How many children can water ski by age 5, slalom by age 7 and ski barefoot by age 9?

How many seventh-graders have the mind to score 910 on the PSAT?

"I feel like I lost my guidance counselor," said Steve. "He was such a little adult. He very seldom complained. No one can know how much medicine he had to take and how many times he had trouble breathing."

Donnie ended his column this way.

Steve recalled the day when Charlie first skied barefoot. How Charlie crashed face down in the water 10, maybe 12 times, only to get up each time and try again until he got it right. All because he had bet his father that he could do it.

"I remember telling him to stop," Steve said.

But nothing could stop Stephen Charles Gane Jr. from enjoying the 13 years and the chance that he was given. Not even cystic fibrosis.

Sara and Steve now live beside the coast of South Carolina. They moved Charlie's ashes from their church in Hickory to their new church in Georgetown, South Carolina.

Charlie's ashes are now interred in the columbarium at their new church, Prince George Winyah Parish, one of South Carolina's oldest churches. Prince George, an Anglican church, held its first service in 1747.

Sara and Steve also have a bench in their backyard in memory of Charlie. It sits near a feeder creek beside a small magnolia tree, a botanical memory from Sara's childhood in Lumberton. Sara grew up with a big magnolia tree in her front yard. Beside the bench is Charlie's grave marker from the cemetery at their former church in Hickory.

There are days when Sara will sit at the bench. So will Steve. When they do, they remember their water bug of a boy.

He was their Davey Crockett. Always will be.

Frank on Frank

The Hope Found in 'Thin Places"

Years after Charlie's death, I was driving back to Greensboro listening to NPR when I heard a story about a young man who had cystic fibrosis.

He had been through two lung transplants and a lot of other kinds of tough stuff because of his disease, and I kept thinking, 'I'm glad Charlie didn't have to go through all that.'

That gave me some consolation for my family, especially Sara, Steve, and Katie. But the more I thought about it, the more it made me realize what we all face at some point in our lives.

What we think is terrible and tragic at the time could later become something incredibly meaningful.

Just look at Charlie's life. He gave us a gift. And his gift was his life. He gave us memories that we all will certainly cherish. And those memories will live with us forever.

See, we all will face losing people we love at some point in our lives. It will be hard. It *always* will be hard. But the people we love who have died will continue to be present with us, and we always will be able to experience that.

You've heard about the idea of 'thin places,' right? It's where the distance between heaven and earth is very thin. It's a term that comes from Celtic Christianity, and it refers to those sacred moments when the separation between us here on Earth and those in heaven is so minimal, so thin that we can sense the presence of God.

We also can sense the presence of those we love as well.

We can find those 'thin places' everywhere — in a church, in a cemetery, in nature, and in your own hometown. We can hear something or smell something or see something, and it will take us back to one of those moments, those memories, that we cherish.

Those moments are almost always unexpected. They come out of the blue. And what a gift that is. Think about how those 'thin places' make us feel. But also think about what we find.

We find hope.

At Christmas, I'll always get together with Sara, Phyl, and their families for a candle-lighting ceremony. Sara got the idea from one of her grief groups, and we do it in the dining room. It's one of the few times all year that we all get together, and we light candles to remember Charlie, my parents, Steve's parents, just those who we love who have passed on. It helps us remember the good memories we have.

With every loss of a loved one, we will grieve forever, and we won't ever get over it. But we learn to live with it.

When I meet with people who are grieving over some terrible loss, I tell them, 'You will heal. You will rebuild yourself around the loss you suffered. And you will be whole again. But you will never be the same nor should you be the same. Nor would you *want* to be the same.'

On the 25th anniversary of Charlie's death, we celebrated Charlie's life and gathered at the Anglican church in Georgetown where his ashes are interred. All of us in our family were there. At the columbarium, Sara and Steve asked me to speak, and I referenced this quote from Ralph Waldo Emerson: 'It's not the length of life, but the depth of life.'

I love that quote because it's what we all want, to have a depth of life that means something. Charlie's life was like that. Look how he lived. And how he lived gave us this great gift of memory.

When we lose those people we love, we need to remember the gifts they gave us. Yes, an emptiness will always be there. It'll feel like a hole in your soul, no doubt. But it's there because of our love. It's the love that creates the pain and emptiness, and we don't want to change that.

As far as our relationship with God, especially in the initial phases of grief, we just have to put one foot in front of the other. But it's our faith and our trust in God that allows us to do that and go on.

So, when we lose someone, we can't be consumed by rage. That never helps. But what does help is knowing that healing will take place. We'll have to be on the lookout for those 'thin places.' We'll find them. And when we do, we will hear things we need to hear, see things we need to see and feel things we need to feel. We'll catch a scent in the air that brings back some memory, and a smile will come across our face.

And when that happens, mark that moment. You know why? We're beginning to heal.

Activists protest the death penalty outside the Supreme Court. The cases of at least nine death row inmates are on the court's docket.

High Court Hears 3 Death Penalty Cases

Capital Punishment Accounts for Larger Share of Justices' Smaller Workload

By Robert Barnes
Washington Post Staff Writer

It was death penalty day yesterday at the Supreme Court, coincidentally 30 years to the day since Gary Gilmore became the first person to be executed under the country's modern capital punishment laws.

The court heard three death penalty cases from Texas even as executions are on hold in an increasing number of states, from Maryland to California, and as the number of new death sentences continues to fall.

The work of the court so far this term shows that the complicated legal process that attends executing a murderer — the balance of state laws and federal constitutional guarantees — can take decades to unspool. Even a trip to the Supreme Court is sometimes not enough to settle the issue.

The cases of at least nine death row inmates nationwide — who are not proclaiming innocence but are protesting their sentences —

bade the execution of those who were younger than 18 at the time of their crimes. But Berman, who writes regularly for and runs the Sentencing Law and Policy blog, said the court's decisions in most death penalty cases affect only a handful of people in the states from which the cases arise. He would like to see the court spend time on other sentencing disparities "that affect thousands of people every day."

Indeed, the Texas cases heard yesterday had all been decided more than 15 years ago, when Texas juries were asked to answer only yes or no to two questions when deciding whether to impose death. They were asked whether the killing was deliberate and whether the killer constituted a continuing threat to society.

Several Supreme Court decisions have said that jurors also need to consider mitigating evidence, such as the IQ of the defendant or an abusive background.

In 2004, the court decided 7 to 2 in the case of LaRoyce Smith, who had murdered a Taco Bell manager in Dallas, that there were broad prob-

been presented more straightforwardly, it was in the best position to decide that such evidence would not have affected the jury's decision to sentence Smith to death. And Roberts defended the state's interpretations. "Why do we remand these cases for further proceedings not inconsistent with our opinion if there's nothing further to be considered?" he asked.

University of Texas law professor Jordan M. Steiker, representing Smith, said that the Texas court's actions were indeed contradictory and inconsistent.

Texas Solicitor General R. Ted Cruz said that complying with the Supreme Court's evolving decisions governing the death penalty "is not an easy task, and state and federal courts have struggled for two decades to draw the appropriate lines."

That struggle is evident on the court's docket, in which most of the death penalty cases come from the U.S. Court of Appeals for the 5th Circuit, which covers Texas and much of the South, and the San Francisco-based U.S. Court of Appeals for the 9th Circuit. "The Ninth looks so

In January 2008, Frank and others who oppose the death penalty unfurled a huge banner in front of the U.S. Supreme Court and made the front page of the metro section in The Washington Post. Moments later, they were arrested.

Chapter 15

"O'er The Land of the Free"

"The love of power can be pretty tenuous. It's here today, gone tomorrow. But what's greater than the love of power is the power of love. It's much more long term. Think of it this way. Not many people are talking today about Augustus Caesar, Rome's first emperor. But a lot more people are talking about Jesus. He was the victim of capital punishment, and he is remembered for His message on the power of love."
The Rev. Frank Dew

Frank can't sleep.

He buries himself deeper into a sleeping bag in the basement of the Dorothy Day Catholic Worker House in Washington, DC, and in his mind, he sees himself on a sidewalk in downtown Greensboro. He's in his hunting shoes and Wake Forest ball cap, holding a sign that says "No Killing In My Name" and hearing cars honk and wave and holler at him during late afternoon traffic at the corner of West Market and South Elm/Eugene.

On that sidewalk, Frank is cold. In that basement, Frank is cold, too.

"Oh, man, it's going to be freezing out there tomorrow morning," he keeps telling himself. "I *hate* the cold."

It's January 2008, the weekend before the Martin Luther King Jr. holiday on Monday, a weekend of celebration and a weekend of heavy coats. The highs won't even go above freezing when Frank drives up to DC to protest the death penalty, 30 years after the U.S. Supreme Court reinstated capital punishment. He joins nine other protesters — seven men; two women — and he stays in Northwest Washington, in a house named after social activist Dorothy Day, the founder of the *Catholic Worker* newspaper. Like Frank, Day put her faith into action. Starting in the 1930s, she helped the poor, aided the vulnerable and pushed constantly for what she called a "revolution of the heart" until her death in 1980.

Frank does like her kind of revolution.

"We cannot love God unless we love each other," Day once said, "and to love we must know each other."

Frank believes that. So, on Monday morning, he's going to stand on the white marble steps outside the highest court in the land, and he's going to protest the death penalty. For more than a decade, he has worked within the system to try and make change. He has met with leaders in Greensboro and in Raleigh, and he has tried to convince them to stop what he calls a "state-sanctioned execution." Now, Frank is going to fight against the system to try and make change. And he's going to do it on a morning that would make his fingers numb.

Frank is never what he would call a "rabble-rouser." But he's fed up with the hypocrisy he sees from those pulling the levers of power. All he has to do is remember listening one night to WPTF on his way home from Raleigh after talking with Gov. Jim Hunt about the death penalty. Frank thought he had made an impact. Hunt was a Presbyterian, and Frank felt listened to. On his ride home, he heard on WPTF that the man he lobbied to save had just died by lethal injection that night.

More than a decade after that conversation with Hunt, that revelation still leaves a bitter taste in Frank's mouth. All he has to do is think about history.

In 1959, the General Assembly of the Presbyterian Church (USA) stated, "the use of the death penalty tends to brutalize the society that condones it." In 1978, the General Assembly reaffirmed its stance: "Capital punishment is an expression of vengeance which contradicts the justice of God on the cross." In 1985, the Presbyterian Church (USA), reemphasized these positions and declared, in their words, "our continuing opposition to capital punishment."

What did that really accomplish? Frank doesn't have an answer, and that really bothers him. Frank knows he has to do something more than stand on a sidewalk in downtown Greensboro and hold a sign. He knows he has to do more than drive to Raleigh to cajole governors who are Presbyterians to stand with their faith and oppose the death penalty. He knows he has to step up his opposition and go to the ultimate power center, the place that reignited capital punishment.

But he knows there's going to be a price paid for that. Frank knows he's going to be arrested for the second time in his life, and his personal lesson in civil disobedience is going to be way different than what happened in a parking lot of a K-Mart distribution center in Greensboro.

"Bill, don't worry. I've got carpool covered."

Frank knows there's no Bill Ingold in DC. Frank won't know any police officer in DC. But he knows why he's there. Art Laffin.

Art Laffin. Photo credit: Courtesy of Dorothy Day Catholic Worker House.

* * *

Inside the small chapel at Greensboro Urban Ministry, talking to a room full of men and women, Art starts with a question.

"If anyone here knows someone in jail or prison, raise your hand."

Every hand in the room goes up.

"OK, does anyone here know someone who has been murdered?"

Only a few hands drop

"You and I have something in common," Art says. "I know someone who has been murdered. It was my kid brother. His name was Paul. Let me tell you about Paul."

For a decade in their hometown of Hartford, Connecticut, Paul had worked as the associate director at a place known as Mercy Housing and Shelter. Mercy was similar to GUM. It helped those without homes find shelter, food, help, and hope. On the third Monday in September 1999, Paul was leaving Mercy when he was approached by a man named Dennis Soutar who frequented the nonprofit's soup kitchen. Dennis stabbed Paul to death.

Dennis was deemed mentally incompetent to stand trial. He was sentenced to serve 60 years at a public hospital in Connecticut that treats people diagnosed with mental illness.

If Dennis had been found competent to stand trial, he would have faced the death penalty in Connecticut. Surprisingly, Art and his mother didn't want that at all. They appealed to everyone to show mercy. They prayed for Dennis. They wanted him to heal. They met with Dennis' family and told them to convey to Dennis their prayers for his well-being. When Art eulogized Paul during his memorial service, Art asked for Dennis to receive the care he needed as well as others dealing with mental health issues.

Art didn't want anyone else to lose their lives like Paul. In front of the Connecticut General Assembly, lobbying for elected officials to repeal the death penalty in his home state, he explained why he felt the way he did.

"Killing Dennis Soutar will never bring my brother back," he told the legislators. "It will never bring healing or closure for me and my family. The pain of Paul's murder will always be there (and) certainly, individuals, and even corporations and governments who commit violent acts must be held accountable for their actions and make restitution to the victims' families.

"But we must never sanction killing those who kill, no matter how brutal the crime. Rather, we must always seek the way of restorative/transformative justice."

After his brother's death, Art advocated everywhere against capital punishment. The T-shirts he wore sometimes said it all. During some death-penalty protests, he'd wear a black T-shirt bearing a quote from Dorothy Day, "The only solution is love." Or sometimes, he'd wear a white T-shirt that said, "An Eye For An Eye Makes The Whole World Blind."

No matter what he wore, his message was the same: Capital punishment is racially biased, innocent people are put to death, poor defendants don't receive adequate representation, and it costs more to execute someone than sentence them to life in prison.

His stance on the death penalty brings Art to Greensboro as part of his campaign. He comes with other people who have lost family members to murder, and they are traveling nationwide to speak out against the death penalty. Art speaks during the afternoon worship service at New Creation Community Presbyterian Church. He also speaks at GUM in front of a room full of men and women, many of whom, like Art, are members of a club no one wants to join.

"We need to appeal to those in power who can make a decision and convince them to do the right thing," Art says inside the chapel at GUM. "Uphold God's command, 'Thou shall not kill' and put justice above the law."

As Art speaks, heads nod. Frank sits off to the side, and as he listens, he realizes he's found a fellow advocate.

He and Art are first cousins in the same fight.

* * *

At first glance, Art doesn't draw attention. He's balding, with a high forehead, a wide girth and a round, kind face. Yet, when Art speaks, people notice. He speaks with the conviction of a man on a mission. He wants to change minds and change hearts. He's a member of the Dorothy Day Catholic Worker, a nonprofit headquartered in the Dorothy Day House. He's become known nationwide as an organizer, a writer and a speaker in the faith-based, nonviolent movement pushing for peace, social justice, and an end to poverty and war.

Art was a student of Henri Nouwen, the well-known Dutch priest, and he spoke at Nouwen's funeral. The teacher and the student were a lot alike. As Frank listens to Art speak at his church and at GUM, Frank recalls how he met Nouwen in the early 1990s at Church of the Saviour in DC, Frank's spiritual blueprint for New Creation Community Presbyterian. Back then, Frank could feel Nouwen's conviction when he wrapped his arms around Frank and whispered in his ear, "Hold onto your calling."

A decade or so later, Frank feels that same kind of conviction from Art. Whenever he speaks, Art emphasizes that the death penalty only creates another grieving family and fuels the cycle of violence. And to honor the memory of his kid brother, Art has lobbied people in all kinds of places to convince them of the need to stop the death penalty.

He did it inside a chapel at a homeless shelter in Greensboro.

He did it in front of the U.S. Department of Justice in downtown Washington, DC.

He did it at a gathering of fellow Catholic social activists in Silver Spring, Maryland.

In a talk he titled, "Citizenship and Catholic Values," he told them in the fall of 2004 to heed the advice from people like writer Henry David Thoreau, India's leader Mahatma Gandhi and the French Catholic social activist Peter Maurin.

Art said:

"Gandhi said 'Be the change you want to see in the world.'" Peter Maurin said, 'The future will be different if we make the present different.' Thoreau said: 'Cast your whole vote, not a strip of paper merely.'

"Thus, I believe in voting with your life. I believe that what we do every day is a way of casting a vote.

"Practicing personalism and voluntary poverty, doing the works of mercy, serving the poor, nonviolently resisting violence and state-sanctioned killing, living simply and sharing your resources, caring for and being good stewards of the earth, standing for and working in solidarity with the victims and trying to create the beloved community, are the best ways I know how to participate in the political life of our society and world."

After speaking at GUM and at Frank's church, Art stays with Michie and Frank. After he leaves, Frank starts thinking more about what else he can do to oppose the death penalty. And that's what gets Frank thinking about a trip to DC.

Frank believes in the power of forgiveness. He knows what it can do for others and entire institutions. He has preached that message so many times in front of so many congregations. That includes a handful of kids. And whenever he speaks to them about forgiveness, he talks about a pencil.

"We all make mistakes, and it's nice to have an eraser when we mess up," he tells the children gathered at his feet during a recent service in Greensboro's Sedgefield Presbyterian Church. "We already have God's forgiveness. That has helped us get on the right path. When we have God's mercy, think of what we can do when we show that mercy and forgiveness to others. We become like that pencil I talked about. We can use our eraser and erase any bad feelings when people mess up. That is forgiveness."

A year or so after Art speaks in Greensboro. Frank channels his pencil story and drives to DC. It's the third weekend in January 2008, the weekend before the Monday when many celebrate the birthday of civil rights leader Martin Luther King Jr.

Like King, Frank discovers mercy — and hate.

After sleeping in a chilly basement at the Dorothy Day House, Frank and the others are driven to the U.S. Supreme Court, and as they huddle in their heavy coats, they park themselves on the white marble steps and begin to chant.

"Stop Executions!"

"Stop Executions!"
"Stop Executions!"

One of the protesters pulls out a banner from underneath his coat, rolls it out and gives it to other protesters to hold. It's 10 feet long bearing two words written in black: "Stop Executions!" Onlookers can easily see it from the other side of the street or even halfway down the block. It is far from subtle, and their banner — and their presence — is noticed immediately by those who have little patience for any kind of protesters, even peaceful ones.

As Frank and the others continue to chant, the Capitol Police arrive. The police officers tell Frank and his fellow protesters four times to stop and put away their signs.

Four times.

"OK, this is your final warning," one of the officers tells them.

The officers don't want to go for five. They simply converge on the group, and Frank immediately knows their Capitol Hill protest is nothing like Greensboro.

"OK, I think we've made our point," Frank tells himself. "These people are serious."

Seconds later, Frank has his arms behind his back and his wrists bound by plastic tie handcuffs. No arms in front like what his friend, Bill Ingold, did for him in Greensboro. Nope, there is no Andy Griffith kindness here on this influential sidewalk in DC. It's all business. And business means that Frank and the others are marched single file toward a van.

"You guys are going to get the behind-the-scenes tour today," one of the officers tells them.

Frank thinks he'll be out by the afternoon. They'll get processed, go before a judge and he'll be back at the Dorothy Day Catholic Worker House for dinner.

That doesn't happen.

* * *

In a room somewhere deep inside the Supreme Court, Frank and the others stay for hours. The Capitol Police are cordial. They even remove the plastic-tie handcuffs from their wrists when anyone needs to go to the bathroom. But other than that, Frank and the others just wait for something to happen. Anything. But nothing does. Hardly anyone notices them other than the guards standing outside. Then comes the announcement from a Capitol Police officer.

"Alright, we have to take you all to the DC Jail for the night," the officer says. "We need to load you all into a van."

The DC Central Detention Facility is a 10-minute drive from the U.S. Supreme Court. Built in 1976, DC Central sits beside RFK Stadium and a few blocks from the Anacostia River. It's a big box of a building that can hold as many as 2,150 inmates. The DC Jail is part of DC Central, and the inmates who are held there have been sentenced for a misdemeanor or are waiting to see a judge.

When Frank and the others arrive, the women are separated from the men, and the men are kept in single cells. Jailers take their shoelaces, their belts, their keys, their wallets, just anything they had in their pockets. Jailers give them dinner — a bologna sandwich with a strawberry Kool-Aid — and take them to where they would stay the night. Frank hears the metallic clang of a turned jailhouse key behind him, and he finds himself in a small, claustrophobic cell that feels like a metal can. Inside the cell, behind a door with a small steel-mesh window, is a metal toilet, a metal tub, and two metal bunks. The air smells like a day-old sweaty sock, and the fluorescent tubes lining the ceiling cast everything in an eerie white-yellow glow.

All night long, under a glaring bright light, people in the jail scream and yell.

Frank calls out to the other protesters held in cells nearby. He wants to make sure they are OK. They are. Frank is, too. Yet, as the night drags on, Frank wonders what will happen next. He has no idea. Later that night, Frank gets a roommate. He's a Hispanic man in his 30s. Frank is sitting on the bottom metal bunk when the jailers bring the man into Frank's cell. Frank talks first.

"What you in for?" Frank asks.

"An outstanding warrant," the man says. "I was just walking along on the street when the police stopped and arrested me."

"Oh, that sounds a little scary," Frank responds. "They just stopped you?"

"Yeah," the man says. "Just stopped. Handcuffed me right there. What you in for?"

"Oh, nine of us were involved in a protest in front of the U.S. Supreme Court," Frank says.

"What were you protesting?" the man asks.

"The death penalty," Frank says. "We believe it's wrong. It goes against everything in our faith."

"Faith," the man says. "Like religion?"

"Yeah, like religion," Frank responds. "I'm a minister."

The man laughs.

"With your white beard," the man says, "you look like Santa Claus."

"I've gotten that before," Frank says, chuckling.

The man begins looking at his shoes. A few minutes later, he looks up.

"I'm glad to know that," the man says. "I'm glad to know you're a preacher. And you got locked up for what again?"

"Protesting the death penalty," Frank responds. "We were chanting, 'Stop executions! Stop executions!' I guess you can't do that in front of the Supreme Court."

The man laughs again.

"Wow," he says. "That's pretty cool. A minister. Protesting in front of the Supreme Court. They handcuff you?"

"Plastic ties on our wrists and put them behind our backs," Frank says, holding up both wrists.

"They did that to you? A preacher?" the man asks.

"Yeah, they did," Frank says. "Sometimes, you have to do what you got to do. You have to stand up for what you believe in."

The man nods and starts looking at his shoes again. He doesn't say another word. Minutes later, he climbs up in the upper bunk and begins to snore. Frank, though, can't sleep. He shuts his eyes and listens to the screaming and yelling. Finally, he sleeps for no more than an hour. When he wakes up, the chaotic din inside the jail has subsided. Soon, jailers begin walking back and forth in front of his cell. Frank figures it is morning. Has to be.

"Alright, take a leak," said a jailer who stops at their cell. "We're taking you to the courthouse."

The jailer walks away. Frank already feels a bit wobbly from his lack of sleep in a jail cell bathed all night in a bright spotlight. He also feels ill at ease, not knowing how long he will have to wait or when he can leave. He doesn't even know what time it is. Then, it hits him.

"Michie," Frank tells himself. "Jeez. She has no *idea* where I am. And when was the last time I talked to her? Heck, I can't remember. I know she does. How is she doing?"

He'll soon find out.

* * *

Michie Dew along with their son, David, often accompanied Frank to his various rallies in North Carolina. Frank protests became their protests because they too believed in standing up against what they believed was wrong. Photo credit: Courtesy of Dr. Michie Dew.

For 36 hours, Michie hasn't heard from Frank.

At first, she's a bit anxious. When Frank was arrested at the K-Mart protest, she remembers how he had his hearing and he got home that same night. But this time? Nothing. Now, she knows Frank can't call if he is in the DC Jail. But the weather that weekend turns nasty, and a storm turns North Carolina and Virginia into an ice rink. A thin sheen of ice covers everything. As the hours reach double digits with no contact from Frank. Michie worries that he tried to drive home in the weather mess. And the more she thinks about that, the more her worry turns into fear.

Finally, Michie has had enough. She calls the jail. She reaches a jailer. Dr. Michie Dew doesn't mince any words.

"Look, I'm afraid that my husband is dead lying in a ditch somewhere in Virginia, and I don't know if I need to call a state trooper to have them looking in a ditch for his body or what," she says, trying to tamp down her rising anxiety. "So, can you tell me if he's there?"

Frank is, she's told.

"Thank you," Michie says, relieved. "Thank you. I'm just glad he's not dead in a ditch."

She hangs up. Questions still linger.

"What is going on?" she asks.

In the federal courthouse, Frank feels claustrophobic once again.

He meets up with the six other male protesters, and they're kept in a holding cell inside the courthouse that looks like a cage at an old-school zoo. The holding cell is simply a box. One side has a wall; the other three sides have bars from the floor to the ceiling. A waist-high toilet is in the corner, and anyone who needs to go can have a crowd watching them. What makes it worse is what Frank hears just beyond the bars. The U.S. Marshals bark, curse, and shout orders at everyone coming and going into any holding cell. After sleeping for less than an hour, Frank feels like he's landed in another world, a world he knows nothing about.

"So, *this* is what it's like?" Frank tells himself.

The U.S. Marshals walk constantly back and forth in front of Frank's cell. They walk with purpose, taking quick steps to somewhere, eyes forward, shoulders back, in their dark blue uniforms with "U.S. Marshal" stenciled in yellow across their backs. Their job is to be the watchdog inside any federal court facility, and they provide security for the judges and other court personnel. So, every few minutes, Frank will see a dark blue uniform walk by. Later that morning, one of them stops outside their cell. He has a Washington Post newspaper under his arm and turns to face Frank and the others.

"Hey, you guys made the paper," the U.S. Marshal says.

He displays the Metro section of The Washington Post, and there they are. It's a picture of Frank and the others standing on the steps of the U.S. Supreme Court, holding the 10-feet banner that says "Stop Executions." The photo anchors the entire page.

The photo catches the attention of one of the other men inside Frank's cell. He isn't one of Frank's fellow protesters. He's a Black man, and like Frank, he is waiting to see a judge. When he sees the photo, he starts jumping up and down.

"We made the paper! We made the paper! We made the paper!"

"Yeah, we made the paper, didn't we?" Frank says, looking at him. "We're the Supreme Court Nine."

The man ignores Frank. He just continues yelling, jumping up and down.

"We made the paper! We made the paper! We made the paper!"

Everywhere Frank looks, he sees inmates in orange jumpsuits, and every one of them is either Black or Brown. Other than Frank and the eight other protesters, the only other white people Frank sees are the U.S. Marshals. As a man who makes his living preaching from a pulpit and having control over what happens around him, Frank is way out of sorts. He's inside the depths of a federal courthouse one block west from the U.S. Capitol. But he could be on the moon for all he knows. Inside this caged box, he has no semblance of control. He feels forgotten, and no one walking outside the bars seems to care.

As he waits to head into the courtroom, Frank is a bit unnerved because he has no idea what time it is, and there is not a clock in sight.

He's had no semblance of time since being arrested the morning before on the steps of the U.S. Supreme Court. Time seems nebulous, an abstract concept, and it only adds to his sense of feeling forgotten. So, when he sees a female U.S. Marshal walking by, a woman with what he believes is a kind face, he thinks he can ask her.

"Excuse me, ma'am," Frank says. "Do you have the time?"

The woman stops, turns on the balls of her feet and faces Frank.

"I'm not on your fucking agenda," she barks. "This is our time, and we'll keep the time."

"Thank you, ma'am," Frank responds.

Later that afternoon, Frank and the six other male protesters are taken from the holding cell to the courtroom. They meet the two other female protesters, and like they have done all day, they wait. This time, U.S. Marshals put shackles on their ankles and put plastic-tie handcuffs on their wrists. Frank looks at his ankles, his wrists and remembers what he told the young Hispanic man in the cell at the DC Jail: Stand up for what you believe in.

At the moment, though, Frank feels beaten down. A silence settles over Frank and the group. Flanked by U.S. Marshals, they wait for the chance to see a judge. They're all like shoppers in line at a grocery store, everyone looking forward, their mouths a straight line.

A U.S. Marshal breaks the silence.

"You know, whenever we see a bunch of white people here, they are either protesters or prostitutes," he says. "You all sure don't look like prostitutes."

Frank looks at the U.S. Marshal. He wants to say something. But he stops himself and looks at the courtroom's closed door in front of him.

"Is that a compliment — or not?" Frank asks himself.

Minutes later, the door opens, and Frank and the others shuffle into the courtroom. The sh-sh-sh syncopation of shackles around their feet echoes in the windowless courtroom.

"I'm not a nobody," Frank tells himself, taking short steps so he wouldn't fall. "But I am closer to nobody than I've ever been in my life."

The next morning, Frank is Greensboro-bound.

Despite the freezing temperatures, he rolls down the window and breathes in the frigid air of Virginia.

"How did I end up here?" he asks.

The night before, Frank walked out of a federal courthouse into an icebox of a night. During a 20-minute hearing, a federal judge warned them not to return to the U.S. Supreme Court, and he told them they would have to come back in a few months to hear their fate.

Frank gets back his shoelaces, his belt, his wallet, and his keys. He doesn't have to post bond. He and the other protesters are represented by lawyers brought in by Dorothy Day House. After the hearing, Frank calls Michie to let her know he's OK. They all get a ride back to the Dorothy Day House and sit around for a welcome-home dinner of beans, rice, and salad. Afterward, Frank and Art walk to a bar nearby to watch a college basketball game.

Yes, a Wake Forest basketball game.

Frank spends one more night huddled in a sleeping bag in a chilly basement. Then, he heads home.

Frank can't get over how claustrophobic and powerless he felt in jail. But what really gets him is how callous the U.S. Marshals were and how they used language to intimidate and to control. And he can't get over how the young woman, the U.S. Marshal, reacted when he asks her for the time.

"She morphed into a dragon," Frank says today. "I kept thinking, 'Good grief, what is her life like? Is she like that 24/7? Are they all like that 24/7? Can they ever really turn it off?'"

When Frank gets home, Michie meets him at the door. She can't get over how tired and worn out he looks. They hug, and Frank responds with just a few words.

"I'm glad I'm home," he says.

A few days later, Frank talks with his son David. He's 22, a student at Wake Forest. And like he did a dozen years before, David had a question for his father. It's about his grandfather, Frank's dad, David's Bobo.

"When are you going to tell Bobo?" he asks.

"When it's all over," Frank says.

That happens a few months later. Frank and Michie go back to that same DC courtroom and stand in front of a federal judge. Once again, Frank feels powerless.

"You know I can sentence you to active time," the judge tells him.

"Yes, your honor," Frank responds.

The judge pauses. Frank listens. Standing in court and hearing what his beliefs could do to his body and his mind, Frank can feel his fear from the tension knotting his shoulders. He knows he could spend two months in jail and pay a fine of possibly up $5,000. But he knows it has all been worked out, choreographed like a dance. But this dance is no fun for Frank. He feels like a statistic, a man known only for the charges written on a piece of paper. Frank has become "a nobody" once again.

"OK," the judge says, looking at Frank. "Let's do this."

The judge rattles off a litany of next steps. He stresses that Frank cannot go back to the U.S. Supreme Court, according to the agreement worked out. He drops the misdemeanor charge of demonstrating in front of the U.S. Supreme Court, and Frank pleads guilty to delivering a speech on the court's steps. Frank pays no fine.

Frank walks out of the courthouse a free man. Immediately, he remembers what had happened that cold Monday in January.

As Frank and the eight other protesters stood outside the Supreme Court, the judges inside heard a death penalty appeal from Texas. They denied it. They went home to dinner, Frank and the others went to jail, and the man in Texas went to his death.

On the drive home after his court hearing, Frank rolls down the window once again. He thinks about the judge, the sentence, and the idea of applying for a job and having to say "yes" to being convicted of a crime.

"Yes," Frank says to himself, shaking his head. "I'm a convicted orator."

He then thinks about, of all things, the words written by an amateur poet long ago. He has sung those words at every football and basketball game at Wake Forest. He'd take off his Wake Forest ball cap, put his hand over his heart, lift up his chin and belt it out like a hymn in church.

O say can you see, by the dawn's early light
What so proudly we hail'd at the twilight's last gleaming,
Whose broad stripes and bright stars through the perilous fight
O'er the ramparts we watched, were so gallantly streaming?
And the rocket's red glare, the bombs bursting in air,
Gave proof through the night that our flag was still there,
O say does that star-spangled banner yet wave
O'er the land of the free and the home of the brave

On his road home, though, he begins to see those words a lot differently.

"Land of the free,'" Frank tells himself. "How ironic is that?"

Frank can now answer that. He has seen it firsthand. So has his friend, Meg Eggleston, one of his church members. They both have quite the introduction to America's criminal justice system.

But Meg's introduction is a bit different. It has a name, a face, and a family. And it's something she'll never forget.

Frank on Frank

"Hate Won't Win"

What is the most universal symbol of Christianity? A cross, right?

Well, that's one of the things I find so ironic about the Christian faith. The Romans killed people by using the cross. I mean, the cross is a symbol of a state-sponsored execution. That is *exactly* what took Jesus' life. He gave his life. But it also was taken from him.

I would think the *last* place you'd find support for state-sponsored executions would be a church with a cross as its symbol. But we all know that's not true. I think what drives people to support capital punishment is their love of power. They look at it as part of their job, and politically they support capital punishment because they want to keep their job.

But that can be such a gamble.

The love of power can be pretty tenuous. It's here today, gone tomorrow. But what's greater than the love of power is the power of love. It's much more long term. Think of it this way. Not many people are talking today about Augustus Caesar, Rome's first emperor. But a lot more people are talking about Jesus.

He was the victim of capital punishment, and he is remembered for His message on the power of love.

Think of some of the last words he said when he was nailed to the cross.

'Father, forgive them; for they know not what they do.'

Forgive them. Think of what that tells us.

Jesus forgave the people who persecuted Him, tortured Him, and sentenced Him to die. There is such power in that. It's the same kind of power in a story I've used in sermons. It's a story of two prisoners recently released from a Nazi concentration camp following World War II, and the first prisoner asks the second prisoner, 'Have you forgiven the Nazis?'

The second prisoner looks at the first prisoner in disbelief.

'No!' he says.

The first prisoner just shakes his head.

'Until you forgive them, you are still in their prison.'

You are still in their prison. Those are strong words.

If we are not able to let go of the wrongs done to us, then we are essentially still imprisoned by the wrongs that *were* done to us.

Every relationship has breakdowns, and every relationship requires forgiveness. It's the glue that holds relationships together. Without forgiveness, relationships unravel, and we become imprisoned by our anger, resentment, and bitterness. If we don't let that go, we will never be released.

In 2 Corinthians 5, verse 18 the Bible talks about how God, through Jesus Christ, has given us what He calls 'a ministry of reconciliation.' Now, there is a difference between forgiveness and reconciliation. Forgiveness we can do unilaterally, but reconciliation requires two parties. A great example of reconciliation is what happened in the summer of 2015 in Charleston, South Carolina.

A man walked into Mother Emmanuel AME Church and joined a dozen parishioners in a prayer meeting in the church's Bible study room. An hour later, he pulled out a 45-caliber handgun and killed nine of them. A few days later, in a Charleston courtroom, members saw the man face to face for the first time.

One member said, 'I forgive you.'

Another member said, 'Hate won't win.'

That is what forgiveness really means. It is not only forgiving him. But it set up members of Mother Emmanuel to free themselves from hatred.

Now, let me tell you about Rick Tatum.

He was one of the more active church members at New Creation. I had met him at Greensboro Urban Ministry. He was homeless, and I encouraged him to come to our worship service Sunday afternoons at Presbyterian Church of the Covenant near UNCG. I even picked him up every Sunday. He first started coming for the food we provided after our services. But what kept him coming back was the church. I remember him telling me, 'You all welcomed me.'

When we moved our worship service to First Presbyterian across town, he continued to come, and he helped set up chairs and put them away after every service. He was such a big help.

A few years later, Rick was caught on video stealing sound equipment and a TV from the church. When it happened, I was angry. But more than that, I was embarrassed because I thought it reflected badly on our congregation. It was just that someone associated with our church had committed a crime in the very place that welcomed us with open arms.

But First Presbyterian didn't kick us out. It could've. But it didn't. The church's business manager who I worked with through this whole thing didn't even bring it up.

Rick spent some time in prison for what he did. I believe it was six months. I went to visit him because I wanted him to know that he would not be cut off from our fellowship for what he did. I also wanted him to know that I forgave him and our church — his church — forgave him. When he got out of prison, we welcomed him back.

As Christians, we are called to forgive others. And yes, that can be hard. But we don't want to be imprisoned by our own resentment and anger. And when we forgive others, we also can forgive ourselves.

See, we often hold ourselves to a higher standard than we hold other people. We can understand and expect other people to mess up. But not us. When we do mess up, we beat ourselves up over it. But there are so many ways in which we all fall short every day. Myself included. Yet, when we forgive ourselves, we can get untangled from the web of tough emotions that can encircle us.

Forgiveness begins with God's grace and mercy. We love because God has first loved us. And God's love has been there from the very beginning. It's like the love of a good parent. That never goes away. And we all need to remember we are not living our lives to *earn* forgiveness. We are living our lives *in response* to God's love.

So, our love — and therefore our forgiveness of others — is based on God's forgiveness of us — and for us. I like to say that we are given opportunity every day to say, 'Thank you, God!' We can thank God by loving others and being gracious toward others. And when we love and forgive others, we also are loving and forgiving ourselves.

The day before his scheduled execution, Meg Eggleston got to meet Elias Syriani for the first time face to face without a thick pane of glass separating them. As they met and talked, two guards stood nearby. Photo Credit: Courtesy of Meg Eggleston.

Chapter 16
"Where is God in all this?"

"Our faithfulness in God often takes us to places we never imagined we would ever go or do things we never even thought we'd carry out. That journey often is painful. It's also incongruous with the world around us because we're doing things other people don't want to do. Yet, there is so much meaning in doing such things that make us uncomfortable. It makes God more real to us."

The Rev. Frank Dew

Frank looks up from his desk, and there she is. His friend from New Creation. On many Mondays and Fridays, she has stood with him on the sidewalk in front of the new courthouse in downtown Greensboro. Like Frank, she's held up some homemade sign and pushes for everyone to see what she wants them to believe.

Let's end the death penalty in North Carolina.

She always is a picture of grace, the slender woman with the relaxed Southern accent. Frank recognizes that accent. Like Frank, she grew up in small-town North Carolina. Her home? Edenton, a small historic town in eastern North Carolina tucked beside the Albemarle Sound. She is four years older than Frank, and they both spring from a home where mothers reared their children to believe in the Golden Rule, no matter who they were or where they worshiped.

But on this particular afternoon, when his friend barges into his office, she looks frazzled. She later feels like she came across, in her words, "a little arrogant." No matter. She needs help, and she knows where to turn.

"This is a lot," she tells Frank. "This thing is getting to be a lot. You got me into this, and I need your help now."

Frank listens. And the more he listens, the more he tells himself, "Wow. I've gotten her way deeper than either one of us imagined."

It all started with a simple question Frank asks a lot of his parishioners.

"You want to try this?"

And Meg Eggleston said yes.

* * *

Meg was simply looking for something to do.

She had retired from teaching and had taken a few classes at the Servant Leadership School headquartered out of Greensboro's Holy Trinity Episcopal Church. She met Frank there and heard about his church, New Creation Community Presbyterian Church. She started going and appreciated what Frank said on Sunday afternoons around a circle of chairs.

Meg also appreciated how all the members shared a meal after their service in Presbyterian Church of the Covenant near UNCG. The food served came in bowls and casserole dishes from people's homes. But what really caught Meg's attention was who came.

They were local folks with no address. They lived under an overpass, in a tent in the woods or on a single bed at Weaver House at Greensboro Urban Ministry. Frank welcomed them all. Even when they walked in bleary-eyed and hazy from too much alcohol, Meg noticed how Frank interacted with each one of them with ease. He knew them by first name or by face, and he had helped more than a few navigate through some rough patches in their lives. Meg watched it unfold from her folding chair in front of a plate of food pulled from New Creation's potluck supper.

What she saw showed her what she believed a church should do.

"It was about Jesus," Meg says later. "It was what I felt churches needed to be. It needs to be about ministering to people."

So, Meg kept coming.

As she got more active, Frank invited her to join a weekly

gathering with members of the local chapter of People of Faith Against the Death Penalty. In 1994, after 22 years of teaching, she moved from Madison to Greensboro, and she was looking to volunteer in her new city. That's how she found New Creation, the Servant Leadership School, and her spot on the sidewalk with Frank holding a sign and protesting the death penalty.

Soon, she wanted to be involved more. After several conversations with her friend, Nell, Meg got an idea. Nell told Meg about her new pen pal, a man in a wheelchair on North Carolina's death row.

"Nell, I would like to be a pen pal, too," Meg said. "Tell your guy that I would like a pen-pal."

"Well, they're always looking for people to do it," Nell replied.

Nell helped. She asked her pen pal to recommend a fellow inmate who would like a back-and-forth correspondence with someone beyond their cell. Nell's pen pal told her about the man who held the door for him, who always spoke kindly to him, and who talked openly about his faith. Nell gave Meg the man's name, and in the fall of 2001, she began to send him letters. Right away, she told him she wasn't interested in any kind of romance. No way. She was a mother, a grandmother, and she wanted to support him — but not his act. With every letter, she ended it the same way:

> *God loves you and so do I.*
> *Your sister and friend,*
> *Meg.*

His first letter to Meg was a card. The one thing Meg noticed immediately was how beautiful his handwriting was. It looked like calligraphy. In it, he talked about his Assyrian Christian faith, and he asked about her and her family. He included his correspondence in a card with this message on the front:

> *If you need someone — a friend to confide in, you can always turn to me.*
> *If you need a word of comfort or a shoulder to lean on, you can always reach out.*

And I'll be there.

Like Meg, he ended every letter the same way:

Your brother and friend

That was how Meg met Elias Syriani.

From their first correspondence, she felt a kinship. He was kind, reverential and open-armed about any kind of friendship beyond the walls of his cell. Yet, if anyone reads the bare-bones summary from the state Department of Corrections, it reveals a much different picture of the father from Charlotte and what happened on July 28, 1990.

"Syriani and his wife, Teresa Yousef Syriani, were separated. Syriani was living in a motel, and his wife with their children in their home. There was evidence of past physical abuse by Syriani against his wife. One night shortly before midnight, Syriani drove to their home. As his wife drove her car onto a nearby street, Syriani blocked her way with his van. Defendant got out of his van, gestured, and chased after her car as she put it in reverse.

"As his wife sat in her car, defendant began stabbing her with a screwdriver through the open door or window, while their ten-year-old son, John, sat in the seat beside her. John was unable to stop his father, got out and ran home to get his older sister. At least two neighbors watched from their homes as defendant stabbed his wife and then walked away.

"Teresa Syriani died 28 days later. She suffered numerous stab wounds in the attack, the fatal wound a three-inch deep puncture wound to the right temple. Syriani stopped at a nearby fire station for first aid, claiming he was battered by his wife. He was covered in blood but had only some light scratches on his arm and shoulder. Police were called and he was arrested.

"The murder weapon, a screwdriver, was never found."

Elias stabbed his wife 28 times.

* * *

Meg starts writing letters to Elias once a week. She sends him photos of her grandchildren and crayon drawings her two grandchildren created. One time, she sends him a heart-shaped leaf from a walk in her neighborhood. Meg wants to give Elias a sensory touch of nature, and like nature, she tells him we can all be reborn. In their letters, they both open up to one another.

Meg tells Elias about her family, her grandchildren, her son in the Army, her career teaching first- and second-graders and her time on a sidewalk in downtown Greensboro protesting the death penalty.

Elias, who Meg called El-E-us, tells Meg about his life growing up poor near Jerusalem, singing Arabic at a radio station in Jordan and coming to the United States with his wife to find a better life.

He talks about his children's dog, Cookie, how the family later moved to Charlotte and how he worked as a machinist. After work, he used to gather his four young children in his lap and have them pick the steel shavings from his hair. Like Meg, Elias is a picky eater. And like Meg, he views his Christian faith as his anchor. He speaks often to Meg about his faith. He also tells her he asked God for forgiveness for his mistakes.

"In the beginning, he tried to convince me that he shouldn't be on death row for killing his wife," Meg says years later. "That was a tight rope to walk because I didn't want him to think there was any room for that (conversation). I simply wanted to keep an open flow and let him know I was there to support him, but I wasn't there to support the act."

In the fall of 2001, Elias' sister is scheduled to visit him. But because of the fallout of 9/11, when Islamic terrorists turned airplanes into bombs, his sister doesn't. She fears flying because she worries her dark skin and foreign-sounding name will turn her into a target for bigoted rants — or worse. So, she stays home. But Meg comes.

Meg drives from Greensboro to Raleigh to visit Central Prison. Meg was, in her words, "nervous as all get out." She doesn't know what to expect in her first visit to prison to see a man on death row. But Elias makes her feel comfortable immediately with his gentle nature and disarming smile. They sit face-to-face inches from one another, separated by a thick pane of glass.

Like with their letters, they share stories. They share a bit of themselves.

"God sent you," Elias tells Meg, "because my sister couldn't come."

Meg doesn't say a word. She continues to listen.

Meg Eggleston began pen pals with Elias Syriani. This letter contains a leaf Meg found during a walk in the woods near her family's mountain home in western North Carolina. Photo Credit: Courtesy of Meg Eggleston.

* * *

The more they talk, the more Meg thinks of the classic sit-com series, "I Love Lucy." With his high forehead and round face, Elias reminds Meg of Ricky Ricardo, the character played by Desi Arnaz in the long-running show. Meg and Elias talk for an hour. When it comes time for Meg to leave, they both place one of their hands on the glass, palm to palm, in a friendly gesture of goodbye.

A few days later, Meg gets another letter from Elias. In sentences illustrative of someone struggling with English and emotion, he writes:

"Before I saw you, I always pray, asking God to help me with my English language and how to share with you just a little about much I would like to say. Thank God I did, and everything was just alright to me. When you were excused to leave, I wish the time would turn back to 1 o'clock again for another more

hour."

The weekly letters continue. The monthly visits, too. Their friendship grows.

"I saw that he was not the act he committed, but he was an individual who sought love and had gifts," she says. "He was a musician who cared about his family, and he became a friend. I don't think I had a whole lot burdening me back then, but I knew anything I had on me I knew I could tell Elias about those things, and he would listen."

In the summer of 2004, Elias' four children — Janet and John, Sarah and Rose — come to see him. Sarah is married and living near San Francisco. John sells cars at a dealership near Chicago. Rose is working with a research firm in California and living with Sarah until she can find a place of her own. They are all in their 20s, all getting on with their lives. And yet, they want to see their father. Their anger has waned. But they don't forgive him. Then, they get to prison and see him smiling at them behind the glass.

"I don't quite know how to say this," Rose told the Charlotte Observer in November 2005. "None of this justifies what he did. There is no way to justify it. But now we're able to pick up these wonderful pieces of our lives, these things we had put away. It's not our fault any of this happened. We just have to find out a way to live. Our mom and dad did love each other. And the love they had together …."

Sarah breaks in: " … created us."

"Yes," Rose said. "Created us."

As they get to know their father again, they also get to know Meg.

"The changed man we were sitting across from did not only experience God's work but had actually been touched by an angel," Sarah told the News & Record, the daily newspaper in Greensboro, N.C., in November 2010.

That angel, she says, is Meg.

"Some people might say their friendship began by mere

coincidence," Sarah adds. "She was in his life to teach him something."

At first, Elias has a hard time acknowledging what he did was wrong. He feels women have to stay in their place and not venture beyond the home and get a job, make money, and become more independent as Teresa, his wife, had done. As Meg listens, she knows she has to say something.

"Think about your own mother, Elias," she tells him. "You loved her. Then, think about your children. They loved their mom like you loved your mother, and you took her away. You have to own up to that."

Elias does — finally. Then, he's ready to meet with his children. He asks for forgiveness. They grant his request. And cry. They tell him they still love him.

So, Meg does become a teacher of sorts for Elias. And like Elias, she has learned something, too. But not without a lot of heartache.

Elias Syriani got to talk with all four of his children while in Raleigh's Central Prison In this photo, left to right, he is with Rose, his oldest daughter; Sarah, his middle daughter; and Janet, his youngest daughter. Photo Credit: Courtesy of Meg Eggleston.

* * *

First, the letter.

Elias writes it on a Monday in October 2005. Meg opens it later that week. What she read rattles her.

"It's so hard sometimes with the human judgement using the power of His Will and unbelievable the news I heard a few days ago of three men scheduled for their execution less than a week or two together, and I am one of them."

Meg goes to see Elias, and the man she knows through the thick pane of glass — the gentle man with the disarming smile — is gone. He's anxious, sad-eyed, beside himself with worry and fear. Meg tells Elias she'll get her minister to come.

She knows Frank will come, and she also knows Frank will help. He has helped so many others, she tells Elias, and Frank can help him.

After their hourlong conversation, Meg drives straight to Greensboro Urban Ministry. She doesn't know if Frank is there. She can only hope. She needs his steady counsel. She needs someone to understand. And she knows Frank, an opponent of the death penalty since his days at Lumberton High, will understand.

She finds Frank in his office.

"This is a lot," she tells Frank. "This thing is getting to be a lot. You got me into this, and I need your help now. Will you go see him?"

"Of course," Frank responds.

* * *

At the Central Prison, Frank sees through the glass a stoop-shouldered man despondent over his fate. They talk, Frank prays, he listens, and they talk some more. Frank leaves feeling drained and understanding even more what Meg is going through. When he visited Gov. James Martin and Gov. Jim Hunt about the death penalty, he talked to them about inmates he didn't know. He appealed to their faith, not a face of someone he met. But this is different. Frank looks into the eyes of a man scheduled to be killed by the state of North Carolina on a Friday in November, six days before Thanksgiving.

As he drives home, he recalls those surreal moments after visiting with the two governors. He hits I-40, feeling optimistic over their conversations and then hearing over the radio two more executions have been carried out in his home state.

Now, here comes one more.

Elias' children go on "Larry King Live" and "Good Morning America" and appeal to Gov. Mike Easley to commute their dad's sentence to life in prison. They go to the governor's office and talk to him personally about saving their dad from a lethal injection of a drug that will stop his heart.

Hope is slim, they know. Still, they believe. They believe Gov. Easley can save their dad. He has granted clemency twice since taking office in 2001, and North Carolina governors have granted clemency only three other times since the state resumed executions in 1984 after a hiatus while the U.S. Supreme Court determined its constitutionality. They want their dad to make that list.

Meg has a front-row seat for what she called an "amazing picture of forgiveness."

"I was blessed to land in the middle of this amazing opportunity," Meg says. "I see it as a blessing because of my connection with Elias' family. I got to see positive love show itself in the darkest of dark places. It's there.

"And it was such a powerful thing for Elias and for me," she continues. "The way we were able to come together, particularly having him get in the right frame of mind and acknowledge what he did was wrong and receive his children the way he did.

"I've always had a strong sense of spirituality, but this definitely strengthened my faith, and I definitely believe it was destined to happen. This is what I was put here for."

* * *

The day Meg will always remember: Nov. 17, 2005, a Thursday night.

At Pullam Memorial Baptist Church in Raleigh, Meg is getting ready to speak at a prayer service for Elias. She's going to tell the people who come about the Elias she knows. Then, she gets the word. Easley is not going to commute Elias' death-penalty sentence.

Immediately, she sits down and starts to cry. She can't believe it. A man she has become close to. A man she saw as her brother. A man she has listened to and who shared with her his innermost thoughts. In a few hours, he is going to die.

"I can't stand up," she tells her daughter, Cherrianne "Che" Hooks, who's beside her.

Meg gets herself composed and looks out over the room full of expectant faces. She has to tell them about the Elias she knows. She has to. Right now.

"Let me share this with you," she says.

She begins to read what she wrote about Elias. She can't continue. Meg's husband Don has a copy and finishes reading what Meg wrote. Meanwhile, Meg sits. All she can think about is getting to Central Prison as fast as she can. She has to be there for Elias, for his children and for her.

Minutes later, Frank calls Meg. Che has her mother's phone. She takes the call and tells him the news. Frank doesn't hesitate.

"I am on my way," Frank says.

Meg always knew Elias could never get out of prison. But like Elias' children, she hoped a miracle could save his life. When it doesn't happen, she remembers her conversation with Elias — and his request.

"I'll be with you during the day, and I'll be with you in my heart," Meg tells him. "But is my physical presence that important to you?"

"It would be good to be able to look into your eyes when it happens," Elias responds. "If you can do it, I want you to do it."

Meg, Don and Che drive to Central Prison. Meg is in shock, torn in two different ways, torn for others, and torn for herself. She never thought it would happen. But it did. And it was going to happen tonight.

"I've got to witness this now," she keeps telling herself. "I've got to keep my promise."

She wants to see the children. She wants to make sure they're alright. They aren't, especially Janet, the youngest. She expects to have her dad with her for a long time. Janet knows that won't happen when she gets the news. At Central Prison, she collapses right in front of her father. So does Sarah, who's five months pregnant. They all hear their dad is going to die by lethal injection at the time they're seeing him. That visit, they realize, will be their last. Janet and Sarah stay on the floor sobbing. What Elias sees crushes him.

Elias then turns to Sarah's husband.

"You have to get them off the floor," he pleads.

When Janet and Sara clamber from the floor, Elias turns to everyone in the room.

"You all need to leave town!" he says. "Please don't stay here for this."

Meg sees Elias' children afterward. They're stunned, sobbing, in shock. They tell Meg they want to get off the grounds of Central Prison. They do a few interviews outside. Then, they're gone. But Meg stays. She has a promise to keep.

Around 10 p.m., Meg gets a call from Frank, and he tells her no one is going to let him into Central Prison. So, Meg goes looking. She wants to find Elias' defense attorney, prison officials, just anyone who will get Frank in. When she finds someone who can help, she becomes forceful, yet civil, polite, yet firm. She has a request.

"That's my minister," she says, pointing to Frank. "I need him to be with me. I may be Elias' spiritual advisor. But Frank is mine."

Meg, Che, and Don Walk into the prison. By their side is Frank. He waits with them until they are led into the witness room.

Such a small room. Meg notices that right away when she walks in with Don.

It's a tiny cubby of a space, this witness room to the death chamber. A thick pane of glass separates them. They'll sit inches away from what North Carolina sees as its death chamber. Meg is in Seat No. 2; Don in Seat No. 3. Frank isn't allowed in. Around them are two Charlotte detectives, six prison employees and five reporters.

"Where is God in all this?" she keeps asking herself.

Meg tells the prison warden she will need to be escorted out once Elias' eyes close and he's unconscious.. She says she can't be in the same room and watch Elias die.

"I care about him," she tells the warden.

Inside the death chamber, she waits. She wants to see the door open on the other side of the glass. She wants to see Elias one more time and honor his request. Still, with each passing minute, her anxiety grows. She tries to pray. She can't. She feels there is no God in this room. Only evil.

Dear Meg,
This is a little note to say I am so thankful for all the great things that you do.
God loves you always. I do, too.
Your brother and friend
Elias

That's Meg's last card from Elias. The card he chooses carries this message:

The seeds of our faith
Planted in prayer
Will bring forth life
And growth into fruit
That is eternal.

On Friday, at 1:40 a.m. in the witness room, the lights dim. Ten minutes later, Meg sees him. A blue sheet covers his body; two pillows prop his head. Elias comes into the death chamber, lying on his back, strapped to a gurney. He comes in smiling.

"I love you," he says to Meg and Don. "I love everybody."

Elias then trains his eyes on Meg and Don and begins mouthing each word carefully.

"I want them to be happy."

"I really loved her."

"Fifteen years."

Elias killed his wife Teresa in July 1990. In November 2005, in his last prepared statement, Elias writes: "I want to thank God first for everything that happened in my life. I want to thank my children. I want to thank my family, especially my sister, Odeet.

"I want to thank all the beautiful friends who share with me my sufferings for 15 years and four months and they so encouraged me, specifically Mr. and Mrs. Meg Eggleston who become a sister to me. She helped me a lot to accept everything. I thank everyone from the staff, nurses, chaplains. I thank everyone."

At 2 a.m., Elias gets his first injection. He smiles at Meg and Don and says, "With all my heart."

Those are his last words.

Elias looks up at the ceiling, and under the blue sheet, his chest heaves once. His head sinks onto the pillow, and he closes his eyes. Meg knows then. Time to go. She feels overwhelmed by emotion that she has tried to keep in check all night. Right then, she can't. She stands up, her hands flutter. A prison guard comes to help, and he escorts her from the room. Don stays. Nearby sits Tommy Tomlinson, the columnist from the Charlotte Observer. They both witness Elias' last breath. Tomlinson unveils Elias' last moments in 14 paragraphs. Here were his last two:

"The next chemical was Pavulon, a paralyzing drug. The last was potassium chloride, which stops the heart. The blue sheet no longer moved. Donald Eggleston whispered: "Oh, dear God." The heart monitor in another room had to run flat for five minutes before death was official.

"For a long quiet time, there in the dark room, we watched him lie still. Fifteen years ago, Elias Syriani killed his wife. Friday morning, the state of North Carolina killed Elias Syriani. At 2:12 a.m., the curtain closed."

* * *

At the prayer vigil outside Central Prison, Frank waits for Meg, Che, and Don to emerge. When they do, Don walks toward the prayer vigil, toward a few reporters. Meg and Che Walk away. Frank catches up with them. Meg turns. A familiar face. She smiles.

"Frank, do you need a ride to your car?" she says.

Frank smiles back.

"That'll be great," Frank responds.

Once in the car, Frank feels he has to support Meg in any way he can. He starts with a statement.

"Tell me what happened," Frank says.

"I can't talk about it," Meg responds.

Frank doesn't say another word. Neither does Meg. She and Che drop Frank off at his car and drive straight back to Greensboro. She crawls into bed with one thought in her head.

"I didn't expect this to happen," she tells herself. "And it did. It's so wrong. So wrong! Why?"

Meg falls asleep.

A year or so later, at a spiritual directors' conference in Seabrook Island, S.C., Meg is overwhelmed by emotion once again. She and others attending the conference are going to watch several scenes of "Dead Man Walking," the 1995 film about a nun who becomes pen pals with a death row inmate and advocates to have his sentence reduced. But Meg can't watch it.

Too close to home.

She leaves to calm down. "Dead Man Walking" reminds her too much of Elias, of his children, and that early morning in a horror film of a room where she watches him close his eyes for the last time.

Too much. Just too much. Meg begins to cry.

That's when she sees it. The crane. A big white beautiful bird. Just standing there on the grounds. She walks toward it, pulls out her phone and takes a picture. She can't believe it. It's because of what she remembers.

When Elias was alive, Meg had told a friend of hers about him and their pen-pal relationship. That's when her friend had discovered Thomas Merton's poem, "Elias — Variations on a Theme." In the poem, Merton writes about Elias, the prophet and miracle maker from the Bible. When Meg's friend read it, she sent Meg eight lines and wrote, "Meg, I found this poem and it goes with what you're going through."

Under the blunt pine
Elias becomes his own geography
(Supposing geography to be necessary at all),
Elias becomes his own wild bird, with God in the center,

His own wide field which nobody owns,
His own pattern, surrounding the Spirit
By which he is himself surrounded:
For the free man's road has neither beginning nor end.

Meg takes the crane as a sign from Elias. He's telling her, "Everything is going to be alright."

Everything is going to be alright.

The poem is affirmation that what Meg feels is right. Just right.

She tells Elias' grown children about seeing the crane in South Carolina. The photo of the crane and the lines from Thomas Merton's poem are now in a frame, and it sits somewhere, maybe on a mantle, in the homes of Elias' children.

Meg gave it to them as a gift.

Today, when Meg thinks about her photo and those eight lines from Merton, she remembers a verse from the Book of Psalms that gave her solace on that emotional Friday morning in November 2005, six days before Thanksgiving. That verse mentioned how we may weep, but rejoicing will come. Meg feels that. And she believes Elias can feel that, too. Like the wild bird in Merton's poem, Elias has become his own geography. He is free.

This is a birthday card Elias Syriani sent to Meg. Photo Credit: Courtesy of Meg Eggleston.

Frank on Frank

"Press On!"

I've always thought being a minister is actually like being a coach.

Coaches don't get out on the field or on the court, but they encourage others to participate. Ministers do the same thing because they want their parishioners to get involved in their community in some way so they can hear their own calling. But that's one of the hardest parts of ministry. When people do that, they follow a path that can lead to a deeper, sometimes painful place.

A lot of ministers are tempted to relieve people of their pain. Take Meg. I could've said, 'Meg, you really don't have to do this!' But I never said that. I mean, she knew that. At a deeper level, though, she knew she had no choice. She wanted to follow her faith.

When we ministers see their parishioners or anyone in pain, our immediate reaction is to take them away from that pain. Make them feel better. I know that feeling comes from a good place, but when we do that, we end up short-circuiting their faithfulness. You have to let people go through it.

Our faithfulness in God often takes us to places we never imagined we would ever go or helps us do things we never even thought we'd carry out. That journey often is painful. It's also incongruous with the world around us because we're doing things other people don't want to do. Yet, there is so much meaning in doing such things that make us uncomfortable. It makes God more real to us.

Even the perceived absence of God, like what Meg perceived inside North Carolina's death chamber, makes God more real. It's like when someone you love is not there or anywhere near you, and as a result, that love becomes deeper because of the heartache and pain.

For example, think of it this way: Say you're in love with someone, and you part company, and you're not going to see them for a week or a month, the feeling you have for them is more intense. That's heartache, and it brings to mind the phrase, 'Absence makes the heart grow fonder.'

That's the problem with love.

In my sermons over the years, I've mentioned this story several times. It's about that person who says, 'You know I think I am ready for a new relationship, a new romantic relationship, but I just don't want to get hurt.' And that's the problem. Whenever we love, we are vulnerable. It's like verse 7 from 1 Corinthians, Chapter 13: 'Love bears all things, believes all things, hopes all things, endures all things.'

I've been the father of a bride once. But I've married a lot of people, and I've come to believe the words in Chapter 13 are so timeless. Particularly its last verse: Faith, hope and love, these three, they do knit together like a knot. But the greatest of these three is love.

Meg discovered that the hard way, the painful way.

She's a classic example of how in life we start out doing something good — like writing to someone in prison — and that good deed can lead us to a deeper place. At each stage in our lives, we have to make up our mind if we want to continue.

As Z Holler, my friend and the longtime minister at Presbyterian Church of Covenant, used to say all the time.

'Press on!"

Yes, press on!

Well, when we do that, the next thing we know we find ourselves in places or doing things we never imagined we would — or could — – do. And Meg did. And she did it out of love and faithfulness to God. And from that love, Elias found meaning and purpose in the little bit of life he had left.

It's understandable when Meg asked, 'Where is God in all this?' She was — all of us were — up against something in 2005 that was more than just one individual or a group of individuals. It was a system that had been in place for decades.

Think about the public support for Elias. Elias' kids wanted his life spared, and the DA who prosecuted him supported that, too. Elias' kids even went on 'Good Morning America' and 'Larry King' on CNN and told the world about how they had forgiven their father and wanted him to live. It was quite amazing. Such an amazing example of forgiveness. Nobody wanted Elias to die. But it happened.

I've been in ministry for a long time, and I've come to understand that there are systems in place that have a gravity about them. And that gravity is something hard to reckon with. They can cause things to happen even when the good will of many individuals don't want it to happen.

It's like what Reinhold Niebuhr wrote in his book, 'Moral Man and Immoral Society: A Study in Ethics and Politics.' He talks about how we can do things in groups that we would *never* be inclined to do as individuals. It's that idea of mob mentality. Niebuhr's book came out in 1932, and how much has really changed? Not a lot.

So, on that Friday morning in November 2005, it seemed that God was absent. But after the execution, Meg and Don came out, and the passage from the Book of Psalms became real for them. Meg told me that later. Here's the verse:

> *For His anger lasts only a moment,*
> *but His favor lasts a lifetime;*
> *weeping may stay for the night,*
> *but rejoicing comes in the morning.*

What Meg and Don latched onto was that joy coming in the morning. Elias was going to be able to leave prison. But he was going to leave in a different form, set free even by the act we all were fighting.

That act was painful for so many of us. But when something like that happens, when the good will of so many people can't stop it, I remind myself of that inscription found on a wall in Germany at the end of World War II:

I believe in the sun when it's not shining.
I believe in love, even when feeling it not.
I believe in God even when he's silent.

Frank traveled to South Africa to visit a young man who New Creation helped receive a college education at UNC-Greensboro. New Creation paid for it. Photo credit: Courtesy of Ali Mabitsela.

Chapter 17
The Lessons from Ali

"We have more in common than what divides us. The things that divide us are surfacy things like skin color or nationality or language. Those kinds of things. But once we get below the surface, the deepest and most basic things are what we have in common. Those are our aspirations of life and liberty and the pursuit of happiness.
We all share that. It's what makes us human."
The Rev. Frank Dew

Finally, they arrive.

Bleary eyed from 15 hours in the air, Frank looks out the window and sees a rolling stretch of green and a cluster of gleaming buildings that make up South Africa's "mother city" — Cape Town, the country's legislative capital. It's snuggled into the elbow of the Atlantic and Indian oceans and tucked beside a flat-topped mountain with peaks bearing names like Lion's Head, Devil's Peak, and the Twelve Apostles. Those names sound like they come straight out of a fairy tale. But this is no fairy tale trip for Frank. As he flies into Cape Town International Airport, Frank knows he isn't bringing his family or 11 of his fellow parishioners from New Creation to see a country in transition. They are coming to see a young man in transition.

After flying from Raleigh to Miami to South Africa, Frank is getting ready to land in a country more than 8,000 miles from Greensboro. And it isn't just that he and Michie, David and Christie, along with a handful of church members, are coming at Christmas —

— and it's summertime in South Africa. That is weird enough. No, it's 1996, the second year of Nelson Mandela's presidency, the first Black president of South Africa and a man working to heal the decades-long wounds of apartheid, South Africa's version of Jim Crow.

That's how Frank sees it.

Frank grew up with Jim Crow, and he saw firsthand how enforced or legalized racial segregation had created two distinctly different versions of America where avenues of opportunity weren't open to all. Those two different versions of America still exist every time Frank listens to the hard luck stories he hears at Greensboro Urban Ministry. But Frank has hope for his America. Like his every-day uniform of light blue shirt, khakis and running shoes, Frank sees hope as part of him. So, he naturally has hope for South Africa. He finds hope in the pages of a book, a 656-page book he brings with him on his trip. It's "Long Walk to Freedom: The Autobiography of Nelson Mandela." Mandela's words show Frank healing can happen.

"I reminded people again and again that the liberation struggle was not a battle against one group or color, but a fight against a system of repression," Mandela writes. "At every opportunity, I said all South Africans must now unite and join hands and say we are one country, one nation, one people, marching together into the future."

Marching together into the future. Frank does like that phrase.

Frank longs to see that happen on his side of the world. But can it? Frank sometimes has his doubts. But he doesn't doubt what one small church can do for one well-meaning young man with a bright future. That effort first takes root on a Sunday back in 1987. A Presbyterian minister from South Africa comes to New Creation and tells parishioners how he finds hope amid the darkness of apartheid.

Afterward, a church member poses a four-word question to the minister. Those four words end up changing a young man's life.

What can we do?

* * *

The Rev. Maake Masango with his wife, Pauline, at a ceremony honoring him for his half-century of being a pastor. Photo credit: Courtesy of Ali Mabitsela.

It's a Sunday afternoon in 1987 when the Rev. Maake Masango comes to New Creation. Kathy Carpenter, one of New Creation's founding members, invites him She and Masango have been students together at a school Presbyterians know by its acronym — PSCE. They both received master's degrees in Christian education from Presbyterian School of Christian Education in Richmond, Virginia, and Kathy knew her friend would deliver a message that her church members needed to hear about racism on the other side of the world.

Established in 1943 by the all-white government, apartheid created a system of legislation that favored whites and undermined non-whites in everything that created a meaningful life. Apartheid separated non-white South Africans from anything that would give them influence, power, wealth, or even a good education. Part of that system was legislation that allowed the government to relocate Blacks away from the urban areas as cities began to spread. Blacks were forced to move into townships or homelands where opportunities didn't exist, and poverty did.

That legislation was loaded with heartache for Masango. He and his family were forcibly moved six times because of apartheid. His home was bulldozed. Masango and his family watched it happen. He and his family along with their furniture were then trucked to their new home.

On that Sunday afternoon, in the fellowship hall at Presbyterian Church of the Covenant near UNCG, Masango unveils for Frank and his parishioners what apartheid has done to his country.

Limited job opportunities. The government requires Blacks to obtain travel passes to come into South African cities for employment.

Limited education. The government creates different classes of schools — one for whites and the other for Blacks, Indians and people of mixed races. Obtaining an education for Blacks, Indians and people of mixed races — what Masango called "colored" — isn't about getting ahead. It's about getting an education, so they remain subservient and take instruction from whites.

Limited future. Someone like Masango can go to a university, but he is only allowed to take courses to help him become a minister, a teacher, or a nurse. That's it. So, Masango becomes a minister. In 1975, he was ordained by the Presbyterian Church of South Africa and went to serve as pastor at a rural church.

It's only through a chance encounter in 1978 with a group of women from Presbyterian Church USA that Masango's future changes. He spends several weeks showing them around South Africa, and the next year, the women he met award him a PCUSA scholarship that allows him to come to America and attend Columbia Theological Seminary in Decatur, Ga., and later the PSCE where he meets Carpenter.

Masango goes to Columbia Theological Seminary and the PSCE so he can learn how to live with whites and work with whites because he believes his home country will change for the better because of the growing anti-apartheid movement. Despite the assassinations and long prison sentences, he sees a future where apartheid will be no more, and at some point, his country will have to come together — Blacks and whites, Indians and "colored" — as one.

As a minister, Masango knows what he has to do: Love the people he once hated to bear witness to the red-letter words from Jesus in Matthew 5: "You have heard that it was said, 'Love your neighbor and hate your enemy.' But I tell you, love your enemies and pray for those who persecute you."

After serving five years as the director of Christian education for the Presbyterian Church of Southern Africa, Masango comes back to America to see friends like Kathy Carpenter. He also wants to speak to churches like New Creation. He wants to spread the news that he sees hope amid the darkness of apartheid and that his homeland is ready to heal.

After his talk, one of Frank's parishioners asks the question.

"What can we do?"

Masango has an answer ready.

"When the day comes for Blacks to have positions of power — and that's not an if, but when — they need to have a good education," Masango says. "They need to have good experiences with whites. The way you can help that happen is invite one of our students to go to your school, your university, right here with you."

Right away, Frank knows that's quite the charge. So do his church members.

That's not like writing a letter to your local congressman or going to a City Council meeting to advocate for affordable housing or standing on a sidewalk in downtown Greensboro holding a sign to protest the death penalty. What Masango is recommending is much more involved. It's a big ask for a small church of no more than 50 people. But it's also a big opportunity. Frank sees it as a way to help educate a young Black student and his own congregation. Together, they all can better understand one another, see firsthand how race affects everything around them and figure out ways to overcome that.

Yet, Masango's recommendation deals with something concrete

— money. At New Creation, members sign a covenant every year to demonstrate their faith through specific actions, and Masango's recommendation was definitely one. So, Frank being Frank becomes the teacher.

"What we're doing is what I would call incarnational ministry," he tells his parishioners. "That's a theological word, I know, but think of it this way. We're putting skin in the game. We're putting skin on our love and embodying our love in such a way that we're going to stand with and walk beside whoever Maake recommends that we support. That, in itself, is a ministry.

"We need to stand with and walk beside people who have different life experiences than our own. When we do, think of what we learn. And think of how we'll see life. We'll see it from their vantage point. We won't have to read about it or study it. We'll experience it!"

Think of it, Frank says, like being a player in a locker room. You're watching a coach draw up X's and O's, but you're not getting a chance to get into the game. And New Creation will get into the game, and parishioners see what Frank calls "real faith" in action. Moments have meaning and epiphanies of faith reveal concrete details that they see, feel, and hear.

"Don't be conformed to this world," Frank likes to say, "be transformed from this world."

That's a favorite line from one of Frank's sermons. He paraphrases a verse that comes from a letter Paul wrote to Christians in Rome. Paul urged them to step away from living like every other pleasure seeker. Be different and look within to see and understand what God has in store for their lives. In Romans 12:2, Paul wrote: "Do not conform to the pattern of this world but be transformed by the renewing of your mind. Then you will be able to test and prove what God's will is—his good, pleasing, and perfect will."

Helping a young South African get an education would make that verse come alive for Frank and so many other parishioners, parishioners like Barbara Clawson.

Barbara, one of New Creation's longtime members, remembers

what she learned when she left her family's Iowa farm to live with Japanese families for five months as part of a program created by 4-H and the Cooperative Extension Service. Twelve years after World War II and the two atomic bombs dropped on Japan that ended the war and killed hundreds of thousands of people, Barbara learned lessons about forgiveness, hope and seeing the world through a different lens.

She sees Masango's recommendation as a way for New Creation to get beyond the white-centric viewpoint of America and have an in-depth relationship with someone so much different from everything she and others in the church knew. The way Barbara sees it, Masango's recommendation will change their church in the best of ways.

"I think it's critical for us to survive as a civilization," Barbara would tell parishioners during any conversation about this big ask. "We need to understand and grow to care about people who are different than we are."

Fundraising begins, and by 1991, New Creation has raised $100,000 from its members and other local churches. When they contact Masango, he knows who to send. It's a young man who used to be one of his students when he taught Sunday School. He's the middle son of a police officer dad and a teacher mom, and he's become a youth leader who's teaching Sunday School, directing the church choir, and overseeing the church's Sunday School classes. But like many young Black South Africans, his future is capped. His college education is cut short when he's 20. In 1983, riots erupt across South Africa over the country's new constitution that gives Blacks no political rights. He ends up having to leave the university and going to a vocational college, getting a diploma in electronics and dreaming of doing more and wanting to be more.

So, yes, Masango knows who to send. His youth leader. His church choir director. His Sunday School superintendent.

Ali Mabitsela with Rick Betton, a longtime member of New Creation and Frank's running partner. Courtesy of Ali Mabitsela.

* * *

Ali is 28 when Masango tells him of his plum opportunity. But Ali isn't ecstatic — at least not at first. He's scared. He's never been out of Africa before, and he envisions America as this far-away land he hardly knows. And now, he hears he's going to fly — for the first time — and he's going to America to a North Carolina college in a city called Greensboro. And he's going to live with whites.

Whites!

The whole idea freaks him out.

"I work with white people and Afrikaners, but we never share anything," he tells himself. "They have their own bathrooms, and we have our own bathrooms. And now, I'm going to a city I've never been to, in a country I've never been to and live with white folks for three or four years? How am I going to survive? Am I going to be a servant? How am I going to be treated?"

He has no idea. But he trusts Masango, and he boards a plane bound for Atlanta. When he lands, he meets Masango and Masango's wife as well as a white woman. She introduces herself as Kathy.

Kathy Carpenter, Masango's former classmate from PSCE, helps make Ali feel comfortable immediately. She has this easygoing demeanor and a ready smile that helps Ali relax during what he sees as so surreal. Kathy drives Ali from Atlanta to Greensboro and straight to Presbyterian Church of the Covenant where Ali joins a celebration in the fellowship hall. And it's all for him. Ali walks in and wades into a crowd of people. All white people. He's surrounded by white people. Everywhere he looks are white people. Ali's relaxed mood evaporates, and he armors up to keep his emotions in check. But the white people around him do not. Like Kathy, they wear smiles and meet Ali with open arms and open-ended questions about him, his family, his interests, and his thoughts for his future.

They care about him.

A Black man from South Africa.

They care about him.

These strangers in a city and a state that Ali can't even point to on a map.

Ali feels himself start to relax. He is simply dumbfounded by how welcoming everyone is.

"Is this for real?" he asks himself.

As Ali takes in the scene around him, up walks Frank.

"Welcome," he says, smiling, his arms spread wide. "This is your new home."

After the celebration, Frank and Michie take Ali to their home in Greensboro's Sunset Hills neighborhood, and he moves into the bedroom downstairs. He becomes the newest member of the Dew family. David and Christie can't wait. They tell him so. David is 6; Christie, 5; and they see Ali as the big brother they never had. Over the next four months, Ali becomes their playmate, their friend.

Ali watches "Teenage Mutant Ninja Turtles" with David, and between commercials, Ali answers David's questions about South Africa.

"Do you have houses?"

"Do you have cars?"

"What is your family like?"

David's questions continue to come with each Teenage Mutant Ninja Turtle episode. David is the quiet one. Christie ... is not. Ali will hear Christie holler, "Carry me!"He'll pop her up on his shoulders and take her everywhere. Wherever they go, Christie introduces Ali with the verve of a ringmaster at a circus.

"This is my BIGGEST big brother! This is THE Ali."

Ali enjoys hanging with David and Christie because they remind him of his own nieces and nephews. But there are times in the Dews' house when Ali grows quiet. When he does, Michie will see his far-away gaze, and she'll turn from Michie the Mom into Michie the Psychologist.

"Ali, are you alright?" she'll ask. "Are you missing home? Want to talk about it?"

Ali always does. Michie becomes Ali's go-to person for anything he needs, especially anything that eased his heartache from missing home.

As for Frank, he becomes Ali's tour guide, his teacher, and his big brother. Ali climbs into Frank's car, and Frank drives Ali around Greensboro, introducing him to everybody. Frank gives Ali a crash course in American culture, American politics and, of course, the all-important need to pull for Wake Forest in everything.

After four months with the Dews, Ali moves into his one-bedroom apartment a block from UNCG. He becomes a supervisor with UNCG's Campus Recreation, joins its Foreign Student Association, and gets involved with its Presbyterian campus ministries. During his time in Greensboro, he has only one run-in with racism. It's when he was a senior supervisor with Campus Rec. One day, a few of his employees tell him someone at the gym isn't following the rules. When Ali approaches him about the complaint, he discovers a man angry at the world.

"No Black man is going to tell me what to do!" the man shouts at Ali.

Ali diffuses the situation quickly. In a quiet tone his employees have come to respect, Ali reasons with the man and tells him he has to leave. He does. After a disciplinary hearing, the man is suspended from Campus Recreation for a few days. That one dust-up is the only instance Ali ran into something that made Greensboro feel like South

Africa. Other than that, Ali feels welcome everywhere he goes.

He also feels welcome at New Creation. He gets active in every aspect of Frank's church — from its campus ministry to its mission trip to Mexico. He feels like he belongs, and he can feel himself being more assertive as he edges closer to 30. He sees his grades improve with every class he takes. He is making As and Bs in courses like calculus, and he becomes more confident, more open, more of his easygoing, jovial self. Ali feels it. Parishioners at New Creation see it.

"We never had to worry about Ali on whether or not he was making good use of his opportunity," Barbara Clawson, a retired UNCG professor, says today. "We never had to say anything. Ali was eager to do well at UNCG. But you could tell he was aware that he needed to take his studies seriously. We just tried to make him feel at home and accepted him for who he was."

Every week in Greensboro, Ali discovers something new, something uniquely American that he'll tell his family back home. And yet, there are moments when Ali realizes that apartheid isn't on the other side of the Atlantic. It's right there beside him, like a shadow just over his shoulder he can't shake.

Ali looks back and forth, his eyes darting from side to side, as he sees police officers lining the sidewalks of South Elm Street in downtown Greensboro. Right away, he remembers that Tuesday afternoon in 1980. Police officers in South Africa fired tear gas at 8,000 Black schoolchildren when they were protesting against getting an education that separated them from everyone else, especially white schoolchildren. Ali even felt the sting of tear gas once.

So, in 1992, as he walks beside Frank, Ali keeps his head down. He doesn't want the police to notice him, not even in a crowd of 1,200 protesters. He just wants to be invisible.

"Why are the police here?" he asks himself. "Why did I come?"

Frank invites Ali to participate in the protest march because he wants Ali to have a sense of what it's like living in America and having the right to protest what you believe is wrong. And Frank definitely thinks what the Guilford County Board of Commissioners is doing is wrong. Commissioners decreased the county's property tax by 3 cents and became one of only two of North Carolina's 100 counties to cut property taxes in 1991. Yet, to make that happen, commissioners sideline programs in most county departments, including programs that help the most vulnerable in the county — social services, health, and mental health.

So, Frank and others from New Creation join the rally to protest the county commissioners' program cuts. Ali agrees to come. But as he marches down South Elm Street, his reluctance begins to rise. Frank notices it right away.

The anxious looks.

The darting eyes.

"You alright?" Frank asks.

"What is going to happen here?" asks Ali, his eyes ping-ponging from one side of South Elm to another. "Is there going to be a confrontation?"

"Oh no, Ali," Frank answers. "They are here to help us and protect us."

"Well, that's not been my experience back home," Ali responds.

He explains to Frank his own run-in with police and getting tear-gassed when he was much younger. Police, Ali tells Frank, are not seen as protectors. He and his young friends threw stones at the police and the police tear-gassed them.

"Don't worry," Frank says after hearing Ali's story, "you're safe. We're safe. And I'm glad you can have a different experience with us."

A year or so later, Ali goes with Frank and other parishioners to Mexico for a week-long outreach trip. Ali sees the trip as a chance to see another side of the Americas. Plus, he has been studying Spanish at UNCG, and he wants to practice what he has learned. It is one of five outreach trips New Creation has taken to Mexico, and on this particular excursion, Ali and others help build a foundation for a guest house near a clinic for families with sick children.

Throughout the trip, Ali stands out. Mexicans have never seen a Black person as black as Ali. They stare at Ali, and during a meal at a restaurant, Mexicans ask if they could touch his curly hair. Ali agrees. That includes a little boy sitting nearby and staring a hole through Ali.

"Yes," Ali says, smiling, "You can feel my hair."

Ali's smile dims, though, when he goes to the South African embassy in Merida, the largest city in southeastern Mexico. He has to extend his American VISA so he can return to Greensboro. He hopes it'll be quick. It's not. He stays two hours. Hew has to prove to the embassy officials he is a UNCG student. They don't believe him. They end up calling UNCG's international student center to double-check all the evidence Ali provided them. The embassy officials keep Ali until they receive faxes from UNCG confirming Ali's identity.

That is one side of Mexico. Now, to the other side.

The longer Ali is away, the more Frank hears the Mayan Indians and the other Mexicans they're working with ask about him. Soon, the Mayans and the Mexicans form a prayer circle and pray for Ali when he goes to the South African Embassy. To Frank, that moment reminds him of what Paul wrote in one of his first letters. Worried about the Galatians moving away from the gospel of Jesus Christ, Paul urged them to remember that we're all equal, no matter our gender or our country of origin. Frank knows the verse well: "There is neither Greek or Jew, there is neither slave nor free, there is no male or female, for you are all one in Jesus."

Galatians 3:28.

As he stands in that prayer circle in a small village in southeastern Mexico, that verse becomes real for Frank.

It's quite the contrast to what he sees and feels when Ali returns.

"How did it go?" Frank asks.

"They didn't take things at face value," Ali tells him. "I felt like a criminal. I felt I was back in South Africa."

"I'm sorry, Ali," Frank responds.

Frank can tell how bad it was by Ali's demeanor. Ali's eyes were downcast eyes; his shoulders drooped. The confident young man Frank has gotten to know has run face-first into the racism of the world. Yet, as the Mexicans and Mayan Indians circle around Ali, Frank knows that one of his favorite verses from Galatians lives in them.

He just wished it would live in everyone.

* * *

After four years in Greensboro, Ali Mabitsela graduates from UNC-Greensboro with a business degree with the help of New Creation Community Presbyterian Church. Photo credit: Courtesy of Ali Mabitsela.

Even before Ali graduates with his business degree in the summer of 1993, he's constantly thinking about who he left back home.

Like his mom and his Aunt Sylvia. When he left for Greensboro, he tells them: "Don't you pass away before I get back." They all three cry. But he means it. His biggest fear is that his parents will be no more, his Aunt Sylvia will be no more, and everything will be different when he returns. He does feel like he has grown so much in Greensboro, especially traveling to Mexico, getting involved at UNCG and New Creation, living comfortably around whites and finally getting his college degree at 31.

But Ali longs to go back home to South Africa to see and feel and touch what had always been a part of him — and always would be.

Yet, leaving Greensboro is tough. He has gotten close to Frank and Michie, David and Christie and everyone else from New Creation.

The day before he leaves in October 1993, he talks with Frank about his pangs about leaving. As he always does, Frank listens. Then, he responds.

"If you want to come back," he says, "let's see how we can help you come back."

Ali isn't thinking about that — at least not yet. He's thinking about his flight across Atlantic, back to his family. The next day, at Piedmont Triad International Airport, a group of 10 from New Creation come to see Ali off. They hug and cry and tell him how much he has given them. Ali can't help but tear up, especially when he hugs Frank.

"Thank you," Ali says, his voice barely above a whisper

"No, thank you," Frank responds. "You had the courage to come, and you shared your gifts with us. And we will continue our connection. This will not be the last time."

After more hugs and more goodbyes, Ali walks down the concourse. Frank can't help but think about when he will see Ali again. He has become a member of their family, a member of their church, a young man who shows Frank the real definition of courage: It's not the lack of fear that defines courage. It's doing the right thing when you're fearful.

Ali was fearful. And look what happened. He never thought he would get a degree after the riots in South Africa. Greensboro provided that. And when the excitement settled and his new worry rose about having enough money to live on, he remembered what members of New Creation said and what Frank said.

"As long as you work hard, that is our contribution to South Africa."

As he flies from Greensboro to New York City to Johannesburg, Ali's mind settles on home and the many questions it brings.

"What will my nieces and nephews look like?"

"Will I even recognize them?"

"Will my girlfriend recognize me? Will she even remember me?"

"Am I going to be able to readjust? How am I going to

readjust?"

"And will I even recognize my own country?"

Ali doesn't know. But who would? Ali's old South Africa is no more.

Six months after boarding a plane in Greensboro that takes Ali back to South Africa, 20 million South Africans stand in line for hours to vote in South Africa's first democratic election. A sense of euphoria grips voters everywhere, especially those who have opposed apartheid. The turnout speaks volumes of that expectant energy. Nearly 87 percent of all registered voters come to the polls in April 1994. The election takes place over four days, and when the votes are counted, out goes South Africa's National Party that has ruled the country since 1948. In comes the African National Congress, which won nearly 63 percent of the vote. The geographical foundation of apartheid — the 10 ethnically determined homelands — is dissolved, and that land is incorporated into nine new administrative regions.

A few weeks later, the moment that seems like a miracle arrives. Nelson Mandela, the president of the ANC, is inaugurated as the president on May 10, 1994. The bloody revolution people expected doesn't materialize, and the unimaginable happens. A Black leader imprisoned for 27 years and a white leader willing to change work together for a new South Africa.

On his Inauguration Day, in front of hundreds of thousands of people from all corners of the world, Mandela speaks of reconciliation rather than retribution. He says:

"We understand it still that there is no easy road to freedom. We know it well that none of us acting alone can achieve success. We must therefore act together as a united people, for national reconciliation, for nation building, for the birth of a new world.

"Let there be justice for all.

"Let there be peace for all.

"Let there be work, bread, water, and salt for all.

"Let each know that for each the body, the mind and the soul have been freed to fulfill themselves.

"Never, never, and never again shall it be that this beautiful land will again experience the oppression of one by another and suffer the indignity of being the skunk of the world.

"Let freedom reign.

"The sun shall never set on so glorious a human achievement!

"God bless Africa!"

This is the South Africa Ali returns to, and in a country that is changing so much, Ali finds himself in a country where the faces haven't changed at all. When he steps off the plane, he sees so many people he loves. His mom. His dad. His Aunt Sylvia. His nieces. His nephews. And with everyone, the questions come.

"What's the United States like?"

"Did you really live with white people?"

"How was the university?"

"Did you go to New York City?"

"Did you go to Washington, DC?"

"Did you really drive on the left side of a car rather than the right side?"

The questions continue late into the night at a welcome-home party. One of the questions that's asked several different ways is about the parishioners at New Creation and the family Ali lived with for four months.

Ali talks about carrying Christie on his shoulders, watching "Teenage Mutant Ninja Turtles" with David, having a confidante in Michie, and a tour guide of America and big brother in Frank. He talks about how he went to Mexico, visited DC, marched in a protest — and the police protected him.

Ali emphasizes that strangers opened their homes to him wherever he went, and because of that reception, Ali talks about the grace he found and the gratefulness he felt. His experience in Greensboro changed him, and when his friends and family asked about how, Ali mentioned a phrase in Sotho everyone in the room knew.

Motho ke motho ka Batho ba bangwe.

They made me trust again, Ali says, my friends in Greensboro.

* * *

Barbara Clawson and Ali Mabitsela became fast friends in Greensboro. Photo credit: Courtesy of Ali Mabitsela.

On his first morning in South Africa, Frank wakes up thinking about the past 24 hours — leaving Greensboro, driving to Raleigh, flying to Miami, landing in an airport on the other side of the Atlantic and walking out to see the familiar face of Ali and the smiling faces of his family and church members.

The last time Frank saw Ali was the summer of 1994, standing at Piedmont Triad International Airport, surrounded by tearful church members, and trying to bring a little levity in an emotional moment.

"When can we come visit?" Frank asked.

That time arrives at Christmas 1996.

He and Michie spend their first night in South Africa with Ali's sister and her family in the black township of Atteridgeville west of

Pretoria,South Africa's administrative capital. When he wakes up, Frank tries to get acclimated. He's in an unfamiliar place at an unfamiliar time. It's Christmas in the summer. But a familiar sound he recognizes everywhere grounds him.

It's the sound of a lawnmower. He peeks out the window and what he sees amazes him.

A white man is mowing the grass in a Black township.

"Wow," he tells himself. "How things have changed."

Barbara Clawson feels that, too. She and her mother, Hazel, are staying in Atteridgeville with a family from Ali's church. The next morning, the family takes Barbara and her mom to visit the police station where residents from the township, people they know and trust, are working. Barbara can tell they are proud of that. But seeing a police station first thing shocks Barbara. It's because of what she remembers when she first visited South Africa in 1989.

"Back then, we would no more have gone to the police station than walking on the moon," Barbara says today.

In 1989, Barbara had gone as a delegate from the Salem Presbytery to visit a Christian health center in the Democratic Republic of Congo. She then extended her two-week trip to see some of the other projects Presbyterian Church USA was supporting in South Africa.

She spent a day with a Presbyterian elder who lived in Soweto and visited one of the homeland areas where the government had sent Black South Africans to live.

The oppression was palpable, filling ordinary moments with buckets of tension. As the Presbyterian elder drove Barbara around Soweto, he would see a police car and yell, "Duck!" He explained to Barbara that it would be, as he said, "problematic" for him to be seen with a white woman. At the end of the day, the elder asked, "Would you have dinner with my family?"

Barbara did. When he took her back to the hotel, she thanked him. Weeks later, when she returned to Greensboro, she realized how big of a risk the Presbyterian elder took in asking her to stay for dinner. It's against the law for whites to be in Black townships after dark. The elder's response to her at the hotel when he dropped her off made even more sense.

"Don't thank me," the Presbyterian elder told her. "You have helped me feel whole."

Barbara sees how South Africa changed from what she remembers from a few years before. Frank sees how South Africa changed through the pages in a book.

Before the trip, he begins reading "Long Walk to Freedom: The Autobiography of Nelson Mandela," and he brings the inches-thick book with him to South Africa. Frank knows his trip would be the motivation he needs to plow through such a barbell of a book. He reads it, though, because he wants to get a better sense of how a country's despair turns to hope and how one man's fight leads to freedom.

With every turn of the page, Frank isn't disappointed.

"I always knew that deep down in every human heart, there is mercy and generosity," Mandela wrote. "No one is born hating another person because of the color of their skin, or his background, or his religion. People must learn to hate, and if they can learn to hate, they can be taught to love, for love comes more naturally to the human heart than its opposite.

"Even in the grimmest times in prison, when my comrades and I were pushed to our limits, I would see a glimmer of humanity in one of our guards, perhaps just for a second, but it was enough to reassure me and keep me going.

"Man's goodness is a flame that can be hidden but never extinguished."

Frank looks for that flame and God's grace everywhere he goes during his two weeks in South Africa. He and his family find it in moments many might find tedious — visiting a government building, making bricks out of mud and straw, and lying atop the roof of a school bus staring at the stars.

So many moments. Except for maybe one. It involves an angry elephant, and it's a bit much.

Christie remembers. Even today.

* * *

Sitting in the back row on the left side in an open-air safari vehicle with her mom, Christie spots the elephant with the broken tusk. He's well-known at Kruger National Park, one of the largest game preserves in Africa. He's a bully of an elephant who lost his tusk in a fight somewhere in the park. And that's a lot of park. Kruger is the size of Delaware, Rhode Island and Connecticut combined. On this particular day, he stands 40 or 50 yards away from the safari vehicle carrying Ali and the 15-member crew from New Creation. And who is the closest? Christie, the petite 10-year-old with a closet full of American Girl dolls and a poster of actor Ben Affleck from the film "Armageddon" on her bedroom wall.

"Mom," she says, turning from the elephant to Michie. "That elephant is not eating."

"What?" Michie responds.

"It's not picking up anything, and it's not putting anything in its mouth," Christie says, pointing to the elephant. "That's just weird."

As if on cue, the elephant looks up and charges the safari vehicle. Christie begins screaming, holding onto her mom, almost climbing into her lap. Christie feels the ground shake as the two-ton elephant bum-rushes the vehicle. To her, it's like the whole world is rumbling. The guide, who has turned off the safari vehicle so everyone can look at the animals around them, turns the key and the engine roars to life.

VROOOOM.

The guide guns it.

"Go! Go! Go!" Michie yells from the back.

Christie never looks back at the elephant. She holds onto her mom, listening to the roar of an engine drown out the thump-thump-thump of the elephant's feet.

Today, Christie looks back to that time in Kruger National Park as magical. She saw a giraffe whose knees bent backward as it leaned down to drink from a watering hole. She and David saw a male lion sunning himself at the hotel pool as two lionesses strode casually around him.

And of course, she watched in horror as an alpha elephant with an attitude charged toward her and made the ground quake with its weight.

All that is still vivid for Christie. Today, when she and her husband, Adam, take their two boys and daughter to a zoo, one of them will often bring up her trip to South Africa, the elephant, and a giraffe with backward bending knees.

"That's so cool, Mom," her son, Sawyer, told her once.

"I've never had an experience like that before," she says. "It's sort of burned in my brain. It's always going to be there."

And elephants?

"Oh, I'm still terrified of elephants."

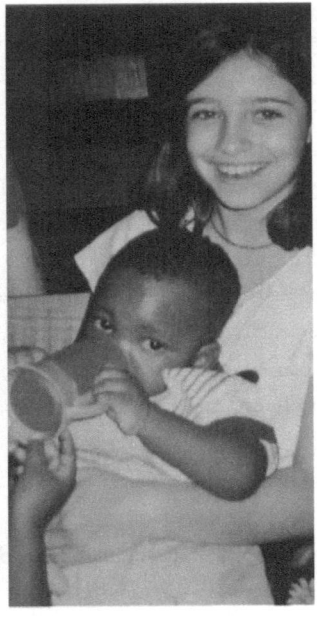

Christie Dew enjoyed much about South Africa. Except the elephants. Photo credit: Courtesy of Ali Mabitsela.

* * *

For Christie, it's the elephant she'll always remember. For David, her brother, it's the night sky.

He spends hours bumping along dirt roads in a school bus with his sister, Ali, and everyone else from New Creation. Their destination: Kruger National Park in the northeastern corner of South Africa. When they arrive, it's dark. Middle-of-nowhere dark. The park has already closed, and all everyone can do is sit in the school bus parked 10 feet from the gate and wait for the park to open at daybreak. David feels really cooped up. He's 11, a sixth-grader who likes to play street hockey in front of his house back in Greensboro. David wants to move, just do anything other than sit on a bus with nearly a dozen adults and hear them sing and tell jokes before they start to snore. His dad senses David's anxiousness, too. He has an idea.

"Let's climb onto the roof," his dad says.

David clambers through a bus window with his dad, and when he gets to the roof, he can't get over how many stars he sees. He lays on his back beside his dad and looks straight up.

"We have never seen stars like this have we?" his dad says.

They have not, especially in Greensboro where the lights from nearby UNCG can turn a night sky above their home into a light blue or a dirty beige. But in South Africa, in a park encompassing 7,580 square miles, what they see is a black canvas speckled with millions of stars that seem to sparkle.

Frank and David don't say a word. They just watch. Today, David and his dad still remember that night.

"At the time, I had trouble quantifying God," David says today. "I wanted something fact-based, some evidence that God existed. But on that roof of that bus, I felt that for the first time. It made me realize there is a God. How could we all exist without it?"

For David, it's the light from the stars he'll remember. For his dad, it's paradox found in that light.

"The stars were more evident because of the darkness, and that is a lesson in itself," Frank says. "The darkest of times can help us see the light more clearly. Here we are a speck on our planet, and our planet is a speck in the universe, and our lifetime begins and ends in the blink of an eye. How could we feel significant and meaningful with that in mind? And how is it that God is mindful of us when we're just a speck on our planet and our lives will end in a blink of an eye?

"Yet, when we find ourselves in that kind of paradox, we can experience God."

* * *

Ali can't wait to show the Dews and the other parishioners from New Creation his home. They had opened their own homes to him, and he wants to open his own world to them. He also wants to dispel the question he heard sometimes in Greensboro.

"When you walk down the street are elephants on the other side?"

South Africa is no jungle, and Ali is no longer who he used to be. He's no longer an electrician. He becomes the first Black person to be hired as a work study officer by the Apartheid Department of Finance. After the 1994 election, his department hires two more Black people as well as Indian. Ali loves what he sees — and feels. He has a purpose. He is helping transform his home country into a place where equity and inclusivity have begun to take root. Because of his experiences in Greensboro, he has begun to trust the government. He also has begun to trust whites. He sees his future and his country's future as bright, especially for those who have been oppressed for decades.

That, Ali believes, is no longer so. He feels that after coming back home.

"Our humble upbringings didn't make us to be nothings in life," Ali tells himself.

Ali wants to show that sense of hopefulness to the Dews and everyone else who comes from New Creation.

He shows them Soweto, the township of 1.3 million people where both Nelson Mandela and Bishop Desmond Tutu lived on the same street.

He shows them Attridgeville, the black township where he grew up.

He shows them the southern tip of South Africa. It's the rocky outcrop known as the Cape of Good Hope, the spot where baboons scurry across the ground like squirrels and the dark blue water of the Atlantic crashes into the emerald green water of the Indian Ocean and creates a constant roar.

He shows them the Union Buildings. They are the imposing structure built from light sandstone that represents the official headquarters of the South African government and the president of South Africa in Pretoria. In 1996, that's Mandela.

"This is what I told you about in Greensboro," Ali says to the group when they stop at the Union Buildings. "I couldn't even go in here before I left South Africa. And now, you are here, we are inside, and our president is not a racist. Apartheid is gone, we have a president we can call our own, and I know that my children will grow up in a free South Africa, and they will be able to tell stories of how we fought for us to be here."

Like other members of New Creation, Barbara Clawson is impressed. Like she had done with New Creation's Nicaragua trip in 1993, she helped arrange their trip to South Africa. It's no small thing, as she knows, to put together an itinerary for a mission trip. But Ali does. And does it well.

The other thing that impresses Barbara is how much Ali has matured. He is so at ease leading a group of North Carolinians through his country — from Attridgeville to the Cape of Good Hope to Kruger National Park. She also notices how much he's his old self, which she had grown to know so well in Greensboro. It isn't anything he says during their two weeks in South Africa. It's how he looks.

It's his wide smile. That hasn't changed.

* * *

In Attridgeville, when she and her family are visiting Ali and his family, Michie can feel the stares. She's walking down the dirt street to the corner store for a soft drink when people start coming out of their houses to stare. Not an at-the-zoo stare. No, an after-an-accident stare.

It isn't hostile. People are mainly curious. So, Michie being Michie, she smiles and waves back.

She runs into that same response when she and others in her group board a BMW bus bound for Attridgeville. Blacks look at her with her blonde hair, and they think she is an Afrikaner who has gotten lost. An Afrikaner wouldn't *dare* step into a bus crammed with Blacks.

"Hey," the driver shouts, "you're on the wrong bus!"

"No, they're Americans," Ali tells the driver. "They're with us."

Immediately, the Blacks in the bus begin to cheer.

"Go USA! Go USA!"

The response makes Michie remember the time when she was a teenager, and she had just moved from Sanford to Lumberton with her family. She was standing in her front yard, talking to her neighbor, a white teenager who lived across the street. During their conversations about teenage life in small-town North Carolina — what to do and where to go — he told Michie about his take on race and class.

"You know," he said, "God made Blacks inferior to whites and didn't want them to have access to life's privileges."

Michie feels that in South Africa. And as she walks to the corner store in Attridgeville to buy a Diet Coke, she sees it unfold on both sides of her with every step she takes. Blacks walk out of their homes to stare, and she just waves and smiles.

"This is sad," she tells herself later. "There is such segregation here still that such a usual event of walking down the street would cause people to come out of their house and look.'"

During their stay in South Africa, Michie and everyone else carries out classic mission-trip work. They become a construction crew. They turn mud and straw into bricks and build a bathhouse for Ali's Presbyterian church. As Michie is working, she runs into something she didn't expect.

"You don't have to do this," a Black South African tells Michie. "You're a pastor's wife."

In South Africa, a pastor's wife is akin to royalty. Black South Africans even have a name for Michie. They call her "First Lady." So, when she's told that she doesn't have to get dirty building bricks or washing dishes, she has a response ready.

"It's OK," she says. "I don't mind working. I want to help you."

The next day after building bricks, Michie and Frank go with Ali and take David and Christie with them. David and Christie first pan for polished stones at a gem mining farm on their way to visit one of the shantytowns outside Pretoria. David and Christie get a bagful. When they all walk into the shantytown, David and Christie see a scene that makes them numb.

They see Blacks living in cardboard boxes, and they smell burning trash and charcoaled meat wafting through the air like perfume. Young Black children — some wearing clothes, some not – – then begin rushing up to them. Christie still has her bag of rocks. So does David. As the children crowd around them, Christie and David start handing them their polished stones. It's almost unconscious, not a word spoken other than "Hi, here you go."

The children around them are speechless. Their eyes, though, light up.

As Christie heads back with Ali and her family to Attridgeville with an empty bag, she keeps going over in her mind what she sees and how it makes her feel.

"Gosh, I hope that could bring them joy."

On the last few days in South Africa, Frank does what he always does. He preaches.

He preaches at Ali's church, and in his message, he thanks them for their generosity and educating him and everyone from New Creation about their struggles. He tells them how America can use South Africa as a valuable lesson in understanding how truth and reconciliation are crucial tools in moving forward no matter where you live.

"It's neat to feel that connection with our church and your church and the larger church with Maake Masango," Frank says. "And you know, it all happened because of four words, 'What can we do?' That's how we met Ali. And that's how we met all of you. It shows us that no matter what passport you may be carrying we all are citizens of God's kingdom. Amen?"

"Amen!" the congregation responds.

Before Frank preaches, Ali's pastor has a question for him.

"What do you mostly remember about Frank's sermons?" he

asks.

Ali thinks about that for a minute. But after four years of sitting in the round circle of chairs in the fellowship hall at the(delete) Presbyterian Church of the Covenant and hearing Frank preach, Ali has a good idea of how to respond.

"His message is unique," Ali says. "So many pastors will say, 'If you don't do this, you are going to hell!' or 'If you don't tithe, you're going to hell' or 'If you don't love one another, this will happen.' But Frank says, 'Do right and be right with God.'

"Frank's sermons are all about bringing hope to people, and after listening to Frank preach so many times when I was in Greensboro, I found that was the theme of Frank's ministry.

"One of his sermons that sticks with me is when he said, 'Don't be conformed to this world. Be transformed from this world.' That means you don't have to be like everybody else. You don't have to fight like everybody else. Do what you think is right.

"Yes, there are many bad things happening. And yes, the economy is not doing well. But Frank tells us, 'It's OK. God loves you. There is hope in times of darkness. That is enough.'"

Ali's pastor listens. He doesn't ask a follow-up. He simply nods and smiles.

Frank on Frank
We Are One Family

What still sticks with me today is how much Ali trusted us.

He came to a different country and a different culture, and he modeled for the rest of us what trust looks like. And that allowed him to benefit from his experience here in Greensboro and at UNCG, and then he goes back and shares with his community what he had gained here.

A few years later, we sponsored our second student from South Africa, Kefilwe Rathabe, and we raised $100,000 again as a church. She graduated from UNCG, went back to South Africa, and from what I remember, Ali gave Kefilwe her first job.

See? Look what happens when we're willing to trust. That is such a catalyst for living life. Trusting in God and trusting in others. Think of it this way. Every day we go through a green light *trusting* that the people on the other side of the street will stop. It's like that verse from Hebrews, Chapter 11, verse 1: 'Now faith is the substance of things hoped for, the evidence of things not seen.'

Everyday life is full of 'evidence of things not seen.' Just examples where we're called to trust one another. Those everyday examples remind us of the power of ultimately trusting in God and knowing that God does have a plan and a purpose for each of us.

After visiting South Africa, I came away with a greater clarity about our own racial history. For example, the more I learned about what they called the Black homelands — the parts of the country like Soweto and Ali's township of Atteridgeville, where Blacks were sent to live and separated from everyone else — the more it reminded me so clearly of what we call Indian reservations. We moved Native Americans onto homelands we called reservations, separating them from mainstream American society. Then think of the whole process of racial segregation. With that came a second- and third-class citizenship where rights and benefits were restricted for people who were not white.

So, being in South Africa helped me to see even more clearly what we had been doing throughout our history and what we're still struggling to recover from today.

That's why Michie and I wanted David and Christie to visit the shantytown with us and Ali. We wanted them to understand the reality of not only South African history but also the reality of our own history. That is critical in moving forward toward any kind of reconciliation. When you tell the truth about what has happened and what has been, true healing can happen.

Remember, it doesn't require another person's cooperation to forgive. We can always forgive unilaterally so any forgiveness doesn't depend on someone else saying, 'I'm sorry.' But reconciliation, that's different. It does require a coming together of both parties to say, 'I'm sorry.'

But you need truth before you can get to reconciliation, and that has happened to a large degree in South Africa. We in America haven't done that. We can't even agree on our common history, and we're still wrestling with that today.

It's so ironic, I think. Germany has done a much better job with their Nazi history in order to move forward. They have not glorified it like what we have done with our Confederate statues. They have memorialized their history so they can learn from it and not repeat it ever again.

We, on the other hand, have sold ourselves on this mythology about the Civil War. That is not dealing with reality. I mean, when she was running for president, Nikki Haley had trouble saying the primary issue of the Civil War was slavery — and she said that in the year 2024.

When people ask me if I have hope for our country and its future, I say we don't get our hope from the evidence — or lack thereof — around us. We get our hope from God. God is our hope. God loves us and is faithful to us, and even when what we see around us is not good, our hope needs to rest with God. The Bible reminds us that the light has come into the darkness, and the darkness has not overcome it.

In Matthew, Chapter 28, Jesus says we should all go out into all nations and make disciples. That's the Great Commission, and that really means being witnesses to God's love and the difference that love has made in our lives. And we can give witness to that love by the way we live.

Such a powerful example of that is what we saw when we were on our mission trip in the Yucatan in Mexico. When Ali went to get his VISA passport and got held up, the people there were praying for him. And that happened without any prompting from us. It was prompted by our hosts, who were Mayan Indians in this rural village in southeastern Mexico. With all the differences we experienced then — and now — their response makes me realize that there is a universal connection when it comes to being citizens of God's kingdom.

Or, as I like to say, 'kin-dom.'

I use that word because it reminds me that we belong to God, and we belong to each other. The word 'kin-dom' reflects what Martin Luther King Jr. called the 'Beloved Community.' That community exists because of our relationship with God, and because of that shared connection with God, we have a shared connection with each other that is much deeper than our differences.

We're in one of those times right now when people are exploiting differences for their own advantage. Fear is a great motivator, and if you can convince people to see differences as something to fear, you then have a lot of leverage over them.

So, how can we counter that kind of exploitation? I say we need to appeal to, as Abraham Lincoln says, 'the better angels of our nature.' We need to recognize that the most important things we share as human beings are that we share a Creator God, our Parent God. We belong to the same family, and God brings us all together.

So, we have more in common than what divides us. The things that divide us are surface things like skin color or nationality or language. Those kinds of things. But once we get below the surface, the deepest and most basic things are what we have in common. Those are our aspirations of life and liberty and the pursuit of happiness.

We all share that. It's what makes us human.

After starting New Creation Community Presbyterian Church in 1985 in his Greensboro living room, Frank Dew decided to step away and retire as the church's pastor and as the chaplain at Greensboro Urban Ministry in 2016. Photo credit: Courtesy of Divinity, Duke University's magazine.

Chapter 18

Connecting the Dots

*"Life is not something earned or deserved by who we are or who we have become based on what we've done. No, life is a gift, and it boils down to what has been given to us. Life is not trying to live up to something; life is in **response** to something. God's love. We love because God has first loved us. **That** is our gift."*
The Rev. Frank Dew

It's right before 5 when Michie looks for a seat in the circle of chairs.

She has followed this Sunday afternoon routine so many times that she can close her eyes and find her spot inside Redhead Hall at First Presbyterian Church near downtown Greensboro. Redhead Hall has housed her church, New Creation Community Presbyterian, for a decade. Every Sunday afternoon, she does the same thing: Walk in, smile big, and catch up with members like Barbara Clawson or Margaret Young. Then, she slips into the circle, finds her seat and listens to her husband Frank talk about Jesus.

But this Sunday afternoon, the last Sunday in 2016, is different.

Michie is mute. She doesn't stop to talk to Barbara or Margaret. She can't even look at them. She can't talk to anybody. If she does, Michie knows she'll tear up and cry. This Sunday will be the last Sunday Frank preaches at New Creation as its full-time minister.

New Creation is Frank's church; New Creation is her church; and Frank is going to say goodbye.

What a way to end the year.

Frank started New Creation in the fall of 1985 when he and Michie lived off Longview Street in Greensboro's Lindley Park neighborhood. New Creation began in their living room. He then moved to the fellowship hall at Presbyterian Church of the Covenant, the church situated between UNCG and Greensboro College, where Frank's running partner and longtime friend, the Rev. Z Holler, preached. After Holler retired, Frank relocated New Creation a few miles away to Redhead Hall at First Presbyterian, the historic church founded in 1824 by 12 people, four of whom were enslaved.

Frank had always wanted to create a church where members lived their faith. He and his members have.

A month after starting their living-room church, nearly 25 members along with Frank drove C(??) and protested apartheid by holding their homemade signs in front of the South African Embassy. That protest set the tone for a progressive church where social justice took center stage, and members represented the rainbow of Greensboro.

Gay and straight.

Black, white, and brown.

Middle class to working class to people with only change in their pockets and the shirts on their backs.

Parishioners for New Creation come from all corners of the city. That includes a tent in the woods. That's what Frank wanted; that's what Michie loved. But 31 years after building New Creation from a living-room brainstorm with a flipchart at his elbow, Frank is ready to retire. He is going to step away from New Creation and a profession that he first thought about as a teenager. A calling that has occupied his Sundays — and his almost every waking thought — for more than 40 years.

Michie watched it all unfold. She had a front-row seat. Or really, she was on the field.

Ever since they first met in the narthex of their home church in Lumberton, First Presbyterian, Michie got involved in almost everything Frank did from a faith standpoint. When they met, Michie was a high school senior, Frank was a junior at Wake Forest. After their marriage, Michie became Dr. Michie Dew. She earned a doctorate in psychology from UNC-Chapel Hill, opened her own practice in Greensboro and advocated in court for those who had no voice. Frank did the same thing, except from a pulpit, a sidewalk in downtown Greensboro, a jail cell in DC and outside the walls of Central Prison in Raleigh. Michie was the yin to Frank's yang, and in every church he pastored, Michie was there to guide, volunteer, counsel, support, and like any good church lady, bake casseroles and bring them to people in need.

On that last Sunday in 2016, Michie knows she has to be like Frank. She has to say goodbye, too.

She slips into the circle of chairs inside Redhead Hall and sits in front of Frank, a few chairs from his right shoulder. She doesn't catch anyone's eye, not even Frank's. She can't. She knows the tears will come. When Frank begins the service, Michie looks at nothing, no one. She just stares at the floor.

"I couldn't tell you what he preached," Michie says today, a touch of emotion in her voice. "I just felt such intense sadness. I knew it would be different. The relationships with everyone at New Creation would go on, but it wouldn't be the same when you're not with them multiple times a week. So, I just cried through most of the service.

"Frank felt it was the best thing for the church, but after being part of such a prophetic church for so long, it's hard to be in another church that is afraid to speak the truth."

Frank and Michie Dew celebrated their 50ᵗʰ wedding anniversary in August 2025, and as she built her psychological practice in Greensboro, she watched Frank build two congregations, a chaplaincy program, and work in various nonprofits to help those without. And in 2016, she watched him step away much of that. Or would he?

* * *

"When are you going to retire?"

At first, that question always made Frank uncomfortable. But that question he fielded from his friends as well as parishioners at New Creation convinced him to reflect on what he had created and what he had hoped to continue.

New Creation was attracting more people from all walks of life to its Sunday afternoon services at First Presbyterian. Frank was glad of that. But what concerned Frank was New Creation wasn't bringing in any young people. He knew young people could help grow New Creation and keep it going for years to come. But Frank didn't see a single young face in his circle of chairs, and the more he thought about his aging congregation, the more he thought of his dad.

Luther Dew, a World War II vet, had come home to North Carolina to get married, start a family, and build and sell homes in Lumberton on both sides of the Lumber River. When Frank was getting ready to graduate from Lumberton High, his dad lamented on what that big moment meant to him and his profession. He told Frank he could see the day coming when he no longer would have the shoulder-to-shoulder connection to young families who wanted to become first-time homebuyers because Frank and his two sisters, Sara and Phyl, would be soon beginning their lives away from Lumberton.

In 2016, as Frank edged deeper into his sixth decade, he understood more than ever how his dad felt. With David and Christie grown, married, and starting their own lives, Frank had lost his connection to a younger crowd.

Just like his father.

"I could ride a unicycle standing on my head, and I'd not attract *any* young people to New Creation," he once told Michie. "Maybe it's time for a new generation."

Frank would mention his concerns to Michie at the most pedestrian of times. They'd be walking to the car, getting ready to go to the grocery store, when Frank would drop his I-want-to-retire bomb. But Michie was used to it. When it came time to contemplate the big turning points in his life, Frank was a man of few words. He wouldn't sermonize. He would think. *Forever.*

When he'd mention something huge in his life, Frank would only say two or three sentences. That's it. As a psychologist, Michie was attuned to such nuances. As Frank's forever partner, she also was attuned to such nuances coming from him. But as the months went by, Frank talked more openly about leaving New Creation and seeing it as a way for the church he created to grow.

But he wasn't talking just about leaving New Creation. He also was talking about leaving Greensboro Urban Ministry.

Frank had been the chaplain of Greensboro Urban Ministry for 22 years. Frank had loved his work at GUM, and he loved what the chaplaincy program had become. All he had to do was walk through the single-story building off East Lee, now Gate City Boulevard, and see for himself.

Frank created the chaplaincy program in 1994 and brought in interns like Vicki McCain from various seminaries in North Carolina.

He turned a windowless room a few steps from Potter's House into a chapel and created a daily noontime service.

He created a Stephen Ministry and brought in loads of lay ministers like Mike Sasser to provide one-on-one care for those in the shelter.

He recruited Tony Brown and Bernard McCoy to start a program where shelter residents could talk about their addictions and rough turns that had wrecked their lives. With the help of Tony and Bernard, shelter residents felt empowered to change. Tony and Bernard called their program "Making A Difference." The title did seem to fit.

Frank had helped turn GUM into a spiritual oasis for those who felt lost. He also created a spiritual oasis for himself.

There wasn't a day he didn't have a conversation with someone at GUM that would transform into a potential topic for a sermon. It happened all the time. He'd be walking into Potter's House or through the cavernous warehouse with its shelves of food and hear, "Hey, Pastor!" Frank knew someone needed help.

But being the chaplain for GUM was like being a chaplain at a hospital. Frank had to be on call all the time and be there every day. He had to be *on*, and there were times his constant treadmill wore him out.

Then came a situation that made it all clear.

Frank wanted to give raises to his two chaplains, the Revs. Helen McLaughlin and Andre Spells. But Frank was told that couldn't happen because of budget constraints. So, Frank found a way. He simply retired. He knew GUM could split his salary and give raises to the two chaplains.

Frank could leave on his own terms and support Andre and Helen in the process. Now came the time to talk to Michie.

When the need for big conversations arose, Frank did what he often does. He'd sit down with Michie in their wood-paneled den off Camden Road in their usual spots — Frank in his favorite chair; Michie on the couch.

And when it comes time to talk about leaving New Creation and Greensboro Urban Ministry at the same time, THAT is a big conversation. Right there, in the den, in their usual spots. Frank begins.

"You know, somebody at New Creation asked me last night when I was going to retire, and I wasn't sure she wasn't encouraging me to retire or maybe the church wanted me to think about that. But it kind of got *me* thinking.

"I don't want to hold on to being the pastor at New Creation too long just because I enjoy doing it. Maybe, it's time to think about finding someone younger who might be better connected with a younger generation — and not have to ride on a unicycle standing on their head."

"And to be honest, I've been thinking about that this past year. It would be nice to have more flexibility and more freedom to be able to, you know, go fishing when I wanted to and not have so many constraints on both of us. Sundays do come around every week.

"I really enjoy what I'm doing, but I'm yearning for more freedom, just more flexibility than being a local chaplain. Just freedom to travel. Freedom to see David more. Freedom to visit Christie more. Freedom to see our grandkids. And we both know we've never been dependent on my income "

Michie earned the first doctorate in her family, and for three decades in Greensboro, she had established a busy practice as the co-owner of Carolina Psychological Associates. A busy practice meant a healthy practice, and that meant money in the bank. But as Frank talked, money wasn't the only thing she was thinking about.

"Are you sure you want to do this?" she asks.

"Yeah," Frank responds.

"But New Creation means so much to you," Michie says. "You sure?"

"Yeah," Frank responds.

"You know, if you do one instead of both at the same time it will impact your pension," Michie says, "GUM does pay part of your salary."

"I know," Frank says.

"And your pension is based on what your church salary is," Michie says.

"That's true," Frank says.

Michie, always the practical one.

"Leaving New Creation and GUM," Michie says. "At the same time. You sure you want to do this?"

"I am," Frank says. "It's clear to me that this is the right thing to do. For the Greensboro Urban Ministry. And the church. It's time for a new person, a younger person to come in there at New Creation."

As Michie listens, she time-travels back to the other big decisions in their lives together as a couple — Trinity Avenue Presbyterian in Durham, to Vandalia Presbyterian in Greensboro, to New Creation, Greensboro Urban Ministry, Nicaragua, South Africa, a jail cell in DC. All those experiences have one thing in common: Frank is going to do what Frank is going to do.

"Frank," Michie says, "If you want to retire, that's fine by me."

In a fall 2002 issue of Divinity, Frank posed in the Potter's House, the cafeteria inside Greensboro Urban Ministry where he had many conversations with those without homes and those whose prayers included this poignant line: "Thank you for waking me up this morning!" Photo credit: Courtesy of Divinity, Duke University's magazine.

* * *

After his last sermon at New Creation, Frank walks away. His parishioners have given him a retirement gift of a fishing vest, and Frank knows he'll give that vest a workout. He also knows he has to give *himself* a workout. He needs new responsibilities that give his life purpose because of two questions that have pestered him for months.

"Who am I?"

"And without those identities, what good am I?"

He thinks he finds at least *something* that could give him an answer.

Frank continues co-teaching his public ministry course at Wake Forest as well as teaching his "Radical Jesus" series at the Servant Leadership School in Greensboro. He becomes a fill-in preacher at various Presbyterian churches when their ministers are away, and he finds a home for the tools of his spiritual trade.

Frank talks with the Rev. Kim Priddy, the new minister at Sedgefield Presbyterian in Greensboro, and turns one of its spare offices into what he calls his workshop. The office at the end of a hall becomes home to all his books, his mementos, and four, four-drawer filing cabinets containing notes on every sermon he has ever given.

Frank turned a spare room at Sedgefield Presbyterian Church into his office that held much from his 50-year ministry career.

Frank steps up his work with Bread for the World, a nonprofit he's been involved with for more than 30 years. He also becomes what Salem Presbytery calls an "engagement pastor," which means he turns into a coach of sorts for ministers at 21 Presbyterian churches in Guilford and Randolph counties.

He chairs the Hunger Committee with Salem Presbytery, joins the Hunger Program Advisory Committee with Presbyterian Church USA and becomes a board member on the North Carolina Council of Churches. He also gets a new a business card.

Frank becomes the Peace and Justice Advocate for Salem

Presbytery. On his new business card is his phone number, his email and three words: Inspire. Equip. Send.

For decades, Frank has been one of the well-known faces of social justice in Greensboro. So, when anyone asks Frank how his retirement is going, he mentions fishing, his new fishing vest or his frequent trips to the family's beach house in Ocean Isle and his flights to Chicago see his grandchildren, Christie's kids, Sawyer, Myles and Posie. And if anyone prods further into Frank's post-pulpit life, he'll mention his other spiritual duties.

After listing his litany of new responsibilities, the people who ask often laugh.

"Frank," they'll say. "Are you really retired?"

"Semi-retired," he'll respond. "I'm still trying to figure out what that means. It's amazing what people will let you do when they don't have to pay you. But you know, the great thing about ministry? We're *always* going to be called to ministry."

As Frank begins his new roles, he still searches for what else he thinks he could do. He doesn't talk about it. Yet, he's always on alert. Michie notices that right away.

"We all knew he wasn't going home to sit in an easy chair," Michie says today. "That's not Frank. But the first six months of his retirement was a period of discernment, and whenever that is happening in anyone's life, you feel a bit in the dark. But for Frank, it wasn't dark as in the sense of a mood. It was dark as in the sense of 'What's next?'

"He was worried about being irrelevant. In his mind, he was still a pastor. But he was over on the sidelines, not making an impact like he once did. And when you have been working your whole life and then have nothing on your schedule, that's always tough. That was tough on Frank. It's that idea of 'Am I going into the Land of Irrelevance?'"

Frank likes his volunteer work with everything from Salem Presbytery to Bread for the World, and he enjoys his occasional Sundays as a stand-in minister at local churches.

But he has this spiritual emptiness that he can't ... quite ... fill.

As his retirement goes from months to years, he realizes he misses GUM. He misses running into a sermon topic around every corner and seeing verses of the Bible take human form and become the faces, names and stories of present-day. He misses the Tuesday nights. He misses being with Tony Brown and Bernard McCoy and seeing how they nurture everyone with more than just chicken bathed in mushroom gravy.

Frank wants to find that spiritual ... something. Then, it comes. Out of the blue.

It's a weekday in 2022, and Frank is in his black Ford Mustang driving to an appointment or some errand in Greensboro. His iPhone rings and he sees on his dashboard computer screen a number he doesn't recognize. But he knows the area code: 202.

"Hmm, DC," Frank tells himself. "Who do I know in DC? Must be from Church of the Saviour. Wonder what they want?"

Frank answers.

"Hello?"

A voice from his past fills his black Ford Mustang.

Frank met Kim Montroll years ago at Church of the Saviour in Washington, DC. Kim now serves as the church's Catalyst at Large in helping communities nationwide start what has become known as a Recovery Café.

In 2016, Church of the Saviour started a Recovery Café in a row house along the Anacostia River in Northwest DC and created a safe space, a drug- and alcohol-free space, geared to help people in crisis, and fill their stomachs and feed their souls.

Kim is one of the program's founding board members, and she tells Frank how they are expanding the Recovery Café model nationwide to help address such societal ills as systemic racism and connect people to a space she sees as "profoundly loving, inclusive and honoring of all."

"Frank, do you know anyone who might be interested?" Kim asks.

Frank smiles, unconsciously gripping the wheel tighter because of his enthusiasm.

"I do, Kim," he says. "I certainly do."

When he was the chaplain at GUM, Frank didn't know everyone's name. But he could recognize faces or even clothing that a person always wore.

If Frank saw a hat or a jacket or a shirt that sparked a memory, he used that as a conversation starter to help him find common ground with the many guests coming through GUM. It always worked. But sometimes, it created a bit of magic that convinced Frank something bigger was at work.

Like this time.

* * *

Seven years into his chaplaincy at GUM, Frank sees a man wearing the recognizable red-and-gold jacket of his favorite team growing up in Lumberton. Frank was a big fan of the Washington Redskins, and on Sunday afternoons, every Redskins game was appointment television for him and his dad. They never missed a game on TV.

So, when he sees the jacket, Frank sees an opening.

"Love your jacket," he says, walking up to the man. "I was always a Redskins fan as a little kid. I'm Frank. What's your name?"

"Robert," the man responds.

"Robert, nice to meet you," Frank says, shaking Robert's hand. "Where you from?"

"Oh, I'm from DC," Robert says.

"Oh, my favorite church is in DC," Frank says.

Frank tells Robert about Church of the Saviour. Almost every day after that first conversation, Frank sees Robert in his Washington Redskins' jacket. A month or so later, Robert tells Frank he's going back to his hometown. Frank offers a suggestion.

"You might want to check out Church of the Saviour when you get there," Frank tells him.

Frank doesn't give his suggestion another thought until a year later when he continues one of his routines that feeds his soul and his love for a good road trip.

Frank gets up at 5 in the morning and drives five hours north to Church of the Saviour. He wants to get there in time for the noon worship service to recharge and reconnect with the church's staff, people he has known for years.

When he walks into the church's chapel, he doesn't notice anything right away. It's always dimly lit, and the stained-glass windows only let so much sunlight into the chapel even on a bright sunny day.

The chapel is small, with a circle of chairs tucked into a turret in a corner of the church in Washington's Adams Morgan neighborhood.

When Frank's eyes adjust to the dim light, he can see out of the corner of his eye, a man in a red-and-gold jacket.

Frank looks over.

Sitting right beside him is Robert.

"Oh my gosh," Frank exclaims. "Robert, it's so good to see you! How have you been?"

Robert started coming to Church of the Saviour right after he returned to DC. After the service, Frank hears more about how the church and its outreach services have helped Robert feel anchored again in his hometown.

"Thank you, Frank, for letting me know about the Church of the Saviour," Robert says. "It's been a huge help."

"Sure, Robert," Frank responds. "But you're the one who made the connection. I just told you about it. You made it happen."

Later that afternoon, as Frank heads south back to Greensboro, he can't get over his chance encounter with Robert. And in all places, at the noon service of Church of the Saviour.

"God is connecting the dots," Frank tells himself on the drive home. "That's the flow of the Spirit. Yep, thanks be to God. I'm on the right path."

But that had been years ago.

Would Frank feel the same way today about Recovery Café?

He is about to find out.

Frank on Frank

Finding Our Right Identity

We get so much of our identity from our external stimuli. I mean, people tell us *all the time* who we are. Like, 'Oh, you're a great basketball player,' or 'You're a great wife' or 'You're a great father' or 'You're a great husband' and so on. That is how we know who we are when we ask ourselves, 'Who am I?'

But there is a problem with that.

When we do that, we put our identity into the hands of other people. But there is another kind of knowing who we are, and we have to look inside us and see who we are internally. When we do, we see how God sees us.

So, when someone asks, 'Who *are* you?' we all can reply, 'I am a child of God.'

That is not something the world gives. But that awareness of belonging *to* God is really the seed from which everything else grows. That should give all of us some peace of mind because it's not something that can ever be taken away.

But if it were only that easy, right?

No matter how old we are or where we live, we all identify ourselves with what we do and how other people see us. It's human nature. And it's human nature to hold onto something for too long because of our love of doing it.

You see it in sports, business, everywhere, and it can become a push-pull, a real tug-of-war inside us. We don't want to leave what we love or who we love or leave what we do or where we live because we want to remain relevant.

Relevance. That's the key word here.

We all want to remain relevant, and let me tell you, I sure felt that need for relevancy when I was thinking about retiring and stepping away from the Greensboro Urban Ministry and New Creation at the same time.

Not being a pastor *and* not being a chaplain at GUM. It had me asking myself, 'Who am I?'

Sure, I can say, 'I'm Michie's husband, I'm David and Christie's dad. I'm a Presbyterian minister.' But who am I really?

I am a child of God.

Stepping away from what I enjoyed was really hard. But I kept telling myself that it would give me an opportunity to grow and the flexibility I needed to do things I have never really had time for before.

As we ministers often say, 'Sundays come around every week.' We always have a sermon to deliver.

But my decision allowed me to get more involved with other things I cared about — the North Carolina Council of Churches, Salem Presbytery and Bread for the World. I got the chance to preach at other Presbyterian churches. That included a chance to preach at Vandalia Presbyterian, the first church I pastored in Greensboro when I arrived here in 1979.

All these opportunities gave me a sense of purpose. But it also reminded me of what life is all about.

Life is not something earned or deserved by who we are or who we have become based on what we've done. No, life is a gift, and it boils down to what has been given to us. Life is not trying to live up to something; life is in *response* to something.

God's love. We love because God has first loved us.

That is our gift.

It ain't all about you or me. It's about what God has given us. In the final analysis, it's not about what I have done or failed to do or what you have done or failed to do. It's more about the opportunity we all have every day.

Each day, we have an opportunity to write a thank-you note to God, and we can write it by the way we live. We don't have to live in the past. We can start fresh each day. That can take a weight off our shoulders, and we can say to ourselves, 'I am not you God. Thank you for letting me be me.'

That takes us out of the center of our lives and puts God in the center. That's the rightful order. Good theology always begins with God in the center.

In my four decades as a Presbyterian minister, I've come to realize there is a difference between believing in Christ and following Jesus.

I've been a believer ever since I learned how to walk in Lumberton. But a few years after leaving the Greensboro Urban Ministry and New Creation, I began asking myself, 'Am I really following Jesus?'

It reminded me of what my friend, the Rev. Z Holler, said when he retired from Presbyterian Church of the Covenant, only to help create in 1991 the Beloved Community Center, an organization rooted in Dr. Martin Luther King's legacy of fighting for racial and economic justice and democracy.

Z told me, 'Frank, I want to finish strong."

I did, too. I missed that part of me that had been immersed deep into marginalized communities of Greensboro. Here's what I mean:

Say, you're fishing. You're in a boat in the middle of a lake, you've got your line cut ready to catch that largemouth bass you've heard about, and you realize you left your depth finder on a dock. Without a depth finder, you have no way of knowing how to get an accurate reading of where to find fish.

My retirement helped me realize I needed a new kind of depth finder.

A spiritual depth finder.

The people I met at New Creation and at the Greensboro Urban Ministry helped me see and hear things I missed because of my privilege. I grew up comfortable, a white man raised in the segregated South, and I missed my connection to those 'PhDs in life.'

They helped me hear the scriptures more clearly, follow Jesus more closely, and really feel Matthew 25 inside me once again and hear God say, 'Whatever you did for the least of these, you did for Me.'

Our faith is like two wings of a bird. Birds need two wings to fly, and we need to have both the inward and the outward to really feel the authenticity of the Gospel.

Think about the words of 'Amazing Grace.' It was written by the captain of a slave ship. After he survived a terrible storm, he changed his ways. After he stopped taking slaves to America, he wrote one of the most memorable hymns we still sing to this day.

Think of these two verses.

I was lost, but now I'm found.
I was blind, but now I see.

That's good theology, too. It's what we see; it's what we discover. It reminds us that 'It's not about who we are but *whose* we are.'

That's a different kind of identity than what the world knows.

So, 'Who *are* you?' You know the answer.

Frank brought in friends and former colleagues from his 50-year ministry career
to help start Recovery Café in Greensboro's Presbyterian Church of the Cross.
Recovery Café is a national program created by the Church of the Saviour in
Washington DC to help those struggling with life find a way to heal and connect.
Photo credit: Buck Cochran.

Chapter 19

'Trust and Believe'

*"In the Twelve Steps program of AA, you hear folks say, 'You can't keep
what you can't give away.' What that means is as we share with others, what
we share grows within us. And when we welcome others with graciousness
and show love to those who feel unloved, the more that love and grace grows
within us. Recovery Café helps me reconnect with that love and grace. "*
The Rev. Frank Dew

Frank stands near the door and watches them file in, one or two at a
time. He recognizes more than a few faces. When he does, he shakes
their hands, gives them a hug or talks about the last time they saw one
another. Some of those familiar faces Frank has seen as recently as
last week.

But for those he doesn't recognize, Frank becomes the greeter
in his every-day uniform — powder-blue button-down shirt, khaki
pants and running shoes. After more than 40 years in a pulpit and 22
years in one of the most hard-luck spots in Greensboro, Frank has a
knack for relaxing anyone leery of walking into a foreign place.

And for some, this is a foreign place, the fellowship hall inside
Presbyterian Church of the Cross in east Greensboro.

With everyone who walks in, especially those Frank doesn't
know, he'll go into preacher mode. He smiles big, opens his arms
wide, leans his head back slightly and does what he often did when he
was the chaplain at Greensboro Urban Ministry.

"Come on into the house!" Frank says.

Frank's voice bristles with Sunday morning excitement. And for

good reason. What he hopes would happen has become a reality —
all because of one phone call in 2022.

His friend, Kim Montroll, called him with a question. That one
question led to an answer that changed his retirement. He discovered
what he was missing, a connection that energized him. That phone
call immersed him once again with a population that he had worked
with for decades, and they helped him as much as he helped them.

Frank calls his new connection Greensboro's "new beacon of
hope."

Recovery Café Greensboro, RCG for short.

Recovery Café Greensboro opened in April 2024 after two years
of training and a seed grant of $50,000 to help it get started. The RCG
continues a helping-hand endeavor that began 20 years ago. The first
Recovery Café started in 2004 in Seattle. Since then, a constellation of
Recovery Cafés has opened nationwide and created a network that
helps people traumatized by drugs, alcohol, homelessness, or mental
health struggles.

Recovery Café Greensboro became No. 64, one of only two
south of Washington, DC. The other Recovery Café is in Charlotte.

"Frank, you know what I think you're doing?" the Rev. Mike
Aiken, Frank's college friend and former boss at GUM, told him. "I
think you're building a church without the building."

Sort of.

In 1985, Frank assembled friends in his living room to help start
New Creation Community Presbyterian Church. After Kim's phone
call in 2022, Frank again brought together people he had worked with
before. He liked them, respected them, and together, he believed they
could make a difference in Greensboro and help people heal.

Frank and others involved with RCG began approaching donors
and applying for grants to raise the $150,000 needed every year to run
the nonprofit. Meanwhile, they recruited volunteers to run
workshops, create classes, cook the food, and be a part of the small
support groups held twice a week to help those who need help.

Everyone Frank recruited had a role. And his? Fundraiser.

Before RCG opened, supporters peppered Frank with questions

during an information session at Presbyterian Church of the Cross.

They asked how RCG is any different from Narcotics Anonymous, Alcohol Anonymous or Al-Anon, a worldwide recovery group for families and friends of alcoholics. They could see it was more comprehensive. And sure, they could see how it offers more wrap-around services and how the support of Church of the Saviour, a well-connected heavyweight in social justice initiatives headquartered in Washington, DC, will make it work.

But really, they asked, why add another recovery organization when others are already out there?

Frank had an answer.

"We don't see ourselves in any conflict or competition," Frank would tell them. "We'll add another support program for people in recovery and our focus is to help people maintain their recovery. It all goes back to the idea of the African proverb — 'If you want to run fast, run by yourself. If you want to run far, run together.' So, we'll all run together to help those around us, 'the least, the last and the left out.' And it helps when you have friends involved, doesn't it?"

Frank remembers driving up to Washington, DC, with Tony Brown and Bernard McCoy, the two friends who created the successful recovery program at Greensboro Urban Ministry. They toured the Recovery Café They ate the food, talked to those involved, and participated in a recovery session sitting in a circle of chairs.

Very Church of the Saviour.

And very New Creation Community Presbyterian Church.

"Oh, man, this is what we're used to doing!" Bernard said on the drive home.

"I was really wondering what my reaction would be," Frank added. "But that was really cool, wasn't it?"

"Frank, it was!" Tony responded. "I felt right at home. These were my people!"

Then came the work.

Two years of training and getting organized. A year of attending 90-minute sessions online every week. A year of hearing how to raise money, how to conduct Recovery Café circles, how to listen, how to respond, and how to create a sense of ownership with everyone involved.

The model RCG has created does work, according to a recent study of participants. Eight out of every 10 participants didn't relapse, and they steered clear of drugs and alcohol, saw their physical health improve and stabilized their mental health. And nine out of every 10 participants reported they were more hopeful in going forward with their lives.

Hope.

That's always been one of Frank's go-to words in any sermon. Now, he's going to see if that word can take shape in a fellowship hall in east Greensboro with the people who come and the stories they share.

So, every Monday and Thursday night when the Recovery Café Greensboro opens its doors, Frank stands near the door.

Twice a week, Frank is surrounded by people who made RCG happen. In that small crowd of people are three who were key, three who Frank saw grow in spirit and in confidence with helping others — — and helping themselves.

Tony Brown. He's the site leader.

Bernard McCoy. He's the kitchen manager.

The Rev. Vicki McCain, the pastor of Presbyterian Church of the Cross. She's the treasurer. They got involved because they believe in Recovery Café Greensboro. Its mission statement is written on the banner perched near a cinder-block wall in the fellowship hall. It reads: To provide a refuge, healing, and transformation for men and women traumatized by homelessness, addiction, incarceration, and other mental health challenges.

They do believe in that. They also believe in Frank.

"I love that brother," Tony says.

* * *

On a recent Thursday night, Tony stands near the window in the fellowship hall in jeans, a long-sleeve baseball jersey and a pair of white Converse high-tops. Born in January 1960, Tony looks like a man half his age even with his gray beard and bald head. He's slender, muscled from his every-other-day regimen of doing calisthenics and lifting dumb bells 40 pounds and 20 pounds each. As the people file in, Tony looks over his round glasses, surveying the room like a teacher before class.

Bernard stands a few steps away, wearing a black apron and a relaxed smile. He's beside a volunteer and behind two tables of food he has cooked and prepared for the weeknight session. People queue up cafeteria-style and Bernard serves everyone who comes through.

Vicki is everywhere — from the kitchen to the fellowship hall door, back into the kitchen and then stopping at each of the four tables. She talks to everyone she sees. Before one recent Monday night session, she sits at one of the tables covered with a black tablecloth and talks about the Saturday soccer program the church has organized on the field below the parking lot. Players from six years old to seniors in high school play every Saturday and turn the field into a United Nations of languages.

Vickie always offers a prayer before anyone begins to eat. But not this Monday night. At least not yet.

Tony has a few things to say. He's standing near a framed banner that reads in part, "Recovery Café — A Refuge for Healing + Hope," and in a gruff voice that sounds more streetwise than saintly, Tony begins.

"Everybody has seen the picture of 'The Last Supper,' right? What we see in 'The Last Supper,' that's the important part. But right off the side, there is a kitchen there someplace. Somebody is preparing food. Somebody is getting the table set up. Somebody is getting the whole atmosphere set. Somebody is serving. Somebody like that brother right there."

Tony points to Bernard. Everyone claps.

Recovery Café Greensboro. Open for another night.

Bernard McCoy and Tony Brown take in another weeknight with their good friend, the Rev. JE McCoy. Photo credit: Buck Cochran.

* * *

Tony Brown, the veteran Marine, sounds like a preacher when he gathers people together twice a week at Recovery Café. Photo credit: Buck Cochran.

Like Frank, Tony recognizes many of the faces who come into the fellowship hall. Tony is old-school Greensboro. He grew up off Finley Street near Benbow Park, where NBA great Bob McAdoo honed his game as a teenager on a concrete slab. A few who come to RCG grew up with Tony, or over the years, he has helped them deal with their struggles with drug and alcohol addiction.

Tony understands their struggles well.

Tony is a Marine, an N.C. Central grad and a former Greensboro firefighter who, as he says today, "got lost in the abyss." He sold drugs, and he got addicted to what he sold — crack cocaine. After his mom and aunt died, Tony looked for ways to get sober. He discovered Malachi House II, a nine-month, faith-based residential recovery program for men. He became one of the nonprofit's leaders by raising money washing cars and turning the enterprise off South Elm/Eugene Street into a bonding session for the men who came.

At Malachi House II, Tony roomed with a man who became one of his best friends. Tony's roommate was Bernard McCoy. Bernard grew up in Winston-Salem, the youngest of 13. Born in August 1953, Bernard came of age in a close-knit family whose life revolved around Saints Home United Methodist Church. He rang the church's bell and became an acolyte. At his home off East Twenty-Fifth Street in Winston-Salem, he shared a bed with his two older brothers, Steve and Donald.

Bernard loves to cook, and he learned in the family's kitchen at the hip of his mom, Lovie. After a brief stint in culinary school, Bernard ran a successful catering business. He also ran in a fast lane, chasing what he calls today a "merry-go-round of life." He got divorced and started smoking marijuana and crack cocaine to cope with his heartache and his everyday stresses of life.

Bernard came to Malachi House II to kick his addiction and recover. He also got involved in the Stephen Ministries program at GUM and met Frank. GUM had started an AA program for shelter residents, but it stalled when fewer and fewer people showed up. Frank then approached Bernard about starting a recovery program because Frank knew of Bernard's work at Malachi House II feeding and helping participants. Bernard said yes and asked Tony to join him.

The two began a weekly recovery program for shelter residents, called it "Making A Difference," and ran it for 14 years until the global pandemic shut it down. With the RCG, they're together once again.

"I do love cooking, and I had a little business cooking because I do love to feed people," Bernard tells the crowd before one recent dinner at RCG. "And Frank, he's a mentor to me and Tony. With Frank's help, we started a ministry at the Urban Ministry, and we didn't miss a Tuesday night rain, sleet or snow. They appreciated it, and we appreciated them.

"And now, we're going to get this going, and we'll give God the glory."

The Rev. Vicki McCain met Frank in 2014 through GUM's chaplaincy internship program when she was a student at Union Presbyterian Seminary in Charlotte. Her internship helped her find, as she says today, "real love with skin on it." It also helped her find a mentor in Frank.

"I am going to help you shape and model what God is calling you to do," he told her when she worked as GUM's clinical pastoral education chaplain intern.

Vicki grew up in church. Inside Ebeneezer Baptist in Rocky Mount, she ushered, sang in the choir, attended Sunday School and participated in Vacation Bible School. After graduating from N.C. A&T, she worked as an accountant, got married and started a family. After a 20-year career, she felt led to become a minister. In 2019, she became the part-time minister at Presbyterian Church of the Cross, a spiritual anchor in east Greensboro for more than a half century.

The tan-brick building off Phillips Avenue has been the home for City Council meetings, candidate forums, voter registration drives and countless gatherings. Just beyond a concrete bench one of the church's signs planted in a garden bed of pine straw reads: "Keep Calm Because God Will Make A Way."

Neighbors and churchgoers came together to talk to police about public safety or ask local officials or city staff about ways to bring more economic growth to a section of the city that often felt ignored.

Now, Presbyterian Church of the Cross is home for Recovery Café Greensboro.

The Rev. Vicki McCain, the former corporate accountant, pastors the Presbyterian Church of the Cross and has become one of the architects in helping create Greensboro's Recovery Café. Photo credit: Buck Cochran.

Vicki, born in May 1965, the youngest of three daughters, can rouse a congregation with her sermon. She is charismatic with a gift of creating a phrase that people remember. On the church's website is one of her favorite sayings: "Don't tell God how big your storm is, tell the storm how big your God is."

But at RCG, where she delivers the prayer before every meal, her prayer is more of a meditative moment. Vicki speaks in measured tones, each word like a click-click-click of a pendulum on a metronome. She wants to get the people who come in the right frame of mind for a night of sitting in a circle of chairs and being vulnerable, sharing stories and listening to understand.

This particular Thursday night is no different.

Vicki gets up from her seat and stands before a crowd of 20 or so seated at tables holding plastic foam plates of spicy chicken patties, baked salmon, rice and salad. It's her time. Time to pray.

"We hope everyone felt love when they walked through the door," she says. "We're going to start tonight with silence and close our eyes. I would ask you to breathe in through your nostrils and out through your nostrils."

After 25 seconds of silence, Vicki continues.

"Oh Lord, how excellent You are in all the earth. For Your love, we say thank you. As we dine and fellowship with one another, may we feel Your presence in this space and in this place. We are thankful for these hallowed grounds for this is what you've given us. But you have also given us this day. And we are to rejoice and be happy in it.

"Although we're almost at the close of an evening and a night, we're grateful because you give us this morning a new day. No sin in it. No interruption. Just a gift.

"So, tomorrow, as we move from this space and into a new day, may we look at this day in a different manner. May we look at this day as a new dawning. A day with no sin in it. A day we have been gifted with. A day in which we won't allow people to rob us of our joy, but to move forward in your spirit.

"So, today, we are grateful that we have an opportunity to laugh, to talk and be mindful of the fact that we are all recovering from something. But because of Your love for us, we are forgiven for whatever it is we find ourselves recovering from.

"Because of Your grace, because of Your love for us, we can stand boldly knowing that You still love us, and we are certainly sinners saved by Your grace. And for that, we are certainly grateful.

"So, as the food has been prepared with love, with a lot of thought and intention, may we enjoy this meal. May we meet someone we have never met before. May we journey with someone we have never journeyed with before. And may we be blessed by their presence because after all Your breath was given to dust, which formed mankind.

"While we're here, fill us up physically, emotionally, mentally, and spiritually. May the breath that we take be of Your sweet, sweet spirit. And may we know without a shadow of a doubt that it is You. And that we were called to be together tonight. Now, Lord, may the food that Bernard prepared 'better be good.'

"All these wonderful things we thank you for. In the name of Jesus. Amen. Amen. Amen."

* * *

Twice a week, Bernard McCoy cooks a meal for those who come to Recovery Café.

Photo credit: Buck Cochran.

After dinner, participants meander over to the circle of chairs and couches. They take a seat and wait beside Tony, the site leader. With his elbows on his knees, Tony looks as if he's in prayer. Once nearly two dozen people get seated around him, he straightens up. He's in a place he sees as sacred and safe. He calls it the "Oasis." When he begins each session, he punctuates every few words in the beginning as if a jab to a heavy bag in a gym.

"Welcome to the Oasis. This is a place where you come to be known and to know one another. This is a place where you embrace who you are right now. But you will be held accountable for who you want to be.

"This is a place of love, kindness and a radical departure of what you're used to. What we're going to do today is talk about our challenges, our successes, what we are grateful for, where we're struggling, and what is our goal for the week.

"Most of the time we flow through the week, and we just flow. We don't have goals. Let's take time to establish what we want to achieve for the week and how do we get there. And can Recovery Café help you get there.

"For me, I am grateful that I was awakened this morning. I am grateful that I can see the faces of the people I care about. I am grateful that I have the use of my arms, my legs, and I'm not feeble-minded.

"I'm grateful that every so often God doesn't hit me in the back of the head like He used to get me to listen. Now, He whispers to me. I'm grateful that I don't have to be smacked around anymore.

"I'm struggling with self-compassion. I do more beating myself up. Everything is in here, in my head, and that's difficult. And this is the one thing I should be able to control because I've known this person my whole life and he still gets squirrely.

"I look at my family, kids, other families and home. I have none of that. But what I do have is the love and respect for everyone in my circle. Every single one of you. I'm happy. I'm blessed that God has allowed me to be in concert with you all.

"My success is that I'm here. My successes are the brothers and sisters who have helped me get to this point. My main success is my relationship with God, and my relationship with God is different. He talks to me like, 'Yo, dude, uh-uh. Don't do that.'

"That's how He sounds to me when I'm doing something wrong. I can see Him shaking His head, and He says, 'Yo, I got you, Brah. We're good.' Amen?"

"Amens" ring out around Tony.

"Thanks for letting me share," he says.

"Thanks for sharing," a few others chime in.

The Oasis is open. Another weeknight session begins.

Recovery Café Greensboro became No. 64, one of only two south of Washington, DC. The other Recovery Café is in Charlotte. Photo credit: Buck Cochran.

* * *

The participants who come to the Oasis open up about the pain in their lives. They're honest, vulnerable and bring up details found in any newspaper story or any news website where all too often violence and fear reign.

They mention surviving a drive-by shooting, a home invasion or having a gun pointed in their faces. They talk about surviving cancer, going to jail, battling drug addiction or growing up in homes with no father or no mother or no one at all. They share with everyone their own battles with mental illness and talk about how they feel demons and the devil shadow them everywhere they go.

An older man in a porkpie hat speaks about that on a recent Thursday night.

He speaks in a raspy, thick-tongued voice and talks about how he tried to kill himself nine times. He overdosed on pills, stepped out in front of a car, tried to hang himself and cut his wrists with a butcher knife.

"If you're looking for love and hope, this is where you'll find it," Tony tells the man. "We all give hope to one another, and when you sit in this circle, you can let some of that stuff go. And listening to you, you have some of the same thoughts I have. But here I have hope and love."

"Praise God!" Frank said. "More hope. More love. Keep coming back."

Around the circle it goes. At the end of each testimonial, which could run anywhere from one minute to more than a few, the veteran participants say the phrase that's become the verbal touchstone during every session: "Thank you for sharing!"

"I totaled two cars and walked away with only a bruise," says one woman. "I thank God every day that I'm above ground. Every day is a new day when I'm above the dirt and not laying on a cooling board!"

"Thank you for sharing!"

"I'm no longer high on drugs," says another woman. "I'm high on sunshine and high on Him. He's taught me things I didn't know. Like I've learned you gotta catch the fish before you clean them."

"Thank you for sharing!"

At one recent Monday night session, the discussion going counterclockwise around the circle lands on a man in a black T-shirt with "End Poverty" across the front. He pulls out his iPhone.

"Let me read something that has helped me not beat myself up like I have before. Hold on one second. Let me find it. Here it is.

"'Jacob lied. Moses murdered. Saul hunted down Christians. David had an affair. Peter disowned Jesus. God used every one of these people to build a kingdom. You are never too far gone for God to use. Don't let the devil steal your story. Let Christ rewrite it.'

A flurry of "Amens" erupt around him. He continues.

"So, my struggle is being obedient. My scars are not from drugs or things from that nature. Mine are from life. My parents divorced when I was a year old. My dad left us, and my mother worked for the city of Greensboro. We never had enough.

"Part of my thing is always anger, and it was always me trying to fit in, me trying to level that playing field myself. I'm still struggling. I still get angry. But being able to admit your shortcomings is part of that cycle of healing, especially when you talk about it out in the open in front of strangers.

"You know what? You never can tell what you may say that can help someone else. It's not all about us. God doesn't have any wasted motions. Everything that every one of us sitting around the circle has been through, and if you take the time to share it, you don't know who it's going to help or who it's going to save.

"So, the things we are ashamed of are the things He wants us to talk about because He knows I'm not the only one who has come from that situation.

"I'm a better father because of my dad's shortcomings, and to be a good friend, you have to have some. And I have some great ones. And they're right here! I mean, with all of my faults, with all of my aggression, all of that anger, all that mouthiness, all that 'God Almighty, what is he doing tonight?' my friends, they never ran away.

"So, I'll say to anybody who will listen that the Good Lord don't make no mistakes. He puts you through what you need to grow through. And some things we just got to grow through. We can't just go through.

"Now, we'd love to go through it because you'll get through it faster. But when you got to grow through it, when it leaves some scars, it allows you to share that with other people and help them.

"This room should be filled every Monday and every Thursday. But we have to be obedient and part of being obedient is sharing the things we aren't so proud of. But how can you help someone if you're not willing share?

"We talk about God's grace and mercy, and we're ashamed to share with other people what we've been through. The devil does not want us having this conversation today, that we had the audacity to share our shortcomings and share with other people.

"My goal is to help as many people as I possibly can and sharing my story will help people think 'If he will do it for him, everybody has got a chance.'

"If I can help keep some other people from going through what I've gone through because of my story then all I went through was worth it. He knows what we're going through, and He knows where we're going. All He wants us to do is trust and believe. My goal is to trust and believe."

The people in the circle murmur in agreement, and the signature phrase pops up once again.

"Thank you for sharing."

More stories come. More people open up. One person recites his spoken-word poem he titled "Senseless." His words energize the circle. Heads begin to nod as a few participants start a call-and-response of "Amens" as if on a Sunday morning in church. The poet goes on for about three minutes, rolling out verse after verse. He ends his poem this way:

> *We need to overcome and over-stand*
> *By finding our inner sense*
> *Getting back in touch with our innocence*
> *Utilizing our spiritual sense*
> *Since the world does not make sense*
> *Stop walking around senseless*
> *Stop walking around senseless*
> *Brothers and sisters, stop walking around senseless*

The people in the circle clap.

"Powerful!" Tony says. "Brother Jake you want to pray us out?"

"I think it would be appropriate for Pastor Frank to pray us out tonight," Jake says.

"Sounds good," Tony says. "Pastor Frank?"

Everyone stands up, circles up and holds the hands of people on either side. When everyone bows their heads, Frank begins.

"Sometimes, prayers can be simple. Let's pray. God help us. Help us. Help us."

"Yes, Lord," someone says.

Frank continues.

"Thank you."

"Thank you," a few respond.

"Thank you," Frank says a little louder.

"THANK you," a few more people respond.

"Thank you," Frank shouts.

"THANK YOU," everyone shouts.

Frank continues.

"And all God's people said …

"AMEN!" everyone shouts.

"That is a great prayer right there," someone says.

Recovery Café Greensboro has rejuvenated Frank. Michie sees it in his actions and hears it in his voice. To her, RCG is GUM, the Stephen Ministries and New Creation all rolled into one endeavor under one roof.

"That is who he is," Michie says. "He is walking faith. He is social justice. He lets himself be vulnerable, and he believes everyone is equal and everyone is love, no matter what you've done or who you are."

* * *

As everyone begins to file out, Frank lingers behind. He talks to a few of the participants and catches up with Vicki about finances and moving forward before heading out. In a few days, he'll be back at Presbyterian Church of the Cross, back in the circle, back in the Oasis.

In the Oasis, Frank shares, too.

"I need to grow my trust in God," Frank says during one recent session. "I am reminded of something somebody said years ago. He said, 'The difference between me and God is God doesn't get confused thinking he's me.'

"Every now and then, I get confused thinking I'm God, and it's kinda frustrating when everything doesn't go according to my plan, and I look around and say, 'Not everything is going according to God's plan either.'

"Somebody also said, 'All things work together for the good.' They didn't say all things were good, right?

"So, my goal is to do some things that require greater trust in God from me. I need to practice trusting, and the best way for me to do that is to do something that requires trust."

Every time Frank shares in the Oasis, he remembers the words from Romans 12:2.

"Do not conform to the pattern of this world but be transformed by the renewing of your mind."

The verse becomes real for Frank because of the stories he hears, the people he meets, and the caring community that the Recovery Café Greensboro, or RCG, has begun to create.

But that verse has become real for Frank his whole life.

From Lumberton High to Wake Forest University.

From Duke University to Trinity Avenue Presbyterian in Durham.

From Vandalia Presbyterian in Greensboro to New Creation and Greensboro Urban Ministry.

From Nicaragua to South Africa.

From a sidewalk in downtown Greensboro to a perch outside Central Prison in Raleigh.

From the General Assembly in Raleigh to the U.S. Supreme Court in DC.

And now to RCG.

As he edges deeper into his seventh decade, Frank sees it happening once again.

God is connecting the dots.

Frank on Frank

How To Be Jesus in The World

Someone asked me recently, 'What would you recommend people do when our country and our world is so divisive and so hateful?'

Well, if someone is mad with me, there is that temptation that we have every right to be mad at them. In other words, we respond to them in kind. But Jesus recommends just the opposite. We need to respond with love, and that is what it means to be salt of the earth and light in the darkness.

Booker T. Washington once said, 'I shall allow no man to belittle my soul by making me hate him.' I mean, how can we be light in the darkness if our heart is in darkness?

Now, that doesn't mean you have to *agree* with them or even *like* them. Think about families. Families aren't always in agreement, and *they* don't like each other. But there is an underpinning of love, a connection and a bonding that is beyond like and dislikes. Jesus doesn't say, 'By your agreement, you are my disciples.' No, he says, 'By your *love*, you are my disciples.'

More and more today, we hear about Christian nationalism and how people categorize themselves as being better Christians than someone else or being better people than someone else. That's definitely *not* Christian.

Christianity evokes humility. It's not about putting a nation and its leaders above God and turning them into idols. When people call America a Christian nation and say, 'Let's make America great again,' it implies we were once something we've never been.

That's not good theology. That's not even good history. So,

what do we do when we're faced with something as insidious as that?

We definitely don't conform and return evil with evil. Rather, we become transformed and be the salt and the light that can make a difference in the world. So, what can we do?

Demonstrate in our actions an alternative and be the beloved community that Martin Luther King Jr talked about where we all are welcome, and we all are valued, especially the least, the last and the left out. We then can move forward by being more like Jesus in the world.

We've all read and seen the surveys that tell us people perceive the church to be outdated, and don't have confidence in organized religion. Those surveys, I believe, are generally responding to the larger church model that is wedded to a kind of corporate business philosophy.

Unfortunately, too many large churches are like that today. Their goal becomes maintaining the buildings and their property and raising money for a budget as opposed to setting goals to help the least of those among us and growing a sense of fellowship in doing so.

So, small is the way to go — and the way I believe the future church can not only survive but thrive.

Small enables a group to be simpler. Small enables a group in an existing church to focus on a particular mission that informs the work and worship of what they want to do, like hunger or working with the homeless. And small recaptures the mission-oriented communities that were the early church.

But how small is small?

Well, a group is small enough when they know everyone's name and large enough to throw a party. That puts you in touch with what creates a sense of community. And that sense of community is what helps us to experience being a part of the body of Christ in the world.

We are His hands; we are His feet. We cannot be that as individuals. We have to be together, in community, so we can forgive and be forgiven.

All too often today people are looking for the perfect church. But there are no perfect churches because there are no perfect people.

There are more people like Groucho Marx. You know, he once said, 'I don't want to belong to any club that will accept me as a member.'

But those people who are like Groucho Marx — people we disagree with or even dislike — are the very people who can help us grow. We can learn how to forgive and be forgiven, and we begin to understand what it means to experience grace and to give grace.

We love because God first loved us, and we experience that most often through other people, even people we dislike. We can benefit from their perspective — and the perspective of others — to help us better understand the challenges and the opportunities that come with being together as the body of Christ.

As Paul said, 'One member suffers, we all suffer together; when one member celebrates, we all celebrate together.'

That's what I enjoy about Recovery Café. It's being in community, and for me, it's somewhat selfish. I get to reconnect with a community of people who have helped keep me grounded in the reality of our need for God's grace and mercy and our need for His divine love.

In the Twelve Steps program of AA, you hear folks say, 'You can't keep what you can't give away.' What that means is as we share with others, what we share grows within us. And when we welcome others with graciousness and show love to those who feel unloved, the more that love and grace grows within us.

Recovery Café helps me reconnect with that love and grace.

We all know the two greatest commandments: Love your God and love your neighbor. And loving God looks a lot like loving your neighbor. That right there reminds me — and should remind all of us — to put more good news in the world.

Today, every time something good happens, I feel like three other bad things happen. It's like that feeling you get when you go for a long time without rain, and you keep looking up at the sky and wondering if it'll ever rain again.

That's the way our world feels today. When I think about the climate crisis, I see it as a sort of parable for the toxicity of our current environment. But even when I think about such things, I'm reminded of Clarence Jordan.

He was a farmer in rural Georgia who helped create an interracial Christian farming community where members worked together for the common good. He named his farm Koinonia, which means Christian fellowship, and his work inspired Habitat for Humanity.

Clarence Jordan once said his farm was a 'demonstration plot for the Kingdom of God.' We all can be like that demonstration plot. People would come to his farm, see what was growing, and say, 'Oh my goodness, look at that field! It's producing fruit!' So, it is with people of faith.

People should be able to see our faith in us. We can be that demonstration plot that produces fruit in God's kingdom, by advocating for sound public policy related to hunger or volunteering at a homeless shelter or helping out at the Recovery Café.

I've had enough people come up to me and say what they see happening around them in North Carolina and the world is just depressing. I tell them, 'Join the club!' But I also tell them that hope does exist.

Our hope is to address the lack of good news by sharing good news and being good news. Our hope is to live that out and demonstrate how the alternative community we're a part of can show others what is possible.

And it is possible. Our lives are lived in grateful response to God's grace and mercy. Our hope and our healing is not with ourselves. It is with God. God woke us up this morning, and God gave us an opportunity to experience a new day and move forward in being Jesus in our world.

That is our calling. To be a light in the darkness. To be a demonstration plot. To be a farmer like Clarence Jordan. Plant seeds that can produce fruit in God's kingdom. What a bountiful harvest we all can reap!

Can I hear an Amen?

Sometimes, only a few words are needed, especially writing in blue icing to signify a big event. Photo credit: Courtesy of New Creation Community Presbyterian Church.

Epilogue
Daniel's Cartoon Bear

"You wanna go?"

Frank told me about the 40th anniversary of New Creation Community Presbyterian Church. He and Michie were going. I thought, "Sure." Scheduled for Easter Sunday, April 2025. Why not? I piled into the Dews' SUV that Sunday afternoon and headed toward a first-floor hall at First Presbyterian Church in downtown Greensboro, the faith home of New Creation. Every Sunday afternoon, members gathered to hear a sermon, hold communion, eat food brought in by members, and share epiphanies they discovered, both large and small, in their spiritual lives.

Back in 1985, Frank created New Creation in his living room when he and Michie lived in Greensboro's Lindley Park neighborhood. During my five years working on Frank's book, I had yet to attend one service at New Creation. But after gathering what I needed through interviews, I felt good with what I had. So, even when Frank asked me whether I wanted to go, I wondered if I really *needed* to go. But once I walked in, I knew it was the right move. I saw in 3-D people I had written about and talked to over the phone. There they were: Kathy Carpenter, Gayle Wulk, and Barbara Clawson. Moreover, I felt right away what I had heard about over the past five years — the passion felt in carrying out a vision members believed a church needed to be.

I followed Frank and Michie into New Creation's makeshift sanctuary and met a crowd of about three dozen members, both past and present. Everyone around me began to hug one another, trading stories, giving updates on family and health, and sharing what was next in their lives. It felt more like a family reunion than a church service. Tables in a back corner held an array of homecooked food, and a few steps away was a sheet cake, bordered by a confectioners' sugar garden of yellow and blue flowers, with "Happy 40th Anniversary New Creation Community Presbyterian" written in the decorative cursive of blue icing. Seven tables, with plastic tablecloths of purple, orange, and pink, filled the room. Once the hugfest subsided, everyone sat down. I grabbed a seat beside Barbara. It had been years since I'd seen her. Not much had changed, though, except Barbara's age. She was now 90, still a quiet fighter for social justice.

When the anniversary service began, up first was Frank. At the podium, Frank had some things to say.

"I heard about a church that Kathy Carpenter called Church of the Saviour in Washington, DC, and I said, 'Kathy, we could start a church like that!', and she said, 'Are you crazy?' I said, "I think so. So, let's do it!'"

Many around the seven tables laughed. They remember. Frank continued.

"What struck me about that church was they said membership in the church is discipleship, meaning following Jesus. I remember Reggie Blackburn. Some of you remember Reggie. He said to me the Sunday he joined, 'This is the first church that made it hard for me to join.'"

"Yea" and "That's right" rippled around the room. People nodded. They knew. Reggie was them.

"Discipleship takes us on a journey, following Jesus inward and our relationship with God, and outward in our service in the world," Frank said. "So, discipleship has this inward-outward thing, like two wings of a bird. Each is required to fly. Inward and outward. And that takes us all into ministry.

"Someone once asked me, 'How did you decide to go into ministry?' and I said, 'I didn't know ministry was optional.' I thought we were all called to ministry. It's not something done by the pastor or the staff but rather what we all do in hearing God's call.

"So, what have I seen over the years at New Creation? People listening for and responding to God's call. I don't have 45 minutes. But we could spend it just on that. Listening to God's call in prayer and in community in teaching and studying the Bible.

"You all have done such a wonderful job teaching the stories of the Bible to our children. People can not interpret the story of the Prodigal Son if they don't know the story of the Prodigal Son. Being with the poor. Being with those who are least, last and left out. PhDs in life who have something to teach all of us. And finally, doing social justice.

"The church spends so much time asking, 'Should we do social justice?" And the first thing this congregation did was go to Washington, DC, to stand in silent vigil with the Synod of North Carolina at the South African Embassy. And it was that experience that led us on a journey to Maake Masango who said, 'When whites finally share power with Black people, Black people need to have good experiences with whites, and they need to have an education.' And that's how Ali and Kefilwe came to be here.

"These are the fruits of the Kingdom that I have been blessed by, and that is what has made me a much better pastor because of this community. Amen?"

"Amen!" everyone around him responded.

Photo credit: Courtesy of New Creation Community Presbyterian Church.

The celebration continued with Barbara reading a letter from New Creation's sister church in Managua, Nicaragua. In October 1993, during their first pilgrimage to Nicaragua, Frank and a few members from New Creation connected with St. Paul the Apostle Christian Base Community. That began their spiritual plugin with St. Paul, and more than three decades later, in a letter from the church's newest faith leader named Yamil, St. Paul thanked New Creation for their friendship, assistance, and leadership. At the podium, Barbara read from Yamil's letter.

"Throughout these years, you have been bearers of good news and builders of hope. The apostle Paul taught that the scriptures were written so people would have hope. In Romans 15:13, it says that the God of hope fills people with joy and peace so that they are bound in hope.

"Brothers and sisters, here's to you continuing your mission of giving hope in a wounded world. You must continue becoming a sign of hope that arouses Christian commitment and solidarity in the face of individualistic culture. To raise up a new climate of solidarity and Christian commitment to the poor inspired by the words of Jesus.

"To be prophetic hope in a world without hope. To be a

welcoming and inclusive community. May you be witnesses to the Risen One like those women who first witnessed the Resurrection who made this Good News known to the world.

"Congratulations, brothers and sisters of New Creation Community. May this celebration be a sign of resurrection for you. We love you very much."

While Barbara read from Yamil's long letter, the stories I heard a few years ago about the church's 1993 trip to Nicaragua tumbled forward in my mind like a movie. I remembered those vivid stories from Barbara; from Buck Cochran, the former Navy officer; from Michie; and from Frank. I listened to members circling those seven tables begin to write down their own favorite memories from the past 40 years. Some were downright funny; Some incredibly poignant; all of them earnest. As those memories were read out loud, they reminded me of what Frank had always hoped New Creation would be. He and the other members have succeeded.

Cattycorner from me at our table sat a member named Daniel Brooks. He was drawing something on a yellow slip of paper, a little larger than an index card. I couldn't really tell what he was drawing, but he was intent. After he finished, he slid it across the table to Michie. I looked, and I saw it was a cartoon of a smiling bear holding four balloons. He drew it in two, maybe three minutes. On the yellow slip of paper, he wrote: "To Michie, I've always wanted to meet you ever since Dennis told me about you and Frank. Always, Daniel." He gave it as a gift to Michie.

"I hope you don't mind me doing that," he said.

"I *loved* you doing that," Michie responded.

"If I had a better pen I would've made it better," Daniel said.

The cartoon Daniel Brooks drew for Dr. Michie Dew.

That short exchange teared me up. I don't know exactly why. It just did. But that little moment felt so rich, so selfless, so right. I looked at Daniel's cartoon bear, the message he wrote, and then looked at Michie. I had no words. They were stuck in my throat. After the service, I tried to come up with a few. I sat across from Daniel, asked a few questions, and listened.

Daniel is 73, a college graduate with a sharp mind, a rich baritone and an innate talent to play a few musical instruments. He lives on a fixed income with his roommate, Dennis, in a room in a nursing home in Greensboro. Two years ago, doctors amputated his left leg below the knee because of a bone infection. Since then, he hasn't been able to attend New Creation. Plus, as a man who needs a wheelchair to get around, moving from one place to another is no easy task. He needs to schedule Access GSO, the city's transportation service for disabled residents like himself, a day or so in advance to get anywhere in the city. Each ride costs him $5, and every month,

Daniel works hard to stretch every dollar he receives through disability.

But he didn't want to miss New Creation's 40th anniversary celebration. So, he forked over $5. He had to come because of what New Creation had done for him.

"This is heaven, and I have missed it so much," he told me after the anniversary celebration. "I couldn't help it. It's been so welcoming to me and being so warm and making me feel like they're a friend. It's a feeling. And I love that feeling."

As I walked back to Dews' SUV parked across the street, Frank went on and on about how the anniversary was so New Creation. I asked what he meant, and he talked about the paper plates, the plastic utensils, the people getting up and walking around during the service and the litany of prayer concerns full of compassion and empathy. And the familiar faces. So many familiar faces. There was even one member who came wearing Easter bunny ears on his head.

"That was so New Creation," Frank said.

He said that over and over on the ride home and the days that followed the anniversary celebration. Yeah, I thought. That is *so* New Creation. Giving hope in a wounded world. So New Creation. Right. But that is so Frank, too.

So Frank

Frank and Michie Dew with their grandchildren, left to right, Sawyer, Myles and Posie. The Dews' daughter, Christie Hartman, is their mom. Photo credit: Courtesy of Dr. Michie Dew.

I've had enough people come up to me and say what they see happening around them in North Carolina and the world is just depressing. I tell them, 'Join the club!' But I also tell them that hope does exist.

Our hope is to address the lack of good news by sharing good news and being good news. Our hope is to live that out and demonstrate how the alternative community we're a part of can show others what is possible. And it is possible. Our lives are lived in grateful response to God's grace and mercy. Our hope and our healing is not with ourselves. It is with God. God woke us up this morning, and God gave us an opportunity to experience a new day and move forward in being Jesus in our world.

That is our calling. To be a light in the darkness.

The Rev. Frank Dew.

Acknowledgements

I always knew the Rev. Frank Dew had a story to tell.

I knew that long before I heard his wife Michie call him Right Reverend Hotdog. It was when I walked into his house, stepped into the kitchen and watched him give me the eagle eye. "You're wearing the wrong colors," he deadpanned. Frank had to loan me some of his own Black and Gold swag. And let me tell you, he has LOTS of Black of Gold swag. I sure didn't have enough. Still don't.

That's one of many moments I've had with Frank and Michie over the past five years, and during that time, I've come to believe their story can be a welcome salve for our wounded nation. It can give us courage and hope — and we sure need that, especially at a time when fear and hatred is like the air we breathe. It's all around us. I clung to my own hope as I worked on their book. Drank lots of coffee too. I always saw myself as a newspaper journalist who labored over word count, not page count. Writing a book? Me? Why don't I climb Mount Everest? Or run across a desert? It seemed so out of reach. But I endured. I spent many early mornings, late nights and weekend afternoons seated at my laptop at my kitchen table writing, rewriting and reading out loud sentences and entire paragraphs for structure and rhythm. My writing regimen reminded me of what the legendary sportswriter Red Smith once said: "Writing is easy. All you have to do is sit down at the typewriter, cut open a vein, and bleed."

Bleed. So true. Yet, ask any journalist. Find a story that matters, and you find your fuel. With Frank and Michie's story, I found my fuel.

So, thank you, Frank and Michie. Thank you for your patience and graciousness with my incessant questions. You unveiled much. That includes nearly getting lost somewhere in Kansas, in a city known for making cowboy boots as you looked for an office in a blink-and-miss strip mall on some forgettable highway. Yet, there, in an office with cream-colored walls, you found your son and daughter.

And thank you, David Dew and Christie Dew Hartman. David, your dad's toast at your wedding was poignant. Just wish I could've gotten in the book about how your dad got all kind of college-student raucous after a big Wake Forest win when you were an undergrad. And Christie, your friend Ali remembers the elephant that scared the bejesus out of you in Africa when you were, what, 10? He even sent me a picture of the elephant. But just think, you can tell that story to Sawyer, Myles, and Posie forever.

And Ali Mabitsela, thank you for your pictures. Your dozens of pictures. Moreover, thank you for your time and your astute perspective on the Dews and Greensboro's New Creation Community Presbyterian Church from the other side of the Atlantic in South Africa. And thank you, What's App.

And New Creation, the church Frank started in his Greensboro living room, you have some stout-hearted current and former members: Gayle Wulk, Ginny Hultquist, Fran and Margaret Young, Daniel Brooks, Kathy Carpenter, and the late Virginia Driscoll. She died in October 2024. She was 82. Her obituary described her as "student of life." May we all be so lucky. And of course, thank you to Barbara Clawson, the soft-spoken fighter for social justice. Once again, your insight was invaluable.

And speaking of soft-spoken fighters, Meg Eggleston, your story about your friendship with Elias Syriani on North Carolina's Death Row will stay with me forever. I will never look at cranes the same way again.

And Phyllis Justice and Sara Gane, thanks for spilling the tea on your older brother and sharing how awkward he was when he first met Michie. You were there. And you were there during those tense dinner-table discussions your brother had with your dad. And thanks for sharing with me his nickname: Buzzard. Do love that. And Sara, your story about your son, Charlie. Thank you for sharing what I know was tough. May your big-hearted memories of Davey Crockett never wane.

Thank you, Steve Tate, for reminding me once again how much a force your older sister was. And thank you, Mike Sasser for retelling how your time as a Stephen Minister changed your life. I remember you told me before the story about the guy you and your wife Barbara ran into at Four Seasons Mall in Greensboro. He was as big as a defensive tackle, and he remembered you fondly from the Thursday night support group meetings at Greensboro Urban Ministry, the safe harbor spot we know as GUM.

"Mr. Mike," he told you, "I miss you buddy."

And the Rev. Mike Aiken, thank you for detailing how the chaplaincy program came to be at GUM and your friendship with Frank that began, in all places, at Wake Forest more than a half century ago. And Tyra Clymer, thanks for welcoming me with your signature smile when I came to see the windowless room Frank used as a chapel for 22 years. I first saw it in 2007. It still looks the same.

And the three folks with the collar: the Rev. Cindy Higgins, the Rev. Kim Priddy, and the Rev. David Smith. Thanks for shining a light on Frank and his impact.

And Burt Higgins, thanks for the anecdote on the way to a Wake Forest football game. I love it when I stumble onto something that plays out in front of me like some scene from a play. And Burt, Frank didn't like what you wore either. Join the club. And like with Burt, I stumbled onto a heartfelt scene when I met Cindy Washington on a random Sunday morning in the pews of Sedgefield Presbyterian. Later, I heard yet another side of Frank, Michie and a young Christie asking Cindy to find what she had misplaced, the pink Care Bear Christie called "Happy Bear" because of the rainbow on its chest. Thanks, Cindy.

Spencer Clark, thanks for revealing the wonder and awe of being a teenager in the late 1960s, running alongside Frank and dreaming big. And thanks for the edits and context. You were crucial.

And to my favorite Mark Twain, Bob Foxworth. I'll always know you as Samuel Clemens in your white suit. You are good, especially with that cigar you wield like a lance. But your backstory is even more impactful, I think.

And the crew at Recovery Café, thanks for being so welcoming and letting me sit in on your Oasis and hearing stories of struggle, resiliency, and grit. And of course, what I call the Power Three: Tony Brown, Bernard McCoy and the Rev. Vicki McCain. We all have been coaxed by Frank to do things we never thought we'd do. I wrote a book. Tony and Bernard and Vicki, you all helped Frank start Recovery Café Greensboro. We four all are better for it, don't you think?

And the Rev. Buck Cochran. Not only did you share your story one memorable Saturday from your front porch. You even volunteered without being asked to take photos for Frank and Michie's book. And boy, did you ever take photos with a camera that felt like a tank. Thanks for your talent and your eye for detail.

"Calling; A Memoir of Ministry" will help raise money for Recovery Café Greensboro. Headquartered at Greensboro's Presbyterian Church of the Cross in northeast Greensboro, Recovery Café is a national comprehensive program started by the Church of the Saviour in Washington DC to help those cope with whatever life struggle they face. Recovery Café Greensboro is one of two south of DC. The other is in Charlotte. I'm glad Frank and Michie's book will help support such a worthy cause.

What does Frank like to say? It's that African proverb: "When you want to run fast, run by yourself. If you want to run far, run together." True. All of us on these pages ran together to put "Calling: A Memoir of Ministry" together. Sure did.

Every book we all know needs a good editor. I had three. Dr. Charles Dew, Frank's relative who taught history for years at Williams College. The talented Betsi Robinson, my former editor at the News & Record who helped me navigate my nouns and verbs for years even after I broke her rocking chair in her office.

And of course, my wife, Katherine. She kept me honest. She kept on point. And she never was afraid to say, "Jeri, this is way too much! You have to trim!" Thanks for your candor, Kath. And your guidance. Love you much. Always.

Every book also needs a publisher. That leads me to another serendipity moment with my friend Mary.

I met Mary when I worked at High Point University. She was a digital content creator; I was the university's senior writer; and she convinced me once to read a thick book about dragons. Mary used to have an office right next to mine, and we talked about books and writing — and books and writing. That's how I found out Mary and her husband, Nathan, had a side hustle, Cardinal Hound Publishing, a business to help writers self-publish their books.

So, when one publisher came up empty and Frank wanted to find a way to get the book out quickly to help raise money for Recovery Café, in came Mary and Nathan. They are truly digital natives, business savvy with a computer mouse and a creative mind. Thank you, Mary and Nathan Gallimore. And yes, Mary, I did like your dragons book.

During my years working on "Calling," I had dozens of conversations with Frank. Just dozens. I often told him I felt like I was in his classroom earning a Master of Divinity degree, especially when I got to our conversations about the sections I called "Frank on Frank."

"Frank, we need some Bible here," I'd tell him. "Some scripture. I *know* you got something."

He always did.

So, Frank, thanks for your guidance. Thanks for the lessons. And thanks for your friendship. You have taught me much. Just hope I continue to absorb what I learned. Like this one.

"God woke us up this morning, and God gave us an opportunity to experience a new day and move forward in being Jesus in our world. That is our calling. To be a light in the darkness."

Yeah. Let it shine.

About the Author
Jeri Rowe

Jeri Rowe is a newsroom ex-pat, a South Carolinian and a first-generation college grad who grew up among soldiers and storytellers. He spent nearly 30 years in daily journalism in four states. For nearly a quarter century, he worked as a reporter, editor, and columnist at the News & Record in Greensboro. During that time, he won more than two dozen local, state, and national writing awards. After the News & Record, Jeri spent a decade at High Point University as its senior writer. He told stories in both pixels and print, helping lead projects both big and small and writing and editing everything from books to video scripts. He is now the editor at large at Our State, an award-wining magazine that celebrates the people, places and traditions of North Carolina.

When asked anytime about the importance of getting anything done, the Rev. Frank Dew always mentions the African proverb: "If you want run fast, run by yourself. If you want to run far, run together." These folks surrounding Frank are just a few of those who make Recovery Café Greensboro run efficiently twice a week.

Want To Know More About Recovery Café?

Please Scan the QR Code Below:

Recovery Café Greensboro is an inclusive environment and welcomes people regardless of age, ability, race, ethnicity, religion, national origin, indigenous heritage, gender identity, socioeconomic status, sexual orientation, and life experience.

Recovery Café Greensboro is founded on the belief that every human being is worthy and lovable regardless of past trauma, mental and emotional anguish, substance use disorder or human errors. RCG is another avenue to recovery in addition to traditional treatment programs and self-help groups. RCG also serves as a bridge to help members establish recovery, maintain their stability, reduce relapse, and fulfill their human potential.

Elements of RCG's work include providing members a recovery coach as well as small peer-support circles twice week. Other RCG offerings include service work, community meals twice a week, peer training to help members become peer leaders, and classes in discovering something new, ranging from art and relapse prevention to meditation and creative writing.

www.ingramcontent.com/pod-product-compliance
Lightning Source LLC
Chambersburg PA
CBHW021657120626
46545CB00004B/1274